One Version of the Facts

One Version of the Facts

My Life in the Ivory Tower

Henry E. Duckworth
Foreword by Thomas H. B. Symons

THE UNIVERSITY OF MANITOBA PRESS

The University of Manitoba Press
Winnipeg, Manitoba R3T 2N2
www.umanitoba.ca/uofmpress

Printed in Canada on partially recycled, acid-free paper ∞

Cover illustrations: courtesy of the author.
Frontispiece: author as seen by Bruce Head, RCA, 1981.
Cover design: Kirk Warren
Text Design: Karen Armstrong.

Unless otherwise noted, photographs are courtesy of the author. (WCPI: Western Canadian Pictorial Index.)

Canadian Cataloguing-in-Publication Data

Duckworth, H. E. (Henry Edmison), 1915-
    One version of the facts : my life in the ivory tower
    Includes index.
    ISBN 0-88755-670-1

1. Duckworth, H. E. (Henry Edmison), 1915–
2. Physicists—Canada--Biography. 3. College teachers—
Canada—Biography. 4. University of Winnipeg—
Presidents—biography. I. Title

QC16.D83 A3 2000   530'.092   000-920126-2

The University of Manitoba Press gratefully acknowledges the financial support for its publication program provided by the Government of Canada through the Book Publishing Industry Development Program (BPIDP); the Canada Council for the Arts; the Manitoba Arts Council; and the Manitoba Department of Culture, Heritage and Tourism.

Contents

J.D. Macdougall (McMaster)
W. McLatchie (McMaster)
J.O. Meredith (Manitoba)
J.M. Olsen (Wesleyan)
J.M. Ormrod (Manitoba)
E.M. Pennington (McMaster)
H.E. Petch (McMaster)
R.W. Preston (Wesleyan)
K. Sharma (Manitoba)
F.G.G. Southon (Manitoba)
G.S. Stanford (Wesleyan)
R.L. Stearns (Wesleyan)
J.G.V. Taylor (McMaster)
P. Van Rookhuyzen (McMaster, Manitoba)
A. Van Wijngaarden (McMaster)
V.S. Venkatasubramanian (McMaster, Manitoba)
S.W. Whineray (McMaster)
P. Williams (Manitoba)
W. Wong (Manitoba)
K.S. Woodcock (Wesleyan)
R.F. Woodcock (Wesleyan)

I owe them much, and I thank them deeply.

Preface

I've lived through interesting times. My scientific career coincided with the post–World War II surge in physics and with the public infatuation with that subject. In the following years, when I was drawn into the administrative side of universities, it was the period of their greatest modern ferment and, subsequently, of their severest financial difficulty. In the following pages, I've outlined my involvement in a variety of events, choosing those that might be of general interest. In doing so, I've had to admit that I had parents, a childhood, and a family of my own, but I've tried not to belabour those personal topics.

The title, *One Version of the Facts*, comes from a chance meeting between Leo Szilard and Hans Bethe, both important figures in the development of the atom bomb. When Bethe asked Szilard, "What are you doing these days?" Szilard replied, "I'm writing down the facts relating to the atom bomb: not for publication, but for myself – and for God." When Bethe said, "Don't you think God knows the facts?" Szilard answered, "Perhaps not this version of them." My own version may differ from those of others, but it represents an attempt to be accurate and objective, and it is not a conscious exercise in self-aggrandizement. Much of it is drawn from diaries, which should lend credibility to dates and the names of individuals.

In putting these matters to paper, I've received much help and encouragement from my family: my wife, Shirley, my son, Harry, my daughter, Jane, and my grandson Daniel (who also prepared the index). Further, I owe much to Alexander Gregor, director of the Centre for Study of Higher Education at the University of Manitoba, who convinced me that an account of my experiences, although not themselves scholarly in form or content, might have scholarly interest . I am also grateful to M. Brochu of the National Research Council of Canada, who provided me with material relating to that body; to Roger Kingsley, Secretary of the University of Winnipeg, for more information relating to that institution; to the University of Manitoba Press, in particular to David Carr (director) for his acceptance of the manuscript and his many perceptive suggestions concerning it, and to Carol Dahlstrom (managing editor) for her careful and constructive editing of the final manuscript; to Gerald Miller and his secretary, Carol Janz, for assistance in word-processing; to Professor Gerald Bedford for reading the manuscript and, especially, to Professor Thomas H.B. Symons, for providing the Foreword.

Foreword

The understatement of the title of this book, *One Version of the Facts*, is in keeping with the man who wrote it. Harry Duckworth's colleagues and many friends have long enjoyed, and respected, his wry wit and gentle, infectious, and often self-deprecating good humour. The book has indeed these hallmarks of Harry's engaging personality and style. It tells, nonetheless, of a life of remarkable service and achievement.

It was a fortunate day for higher education and science in Canada when, in 1951, Harry accepted the invitation of Dr. Harry Thode to return to Canada to become a full professor of physics at McMaster University, even though it meant leaving a similar position at a higher salary at Wesleyan University in the United States. There has ensued, for the next half-century, an extraordinary roster of public service, not only at the helm of academic departments and institutions but also on a plethora of the councils, boards, advisory bodies, committees, and commissions that assist Canadians in their thinking and planning for public policies and the programs that implement them. These have included the National Research Council of Canada, the Defence Research Board, the National Library Board, the Science Council, the Canadian Environmental Advisory Council, the Natural Science and Engineering Research Council, the Institute for Research on Public Policy, the Manitoba Research Council, the Royal Society of Canada, the Association of Universities and Colleges of Canada, and many more in both the public and private sectors. In many of these, he has played a leading role, for example, as president of the Royal Society of Canada, as chairman of the Advisory Committee on Nuclear Safety of the Atomic Energy Control Board, and as chairman of the Association of Universities and Colleges of Canada.

The same pattern of service, and of leadership, may be found in the areas of Harry's professional academic work, for example, as president of the Canadian Association of Physicists and, again with an international dimension, as chairman of the Commission on Atomic Masses and Related Constants of the International Union of Pure and Applied Physics, and in assistance given to the work of the National Academy of Sciences of the United States.

In tandem with this extensive activity, indeed at its core, has been Harry's own research and scientific work. Particularly notable are his contributions, through the development of the instruments and techniques for mass spectrometry, to the measurement of atomic masses to a very high degree of precision and accuracy. Work was risky and long term in this area, in which Harry was a pioneer. He is the author of approximately 100 research papers and several books, as well as of numerous general papers, reviews, and published addresses. He was an editor of the *Canadian Journal of Physics*, has received the Tory Medal of the Royal Society of Canada, has been awarded eight honorary doctorates of science and has received a number of other degrees, awards, and fellowships recognizing his academic contributions.

It is, however, Harry's contribution to higher education and his leadership in this field that may well be seen as his most significant area of achievement. As the president of one university and the chancellor of another, and, before that, as department chair, dean, and vice-president, and much else, as chairman of both the Association of Universities and Colleges of Canada and the Association of Commonwealth Universities, and as an advisor to governments on academic matters, he has provided a rare quality of leadership that is both considerate and efficacious. The thoughtfulness, courtesy, care, integrity, and vision he brought to these responsibilities have set a standard that should be helpful to all those who follow in such offices.

Yet, it may well be argued that Harry's contribution as a teacher has been his finest gift. By this, I mean he is a teacher in the broadest and deepest sense, going far beyond the lecture hall and the laboratory to the legacy left by the character of the man, the values he espouses, the example he sets, and the inspiration he provides. In this sense, Harry Duckworth has been a mentor and exemplar to students, colleagues, public servants, and countless others whom he has encountered along the way. This autobiography, like its author, is straightforward, orderly, understated, good-humoured, and deeply perceptive. It is enriched by his eye for character, for detail, and for the telling anecdote. But a number of major themes emerge as the book unfolds. These include: the importance of childhood and family, the values of education, the multifaceted challenges of leadership, and the pervasive importance of good research for the whole of society.

The book offers interesting descriptions, based on personal experience and observation, of post-graduate education in its comparatively early stages in Canada. It provides informative insights into the early days of atomic research. And it takes the reader inside many of the changes and debates that have swept higher education in the second half of the last century. It does this through the eyes of a patient man, gifted with civility and a capacity to see the humour in every adversity and absurdity, who was himself a principal actor on these many stages.

One must be struck in a reading of this book by the fact that Harry has spent much of his life at the centre of things. In part, at least, this was because wherever he was often tended to *become* the centre of things. People gravitated to him, recognizing not only his knowledge, but, still more, the quality of wisdom that he brought to bear, derived from study, research, experience, observation, and reflection. It is a part of this wisdom that he took as much interest and pleasure in the work and attainments of others as in his own.

Harry "admits" in his preface that he has indeed had parents and a family of his own but notes that in this book he will "try not to belabour those topics," seeking rather to write of events in which he has been involved that might be of general interest. The quality of reticence with which he writes of himself is thus extended to embrace his family and family matters. Nonetheless, one cannot read *One Version of the Facts* without realizing how central his family has been to his life and what a part they have played in his activities and achievements.

It is an honour to be invited to write the Foreword to this book and it is a particular pleasure, in doing so, to be able to acknowledge, although so inadequately, the immense debt that a multitude of people in Canada and beyond owe to this good man.

Thomas H.B. Symons, C.C., M.A., LL.D., D.U., D. Litt., F.R.S.C.
Founding president of Trent University
Peterborough, Ontario

One Version of the Facts

Growing up in the Manse: 1915 to 1931

1

Henry Bruce Duckworth, a minister in the Presbyterian Church, and Ann Hutton Edmison, a daughter of the manse, were my only parents, and I was their only child. In the lottery for good parents, I drew first prize.

Although other activities, including school and play, had more immediacy for me, the church was always in the background. My father was not blatantly doctrinaire, but he believed in the Virgin birth, in the divinity of Christ, and that those who loved their neighbours were destined for Heaven. My mother often said that we had our heaven here on Earth but, the night before she died, she whispered to me her father's last words:

> Earth is receding,
> Heaven is approaching,
> Jesus is calling,
> I must go.

She was clearly counting on a celestial heaven to succeed the earthly one. At that time, a confident belief in all aspects of the Apostle's Creed was common in the mainline churches and not only amongst ministers and their wives. Even many years later, my father's sister, my aunt Ella Krueger, crying with grief at her husband's death, blurted to me, "Oh, Harry, if we could only see them going up!"

My father was described in the 1908 *Torontonensis* (the University of Toronto yearbook) as follows:

> Harry first came to light in the late 70's [1 December 1879] in Garafraxa Township, near Fergus. In boyhood, the farm and the country school-house, in youth the woollen mill at Hespeler were his fields of labor. . . .
> He entered Varsity in the fall of 1903 [at the age of 24], handicapped, for he had no high school training. He had the will, however, and the energy

to make things go, and even found time for his full share of college activities. Three times "Y" [YMCA] Executive claimed his support. Debate and football have been his pastimes; Philosophy his course, and after two more years at Knox [the Presbyterian Theological College], the manse will be his home.

Each entry in the yearbook carries an aphorism thought to be apropos. Whilst others read "A jovial lad withal," "Steadfast and still, the same on any object bent," and "Sterling worth gains love and respect," my father's entry hints at darker things: "My life is one dem'd horrid grind." And so it must have been, as he scrabbled to support himself. His most dependable job was Sunday preaching, which he did in more than 200 different rural churches. His last enterprise, aimed at providing a nest egg for his marriage, was the chartering of a vessel and the hiring of a military band for a Saturday evening cruise from Toronto to Port Dalhousie – a splendid plan, grandly visualized, but sabotaged by torrential rain.

Because of that deluge, my father and mother carried debt into their marriage, and both felt that he should delay his full-time ministry until the books had been balanced. Thus, in 1912, they emigrated to Winnipeg, my father became an agent for the Confederation Life Insurance Company, and my mother practised thrift as only she could do. In 1915, they were free of debt and even proud owners of a building lot on Niagara Street in Winnipeg, which they had bought for $2,600 in the pre–World War I land boom. In that year, my father accepted a call to the Presbyterian Church in Rivers, Manitoba; in 1919 he moved to Transcona (six miles from Winnipeg); in 1926, to St. James (a suburb of Winnipeg); and in 1936, to St. Andrew's (Elgin Avenue) United Church, Winnipeg, where he stayed until his retirement in 1948. I appeared during the Rivers period and entered University during the sojourn in St. James. During the Transcona period, the lot on Niagara Street was sold for $1,300, exactly half its original cost.

My paternal grandfather, Henry Duckworth, had farmed in Garafraxa Township, Wellington County, Ontario, until he was forced to sell the farm to honour a promissory note that he had signed for a friend who was in financial difficulty. The family moved to Hespeler (now part of Cambridge, Ontario), where both father and son found employment in the Brodie woollen mill and my father became active in the Christian Endeavour Group of St. Andrew's Presbyterian Church. When my father announced to his father that he intended to enter the ministry and awaited his blessing, it was hardly inspirational: "If you read your sermons, I'll be ashamed of you." My father committed his sermons to memory (two per Sunday) until he was fifty-five years of age. My great-grandfather, Henry Duckworth, was born in County Armagh, Ireland, in 1817 and came to Canada in 1847. My grandmother's family (Loutit) came to Canada from the Orkney Islands in 1851.

My maternal grandfather, Henry Edmison, also a Presbyterian minister, earned his B.A. from Queen's College in Kingston in 1863. In that year, he constituted 1 percent of the B.A. graduates in all of Canada. His M.A., which he received in 1866, must have placed him in an even more exclusive academic group. As his namesake, I inherited his B.A. diploma. It is in Latin on parchment, of course, and is signed by seven professors, led by "Joannes B. Mowat, M.A.," and "Georgius Lawson, LL.D., Ph.D." At least three of the rest have M.D. appended to their names, and one has a D.D. In 1867, following Confederation, the new provincial government withdrew from Queen's the $5,000 grant that the College had been receiving from the provincial treasury. If the College had agreed to federate with the University of Toronto, the grant would have been continued. Valuing its independence and placing principle above money, Queen's struck a committee that successfully raised an endowment of $100,000 to compensate for the grievous loss of the government grant. Henry Edmison was a member of this committee, although my distant recollection of him, combined with family legend, suggests that he may have been the least worldly man in Christendom. He had charges in Waterdown, Ontario, and Melbourne, Quebec, before spending the last twenty-five years of his ministry in Rothesay, Ontario. Whilst at Melbourne, he taught Latin at nearby St. Francis College.

My great-grandfather, John Edmison, was born in Berwick-on-Tweed in 1794 and came to Canada in 1819. My grandmother's family (Lunam) came to Canada from East Lothian in Scotland in the early 1840s.

My mother knew what was expected of a minister's wife and, as a young woman, had often declared to her friends that she would never subject herself to that self-effacing role. But, once my father had changed her mind, she never faltered in her support for him and for the many organizations in his congregations. It used to be said that congregations got two for the price of one. Today some are lucky to get one for the price of two.

I once read in a German encyclopaedia that the father of one of my professors at the University of Chicago, physicist Arthur Compton, was a clergyman and that Compton was "faithful to his father's religion." The entry caused me to ask how "faithful" had I been to *my* father's religion. He would not have wished me to be "loyal" for loyalty's sake, but I hope he would not be disappointed to know that I believe in a prime mover, that I accept Christ's teachings as a guide to life, but, at the end of the day, I do not expect to be welcomed by either St. Peter or his rival, the defrocked archangel Lucifer. Notwithstanding, I have the greatest respect for the life of service that my father led and for his faithfulness to his own beliefs.

Rivers: 1915 to 1919

I spent my first years in Rivers, Manitoba, some 150 miles northwest of Winnipeg. It was a divisional point on the Canadian National Railway (CNR) line, which passed through Saskatoon to Edmonton. It was about thirty miles from Brandon, and there was a train connection. This connection was important because one of my mother's brothers, John H. Edmison, practised medicine in Brandon, her other brother, George A. Edmison, was minister of Knox Presbyterian Church in that city, and her parents had recently emigrated from Toronto to Brandon. I was born in my grandparents' cottage in Brandon at 630–14th Street on All Saints' Day in 1915, with my uncle Jack officiating, and I was taken to Rivers a month later, when mother and son were declared fit to travel.

My knowledge of Rivers is largely hearsay. I remember falling down stairs and riding in a Model T Ford car. Also, I vaguely remember the inside of the church and darting down the aisle to my father in the pulpit. My mother was agile and caught me short of my destination, removing me from the church for a spanking. I guess that's why I remember the inside of the church. On a train trip to Brandon, my mother warned me not to throw her purse out the open window. Possibly misunderstanding her warning, I threw her purse out the open window. In the general confusion that followed, I must have escaped a spanking, because I do not remember the inside of the train. The CNR was apprised of the loss, and a track-repair crew found the purse and returned it to its rightful owner.

I've been told of the 1918 influenza epidemic and of my father's heroic efforts to take food, medicine, comfort, and condolence to those affected by it. And I've been told that word of his ministry was carried by trainmen to Transcona, the recently established headquarters of the CNR for western Canada. He accepted a call to Knox Presbyterian Church in that town in the fall of 1919.

Transcona: 1919 to 1926

Transcona was the ultimate single-industry town. All male residents either worked for the CNR or provided services to those who did. When the workday at "the shops" ended at five p.m. and the great gate swung open, the men poured forth like lava from an erupting volcano, breaking into rivulets as they made their way to their respective streets and homes. Each man knew his place in the pecking order, and tensions in the plant were apt to be continued elsewhere. Lackie Smith of the paint shop was ushering in church when an enemy entered and cheerfully said, "Give me a good seat, Lackie." Lackie's wife overheard and in a stage whisper added, "Give him the toe of your boot, Lackie."

I had Grades 1 to 5 in Transcona Central School, a two-minute run from home. In the Grade 2 classroom (taught by Mr. Honor), the back seats were taken by large boys, or even young men who could speak little English. These were Galicians and Ruthenians who lived on the east side of town, an area not yet provided with sewer and water, and their fathers worked as labourers for the CNR. I now know that Galicia and Ruthenia were regions of Ukraine and that these families were part of the post–World War I Ukrainian immigration, but I never heard the word *Ukrainian* ever mentioned.

World War I was still a recent event, amputees were a common sight, war widows were still being comforted, and children were eager to hear stories of the conflict. One veteran described to me how he had captured eighty German prisoners but, when I repeated the story to my father and he asked the hero's name, I was told not to believe everything I heard. In any event, Remembrance Day (11 November) was a major occasion in the school year and was commemorated by a special ceremony. Miss Barton asked me to read "He was a Private of the Buffs," a patriotic poem of the Henry Newbolt variety. It may have been set in the Boxer Uprising of 1900, not the noblest of British actions in the defence of freedom.

When I was in Grade 4, with Miss Barton, the strap was not used; instead, those who misbehaved (usually boys) were required to stand with their arms outstretched. This punishment was a joke for the first few minutes but soon became no fun at all. It was in Grade 5 with Miss Moir that I was finally given the strap, finally admitted to the select circle of those who had no fear. Actually, I did have fear, because I had often seen the punishment inflicted, and the recipients were obviously in pain, but the prestige to be gained far outweighed the prospect of discomfort. After all, pain is transitory, but pride is forever: I could now swagger with the other "strappees" and claim that it hadn't hurt. Miss Moir was particularly generous in the use of the strap and obligingly made it a public event to be enjoyed by the entire class. It was especially enjoyable when Alfie Mair was the victim. As a result of many such experiences, he had developed the knack of withdrawing his hand just before it was struck, with the result that

Miss Moir would hit herself on the thigh. Each encounter between the two – and they were numerous – became a duel, with Miss Moir determined not to let Alfie pull his hand away from her grip and Alfie, to her frustration, often managing to do so.

It was about this time that I learned to smoke. My father had stopped smoking so as not to give me a bad example, but his pipes and tobacco could be seen on a rafter in the basement. One spring, my friend Murray Matheson and I decided to try our luck. Taking the apparatus to the nearby prairie, we had scarcely begun to enjoy the vice when, in our excitement, we set the dry grass on fire. When stomping failed to extinguish the flame, we had visions of the dreaded prairie fire and rushed to the nearest house that had a telephone. When the mistress of the house answered our frantic knocking, we panted that a man had dropped a match and would she please telephone the Fire Department. With a stern look she asked, "Are you sure it was a man?" Desperate with guilt and fear, we ran home, where I began to feel unwell from the tobacco smoke – very unwell as it turned out – and I crawled under the porch to convalesce. Minutes later, when I was more than half in love with easeful death, the fire chief approached our front door; now more than ever seemed it rich to die. As it happened, the fire chief was consulting my father on some other matter, the prairie fire did not materialize, and I did not expire – but the episode put me off smoking.

In 1925, the Congregational, Methodist, and Presbyterian Churches came together to form the United Church of Canada, the largest Protestant Church in the country. The new church brought together three distinctive religious cultures: the Presbyterians, who stressed doctrine, the Methodists, who stressed deeds, and the Congregationalists (who were not numerous), who stressed congregational autonomy. To overstate slightly: the Methodists didn't care what you believed as long as your behaviour passed muster; the Presbyterians didn't care how you behaved as long as your creed was in order. For example, many Presbyterians saw virtue in whisky, but all Methodists viewed it as anathema.

There were also social differences. The Presbyterians came from the Established Church of Scotland, while the Methodists had been rejected by the Established Church of England. Although it was never said in public, the Presbyterians thought that they were a cut above the Methodists.

Discussions of Church union had begun prior to World War I, but only the Congregationalists had taken action: they had agreed to enter into union whenever the opportunity presented itself. Thus, when the other two were discussing the matter further, they both knew that the

Congregationalists could be counted upon. The decision in the Methodist Church lay with its central governing body: indeed, some congregations were unaware that union was being contemplated. Reid Vipond, sometime minister of Westminster United Church in Winnipeg, told me that his boyhood minister, in southwestern Ontario, made the surprise announcement one Sunday, "By the way, from now on, this will be called the 'Elgin United Church,' instead of the 'Elgin Methodist Church.'"

Things were quite different with the Presbyterians: each church had to decide for itself. Thus, in the year 1924 and the spring of 1925, the *Presbyterian Record* carried lists showing how different congregations had voted. My father, who had preached to 200 of these congregations, and my grandfather Edmison read and discussed these lists with intense interest, and the arrival of a new *Record* was an occasion to drop everything else.

Most, if not all, Presbyterian Churches in western Canada voted for union but, in eastern Canada, although the majority concurred, it was far from unanimous. Many major congregations, as well as numerous smaller ones, remained Presbyterian or, as they were called, Continuing Presbyterian. (Leonard Brockington, eloquent radio personality and former rector of Queen's University, when once called upon to thank a clergyman who had spoken too long, said, "I now know what is meant by 'Continuing Presbyterian.'")

My father and grandfather were in favour of union and were in suspense as to how the Transcona congregation would vote. The decision was made at a Sunday evening service, and I am told that I ran to my father with the cry, "What was the score?" The score was forty to two for union, which compensated in part for the negative vote at my father's home church in Hespeler, which my Duckworth grandparents still attended. The members of the Transcona Methodist Church were told that they had a new name and, in due course, the two congregations merged. In the meantime, my father had preached for a call to St. James, a suburb of Winnipeg.

St. James: 1926 to 1936

Most ministers have a favourite sermon, or "potboiler," which they use when they are guest preaching in another church. My father's potboiler was based on the text "Give me this mountain," words spoken by Caleb to Joshua (Joshua 14:12) when he chose between a fertile valley and a barren hillside. This was the sermon my father selected to preach for a call to Hampton Street United Church in St. James, a congregation known to be looking for a new minister. Some who heard the sermon assumed that it was addressed to them as a congregation and wondered what difficult mountain my father had identified. In spite of this perceived criticism, he received the call and, in the summer of 1926, we moved to 296 Hampton Street in St. James and my father began his new ministry. In 1929, Hampton Street United joined with Parkview United (the former Methodist Church) to form St. James United, with my father as its first minister.

I was sent to Britannia Public School, a quarter of a mile north on Hampton Street, and was placed in the Grade 6 class of Miss Campain, an agreeable woman who read us a continued story every Friday afternoon. One of the stories was Nellie McLung's *Sowing Seeds in Danny* which we all found amusing.

Much more important than school, however, were the soccer games that the principal, Clarence Moore, had organized. All the boys in Grades 6, 7, and 8 were divided into teams that played one another in a regular schedule. One game was completed each day, during the morning recess (fifteen minutes), the last third of the lunch hour (thirty minutes) and the afternoon recess (fifteen minutes). Each day's results were recorded as we trooped in from the afternoon recess. I could hardly wait to finish my lunch in order to return to the fray, and I gradually developed some skill in handling the football. My father, who had played Association Football (as he called it) in college, was only too happy to provide my own football, which we used for games in the back lane. Eventually, I played left wing for St. James Midgets in a city league sponsored by the Canadian Legion. To be in the midget category, one had to weigh less than 112 pounds, and, prior to the official weigh-in at the *Winnipeg Tribune* building, boys were known to have taken castor oil in a desperate attempt to make the weight. I always found myself playing with older, and usually better, players. One, Groves by name, was at least three years older, but he was small for his age and very fleet of foot. We were selected to perform prior to a game between the Winnipeg Selects ("All Stars") and a touring professional team from Kilmarnock, Scotland. Groves ran like a deer, dribbling almost the length of the field and astonishing the sports writers, who hailed him as a football prodigy: but we knew why he was so much better than the rest of us.

Prior to Christmas 1926, Mr. Moore decided to promote six students from each of the two Grade 6 classes to Grade 7. I was the last to be chosen from Miss Campain's class and so started 1927 in Grade 7. I must have held my own: at least, I entered Grade 8 the next year with Miss Gillis. Partly through Grade 7, whilst playing road hockey, I broke my right wrist and was obliged to write one set of examinations with my left hand. This was viewed as a feat of great courage, and I'm sure that my marks included a bonus for effort. During these two years we studied British history; thus, by taking two grades in one year, I missed the parts normally taken in the last half of Grade 6 and the first half of Grade 7. These had to do with the Tudors and the Stuarts, and I have never had them straight. I'm still not sure how many wives Oliver Cromwell had. We didn't study Canadian history until Grade 9; I suppose we had to establish our pedigree first. At the end of Grade 8, we wrote our "entrance" examinations. These were set and marked by the provincial Department of Education, and we waited in suspense for the arrival of the official letter informing us how we had fared. The "entrance," of course, was entrance to high school.

In 1928, my father bought a second-hand Chevrolet car from Mr. James Clark, an efficiency expert with the CNR and a friend from Transcona times. This was to carry us to South Orange, New Jersey (where my Uncle George Edmison was now located), and, the next year, to Vancouver and Victoria. Prior to our departure for the East Coast, my father took me for a trial run on the road from Winnipeg to Headingley, a hamlet eight miles west of Winnipeg. He accelerated to forty-eight miles per hour, the car quivered in every joint, and I was speechless with terror. At that point, he solemnly turned towards me and said, "That's how fast we'll have to travel on our trip." My mother had not been part of the test drive and, as it happened, had other ideas; her ideas usually prevailed. She had discerned a vibration that appeared at thirty-six miles per hour, and this became her sign that my father was driving dangerously: thirty-six miles per hour, not forty-eight, became our top speed.

The first "big trip," which was to cover 5,800 miles, began one evening in early August, following the final of the Sunday School Football League (Junior Division) in which Hampton Street United defeated Epworth United by a score of seven to three. To the surprise of everyone, including myself, I scored three of the goals. After the third, Jimmy Thorburn, our reliable centre half, said, "What's happened to you, Harry?" My exploit was discussed all the way to Emerson, on the United States border, where we pitched our umbrella tent for the first night. Although many towns had camping grounds, it was early days for touring, and we felt a bit like stout Cortez. We passed through Minneapolis, Chicago, and Detroit en route to South Orange, New Jersey. On the last day, we folded our tent at 4:30 a.m. and drove until 10:30 p.m., covering 340 miles in all. As the highway coincided with the main street of every town and city, we were unable to maintain our maximum speed of thirty-six miles per hour for much of the time. We arrived exhausted at Uncle George's on a Saturday night. There, after the usual pleasantries, Uncle George said to my father, "Harry, would you preach for me tomorrow?" My father obliged, undoubtedly using the text "Give me this mountain." My mother did not attend the service but slept for twenty-four hours.

Uncle George and Aunt Elizabeth had two daughters, Mary and Maude, and we had many happy times together. On this occasion, we were taken to Coney Island, where I squandered more than fifty pennies on a vending machine that sold pictures of baseball players. I kept trying for Babe Ruth, the famous Sultan of Swat, but kept getting lesser figures. A couple of days later, we were taken to Yankee Stadium, and I saw the Babe in person. During the game, a foul ball came directly towards my father, who would have caught it had not a woman squawked in alarm and thrown him off balance. But in the last of the ninth inning we forgot the foul ball. The Yankees were down two runs, with two men on base, and Ruth came to bat with two men out. He hit a towering fly ball that fell inches short of a home run.

We returned via Portland (Maine), Quebec City, Montreal, Ottawa, Toronto, Sarnia, the Straits of Mackinac, and Duluth. At that time, there was no highway through northern Ontario. Except when staying with friends or relatives, we slept in public camping grounds and became adept at raising and lowering the umbrella tent.

On the second big trip, in 1929, camping as before, we drove west to Calgary, Vancouver, and Victoria, by way of Spokane. This was a more difficult odyssey, because fewer adventurers had travelled this path. Odd incidents were lodged in the memory of a thirteen-year-old. First, the roads were rough; for example, between Winnipeg and Calgary, only two stretches of hard-surface highway existed – the "test run" between Winnipeg and Headingley, and the fifty miles between Regina and Moose Jaw. The Province of Saskatchewan had squandered its resources on the Regina–Moose Jaw showpiece, and long stretches of the remaining highway had ruts and no trace of gravel. Some of the soil adjacent to the wooden culverts had recently been washed away, and a car travelling at thirty-six miles per hour could receive quite a jolt. My mother, sitting in the back seat, was thrown to the ceiling at one of these culverts and hurt her head. She was annoyed and was scarcely mollified by my father's abject apology when we struck a second culvert and she hit her head on the ceiling again. This was the second worst thing he could ever have done, but, minutes later, he did the worst thing – he hit a third culvert. By the time we reached Calgary, a reconciliation had been partly effected.

To avoid the mountainous Canadian route, which we had been told was perilous, we drove south through Cranbrook to Spokane. An excellent road from Spokane to Seattle crossed the Columbia River Valley. Just over the river, a sign warned that we were commencing a twelve-mile hill. We marked the twelve-mile point and, on the return trip, my father turned the engine off and we did indeed coast for twelve miles.

In Vancouver, friends of my mother took us to Lynn Canyon and later to their house for dinner. I had run back and forth on the suspension bridge until my stomach felt queasy, but I managed to hold off until we reached the house, where I was hugely sick in the front hall.

From Victoria, where we visited the Butchart Gardens, we took an overnight ferry to Bellingham, Washington, and then returned to Spokane, en route to Yellowstone National Park. There we saw Old Faithful and fed bears from our hands. Much of the stretch from Spokane to Yellowstone was rough and barren. Near Coeur d'Alene, we ascended the Camel's Hump, a *very* steep section of highway at the top of an already steep hill. This was no small feat: to change to a lower gear in our model of car, it was necessary to bring the car to a complete stop. We had been climbing the approach hill in second gear, but the engine lacked sufficient power for the Hump itself, and my father barely achieved low gear, whilst operating the emergency brake, before we would have rolled back over a precipice. In a section of Montana, we drove for forty miles without seeing a mammal of any type, and we rejoiced when a cattle beast came into view.

I had entered Linwood High School in 1928. It was a mile from our house, and I came home for lunch regardless of the weather. Mr. Macdougall was the principal, and he taught Latin. At the start, I found Latin so simple and orderly that I felt I could soon converse with the Romans, at least about the Gallic Wars. But soon I could see merit in what an earlier scholar had written in my pre-owned grammar:

> Latin is a language
> As dead as it can be;
> It killed all the Romans,
> And now it's killing me.

Mr. Boyd, whose daughter Daisy later succumbed to the wooing of Mitchell Sharpe, taught mathematics. As we began algebra, the problems were so trivial that I calculated the answers in my head, without following the protocol recommended by Mr. Boyd and which became necessary as the problems became more difficult. As a result, I could not solve the more difficult problems until my mother, who had taught school in Ontario, showed me the technique. I had always admired her, but now I respected her. In Grade 11, when we studied geometry, Boyd gave us a special problem for homework every day, and I rushed home to attempt it.

Miss Megaffin taught composition and English. I was not electrified by these subjects, but I liked her. For a public-speaking assignment in the 1929-30 school year, I chose the topic "Television," which I had seen described in *The United Church Observer* as an important new invention. I committed my speech to memory and began well, but, as I neared the end, I realized that I had forgotten the name of my topic. Ducking my head, I asked a boy in the front row, "What am I talking about?" Without hesitation, he replied, "Television," and I was able to complete my speech with barely an interruption.

Physics and chemistry were taught by Mr. Clark, but I found little interest in those subjects. He took an interest in me, however, and some years later, when I was teaching physics at United College, he invited me to lunch to receive serious advice. A romantic young man, he said, is apt to think that he has met the one girl whom fate has chosen for him. Actually, there are thousands who would do just as well, so one shouldn't jeopardize a career by acting on the-only-girl-in-the-world myth.

Miss McLaren taught French but pronounced all words as if they were English. The single exception was her description of a visit to Paris during which poor children called out, "Sous! Sous!" Otherwise, the subject was an exercise in written rules; we never realized that it was a means of communication.

At the end of Grade 11 we wrote matriculation examinations which, if passed, would admit us to university. From the class of about forty, three of us went on to university. One of the brightest boys, Roberts by name, later called regularly on my mother as a door-to-door bread salesman for Spiers Parnell. And there were others with more potential than I who were happy to secure similarly menial jobs.

My years from the ages of ten to fifteen were carefree, idyllic, and full of adventure. The prairie was a few hundred yards away, where crocuses bloomed in the spring, gophers ran free in the summer, and wild strawberries could be picked in season. The Assiniboine River was there to be swum in; vacant lots provided sites for tree houses and underground abodes; fields existed for baseball, outdoor rinks, and golf; and distant places beckoned, where we could venture on bicycles.

Our own rink was located on Marjorie Street behind Ferguson's house. We collected fifty cents per family for a total of ten dollars, the price charged by the Fire Department for three floodings. The shape of the rink was irregular, because trees were in the way, but we defined it with low boards and gathered in wild expectation for the first flooding. The other two floodings were spaced throughout the winter as the condition of the ice surface required. The Ferguson boy, a thirteen-year-old electrical whiz, ran a line from his house to a single light bulb on a pole. We put our skates on at home and went home to warm our feet. Several such rinks existed in St. James, but most were organized by adults and were rectangular in shape. All, however, were governed by the ten-dollars-for-three-floodings rule, which represented an act of charity by the fire chief but which we took for granted at the time. There were only two indoor rinks in the City – the Amphitheatre (across Osborne Street from the Legislature) and the Olympic (on Church Street across from St. John's College).

One day, in a poplar bluff about two miles away, my friend Ab Marley and I came upon a pile of empty safety deposit boxes. I recognized them because I had accompanied my parents to the Bank of Montreal vault at the corner of Portage and Main, when they were clipping coupons from Canada savings bonds. I told my father of the discovery, he telephoned the police, and within minutes I was directing them to the site. To my slight embarrassment, and to my father's humiliation, the artifacts were discarded lead batteries, and even I could see that I had been mistaken.

Most delivery vehicles – milk, bread, coal, Eaton's – were drawn by horses. An innocent fall and spring pastime for us was throwing snowballs at these beasts of burden. The horses seemed to enter into the fun: at least, they reared a bit and galloped faster. But their drivers lacked a sense of humour and were fast runners. Luckily, I was a fast runner too.

One Monday, when I was still at Britannia School, the news spread that a boy had walked to the city dump on the preceding Saturday, had found all the parts needed for a bicycle, and had ridden it home. The next Saturday Ab Marley and I, equipped with a borrowed bicycle wrench, walked the two miles to the dump. We found where the rats lived, but not where the bicycle parts were kept; it was a long two miles home.

I had two different paper routes: King Edward Street in Grade 10 and Rutland Street in Grade 11. According to the *Winnipeg Free Press*, I was an independent businessman, buying papers from the publisher and selling them to my customers. This was a clever device to ensure that the carrier, not the publisher, bore the loss for unpaid subscriptions. The courts have recently (1998) ruled that carriers are employees, not entrepreneurs, thus putting an end to this long-standing charade.

My friend Ab Marley was my helper on both routes. From the proceeds of this independent business, I deposited fifty cents per week in the *Free Press* Carrier Savings Bank, and we split the rest – about $1.25 per week. This allowed us to buy a piece of cream pie from Mrs. Holland, at a cost of five cents, before starting our delivery and, after finishing, to choose special chocolates, at one cent each, at the corner store operated by Mr. and Mrs. Cartman. Finding a chocolate with a pink centre earned a prize of five cents. One of the neighbourhood boys could spot the pink centres and was always on hand when a new layer was unveiled. Then it was left to the rest of us, hoping against hope, to finish the layer. We were major customers at Cartman's store, where the daily cash intake once fell to thirty-five cents. Somewhat more was sold on credit, to be paid at the end of the month. Mr. Cartman had lost an arm in World War I and was unfit for a regular job.

Twice a year, the *Winnipeg Free Press* had a competition for new subscriptions, or "starts." These could be virgin readers or could be stolen from the *Winnipeg Tribune*, whose carriers were also attempting to secure new starts. The first and third pages of the *Tribune* both carried headlines, and its carriers could brag of "two front pages." We tried to make the most of the "better comics" and "more classified ads," never realizing that John Dafoe's editorials were the pride of the nation. Our contests were invariably won by one kid who could shed tears on demand as he described to non-subscribers the plight of his widowed mother. During one contest, Ab and I targeted a remote area west of Deer Lodge, where the houses were widely separated. In one night we obtained three starts from householders who had never been the objects of high-pressure salesmanship from independent businessmen.

The stock-market crash of 1929 meant nothing to the residents of St. James, which was a working-class community. They knew nothing about the trading of equities and commodities. But they were mightily affected by the economic depression that followed. At that time, the safety net, as we know it, was virtually non-existent. Old-age pensions were twenty dollars per month and could only be got after a humiliating means test. Welfare was in its infancy and the meagre payments were usually tied to make-work programs. Soup kitchens were a necessity. But worst of all, proud men, whom their wives had married for better, not worse, could no longer support their families and were forced to seek charity in one form or another.

The church became a major agent of hope and material relief. Thus, at Christmastime, St. James United Church alone provided more than 100 hampers to distressed members of the community. These were delivered on Christmas Eve, on toboggans, to anxious parents who had been told that the hampers would arrive but were never sure of meat and toys for the morrow until the knock came at the door. The elderly were also on the list, and I once felt the wrath of an older man whose pride would not allow him to accept charity, although the need was everywhere apparent. Some unfortunates tried to register for a hamper at more than one church, unaware that a master list existed to ensure that the limited resources were distributed as fairly as possible.

One family was notorious for cultivating several church affiliations as the Christmas season approached. The father was a remittance man, who received regular payments from his family in England on condition that he stay in Canada. He could be seen in gentleman's garb and carrying a walking stick, whilst his wife and children followed respectfully behind. He, himself, never sought charity, but his wife and children made up for his reticence.

In the fall of 1931, I entered first year at the University of Manitoba. Thereafter, my recreation centred mainly on golf, tennis, and bridge, the latter two with Janet, Murray, and Gladys Conklin. The Tom Sawyer days were over.

College Days: 1931 to 1937

2

In 1931, the University of Manitoba offered arts and science programs as well as professional ones in accountancy, agriculture, architecture, engineering, law, medicine, and pharmacy. Arts programs were also offered by three affiliated church colleges – St. Boniface (French Catholic), St. John's (Anglican), and Wesley (United). These institutions prepared students for examinations conducted by the University. At St. Boniface, the instruction was in French and the curriculum (Latin philosophy) was unique to that college. The programs at St. John's and Wesley followed those of the University, and the college professors participated in the setting and grading of the University examinations. For some reason, it was decided that I should study science, although my enthusiasm for physics and chemistry had up to then been slight and my performance little better. That decision propelled me to the University itself, which was housed in temporary buildings that had been erected during World War I on the site now known as The Mall.

At that time, and indeed until 1961, it was possible to enter the University of Manitoba upon the completion of Grade 11. Thus, in September 1931, two months shy of my sixteenth birthday, I enrolled in first year, taking chemistry, English, Latin, mathematics, and physics.

I went to classes each day with Ronald Paris, who lived on Berry Street, one block away from my home on Hampton Street. We also ate lunch together at the nearby Hudson's Bay cafeteria where, for twenty-five cents, we were given soup, a main dish, bread, beverage, and dessert. Before returning to class, we spent ten minutes in the sports department (for me) and an equal time in the music department (for Ronald). Golf was my passion at the time, whilst Ronald played the trumpet.

I'd like to report that I was stimulated by my university classes, but that was not the case. Chemistry was dull, and the laboratory was heavy with the stench of experiments that had gone wrong. English, with Fletcher Argue, the students' friend, was better, but eighty of us sat alphabetically, cheek by jowl, in a poorly ventilated room, and Duckworth and Dyker completed the back row of Argue's section. Latin was Latin. Dean William Tier and N.R. Wilson taught us mathematics in the adjacent Law Courts Building and failed to arouse my interest. Physics was taught by W.A. Anderson, a former school principal, to a listless class of 250. I could scarcely wait for classes to end and for golf to begin.

On 23 August 1932, the *Winnipeg Free Press* revealed that the University of Manitoba's endowment funds had been embezzled by J.A. Machray, the nephew of the University's first chancellor, Archbishop Robert Machray. One American newspaper used a garbled version of events to titillate its readers: "Archbishop Embezzles University Funds." At that time, financial transactions involving the University had prudently required the authorization of both the chairman of the Board and the bursar, but Machray had fortuitously held both offices. Thus, he was able to divert University funds to cover personal investment losses. The loss to the University, later established at $971,000, came on the heels of a reduction in the government grant from $500,000 to $400,000 and forced the University to reduce salaries and increase tuition fees. I was not affected by the salary cuts, but the higher tuition was another matter.

Wesley College: 1932 to 1935

I was vaguely aware of Wesley College, the former Methodist institution; indeed, I had passed it daily on my way to university classes. But, because I was pursuing science, I had not considered studying there. However, Murray Conklin, who was entering his final year, had learned that Wesley was *not increasing its tuition fees*. Machray had not embezzled its funds (although he had denuded the Anglican Church as well as the University), and there was no government grant to reduce. I could register at Wesley and commute the short distance to the University for whatever science I needed. Accordingly, in September 1932, I presented myself at that chateau-like building on Portage Avenue, where I found myself in the company of many others whom I had known at the University during the preceding year, including my cheek-by-jowl mate, Lyle Dyker. Moreover, I was told of a 10-percent reduction for the children of United Church ministers.

The extent of the migration from "Varsity Arts" to "Wesley Arts" took everyone by surprise. Thus, in each of 1928 and 1935 (my own graduating class) the two institutions contributed a total of 170 arts graduates. In 1928, Wesley contributed 14 percent of this total; in 1935, it was 54 percent. On top of the University's other problems, this was a blow, both to morale and to the treasury.

What did I find at Wesley College? First, of course, I found over-crowding: 400 arts students, 150 collegians, thirty theologues, and thirty staff in a building designed for 100 to 150 students and fifteen profes-sors. But we crowded into classrooms, two to three professors shared an office, and library books worked overtime. Bradley's *Shakespeare* was the major authority on that literary giant, and seldom were its covers closed. I found that I was no longer permitted academic anonymity as professors tried to draw me into discussion and probe my knowledge. This was not especially to my liking, as I wasn't working very hard, but it was a change from the impersonal atmosphere at the University. I found that the student activities – sport, social, intellectual, and cultural – were numerous and open to all: in them and in class, I found friends who have remained so for life.

Wesley College had been founded in 1887, primarily to train men for the Methodist ministry. One of its early graduates (1896) was J.S. Woodsworth. The son of James Woodsworth, who had come to the North-west as a Methodist missionary in 1882, J.S. Woodsworth became Wesley's most famous alumnus, as he applied Christianity to social problems, begin-ning with All People's Mission in north Winnipeg. In 1918, he left the Church to be more effective in helping people, and, in 1921, he was elected to Parliament. In 1933, he was the founder and leader of the Co-operative Commonwealth Federation (CCF, later the NDP). In 1939, he registered the sole vote in the Parliament of Canada against the declaration of war and received an ovation from his fellow MPs for following his conscience.

Woodsworth was the greatest, but by no means the only, Methodist to preach the social gospel. Albert E. Smith was ordained in 1897 and, in the next twenty years, steadily moved to the left until his sermons during the great Winnipeg General Strike of 1919 were tirades against those who profited from the poor. These tirades were delivered from the pulpit of First Methodist Church in Brandon until, under pressure, he was forced to re-sign. Thereupon, he organized the People's Church in that same city. And, in 1920, he and nine others were elected to the Manitoba legislature as members of the Labour Party. The Norris government fell in 1922, pre-cipitating a new election, and Smith stood again as a Labour candidate. Believed to be a socialist, if not worse, Smith inspired fear in the Conserva-tive and Liberal camps, and they sought out my uncle, Dr. John H. Edmison, to run as a coalition or "fusion" candidate. My uncle had delivered count-less babies and was well liked. In the course of the campaign, Smith re-ferred to my uncle, disparagingly, as a rich man. My uncle replied that, if he had more money than the Rev. Smith, he had earned it while Smith was at home, asleep in his bed. We were proud of my uncle's witty rebuttal, but I now realize that Smith was also trying to serve his fellow human beings. In 1923, he moved to Toronto to become involved in labour organizations and, two years later, he and his wife became members of the Communist Party.

The most flamboyant personification of the social gospel, of course, was Salem Bland, a professor of theology from 1903 to 1917, who roused his students from piety to action and, perhaps for that reason, was removed from the College. One of his prominent followers, William Ivens, left the ministry at the time of the Winnipeg General Strike to work for the Labour cause and was one of the ten members elected to the Manitoba legislature in 1920. Stanley Knowles (theology 1933, and long an NDP MP), Carl Ridd (1950, professor of religious studies, social activist), and William Blaikie (1973, and currently an NDP MP) were later embodiments of the social gospel of Woodsworth, Bland, and the others.

In the 1930s, the spirit of the social gospel still imbued the students in theology, and the Student Christian Movement (SCM) was vigorously active. Daily chapel, which was well attended, reminded us of our obligations to others, and our professors had not yet declared that moral issues were off limits. The College was anything but an ivory tower.

Pacifism was a major subject of argument, but usually in the abstract. However, when Adolf Hitler came to power on 30 January 1933, promising to avenge Germany's humiliation at the Treaty of Versailles (after World War I) and to restore it to its former greatness, the prospect of war became less hypothetical. Largely for that reason, the debate in the Oxford Union in February 1933 on the motion, "This House will in no circumstances fight for King and Country," which carried by 275 to 153, received worldwide publicity. Not realizing that it was simply a debate that the affirmative had won, the German ambassador to Great Britain, Joachim von Ribbentrop (who was hanged as a war criminal in 1946), reported back to Hitler that the flower of British youth supported Chamberlain's policy of appeasement. Influenced by the headlines, we also assumed that the result reflected student opinion and asked ourselves, in debates and bull sessions, whether Canada should be involved in Europe's wars. Also, in the event of war, were we prepared to fight? At a rowdy gathering at the house of my classmate Jack Sword, I remember stating that, if forced to fight, I would shoot the enemy in the legs. All of us were pacifists to some degree, but later, when war did erupt, the talk of pacifism vanished and the question of which service to join arose. took its place. In my circle, the navy and the air force won hands down, and I was one of the very few in my circle who did not serve in uniform.

In my second year (the first at Wesley), I took English, chemistry, geology, Latin, and mathematics; chemistry and geology at the University. I continued English, Latin, and mathematics during third and fourth years and filled out the degree requirements with a smattering of economics and sociology. Thus, although I began university as a science student, I left Wesley with a B.A. degree and a few low-level science courses. When I applied for the Rhodes Scholarship in the fall of 1935, I stated that I intended to study Latin, but I did that only because the application form called for a statement of purpose; I still had no real purpose in life.

One of the College songs began with this verse:

> Our College is United,
> Here on Portage Avenue,
> That's where we work for Phelps and Kirk,
> O.T. and Ritcey too.
> Our boys are great in loud debate,
> Our girls in sports and fun.
> Then Hail to Old United,
> We'll cheer her every one.

Arthur Phelps and Watson Kirkconnell (Kirk) taught me English, but what a contrast in style! Phelps was by turn lyrical, provocative, and inspiring but never consistent or systematic. Kirkconnell was factual, thorough, and encouraging and always consistent and systematic. From Phelps we learned that form is often more important than substance; from Kirkconnell we learned that substance is often more important than form. The bright students revelled in Phelps; I inclined to Kirkconnell. One day I found a small notebook filled with phrases and incomplete sentences, which someone suggested might belong to Phelps. When I took it to his office and he grasped it fervently, I had the impression that I was restoring to him his entire lecture notes. At the start of his presentation of each new novel, Kirkconnell would summarize on the blackboard the main facts of the author's life. Years later, I spoke to him about the summaries and supposed that their preparation must have been time consuming. "Not at all," he said. "I copied them from the *Encyclopaedia Britannica*." Phelps, at heart a poet, became a well-known voice on the CBC, whilst Kirkconnell became first a professor at McMaster and later the president of Acadia University in Wolfville, Nova Scotia.

The "O.T." in the College song was O.T. Anderson, an Icelander and the dean who, along with Lee Ritcey, taught mathematics. Ritcey taught the higher stuff, and some good students came from the University to sit his classes. He later became the executive director of the Canadian Mathematics Congress. By the second class, it seemed, O.T. knew the names of all the students. He spoke quietly, taught carefully and, at the end, gave us strong hints as to what was on the examination paper; his pass rate was high.

The president, J.H. Riddell, taught second-year Latin, whilst Kirkconnell taught the higher years. It was probably because of him that I took the subject for four years. Riddell also taught what we were told was sociology. The subject was not well established in Canada at that time, and the examination comprised two parts: one for Riddell's students and one for those who had studied at the University. Riddell placed emphasis on "the interchange of thought and feeling," as did I on the final examination. On one occasion, Mrs. Riddell was invited to play bridge, not realizing that she would be playing for money. When she confessed to her husband that she was in debt, he wrote a cheque but marked it "gambling debt," which he knew the bank would not accept. He managed the College's finances with the same astuteness.

David Owen and Meredith Thompson also taught English. Owen was a graduate of the College and an ordained minister; he taught some English until he found a place in philosophy; he occupied the chair of the Department of Philosophy until his retirement in 1971. In the congenial family atmosphere that existed, Owen brought his baby daughter, Jane, to class and bestowed her on an occupant of the front row. Thompson had come directly from a Ph.D. in music from Breslau, and his arrival caused quite a stir. He gave a public lecture entitled "Student Life in Other Lands," in which he devoted the entire hour to student life at Oxford. In conclusion, he said that if he were invited again, his title would be "Student Life in *Other* Lands."

Although I took no history, French, or psychology, I was aware that Arthur R.M. Lower, Victor Leathers, and Russell Cragg ruled those disciplines, with the assistance of John W. Pickersgill in history and Pansy Bowes in French.

Lower was a distinguished historian and interpreter of current events. He thought nothing of offering unsolicited advice to the prime minister of the day. He moved to Queen's in 1947 and in 1962 was president of the Royal Society, an honour that he described in *My First Seventy-Five Years* as "academically, . . . the top."

Leathers had studied in Paris where, for a time, he shared a room with a young Quebec artist, Alfred Pellan, who enjoyed late-night cafés. As Leathers studied during the day whilst Pellan slept, they co-existed genially but out of phase with one another. Leathers had a forbidding mien, and students were reluctant to respond to his questions in class but gradually learned that a gentle heart beat below the bellicose surface.

Cragg, an ordained minister and master of the arresting phrase, taught a version of psychology that was equivalent to Riddell's version of sociology. Every summer he proceeded to Northwestern University in Evanston, Illinois, to deepen his knowledge of his subject. Later we learned that his academic sojourn coincided with an extended home stand of the Chicago Cubs, who played at nearby Wrigley Field. A frequent guest preacher, he once found himself before a congregation of two. Undismayed, he told them how lucky they were: they would each have one-half the benefit.

Pickersgill was a graduate of Manitoba and had recently returned from Oxford with an accent only partially mastered. He left the College to join the Privy Council Office and ultimately served in the federal Cabinet.

Bowes doubled as dean of Sparling Hall, the women's residence. To help her students remember the gender of *l'arbre*, she said, "Think of a girl up a tree: that's no place for a girl – *l'arbre* is masculine."

Second-year chemistry, which I took at the University, was taught by Paul Hiebert who, although we did not know it, was preparing to immortalize Sarah Binks, "the sweet songstress of Saskatchewan." He taught analytical chemistry, which he appeared to know, but it was not his passion. In the laboratory, we were given unknown samples to identify, using standard analytic techniques. We would take our samples straightway to the reagent shelf in the hope that they would resemble some of the compounds there. Once, I was given a sample of distinctive thin, white crystals and, to my delight, found that they were identical to those of magnesium sulphate (Epsom salts): hours of wearisome analysis avoided!

Were any of our professors eccentric? That depends. I once saw a television interview with two elderly Oxford dons who were asked if they had known anyone who was eccentric. It seemed to me that the interviewer needed look no further. However, the two consulted briefly and agreed that a late colleague may have been so. Every evening he left the high table carrying with him a piece of toast that others assumed formed a bedtime snack. After his death, those who cleared his rooms found a closet full of toast. By that definition, our professors may have fallen short, but they exuded individuality, and their personalities impressed us as much as their learning, in some cases even more.

It was in my final year at Wesley that I attended my first opera production. It was *Faust*, performed by the touring San Carlos Opera, and for thirty-five cents I had a seat in the "gods" at the Walker Theatre, as far from the stage as space would permit. Since that time, and seizing whatever opportunities presented themselves, I've attended some 200 performances in various parts of the world. My census may be of interest: *Carmen*, 16; *La Bohème*, 11; *Don Giovanni*, 8; *Madama Butterfly*, 8; *Faust*, 7; *La Traviata*, 7; *Tosca*, 7; *Lucia de Lammermoor*, 6; *Marriage of Figaro*, 6; *Aida*, 6; *Rigoletto*, 6; *Turandot*, 5; *The Barber of Seville*, 5; *Salome, 5*; and sixty-eight others, seen one to four times each, not counting John Gay's *Beggar's Opera* or Kurt Weill's *Three-penny Opera*. The opera houses have included Bayreuth, La Scala, Vienna State Opera, Berlin Opera, Paris Opera, and, of course, Covent Garden and the Metropolitan Opera. Often the music alone would not have held my attention but, when combined with the spectacle, I've found it hard to resist.

Convocation Hall, which dominated the second and third floors of the four-storey College building, was the scene of all major events – public lectures, plays, musical events and morning chapel. For some reason, Phelps also taught us a second-year course in English in its more than ample confines. Once a year he would instruct "Dad" French, the caretaker, to leave a stepladder standing, which he would absent-mindedly ascend during a lecture, in what was obviously a contrived action, but which caused the girls to giggle.

Carl Pye, the master of the Wesley College physical plant, carried a famous name in science, especially in Cambridge. There, a Pye had co-founded the Cambridge Instrument Company, and his son, W.G. Pye, after serving as instrument maker to Sir J.J. Thomson, had founded Pye's Radio. I suspect that Wesley's Pye shared the same genes, for his mechanical inventiveness was a feature of the College from 1920 to 1963. It was said that President Riddell had a pact with Pye: he was paid a lump sum for salary *plus* fuel. Whatever he saved on the fuel went to his own pocket. With this incentive, he devised a massive furnace that, under a forced draft, would burn almost anything. During my time as a student, he favoured sawdust and rubber tires, which he accumulated behind the College. *Unsightly* is too tame a word to describe the scene, but no one ever complained of being cold. As the fiery furnace was around the corner from the boys' locker room, I frequently paused to marvel at the spectacle. The sawdust was consumed whilst still in the air, but the rubber tires gave permanence to the conflagration. Pye was a bit brusque but never bridled when disciples came to admire his work: I was allowed (or perhaps even encouraged) to feed the flame.

Pye's unorthodox fuel once saved a student's life. Henry Funk had taken a dare to walk from one window to another along a narrow ledge on the fourth floor of the College, but his foot had slipped. As his companions raced down to pick up his body and carry it to the morgue, Funk met them on the stairs; he had fallen on the sawdust and the tires. Surely one human life more than compensated for the months of black, particle-laden smoke that Pye delivered to the City of Winnipeg every winter. I played golf with Funk a few years later at Sandy Hook, and he seemed unaware that he was a legend in the Wesley Hall of Fame.

Gerald Bedford, the University of Winnipeg's historian, has written: "The Class of 1935 may well have been Wesley's finest." Not trusting myself to single out individuals, I shall confine myself to Bedford's selections. He mentions the senior stick and lady stick (student president and vice-president), Neil Morrison and Freda (Porter) Hoole. Neil had his major career with the CBC but later flourished at York University. Freda was elegant, generous and wise, and we all did whatever she told us to do. Donald McGavin, our scholar and permanent class president, became a prominent lawyer and secretary to the International Nickel Company. Jack Sword joined the University of Toronto, where he served two terms as acting president. Tom Saunders, a poet, served the United Church before joining the Editorial Board of the *Winnipeg Free Press*. Lyle Dyker was teacher, curling champion of Canada, and investment expert. Gordon Leckie was a journalist with Federated Co-op and later joined me at the University of Manitoba. Genevieve (Johns) Doidge, the outstanding sprinter, and Helen (Bowman) Hickling, our permanent class vice-president, have had key roles in our class reunions. Frank Pickersgill, who was executed as a spy in occupied France, took some classes with us but did most of his work at the University. In addition, two of our number (Tom Cottier and Jim Marsh) lost their lives in the war, four others (Alex Calder, George Douglas, Julius Eustace, and Bill McKay) entered the Christian ministry, two (Bruce Hunter and Laird Wylie) became medical doctors, many trained as teachers, and all made significant contributions to society. Bedford was quite right!

It was customary at that time for graduating classes to make a gift to the College, say, a lectern or a desk. Our class, led by Freda Porter, was more imaginative, and, through W.J. Phillips's daughter Mary (who was a year or two behind us) made a deal to buy one of his watercolours. There is no record of the price paid, but it would have been between $50 and $100, as we could not have afforded more than one dollar per person. Phillips, of course, is famous for his coloured woodcuts, but the College also possessed a portrait of President Riddell by Phillips in addition to the Class of 1935 gift. When I returned to the University of Winnipeg in 1971, I asked for the watercolour and it was discovered in a closet off the comptroller's office. I immediately promoted it to the president's office, where I enjoyed its view of a country elevator for the next ten years. The last time I saw it, it was in the office of Chancellor Carol Shields: that's as high as it can go.

Gordon Leckie, Jack Sword, and Les Thompson organized a public-speaking club, where we met weekly to orate to one another and subsequently to be criticized unmercifully. Although speaking to a small group of good friends, I was very nervous at the start. We discussed not only the presentation but also the content of the speech. After all, as Kenneth Tynan, the theatre critic for the *Observer* once said, "Look after the sense and the sounds will take care of themselves" (a takeoff on the proverb "Look after the pence and the pounds will take care of themselves").

I also had some coaching from Edna Sutherland, who taught public speaking to the theology students. She had a magnificent voice, and she sought to teach her students how best to use their own voices, quite overcoming the fact that her features were deformed from a malfunction of her pituitary gland. At our first session, she asked me to read some poetry: I chose Browning (for his bravado) and Keats (for his melancholy). She agreed with Tynan, that is, that the emphasis should be on meaning, not on emotion, and she prescribed a series of exercises to strengthen my diaphragm, which I followed for a few years. The principal one was to stretch out my arms as if preparing to catch a child who was jumping from a roof.

Debates were popular and always about serious subjects – capitalism, isolationism, imperialism, protectionism, pacifism, socialism, and the like. On one occasion, I took the affirmative for the motion "That state medicine should be established," and I quite convinced myself of its merit. My two uncles and four cousins who became doctors would have been shocked at my apostasy. Victor Leathers, who taught French, was the judge and commented on my florid style but added that it was excusable at my age. At least, I stuck to my lines, unlike the situation at a school debate when a boy prepared not only his own speech but also that of his partner. When he rose to speak, he forgot his own speech and gave his partner's instead. As he sat down, he muttered to her, "I'm sorry, Sybil." Tears were her only means of dealing with the situation.

Phelps wrote an anti-war play that he offered to the Dramatic Society without divulging its provenance. Dorothy Jones was the female lead, Molly Rogers was the director, and I was a soldier. Dorothy could be dramatic, and Molly was histrionic to the core, but I could never portray anyone but myself. I was chosen because of my voice (thanks to Edna Sutherland). Dorothy smoked a cigar, which took attention from my bland characterization. After the performance, Phelps revealed that he was the author, and many were agog that they had been part of a *world premiere*. I understand that Phelps did the same thing the next year, with R.O.A. Hunter and Lorne Tyndale in two of the roles, but his cover was blown before the performance.

One day, Kirkconnell asked if I would participate in a meeting of the Polish-Canadian Society, which he had organized. Helen (Heaslip) Robertson, a personable and clever member of our class, and I were to speak on two Canadian writers. I was assigned Frederick Philip Grove, then of mysterious origin who, with encouragement from Phelps and Kirkconnell, had written *Search for America, Over Prairie Trails,* and *Settlers of the Marsh.* Kirkconnell was intent on establishing bridges with those who had come from Central Europe, and one of his other activities was to translate selected poems into English. Later, following the war, he became almost obsessed with alarm that Communists were infiltrating Canadian ethnic societies and publications. This was the theme of his convocation address when he was awarded an honorary degree by McMaster University. Incidentally, during the reading of Kirkconnell's citation (which listed his numerous books), Chancellor Carey Fox, unaware that his microphone was live, whispered to President Gilmour, who was to leave on the morrow for the United Kingdom, "That would be good reading for you on the ship."

All this was but prelude to the valedictory address, which my classmates had entrusted me to deliver at the graduates' farewell dinner and dance, held at the Royal Alexandra Hotel in March 1935. After delivering some unmemorable passages, I closed with a poem entitled "The Way," by John Oxenham. As with my other public utterances, I had committed the text to memory and, in my mind's eye, followed the written page. Before reaching the poem, I realized that I had forgotten John Oxenham's name. Not having someone in the front row to ask, as in the "Television" speech, I lamely introduced the poem with the words "As the poet has said" and managed to pass it off without disgrace. A few days after the event, John MacKay, principal of Manitoba College (the United Church Seminary), called me to his office and asked if I had considered studying for the ministry. If he had known how my memory failed in times of crisis, he might not have honoured me with the question.

The University of Manitoba: 1935 to 1937

During the summer of 1935, I took a course in zoology on the chance that I might decide to apply for admission to medicine. Then, C.W. Lowe, a member of my father's church and a professor of botany, pointed out that I had sufficient credits in science to obtain a B.Sc. in one additional year. Accordingly, I registered at the University for organic chemistry and sufficient botany courses to complete the degree requirements. This involved a significant change in venue as, in 1932, the University had transferred the senior years of the Faculty of Arts and Science to its Agricultural College, some eight miles south of the Broadway buildings, which I had attended and which remained the site of the Junior Division for a further eighteen years. The botany courses were all descriptive, emphasizing appearance and other external characteristics. It was the type of science that Lord Rutherford had in mind when he made his brutal statement "All science consists of two parts – physics and stamp collecting." At that time, zoology was also dedicated to externalities and provenances. The botany courses were heavy on fungi, of which Reginald Buller was a world authority and whose intricate sexual habits he had pursued with no respect for their primitive modesty.

Reginald Buller was one of the five professors hired in 1904 to establish the teaching of science in the University. He became world famous for his studies of fungi, publishing seven monographs on the subject. He was the only University of Manitoba professor ever to be elected to the Royal Society of London. Many years later, in 1990, as chancellor of the University, I wrote to older graduates inviting them to contribute towards plaques summarizing the careers of early professors, after whom University buildings had been named. The response was generous and, in some cases, anecdotes were enclosed. One woman reported that Buller entertained his senior class every year at the Fort Garry Hotel. Tea was served, and each woman was given a rose whilst each man received a package of cigarettes. Another recalled misbehaving in Buller's class and being expelled for a week. Indignant, she complained to Dean Tier, who listened sympathetically to her tale and advised her to stay away from class for a week. Buller's entry in *Who's Who in Canada* gave his hobbies as billiards and crossing the Atlantic (sixty-five times). In this respect, I have surpassed Buller with my ninety-two crossings.

The summer of 1935 had been my last year of summer golf; now, in 1936, I had to face the world of work. It was to be in Brandon with the trucking company that my cousin Jack MacArthur had established under the name MacArthur and Son. He had devised a strategy to compete with the railroad. He would pick up goods in Winnipeg at the end of the day and guarantee delivery in Brandon by the start of business the next day. Thus, drivers were involved in the Winnipeg pick-up and the subsequent loading of the trucks before starting off for Brandon at 8:00 or 9:00 p.m. Reaching there an hour or two after midnight, they slept until 8:00 a.m., when they began to deliver their cargoes to the Brandon destinations. In this way, customers in Brandon could telephone orders to Winnipeg at 4:00 p.m. and find them on their doorsteps sixteen hours later, a service the railroad could not duplicate. Loads in the opposite direction, from Brandon to Winnipeg, which were mostly livestock and chickens, also travelled by night. It was a hard schedule for the drivers but, by the summer of 1936, the company was well enough established for Jack to risk hiring his young cousin at the provincial minimum wage of forty-five dollars per month. One of the drivers warned me that I would be a target because I was a relative of the boss. I worked hard, Jack showed me no favours, and that threat soon evaporated.

Scott Bateman, later deputy minister of Education, was another summer driver, but the permanent drivers were a tough lot, or at least pretended to be. One, Bill Tieple, strong as an ox, once had a load of hogs destined for a packing plant in Winnipeg but took a curve at too high a speed. The side of the truck gave way, and the hogs were thrown free. Although it was the dead of night, he scoured the bushes until he had retrieved them all. When he arrived at Swift's in Winnipeg, he had one more hog than he had started with.

Another driver, Gordon Rice, was keen on race horses and, when we took a load of merchandise to Lethbridge once, he arranged to stop in Moose Jaw for a day at the races. We made a prior visit to the stables, where we learned which horses were expected to win. Armed with this informa-tion and emboldened by Gordon's confidence, I bet two dollars on the first race, to win. By the end of the first race, I had lost 4.4 percent of my monthly salary but had seen how the system worked. For the next six races, I bet two dollars on the favourite, to show, and ended twenty cents ahead for the day. We arrived in Alberta soon after Premier William Aberhart had begun distributing twenty-five dollars per month to its citizens, in accord-ance with the principles of the Social Credit Party. This dividend was given in the form of scrip, not cash, and the workability of the scheme depended upon merchants' accepting the scrip at face value. Already some stores had notices in their windows indicating "Scrip not accepted." Although the twenty-five-dollar-per-month gimmick was a failure, the Social Credit Party continued in power for many years because they provided conservative, prudent government.

The first part of July was the hottest period on record, with tempera-tures above 100 degrees Fahrenheit for about a week. People slept in their basements, and ice cream cones melted between the hand and the mouth. Nothing, of course, was air conditioned.

The residents of Brandon ate a lot of tapioca, which came in large sacks, each weighing about 200 pounds (the exact weight was painted on the sack), which were large and awkward to grasp. To lift this sack was the standard test of manhood and, before the summer was over, I had passed the test.

Still aimless, I enrolled in the Faculty of Education in the fall of 1936. This faculty was housed in the upper reaches of the Administration Building and was in the second year of its existence; the initial class had numbered fifty-six and was heavy with members of my Wesley College Class of 1935. D.S. Woods was the dean, and the other full-time member was a personable Scot named H.R. Lowe; many others were involved on a part-time basis. Woods taught us something-or-other, Lowe dispensed educational psychology, Robert Jarman, an exercise instructor, taught us to folk dance, an agreeable woman showed us how to organize a percussion band, and Rupert C. Lodge, head of philosophy, explained that all humanity can be divided into three groups: idealists, realists, and pragmatists. It was pretty thin gruel.

The practice teaching, however, was exciting. I was sent to Norberry Elementary School in St. Vital, to Gordon Bell High School in Winnipeg, and, for two weeks, to Stony Mountain High School. At that time, Gordon Bell was located across Maryland Street from the Misericordia Hospital and was ruled by Mr. Jewett, who dealt with miscreants promptly and physically. The few who threatened to tell their parents were urged to bring them to the school, so Jewett could document the transgressions of their children. A Miss Anderson allowed me to teach a class in English, where I read some poetry with the sincerity that Edna Sutherland had taught me to exude. Stony Mountain was the site of the federal penitentiary in Manitoba, and most of the pupils were children of the guards. The boys, in particular, were large. I led them in a tumbling exercise, and one landed in such a way that matches in his hip pocket were ignited. His friends rushed to the rescue and slapped his seat with such vigour and persistence that he might have preferred the smoke and the fire. During that fortnight, I stayed with the United Church minister, Lloyd Stinson, and his wife; he was another preacher of the social gospel. The principal of the school was Miss Hamilton, who was very kind to me, as were the Stinsons.

College Sports

By the time I had reached University, I was a fair football (a.k.a. soccer) player, and I turned out for the arts team, captained by Tom Easterbrook, who later taught political economy at the University of Toronto. When I was at Wesley, I played with Tom Saunders, John McWilliams, Des O'Brien, Martyn Best, and others. We won the Interfaculty League in 1933–34 with Saunders as captain; the final was played at St. John's College in a foot of snow, but in 1934–35 we lost to Engineering under my captaincy.

One evening, in the spring of 1937, I answered the door to two emissaries from the Winnipeg Scottish Football Club, which played in the First Division of the City League. They urged me to attend their practice game with United Weston. We tied, two to two, with me scoring the two Scottish goals, and I was declared to be their regular centre ("striker" in modern parlance). The officials of the Club had played when they were younger, and they loved to be associated with the game in any way – handing out oranges at half-time, laying out the uniforms on the benches, or massaging sore muscles. The coach, Jock Hastie, had been a professional in Scotland, but his eye had been flicked out by a football lace. Jimmy Murray, the manager, could still control the ball effortlessly and once, when we were a man short, played inside right. He made moves that we had never seen. I played for three seasons and, when the Glasgow Rangers toured Canada in 1937, was a member of the all-star Winnipeg team chosen to oppose them. Most of the league matches were played at Carruthers Park, behind the north Main streetcar barns.

I had not played basketball until my final year at Wesley, when I was persuaded that my height would be an advantage. It would also have been an advantage if I had been able to dribble and shoot. I made the second Wesley team as a guard and two years later earned an *M* on the University of Manitoba senior team. As there were no funds for travel, we played no other universities but competed in the city senior league. At that time, I was six feet in height, which was regarded as tall. The tallest player in the city – and he was in a class by himself – was Dick Flower at six foot six inches, who toyed with us around the basket. Teams rarely scored as many as thirty points in a game.

When I was between the ages of thirteen and nineteen (1929-1935), golf was my passion. Until I was seventeen, I could buy a membership at the Assiniboine Golf Club for five dollars a year, subject to the condition that I could not start a round after 5:00 p.m. on weekdays, after 12:00 noon on Saturdays, or ever on Sundays. A group of us made the most of this privilege – Drew Gibb, Bill Gray, Claud Brereton, Don Brereton, John Punchon, Les Rowland, Ewen Rankin, Don Rankin, and others – often playing two rounds per day. At sixteen, I was second in the Manitoba Junior Championship with a score of eighty-three at Southwood Golf Club. Later,

I obtained a junior membership (eighteen and under) and played to a handicap of six.

Each summer during the early 1930s, my parents and I spent a couple of weeks with my uncle George and my aunt Elizabeth at Sturgeon Point, Ontario, in the Kawartha Lakes. The squire of Sturgeon Point was Sir Joseph Flavelle, the founder of Canada Packers. His mansion was adjacent to those of his daughters, Mrs. Barrett (her husband was head of Simpson's store) and Mrs. J.S. McLean (her husband was then head of Canada Packers) whilst his son Ellesworth, who later inherited the title (Sir Joseph was a baronet), lived 100 yards away. Every morning we went to the Sturgeon Point Golf Course and played in foursomes as circumstances dictated. I frequently played with my cousins, Mary and Maude Edmison, with my uncle and his ministerial friends, Rev. Charles Stewart (of Buffalo) and Rev. Archie Sinclair (of Bloomington, New Jersey), with my contemporaries Don Neelands, Bill McLean, and Don Cooper or, occasionally, with other members of the Flavelle clan, including Sir Joseph himself. He was a charming companion: as Agnes McPhail (daughter of J.S. Woodsworth) once said at a political rally in nearby Fenelon Falls, "He could fool St. Peter." She was known to be against all capitalists, but the residents of Sturgeon Point thought it was an offensive remark to make so close to Sir Joseph's vacation retreat.

Prior to World War I, Archie Sinclair had occupied the pulpit of St. Andrew's Presbyterian Church in Winnipeg, a pulpit that my father later occupied from 1936 to 1948. Stories were still being told of his impetuosity: for example, a shy couple came to the manse to be married. Sinclair, who was at the church, rushed home and told them to stand up. After they had been pronounced husband and wife, it emerged that they had come to *arrange* to be married. Equally obedient was a World War II groom who asked my father to tell him when to kiss the bride. At the appropriate time, my father (who sometimes used lofty language) whispered, "You may salute the bride," which the groom literally did.

In my last summer at Sturgeon Point (1935) I played nine holes in the morning for thirty-six, which was par for the course. My uncle insisted that I return for a second nine holes, which I also played in thirty-six, for an eighteen-hole total of seventy-two. That this established the course record is an indication that few professionals played at Sturgeon Point.

My own direct experience with the wider world of golf was limited to four events: the U.S. Amateur of 1931, the Canadian Open of 1933, an exhibition in Winnipeg by Gene Sarazen and Joe Kirkwood, and an exhibition in Toronto by Joyce Wethered. In addition, I followed every step taken by Bobby Jones.

My obsession with the game had become serious in 1930, the final year of competitive golf for Bobby Jones, the gifted amateur from Atlanta, Georgia. Jones had first achieved national prominence in 1916 when, at the age of fourteen, he had reached the eights of the (U.S.) National Amateur Championship, held that year at the Merion Cricket Club near Philadelphia. Fourteen years later, in September 1930, he returned to Merion to win his fifth National Amateur, having previously won twelve major titles (U.S. Amateur: 1924, 1925, 1927, 1928; U.S. Open: 1923, 1926, 1929, 1930; British Open: 1926, 1927, 1930; and British Amateur: 1930). This triumph at Merion in 1930 completed the Grand Slam, a feat not accomplished before or since. I was virtually sleepless during the final competition.

Jones, who was a graduate lawyer from Emory University and Harvard, continued his connection with golf in various ways. He made instructional films that were widely shown (in our neighbourhood theatre, for example), he conceived and helped realize the Augusta National Golf Club, and, in 1934, he inaugurated the Augusta National Invitation Tournament, now known as The Masters. Jones participated for several years in this event until prevented from doing so by a progressive disease of the spinal column. He died in 1971 at the age of sixty-nine.

A new event for Winnipeg, the long-driving contest took place in Assiniboine Park on the evening of 31 August 1932. A corridor fifty yards wide was marked off in the area now used for cricket, with the teeing ground at the north end. The champions of sixteen city golf clubs reported for duty, together with ten professionals who were to compete separately. Each contestant was allowed three attempts, with the longest counting towards the winner. Three thousand spectators were on hand, unaware of the peril to which they were exposing themselves. For one thing, there was a strong northwest wind, which exacerbated any hooked ball by a right-handed hitter. But, in addition, it soon emerged that some of the club champions must have won their titles on lucky hits.

The first to be called was Edwin Bourke from the Bourkeville Golf Course. This was a nine-hole course in St. James extending from Portage Avenue to the Assiniboine River between Ferry and Douglas Park Roads. All holes were par three and the greens were sand. Edwin was the son of the owner. Beginners played there, and sometimes other men who had promised women they would play with them. It was at the very bottom of the totem pole amongst Winnipeg courses.

Edwin took his place and calmly drove 249 yards, and within the fifty-yard markers. The other fifteen champions then took their first turns, and so it continued until a total of forty-eight attempts had been made. The word *attempts* is not used lightly because, in the course of the competition, three shots were completely missed, and the humiliated competitors were obliged to pick up their balls and return to the end of the line. In all, thirty-four of the forty-eight attempts were either missed, dubbed or hit out of bounds. Invariably, these last were on the east side of the corridor and gave rise to local tumults as spectators sought to avoid being hit. Even Edwin Bourke put his second and third drives out of bounds. But at the end of the day, his first drive had withstood all competition, and the Gold Drive Trophy made its way to the humble Bourkedale Golf Course. The professional competition was won by Kasimir Zabowski with a drive of 260 yards. Twenty of the professional attempts were out of bounds. I do not remember that the entertaining fiasco was ever repeated.

For a decade prior to 1935, Joyce Wethered, of England, had been recognized as the pre-eminent woman golfer of her time, although she had played in only one major tournament during that period, winning the British Ladies' Championship in 1927 against a strong American contingent, headed by the U.S. women's champion, Glenna Collett. But, because she hit the ball so far and so accurately, reports of her non-competitive achievements kept appearing in the press. Then, in the *Winnipeg Free Press* of 16 April 1932, we read the stunning headline "Popular English Lady Golfer will not Marry." This proved not to be a renunciation of the world, but a decision by the thirty-one-year-old Wethered to break her five-month engagement to her fifty-one-year-old fiancé, Major C.K. Hurcheson, whom she had often partnered in mixed play. We, who had been unaware of this romantic attachment, heaved sighs of relief that this threat to her concentration on the game had so narrowly been averted.

Imagine the excitement when news came that Wethered would play an exhibition match at St. Andrew's Golf Club in Toronto on 27 July 1935, as part of a North American tour. Her playing companions were to be C. Ross "Sandy" Sommerville, Bud Donovan, and Ada Mackenzie. Sommerville was from London, Ontario, had been U.S. amateur champion in 1932, whilst Donovan, from Winnipeg, had been playing brilliantly and had recently stood second in the General Brock Open, ahead of Byron Nelson, Walter Hagen, Harry Cooper, and others. Ada Mackenzie was the outstanding woman player in Canada.

We were vacationing at my uncle George's summer cottage at Sturgeon Point, and the ninety miles to Toronto proved no deterrent. My uncle, my father, and I spent an energetic day watching all players but especially the graceful effortless play of Joyce Wethered. Scores were Wethered: 40 + 35 = 75; Sommerville: 39 + 37 = 76; Donovan: 41 + 37 = 78; Mackenzie: 43 + 41 = 84, with Wethered's figure including a triple bogey on the sixth hole. During her tour, she played a total of fifty-three matches – all from men's tees – and was never above seventy-five. And this at a time when women rarely broke eighty! As Bobby Jones said, "She plays like a man, only better." She later married a title, dying as Lady Heathcoat Amory in 1998.

In 1935, my last year of regular play, I was consistently scoring seventy-four to seventy-six, but my juvenile dream of becoming a professional was evaporating. It had been a good run, but the fact that I must earn a living was beginning to intrude. Thereafter, I played only sporadically.

Starting to Earn a Living: 1937 to 1940

3

Stonewall: 1937–38

Stonewall, a town of 1,500 persons, located about fifteen miles northwest of Winnipeg and connected to the City by a streetcar, had advertised for a teacher of high-school mathematics. I had been preparing to teach Latin, but I had taken four years of mathematics and was pretty good at it. Accordingly, I paid a visit to Mr. Stanbridge, a member of the Stonewall School Board who, as it emerged in the conversation, had sat in the legislature with my uncle, Dr. John H. Edmison of Brandon. This coincidence weighed heavily with him, and I left with the impression that I would be offered the job. Teaching jobs, I should add, were scarce at that time and normally paid $500 to $600 per annum. The Stonewall offer, when it arrived, was for $800 per annum!

The job, however, included more than mathematics; it included history in Grades 9 and 11 and music in Grade 9. When I explained that I could not teach music, I was told not to worry, they had yet to hire a teacher for Grades 7 and 8, and music would be made part of that job description. Thus, late every Friday afternoon, Mr. Smith, the man hired to teach Grades 7 and 8, and I crossed in the schoolyard as he headed to the high school to lead Grade 9 in singing and I prepared to teach composition to his class. It turned out that he had no more talent for music than had I, but he had come too late on the scene to negotiate.

It was a four-room high school, one room for each grade. Mr. Newfield, the calm and efficient principal, taught science. Miss Oastler taught mostly English and Miss Smith mostly French. These women were experienced and businesslike but did not socialize in the town. Years later, when I encountered them in a different setting, I was surprised at how personable they were.

I boarded with Mrs. Stratton, whose husband had once been the official trustee, that is, the school trustee for all the schools in the province that did not have their own school boards. But he had committed some misdemeanour that had blighted his career, and Mrs. Stratton, who had thought she was marrying a prominent educator, was now the breadwinner. She had four boarders: Harley and Albert, who worked in the local garage, Reg Noton (from Wawanesa), who managed the local movie house, and me. She regarded me as the star boarder and gave me the large front bedroom, with all meals, for twenty dollars per month. I did most of my lesson preparation, however, on the dining-room table. We had generous, tasty meals served in the atmosphere of a home, not a boarding house, and she never complained about her lot.

One of my first moves in Stonewall was to organize the boys into football teams, as Mr. Moore had done at Britannia School. We were two players short of the forty-four needed for four teams, but Len Billings, the janitor, and I brought the teams up to full strength. As at Britannia, we played during the morning recess, from 1:00 to 1:30 and during the afternoon recess, for a total of sixty minutes. A scoreboard was placed inside the main door and the day's results were entered immediately. Billings had grown up in the United Kingdom, the home of football, and may have been the most enthusiastic player on the field. And it may have been the happiest year of his life. We played all winter, regardless of snow and cold, and I reported to Winnipeg Scottish in the spring in superb physical condition, scoring the team's two goals in the season opener.

I was the room teacher for Grade 10, which had about twenty students, including a dozen giggling girls. I told the girls to stay after school and I explained to them that they were adults and should be beyond giggling. In fact, in the previous century, many of them would already be married. This sobered them momentarily, but a whisper set them off again, even worse than before. Sixty years later, I learned from the whisperer that her remark had been, "Oh, Harry, this is so sudden!"

Once the giggling had died down, I had no problem with discipline: I guess the boys were having enough fun baiting Miss Oastler and Miss Smith to leave me alone. I did ask two boys in Grade 9 to stay after school for some malefaction, and I gave them a choice of staying late for a week or receiving two punches in the chest. They chose the punches and the first, a strong kid, recoiled a bit but survived. Unbeknownst to me, the second was asthmatic, and the first punch left him gasping. I indicated that one punch would be enough, but he thrust out his chest and demanded the second, which, when it came, was not very hard.

Grant Stratton (Grade 12) and his brother, Keith (Grade 10), asked if I would organize a Scout troop. Grant was too old for Scouts himself but could assist as a leader. I had never been a Scout, but I had been a Cub leader in St. James and knew in general how the system worked. There were about ten in the troop, and we followed the assigned program, supplemented by excursions, or "hikes."

On the first hike, I planned a meal of bread plus pork and beans. The two cans of pork and beans were placed in the fire for warming whilst we did other things, until we were interrupted by an explosion and flying beans. The second can was rescued, but we were reduced to half-rations, and the scouts lost some confidence in their leader. The second hike did little to restore that confidence. The planned snack was hot dogs plus cocoa. My mother would have taken a pot for the cocoa and a pot for the wieners, but I decided to cook the wieners and the cocoa together, thus saving one pot. My mother would have known that wieners, whilst being cooked, release an oily substance, but she had never told me that fact. In the event, the hot dogs were all right, but the cocoa was not good. The third and final outing, an overnight camp, passed without incident; we may have taken sandwiches.

At the outbreak of war, both Grant and Keith Stratton joined the air force and lost their lives overseas. Indeed, most of the boys in the school, when they finished Grade 11 or Grade 12, joined one or another of the services, and several others – like Grant and Keith – failed to return. It hadn't struck me so forcibly before, that old men make war but it is boys who die.

Mr. Stratton, father of Grant and Keith, farmed west of Stonewall and was the superintendent of the Sunday school. He asked me to teach a class of boys, all of whom I knew from the school, and many from Scouts. He tried to encourage the memorization of Bible verses by publicly asking each class how many verses they had committed to memory that week. Our results were desultory until I challenged the class to make a superhuman effort for a given Sunday. They rose to the occasion, I heard them say their verses, and we all waited breathlessly for Stratton's question. He followed the usual procedure, getting answers such as five, seven, three, nine, and four, until he came to our class and received the answer 254! Boys love competition. Stratton's contest was not unlike the old Sunday school practice of memorizing one verse each Sunday, the so-called golden text. My cousin Mac(millan) Edmison was in attendance one Sunday when the golden text was "It is I, be not afraid." When my aunt, Ada, asked him to repeat it, he proffered, "It's only me, don't be scared."

The hockey and curling rink was the social centre of Stonewall during the winter; here, games could be watched, food could be eaten, non-alcoholic drinks could be imbibed, first- and second-hand smoke could be inhaled, and any subject could be ventilated. Mr. Small, chairman of the local school board, organized Newfield, Smith, and me into a curling team, and we played once or twice a week during the season.

On the hockey front, we learned of a school hockey tournament to be held in Winnipeg *at the Amphitheatre Rink*. To a boy in Stonewall, this was the equivalent of Maple Leaf Gardens or Madison Square Garden. We entered a team, but I warned the boys that no one who swore could play, no matter how compelling the provocation. Between games, Frank Costello was adjusting his boot when the lace broke, and he said, "Hell!" Without another word, he replaced his skates with his street shoes and spent the rest of the tournament with me on the bench. The team played well against much larger schools. At least four of the boys later played as professionals: Hugh Millar, Lou Medynski, Joe Medynski, and Frank Grabowski.

The visit of the School inspector was a solemn event. He came unannounced and entered the classroom whether the teacher was ready or not. He might observe, he might ask the class a question, or he might ask the teacher to ask a question. One cagey teacher instructed her class, "When the inspector comes and I ask you a question, I want all of you to raise your hands: the right hand if you know the answer, and the left hand if you don't."

When Inspector Knapp appeared in Stonewall in the spring of 1938, he chose to visit my Grade 12 class in analytical geometry; he could not have done better. We had completed the course by Easter and were now doing old examination papers. Even the slowest student could arrange an equation into the form of a parabola, ellipse, or hyperbola and describe its characteristics and orientation. Knapp wrote two or three equations on the blackboard and asked various students to solve them. They were so letter-perfect that he felt it unnecessary to visit my Grade 11 class in Canadian history, where the result would have been completely different.

I treasure the year spent in Stonewall. I was part of a dynamic community, with its own schools, sports, churches, and social life. Many of my classmates at Wesley had come from similar towns, and I had envied them their confidence, their maturity, their openness, and their lack of pretension. I could now see in Stonewall how these attributes had been acquired in such places as Dauphin, Souris, Dominion City, Reston, and Glenboro. When I received a letter from Dr. Riddell in early June, inviting me to return to Wesley College, I read it with mixed emotions, knowing that I would accept the invitation but melancholy because it would take me from my students and friends in Stonewall.

United College: 1938 to 1940

When I reported to Dr. Riddell to discuss his offer, he was in his final days as president of Wesley College. Indeed, they were the final days of the College itself, as Manitoba College (theology) and Wesley College (arts), which had been operating under the same roof as United Colleges, were to be merged formally and called United College, under one principal and one board of regents.

Riddell explained that his lecturer in physics, Stewart A. Johnston, was going on leave and that he had immediately thought of me as the replacement, knowing that I had taken a B.Sc. since we had last met. He did not question my knowledge of physics but simply asked, "Can you handle it?" I answered yes, and we turned to salary. He suggested $1,000 per annum but, when I appeared to hesitate (I was actually gulping), he settled on $1,100. Thus was H.E. Duckworth, who had never studied physics beyond first year, hired to teach at that same level as well as in the college's Collegiate Division (Grades 11 and 12). When I met Dean O.T. Anderson a few days later, he was more specific, asking, "How much physics do you have, Harry?" I replied that I had first year and intended to take second year at summer school. He never blinked.

The second-year physics course at the 1938 University of Manitoba summer school was taught by Harold Batho, who had taken his Ph.D. with Arthur Dempster at the University of Chicago. He was a good, clear teacher, although he had to leave class periodically for a few puffs at a cigarette. I worked as if my life depended on it and was satisfied with the end result. Batho knew my situation but never referred to it and, later, when I began lecturing, treated me as an equal, although the disparity in status and knowledge was huge.

My total teaching load was twenty-two hours of lectures per week plus responsibility for the laboratories. The laboratories were run, however, by two undergraduate science students, Roger Smith and Ben Schwartz, and I spent little time in them. Also, the twenty-two hours represented only two preparations: Grade 11 and Grade 12 (which was the same as first year). The strain was mostly on the voice: on one day, I started at 9:00 a.m. and lectured continuously (except for class breaks) until 3:00 p.m.

The first-year course at the University was still being taught by W.A. Anderson, who had taught me in 1931-32 and who would be setting the final examination. I acquired some old examination papers and saw that they were heavy on short answers and didn't change much from year to year. In every lecture, I emphasized the material that had appeared on previous examinations. At the end of the year, the passing rate for my students was higher than for Anderson's, but his students may have learned more. During the summer of 1939, I attended the University of Chicago and returned much more confident for the 1939-40 session. Former students seem to remember my teaching as satisfactory and appear to have been unaware of my slender knowledge.

During my two years at United College, my students included Harold Thompson (later president of Monarch Life), George Johnson (later lieutenant governor of Manitoba), Duncan Jessiman (lawyer and later senator), Lorne Campbell (later president of the Canadian Law Society), James Duff (later head of the Department of Physics, University of Winnipeg), Comrie McCawley (later a well-known gynecologist), John Gemmell (later head of the Department of Medicine, University of Manitoba), and my cousin Jack Edmison (later a radiologist in Victoria). It's perhaps significant that only Duff continued in physics.

W.C. Graham, ordained minister and distinguished Old Testament scholar, was named principal of the new United College. An expatriate Canadian, he had been professor in the Oriental Institute at the University of Chicago and had actively "dug" in the Middle East. I learned later that he had the nickname "Baal" in Chicago.

Graham's installation took place in St. Stephen's-Broadway United Church, and he spoke on the value of a liberal education. He did not defend it, he asserted it. Indeed, his style was always to attack, rather than to defend. The emphasis on a liberal education was new to me at the time, but I have since listened to countless versions of the same theme, including some from my own lips. Shortly thereafter, he gave a lecture in Convocation Hall on his archeological work, illustrated with slides. The screen was small and the lighting was poor, but we appreciated his enthusiasm, even if we were unable to see the slides.

Once, early in his administration, he was expressing the thanks of the audience to a visiting speaker and invited us to give the Chautauqua salute, at the same time distracting us by waving his white handkerchief. We were too obtuse to realize that the handkerchief bit *was* the Chautauqua salute. As a result, that part of the tribute fell rather flat. If we had been ten or twenty years older and had lived in a major rural town, we'd have known about Chautauqua and the excitement when its troupe of lecturers and artistic performers made its annual visit; it was the cultural equivalent of the Ringling Brothers Circus. Personable young women went ahead to persuade leading citizens to guarantee the cost of the visit, but rarely was the guarantee invoked, so popular was the event. Two of my older friends, Genevieve Brownell and Gladys Thorlakson, both of whom exuded personality, had been amongst the "Chautauqua Girls," who beguiled leading citizens into providing the guarantee.

Graham had not realized how precarious were the College's finances, but he undertook to repair them. In the summer of 1939, following his first year in office, he optimistically approached potential philanthropists in eastern Canada and reported that he had collected a few thousand dollars: "They with their gold to give, doled him out silver." He never faced a new session without worrying about money, an anxiety that undoubtedly shortened his life.

But, against financial and other odds, he led the College with vigour and courage for seventeen years, retiring on 30 June 1955 and dying a few short weeks later, on 31 July, exhausted from strain and effort. He had a cottage at Roche's Point on Lake Simcoe, where he had hoped to spend many more happy summers. I attended his funeral at nearby Newmarket. If it had been held in Winnipeg, it would have been a standing-room-only event, but in Newmarket it was a sad, forlorn affair. His two sons, Roger and John, became professors at Queen's and Western Ontario, respectively. Roger was Arthur Meighen's biographer, and that eminent political figure was one of the few at the funeral.

Incidentally, when I told Graham that I was considering spending the summer of 1939 at the University of Chicago, he was ecstatic and recommended that I make myself known to a friend of his in the Physics Department who had also been raised in Canada, a Professor Dempster.

I was now a junior colleague of some of my former professors and almost the contemporary of some of the newer ones, such as William Morton and Donald Masters (who became eminent Canadian historians), Harry ("Buss") Woods (who became professor of economics at McGill), Gladys Pettingell (German), and Ida Wilkinson (French). The old guard included Lower and Pickersgill (history), Phelps, Kirkconnell, Thompson, Jack Murray, and Alfred Longman (English), Leathers and Bowes (French), Cragg (psychology), Owen (philosophy), Anderson, Ritcey, and Evelyn Mills (mathematics), Swyers (chemistry), and Carl Halstead (dean of Collegiate Division). The professors in theology were E. Guthrie Perry, George B. King, and E.G.D. ("Dink") Freeman (a college friend of my father's). I'm told that the Germans define a professor as one who thinks differently. On that basis, these were all professors, each with his or her own coterie of acolytes trying hard to think differently as well. In this august and idiosyncratic company, I was a colourless, callow youth attempting to remain as inconspicuous as possible.

Although space was in short supply, Graham made a small classroom on the second floor into a faculty room, where tea was on offer in the afternoon and various opinions were allowed to collide. In Chicago, he had lunched regularly at the University's handsome Quadrangle Club, and he was attempting to reproduce some of its intellectual atmosphere in the wilds of western Canada.

Although it was never said in public, the University of Manitoba was the enemy. The head of each department at the College was a member of the corresponding University department, but its professors controlled the curriculum and the examinations. Any changes in procedures or regulations were interpreted by the College in their worst light, and it was suspected that the University would not hesitate to raid the college for staff, although Graham thought he had a bargain with President Smith not to allow this to happen. When I took a position at the University following the war, there was no suitable position for me at the College, but Graham took it badly and wrote me a long letter of discontent. *Paranoid* would be too strong a word, but slights and offences were often discerned where none existed. However, the distrust of the University was a mighty unifying force and, I believe, was sometimes exploited by the administration for that very purpose.

When classes resumed in September 1939, war had been declared and the regiments based in Winnipeg were actively recruiting: the Cameron Highlanders, the Winnipeg Grenadiers, the Princess Patricia Light Infantry, the Strathcona Horse, and the Fort Garry Horse. Each day, some of these units paraded at Minto Barracks and marched thence to their respective headquarters on south Main Street. Their route led past United College, and, from the classrooms that faced on Portage Avenue, we could see the daily lengthening of these columns. The Camerons were in kilts and were led by a pipe band; their columns lengthened much faster than the others, although the new recruits marched in their civvies and had only the promise of future glamorous garb.

Although we were at war, there was no land action. The newsreels at the movies showed detailed scenes of the Maginot Line and assured us of its impregnability. All were lulled by a propaganda-induced sense of security, and classes continued as normal. We were completely taken by surprise by the fall of France in the spring of 1940. Hitler was supposed to have attacked the Maginot Line like a man, instead of effecting a cowardly panzer-led assault through Belgium. This was going to be a nasty business after all. As for me, I was headed for the University of Chicago again, but this time to complete the Ph.D.

The University of Chicago: 1939 to 1942

4

Early in my first teaching year at United College, 1938-39, it became evident to me, if not to the students, that I knew little about the subject I was teaching. Whilst brooding over this deficiency, I learned that my counterpart in chemistry, Lawrence Swyers, who was several years my senior in both age and academic standing, was to spend the summer of 1939 at the University of Chicago, completing the course requirements for the Ph.D. Also, another colleague (and my former professor of mathematics), Lee Ritcey, would be there with his wife and two children in tow, as he worked on his doctoral thesis. I reckoned that if Chicago was good enough for these proven scholars, it was good enough for me.

The University

As I later learned, the University of Chicago was of relatively recent vintage. It had been founded in 1891 by members and friends of the Baptist Church, in particular that eminent Baptist John D. Rockefeller (1839-1937). This industrial behemoth, owner of Standard Oil of America and once said to have been the most-hated man in the United States because of his ruthless destruction of competitors, was the financial good fairy to this new institution. Indeed, whether or not this was part of his intention, the University provided Rockefeller with a wholly acceptable medium for laundering money. Before he died, because of his philanthropy and aided by his practice of giving dimes to children, he had become the "grand old man" of America.

From the start, the University was envisaged as one of international stature, which, although under Baptist governance, would impose no doctrinal requirements on its professors or students. To put it somewhat grandiloquently, it was to be a Baptist gift to the nation and was to flourish under the motto "Let knowledge grow from more to more, and thus be human life enriched."

Much of the new University was modelled after Johns Hopkins University, which had been founded in Baltimore in 1876 with money bequeathed by a railway magnate of that name. The Baltimore institution was a response to widespread criticism that American colleges were removed from society and made no contribution to the prosperity of the nation. The German universities, in contrast, emphasized research and were seen as the reason for the flourishing chemical and other industries in that country. Central to the German system was the Ph.D. Thus, Johns Hopkins University was established to introduce the German Ph.D. to America. Under its first president, Daniel Coit Gilman (1831-1908), research-minded professors were hired and fellowships were offered to graduate students. The first Ph.D.s were awarded in 1878, and very shortly thereafter Johns Hopkins became the preferred destination for aspiring young American scholars. Its Ph.D. program completely superseded the half-baked ones that had been cobbled together at Yale, Harvard, Columbia, Syracuse, Michigan, and Pennsylvania. Incidentally, these hearties, after a few years of condescension, quietly followed the lead of Johns Hopkins but, until the end of the century, that pioneer institution remained the most important graduate school in the country. When it was ultimately surpassed, it was only because it lacked the financial base to compete with its longer-established rivals. Unlike the University of Chicago, its founder had bequeathed a fixed sum for its establishment and had not lived to provide further injections as needed.

Incidentally, the first earned Ph.D. to be awarded in the United States was from Yale in 1851. It was a pale version of the degree that was attracting students from all parts of the world to the great German universities: Berlin, Goettingen, Heidelberg, Leipzig, and Munich.

Under Chicago's dynamic founding president, William Rainey Harper (1850-1906), the University was seen as a research institution that emphasized graduate work but that also admitted undergraduates. The Johns Hopkins influence was clear, although Harper did not emphasize that point. Chicago quickly established its credentials, and, by 1923, it had awarded 1,838 Ph.D.s, second only to Columbia (2,008) and followed by Harvard (1,516), Johns Hopkins (1,372), Cornell (1,033), and Pennsylvania (919). Its rapid growth could be attributed to Harper's energy in attracting outstanding professors, to a generous fellowship program, to his successful courting of Chicago's wealthy families, to his admission of women to graduate studies (at a time when Harvard and others were spurning them), to his four-quarter academic calendar, to his support for academic publications and, above all, to Rockefeller's continued munificence. The Chicago students, who knew where their bread was buttered, had their own version of the Doxology: "Praise John from whom oil blessings flow." By 1937, the Rockefeller "oil blessings" had approached $70 million.

In any event, even before I arrived in 1939, Chicago was no mean university. I had naïvely thought that it was good enough for me. If I had known what I later knew, I might well have asked, "Am I good enough for it?" But, unaware of the potential mismatch, I accompanied my friend Lawrence Swyers with all the confidence of youth.

The Summer of 1939

When we arrived at the Chicago bus terminal, we were met by our friend Lee Ritcey, who had arrived in Chicago earlier and had already secured a room at 6052 South Ingleside for our joint occupancy. He called a taxi, and my bags were put in the trunk. Meanwhile, Lawrence, acting independently, had also called a taxi and given up his luggage to its driver. To have engaged two taxis had not been our intent, but, for a time, it appeared that it would be our fate, as neither driver was willing to surrender his share of our luggage. Eventually, one relented; I don't remember if payment was involved. But the event confirmed our worst fears of the city of Al Capone.

In organizing the academic year for his new university, Harper had not followed the usual two-semester system but had divided the year into four quarters of eleven weeks each. Thus, the summer quarter, which began in June, was not the usual six-week summer school but had an academic reputation and status that was equal to the other three quarters; course offerings were equivalent, and regular professors taught the classes, which met from Tuesday through Friday at the same times each day. This schedule allowed for some recreation on the long weekends and for a good deal of work. A full teaching load for a professor was to lecture in any three of the four quarters.

Lawrence registered for high-powered chemistry courses whilst I registered for third- and fourth-year courses in physics (electricity and magnetism, optics, atomic physics, and heat and thermodynamics), one course more than the normal load. For this I paid $200, with no questions asked – sink or swim! With much effort, I managed to swim and emerged at the end of the summer with a knowledge of physics that was not much inferior to that of an honours physics graduate of a Canadian university. Further, as the summer wore on, and my all-out effort looked to be succeeding, I began to see physics as a possible vocation rather than a simple teaching subject. Indisputably, it was the most exciting of the sciences, and I was demonstrating some mastery of it. On my return to Winnipeg at the end of the summer, I decided to pursue the subject seriously as the basis for a scientific career. Finally, I had a purpose in life.

Uranium Fission

Preoccupied with my regular teaching duties at United College and un-connected as I was with the larger world of physics, I was unaware, before going to Chicago, that the uranium atom had been split in the laboratory of the Kaiser Wilhelm Institute in Berlin. None of my students had asked about it, which suggests that no report had appeared in the *Winnipeg Free Press*. But the topic was more than a desultory one amongst the physics students in Chicago.

I soon learned that, in early January 1939, Otto Hahn (1879-1968) and Fritz Strassmann (1902-1980) had observed that radioactive atoms of barium and lanthanum were produced when uranium was bombarded with slow neutrons. Hahn's long-time collaborator, Lise Meitner (1878-1968), then in exile in Copenhagen, suggested with her nephew, Otto Frisch (1904-1979), that these middle-weight atoms had been formed by the fission of uranium. It had been known from the work of F. W. Aston and A. J. Demp-ster that, if heavy atoms could be made to split, enormous amounts of energy would be released. But until Hahn's discovery, this fantastic possi-bility had been mostly a subject for science fiction.

News of the discovery had been brought to America by Niels Bohr (1885-1962) who landed in New York on 16 January 1939, two weeks after Enrico Fermi (1901-1954) had taken up residence in the United States. Fermi had received the Nobel Prize for physics late in 1938 and had decided not to return to Italy, in part out of concern for the safety of his wife, who was Jewish. Fermi and others in the New York area were told the news and, two days later, it was given wider circulation at a conference in Washington. Thence, it spread like wildfire with the result that the fact of fission was verified in four different laboratories in the United States in time to be reported in the 15 February issue of the *Physical Review*. Mean-while, Frisch himself had confirmed the result in Copenhagen (reported in a letter to the British journal *Nature*, dated 16 January), and Frederic Joliot (1900-1958) had done likewise in Paris (30 January issue of *Comptes Rendus*). Further, it was very quickly observed in both New York and Paris that two or three neutrons were emitted per fission, suggesting the real possibility of a chain reaction in which neutrons released in the initial fission could induce additional fissions, and so on.

Because of the military implications, the American experiments in which fission neutrons were detected were not reported in the open literature until after the war. The French experiments, however, were reported in *Nature*. But, soon thereafter, an unofficial embargo was placed on the publication of anything relating to the subject. Nonetheless, the world of physics now suspected that the time was not distant when vast amounts of energy would be released in a self-sustaining nuclear reaction.

Although the rest of the world was virtually unaware of this impending result, there was concern in the scientific community that Germany would be the first to exploit it for military purposes. In the summer of 1939, two émigré scientists, Eugene Wigner (1902-1995) and Leo Szilard (1898-1964), persuaded Albert Einstein (1879-1955), then at Princeton, to write directly to President Roosevelt, pointing out the military implications. In part, the letter read:

> Some recent work by E. Fermi and L. Szilard, which has been communicated to me in manuscript, leads me to expect that the element uranium may be turned into a new and important source of energy in the immediate future. . . . This new phenomenon would also lead to the construction of bombs, and it is conceivable — although much less certain — that extremely powerful bombs of a new type may thus be constructed. A single bomb of this type, carried by boat and exploded in a port, might very well destroy the whole port together with some of the surrounding territory. However, such bombs might very well prove to be too heavy for transportation by air. . . . In view of the situation you might think it desirable to have some permanent contact maintained between the Administration and the group of physicists working on chain reactions in America . . . [to apprise] (government departments) of further developments . . . [to secure] a supply of uranium ore for the United States [and] to speed up the experimental work, which is at present being carried out within the limits of the budgets of University laboratories. (C.P. Snow, *The Physicists* [London: Macmillan, 1981], 178-9).

Roosevelt's response to this letter from the most famous physicist of the time was to establish a government committee to investigate this potential source of power, with a grant of $6,000 to cover the twelve-month period between 1 November 1939 and 31 October 1940! Nothing of merit came from the committee.

Thus, it was left to the scientific community, working informally, to execute a logical research program until such time as the military took the matter seriously. This they finally did in June 1940, shortly after the fall of Paris.

The Summer of 1940

During the winter of 1939-40, back at United College, I had taken a correspondence course in vector analysis from the University of Chicago. This involved sending in assignments that were carefully marked by Dr. Everett of the Mathematics Department. In the fullness of time, the final examination paper was sent to Dean Halstead of the College, who had been designated as the examination supervisor. He and I sat in the Senate Room one Saturday morning, he dealing with paper chores and I addressing the examination questions. All were straightforward except for the final one, which was completely baffling until ten minutes from the end, by which time I had virtually given up hope. I was saved by a sudden inspiration and hastily scribbled the answer. I had known excitement before, to be sure, but never the peculiar thrill of this mathematical epiphany; it still sends a shiver up my spine.

When Lawrence and I returned to Chicago in June 1940, it was with the intention of staying until we had completed our doctorates. Although his intention was more realistic than mine, I was confident of obtaining at least a master's degree and, with it, could contribute to the war effort whenever called upon to do so. An advanced knowledge of physics was generally viewed as an asset in the waging of war.

That summer, I had lectures from two of the giants of the Department of Physics, Arthur Holly Compton and Arthur Jeffrey Dempster.

Compton (1891-1962) and his brother Karl (1887-1954), who subsequently became the president of the Massachusetts Institute of Technology, were sons of a clergyman. They were undergraduates at Wooster College in Ohio and had taken their doctorates at Princeton. In 1922, whilst teaching at Washington University in St. Louis, Arthur observed that scattered x-rays became lengthened, an effect (the Compton Effect) that he correctly ascribed to a corpuscular aspect of x-rays. This led to an invitation to Chicago in 1923 and a sharing of the Nobel Prize for physics in 1927. A deeply religious man, he was the model of courtesy and modesty. I took a course in x-rays from him in the fall of 1940 and, although we studied the Compton Effect in some detail, it was never referred to by name. In the summer of 1940, however, he was teaching a course in mechanics, and it sometimes struck me that he had not attempted the problems before coming to class. So, it was exciting, and even suspenseful, to observe this powerful mind in action as he publicly fought his way to correct solutions. It was during that summer that he assumed the chair of the Department, which could explain why he had not attempted the problems in advance. Incidentally, an Australian physicist, Joseph A. Gray, who became Chown research professor of physics at Queen's University in 1924, had also observed the lengthening of the wave length of scattered x-rays and felt that he should have shared Compton's Nobel Prize. He had not, however, provided the rationale that was a crucial element in Compton's work.

One of Compton's innovations as chairman was to rotate undergraduate lecture assignments that had been static for years. This action was to stir minds that had been dormant too long. The most adversely affected was George Monk, the perennial lecturer in optics, who was a master of that subject. He had written a well-regarded textbook on the subject, which was used in his class, and he could almost cite page and line references for any point he was making. To be torn from the security of this subject and to be assigned electromagnetic theory was a personal tragedy. In the latter, he would frequently be stumped whilst working at the blackboard, sit down and stare at the problem, and eventually turn to us sheepishly for suggestions. He it was who explained to us, in another context, that as a child he had been forced to change his writing from left to right hand. Since then, he averred, he had been unable to differentiate between right and wrong.

Arthur Jeffrey Dempster (1887-1950), an expatriate Canadian and member of the Dempster Bread family of Toronto, had his bachelor's degree from Toronto in 1909 and his Ph.D. from Chicago in 1916, although most of the preparation for the latter had been done in Germany, before the outbreak of World War I. In 1918, he had constructed a novel instrument (the mass spectrograph) for the study of positive rays, which he subsequently used to discover the stable isotopes of lithium, magnesium, potassium, calcium, and zinc. Francis Aston (1877-1945) had been developing at Cambridge University a different form of mass spectrograph, which he used to observe the stable isotopes of a group of gaseous elements. Aston was awarded the Nobel Prize for chemistry in 1922, an honour that the Nobel Committee should have shared with Dempster. Later, in 1935, Dempster devised a much more precise mass spectrograph with which, amongst many other things, he discovered ^{235}U, the fissile isotope of uranium. In August 1940, I asked Dempster to supervise my thesis, which he agreed to do.

Dempster was self-conscious in front of a class and from the beginning to the end of a lecture faced the blackboard. Also, he cleared his throat continually, perhaps ten times per minute. I occasionally broke the rhythm by calling out, "Question," an interruption that he appeared to welcome. His lectures, however, were clear and included the latest research results from the literature.

On one occasion he made a mighty impression on us, even on those who took pleasure in counting the number of throat-clearings per minute. At the time, he was arranging a meeting of the American Physical Society to be held at the University. Some days prior to the meeting, he brought to class a number of copies of the program, which mostly comprised abstracts of contributed papers. One by one, and this time looking us straight in the face, he led us through these abstracts, providing helpful background comments. It was a tour de force and demonstrated to us his wide knowledge of physics and his familiarity with recent developments in all branches of the subject.

Apropos something, Dempster once told me of an experience that shed light on the dueling societies that flourished in Germany in the pre–World War I era. He and a German friend were walking together when they met another German student. Later, his friend received a challenge from the student, alleging that he had been insulted that Dempster had had his hands in his pockets. Admittedly, at that time and until much later, hands in pockets were considered a serious social affront in Germany, but Dempster thought that putting the blame on his walking companion was a bit much. Apparently, when one was under pressure to meet a dueling quota, even a second-hand affront was an acceptable basis for a sabre encounter.

Not present in the flesh when I was at Chicago, but palpably present in legend, was Robert Andrew Millikan (1868-1953). He had his B.A. from Oberlin, his Ph.D. from Columbia, and had spent time at both Berlin and Goettingen before joining the University of Chicago in 1898. In 1911, after years of careful preparation, he measured the value of the elementary charge, that is, the charge on the electron. For this achievement he was awarded the Nobel Prize for physics in 1923. Two years before this recognition, however, he had joined the newly created California Institute of Technology in Pasadena, California.

I had seen Millikan in Winnipeg in the late 1930s when he spoke at Westminster United Church on the topic "Science and Religion." I don't remember what he said, except that he felt that no conflict should exist between the two. I do recall that he spoke without passion and as one having authority.

The experiment to determine the electronic charge came to be known as the "oil drop" experiment, inasmuch as it involved giving an electric charge to minute drops of oil and observing the behaviour of these "ions" in an electric field. Once such an ion was brought under observation, it was tempting to follow it for as long as possible. On one occasion, he realized that he would be late for a dinner to which guests had been invited. Accordingly, thoughtful husband that he was, he telephoned his wife to say that he was watching an ion and would be home as soon as he could. When the guests arrived, Mrs. Millikan explained that her husband was washing and ironing and would be home soon.

The calculation of the electronic charge involved the value of the viscosity of air. Thus, Millikan assigned two Ph.D. students, separately, to make accurate determinations of this value. The two students were E.L. Harrington (later head of Physics at Saskatchewan) and Lachlan Gilchrist (later professor of physics at Toronto). It was subsequently shown by J.A. Bearden, using crystallography, that Millikan's value for the elementary charge was slightly in error. The error, which Millikan stoutly refused to admit, was eventually traced to the value for the viscosity of air. Thus, Canada must carry some blame for bitter words between Millikan and his critic Bearden. It should be said, however, that Harrington was born in Montana and did not arrive in Saskatchewan until well after he had studied the viscosity of air.

Millikan was one of the most influential scientists of his generation, and his move to Pasadena gave instant credibility and publicity to the California Institute of Technology, which was a reincarnation of the formerly inconsequential Throop Polytechnic Institute. The Cal Tech students enjoyed the public recognition but felt that rather much of the adulation was accepted by Millikan personally. In the mid-1930s, a large steam engine appeared on campus in connection with a construction project. Soon a student had written on its side "Roosevelt for King," whilst a religious zealot found space for "Jesus Saves." Under the latter, a third party added, "But Millikan gets credit."

In going to Chicago for an indefinite period, Lawrence and I had not resigned our positions at United College but had been granted leaves of absence. In August 1940, Lawrence received a telegram from its principal, W.C. Graham, stating that he had been unable to find a replacement and asking that Lawrence return in September to his regular teaching duties. Never have I seen a friend so dejected, so torn between desire to continue his studies and loyalty to his institution. But, as always was the case with Lawrence, the College won and, when we returned to Winnipeg for the inter-quarter break, he took back with him all the possessions that he had so laboriously lugged down to Chicago a few weeks before. Although he returned to Chicago during the next two summers, this part-time effort did not permit him to start an experimental thesis, as had been his intent. Later, when the College might have spared him, the momentum had been dissipated, and an excellent scholar, in the interest of his College, had sacrificed a long-held and partly attained ambition. I was the only one fully to know the anguish that marked his decision.

Meanwhile, it was hardly flattering that Dr. Graham had had no trouble replacing me.

The Academic Year of 1940–41

And so, in September 1940, I returned alone to Chicago, moved into a single room in the apartment, and became acquainted with the other three lodgers: George Zevnick and George Pletch from downstate Illinois, who shared the double room that Lawrence and I had occupied; and Alberto de Marco from Germany. The latter's place of origin was to have more significance after Pearl Harbor.

I was now an honest-to-goodness graduate student. I had eight course credits, two of them graduate, and had managed to scrape an A in each case; I had an eminent thesis advisor; I was about to begin experiments with the very mass spectrograph that Dempster had used to determine the atomic masses from which the energy released in fission had been estimated; and I still had some money in the Bank of Montreal. Until then, I hadn't worried much about money: I had started with about $2,000, which I had assumed would last until the bubble burst. Now that the bubble threatened *not* to burst, the money side became more relevant. Fortunately, I had a good fall quarter and, quite unsolicited, was awarded two small fellowships that paid my fees for the rest of the year.

One of the fellowships required three hours' service per week to the Department. One possibility was to teach one of the many weekly tutorial sections attached to the first-year physics course. Lectures were given by two charismatic staff members, Harvey Lemon and Michael Ference, and problems were discussed in the tutorials. I chose instead to assist Karl Eckart, a theoretician who had an idea for improving the machine on which diffraction gratings were ruled.

From its beginning, the Department had specialized in the accurate measurement of optical effects. In 1892, Harper had brought from the Case Institute (of Cleveland) the celebrated Albert A. Michelson (1852–1931), the authority on the velocity of light and co-author of the Michelson-Morley Experiment, which showed that the motion of the earth had no effect on that velocity. Michelson, who was head of the Department until 1929, had been awarded the Nobel Prize for physics in 1907. Amongst his interests was the manufacture of diffraction gratings for the accurate study of spectra. These gratings were created by ruling, with a diamond tool, thousands of closely spaced lines on a slab of glass. The lines should be uniformly spaced and as close together as possible. The whole apparatus floated in a tank of mercury to isolate it from vibrations.

Eckart and I spent many a peaceful afternoon studying the uniformity of gratings and planning how to compensate for their lack of uniformity. It was a classic case of the blind leading the blind and, although we swore no oaths, there was a tacit agreement that neither would ever disclose our lack of success. As Eckart later went to the Scripps Institute and has since died, I feel free to break the faith.

I was told that an earlier assistant in the grating business had been Karl K. Darrow, later long-time secretary and de facto dictator of the American Physical Society. Although his ultimate aim was to be a theorist, Darrow desired some hands-on experience and registered for a master's degree under Michelson. He soon gained a reputation for awkwardness with his hands. A major project during this period was the construction of a device to compensate for lack of uniformity in the screw that advanced the diamond between rulings. The device was sizable, but its effect was scaled down in use. By its very nature it was non-uniform because it was to correct non-uniformities. When it was completed, Darrow was sent to the machine shop to bring it to the grating room. As he carried it carefully down the hall, one workman remarked to another, "That must be something that Darrow tried to make round."

About 1960, I sent Darrow an abstract for a forthcoming meeting of the American Physical Society. On the following day, I discovered an error in the abstract and immediately sent a correction. A day or so later, I discovered that the correction itself was incorrect and dispatched a second correction. In due course, I received a note from Darrow saying, "I have received your Abstract, with its Correction, and the Correction to the Correction. I hope that these are not the first three terms in an infinite series." Abstracts were never acknowledged by letter, but evidently Darrow could not resist this witticism.

One of the Ph.D. requirements was a reading knowledge of two languages other than English. Lawrence and I chose French and German. We both started with a little French, and he began with a fair grasp of German. My knowledge of German was limited to two words: I believed the word *hell* meant "yellow," which was close, and I was under the impression that *Decterschnockter* meant "handkerchief," which was incorrect. Thus, in a way, I entered at the 50 percent level. Fortunately, the German Department offered a non-credit (but not free) course in scientific German, which 100 of us attended each morning at 8:00 a.m., and I gradually began to get the hang of the language. Lawrence did not attend, as he had better things to do, but he used to give me tips. For example, he taught me not to fear long words, which were endemic in chemistry, but to look for the shorter words that they comprised. I was also helped by Steven Leacock's explanation that a German sentence dives into one side of the Atlantic and emerges on the other side with the verb in its mouth. The formal instruction and the other insights, plus a much-thumbed dictionary, enabled me to translate numerous physics articles in preparation for the reading examination itself, which I passed (along with the French) in the summer of 1941. I should add that dictionaries were allowed in the examination room, and each student was given passages to translate that were related to his or her subject.

It was also necessary to pass a qualifying examination in physics before writing a thesis. As only two attempts were allowed, it was prudent to attempt it as early as one felt confident. Its purview was the whole of physics, at about the first-year graduate level. A well-organized underground provided aspirants with previous examination papers, but there was no guarantee that history would repeat itself. In this connection, I think of the student in Bible who was assured that he would be asked the names of the kings of Israel. When he was asked a different question, he wrote, "I cannot answer this question, but it occurs to me that you might like to know the names of the kings of Israel."

During winter and spring of 1941, I studied the kings of Israel, and everything else that seemed relevant, and succeeded in passing at the first try. Thus, by the summer of 1941, I had satisfied the course and language requirements and had completed the qualifying examination. Only the thesis and final oral remained!

The Academic Year of 1941–42

I commenced the academic year of 1941-42 with the enviable status of "University Fellow," with $800 at my disposal and free of all duties. As with the two earlier fellowships, this windfall had come unsolicited. There were two other university fellows in the Physics Department: my friend Mark Inghram, and a tall, somewhat forbidding man named Fallon or "infallible Fallon," as he was called. Inghram later became a professor at Chicago; I don't know what became of Fallon.

I was now spending long hours in the laboratory, especially in the late evening when the building was quiet and the electrical power was less subject to fluctuations. In the source end of the mass spectrograph, where the atoms were ionized and accelerated, I placed samples of the elements to be studied. Then I attempted to create a vacuum so that the passage of the ions through the mass spectrograph would not be impeded. This latter involved locating and sealing leaks. Next, at the collector end, I inserted a photographic plate to record the arrival of the ions. When all was in order, several exposures were taken, after which the resultant lines on the photographic plate were carefully measured with respect to one another using a travelling microscope. It sounds very commonplace, as indeed it was, but, by the spring of 1942, Dempster declared that I had made sufficient mass comparisons between atoms to serve as the basis for a thesis. If it had not been wartime, I expect that more would have been required of me.

The Manhattan Project

Despite Roosevelt's grant of $6,000, American research to determine the feasibility of an atom bomb did not move quickly until mid-1941, when the British informed the United States National Defence Research Committee, chaired by Vannevar Bush, that: (a) they believed that the "critical mass" for an explosion was about ten kilograms of the uranium isotope of mass 235; and (b) they thought this fissile isotope could be separated from its more abundant companion of mass 238 during passage through a series of permeable membranes ("gaseous diffusion"). This encouraging news, combined with Ernest O. Laurence's (1901-1958) belief that the separation could also be achieved in a massive mass spectrograph, led Compton and others to pressure Bush to greater action, if only to demonstrate that the device was not feasible. In October 1941, the president authorized a stepped-up activity, and, in January 1942, Compton assembled at the University of Chicago an impressive group of scientists to work together as a coordinated group This group activity went by the name Manhattan Project, and things soon began to change in the Physics Department.

For one thing, "security" appeared in Eckart Hall (where I was located) in the person of a guard, an amiable fellow of timorous nature with whom I developed a nodding acquaintance. One night, about midnight, I was crushing dry ice for a cold trap, preparatory to going home. The guard, hearing the pounding, came to my door to investigate but, at that very instant, the pounding ceased. Under these highly suspicious circumstances and all unknown to me, the guard called for assistance in the form of the Chicago Police. Soon there was an imperious pounding on the door and, when I opened it, I was told to stand still or I'd be filled full of lead. And the two uniformed officers were holding in their hands the weapons needed to carry out their threat. Fortunately, I was able to explain my presence before the triggers were pulled, but I was angry with the guard for placing me in the line of fire, and I thought of a few things I should have said to him before he had departed with his reinforcements. At that moment, he returned to make amends, and I had the rare pleasure of saying what I should have said earlier but thought that I had lost my chance.

In another change, a number of graduate students who had started, or were about to start, their thesis work, abandoned it in favour of mysterious other employment, and we saw them only at lunch in the Hutchison Commons. Further, as the year wore on, and although they washed before eating, they bore traces of some black material. This we realized was graphite, a very pure form of carbon. It needed little imagination to surmise that an experiment was under way to cause a chain reaction, the purpose of the carbon being to provide an environment of relatively light atoms (atomic weight = 12) in which the fast neutrons emitted in the fission of ^{235}U could be slowed to the point where they would be efficient agents of additional fissions. At this stage, our graphite-stained friends came to lunch from Stagg Field, the football stadium, where the once-mighty Maroons used to vanquish their Big Ten rivals. After the war it was revealed that the first chain reactor had been assembled under the west stands of Stagg Field and had incorporated almost 400 tons of graphite. No wonder it was called a pile.

Eminent physicists not belonging to Chicago began appearing on the campus. Chief amongst these was Fermi, who had come from New York, as it turned out, to direct the construction of the pile. In the mid-1930s, Fermi had led a group in Rome engaged in bombarding uranium with neutrons and, in so doing, creating new elements located beyond uranium in the Periodic Table. These "transuranic elements," which were the basis for Fermi's Nobel Prize were, in fact, the fission products identified by Hahn and Strassmann in 1939. Thus, Fermi, Segré, Rassetti, Pontecorvo, and others had been producing uranium fission but had not recognized it as such. That might suggest they lacked perception, but the idea of using the recently discovered neutrons to bombard heavy atoms had been a brilliant one. Fermi was probably the outstanding physicist of the period between 1935 and 1950, equally at home in theory and experiment.

The pile did not go critical until 2 December 1942, some three months after I had completed my program and had returned to Canada. Stagg Field and its west stands have since been demolished in favour of the vast Regenstein Library, but the nuclear energy site has not been forgotten: it is marked by an explosive Henry Moore sculpture.

Robert Hutchins: University President

The president of the University of Chicago during my tenure as a graduate student was the celebrated Robert Hutchins, who left Oberlin College to serve as an ambulance driver during World War I. Thereafter, he continued his studies at Yale, where he graduated in 1921, giving the commencement address and being voted the class member "most likely to succeed." A month before his twenty-ninth birthday he was named dean of the Yale Law School. A year later, he was appointed president of the University of Chicago.

Hutchins had formed an intellectual friendship with a young philosopher at Columbia University, Mortimer Adler, who had little trouble convincing Hutchins that the true purpose of a university was to search for and teach the verities that should guide our lives. Adler was soon brought to Chicago to assist in reforming that benighted place, which had been squandering many of its resources on the "collection of data," otherwise known as the natural sciences. Indeed, it was so errant in this respect that its science faculty was judged the strongest in America.

Central to the desired new curriculum was a study of the great ideas of the past, as presented in a selected group of Great Books, which were later marketed by the *Encyclopaedia Britannica*, and are still occasionally to be found in homes, with pages uncut.

To provide a vehicle for the new curriculum, a college was established within the university, where bright young students would focus on the essential truths before proceeding to graduate or professional studies. This infusion of new ideas was strongly resisted within the university but, by the time of my arrival, the college was an accepted part of the landscape.

The University of Chicago itself never adopted the Great Books Program, although some other institutions did. But Hutchins's views had a major influence on undergraduate curricula. The post-war rush to courses entitled Humanities and Western Civilization owed much to his influence but, to a large extent, he was a prophet before his time. I often heard the name of Hutchins, mostly in a pejorative context, but I never saw him in person. Obviously, we moved in different circles.

American Selective Service

In September 1940, although the United States was not yet at war, the United States Congress decreed that all men between the ages of twenty-one and thirty-six should register for the draft, and from that pool conscripts would be drawn as needed. It was anticipated that 900,000 young men would be called up each year. When I had returned to Chicago in June 1940, I had done so on a permanent visa. Thus, in October 1940, I found myself under the watchful eye of the new United States Selective Service.

This agency was organized by districts and, when the call went out for more men, each district was obliged to deliver its stated quota. Each district was provided with national guidelines for the deferral of candidates, but the final authority rested with the District Draft Board. At the start, the draftees were mostly men who were not gainfully employed, and the local draft boards had no difficulty filling their quotas. Those circumstances, combined with my status as student, rendered me immune, at least for the time being. Further, I was told that my board had asked what a physicist was and had been told that a physicist was an engineer, which was as high as one could rate in wartime value. Thus, although I reported regularly to my draft board, it was a perfunctory exercise.

After the Japanese attack on Pearl Harbor (6 December 1941), and the entry into the war of the United States, the climate changed. Draft quotas rose rapidly, and draft boards re-examined their list of deferees. My board seemed to lose patience with those who were attending university, at least with me. By this time (1942), a corresponding selective service had been established in Canada. This agency had reviewed my status, had been assured by the University that my work was nearing completion, and had encouraged me to complete it. My explanation to the South Chicago Draft Board that I was under Canadian authority did not sit well, as board members knew that I was under *their* authority. Their solution was to recognize me as a Canadian and to escort me under military guard to the border, where I would be handed over to the Canadian Army. Desperate, I contacted the British consul in Chicago, who somehow extricated me from this forced march, and I had no further difficulty in the few months remaining. It had all stemmed from the fact that, for convenience, I had chosen to study under a permanent visa.

Encounters with Blacks

My contact with Blacks in Canada was limited to sleeping-car porters. I had the impression that these fun-loving men were following a chosen vocation, so anxious were they to oblige. Obtusely, I failed to realize that they were performing one of the few jobs that were open to them and that jollity was part of the job description. In Chicago, on the other hand, the Black population was large, it comprised men, women, and children, and the restrictions on their lives were evident even to me.

Prior to the American Civil War (1861–1865), there was little opportunity for Blacks to obtain higher education. In spite of the existence of three Black colleges and the occasional charity of white institutions, only twenty Blacks had qualified for degrees by 1860. Following the Civil War, however, northern churches and Congress itself took steps to establish Black colleges where teachers could be trained and future Black leaders could be educated. Chief amongst these were Fisk University (Nashville, Tennessee, 1866) and Howard University (Washington, D.C., 1867), but from the start these institutions were poorly funded and operated in the academic shadows, and they had little contact with white universities and colleges.

In only one of the fifteen courses that I took at the University of Chicago was there a Black student in class. He was on the staff of Howard University and was attending a summer quarter. The course we shared was a senior-level course in electronic and nuclear physics, taught by Barton Hoag. He seemed a bit self-conscious but, otherwise, was much the same as the rest of us.

Early in my sojourn, whilst riding on the El (the Elevated Railway), I rose to give my seat to a Black woman, as I would have done in Winnipeg for any adult of the opposite gender. I was a bit of a show-off in that respect. But in Chicago, this provoked a scene of huge embarrassment. The woman was the most embarrassed: she could not bring herself to accept the offer and was aware that many hostile eyes were watching her reaction. Others in the neighbourhood were embarrassed that one of their own would so demean the White race. And I was embarrassed that I had caused such distress to an innocent fellow human. The two of us moved off in opposite directions; I don't know who got the seat.

I sometimes ate at a restaurant on Sixty-third Street and was known to the proprietor. One evening, before entering the restaurant, I was accosted by an elderly Black man who had fifty cents in his hand. He had walked from Gary, Indiana, was hungry, but no one would sell him any food. Would I buy some food for him? "I'll do better than that," I said. "I'll buy you a meal." As we entered the restaurant, the proprietor was much less friendly than usual, but he did show us to seats at the counter, where we were served and ate our food in silence. Thereafter, the proprietor was distinctly cool towards me, and I decided that the system was too entrenched for me to change.

If the elderly Black man had only known, he could have crossed Cottage Grove Avenue and found a large Black community. I did so one evening, to see the movie *Abe Lincoln in Illinois*, with the Canadian actor Raymond Massey playing the title role. Not far into the film, it broke, and the lights were turned on whilst the film was being repaired. In the well-filled theatre, I was the only white face. I was looked at with curiosity but with no malevolence. Before it was finished, the film broke about twenty times.

Such were my glimpses of the "free north" between 1940 and 1942.

Social Life, Entertainment, and Sport

I had some contact with girls, but not much, and none of it serious. I corresponded regularly with Katherine McPherson of Winnipeg, and we looked forward to seeing one another at the end of each quarter when I returned to Winnipeg to see my parents and to have my shirts laundered.

One quarter, Mark Inghram persuaded me to attend a dancing class at Ida Noyes Hall, a women's residence. He was already a master of the art, and even I gained some knowledge of conventional dance steps, especially the fox trot. When I returned home following that quarter, I astonished Kay with the flourishes with which I could embellish that popular dance step. However, I often had to confirm with her that the band was playing a fox trot before I went into my act.

Time and money constraints prevented me from partaking much of the cultural life of Chicago. I saw Maurice Evans in a touring production of *Twelfth Night*, I was taken to a hilarious performance of *Life with Father* and to the union-sponsored *Needles and Pins*, and I attended a noisy musical, *Lousiana Purchase*, starring Al Jolson and his wife, the winsome dancer, Ruby Keeler; she was the drawing card for me.

I also attended a moving concert by the Black contralto Marian Anderson, who, according to Toscanini, "had a voice that comes once in a hundred years." She was born to poor parents in Philadelphia, her voice was recognized in a local church choir, and she had her first professional success in Europe. In 1939, the Daughters of the American Revolution (DAR) prevented her from singing in Constitution Hall in Washington. Eleanor Roosevelt resigned from the DAR in protest and arranged for Anderson to sing from the steps of the Lincoln Memorial, where a crowd of 75,000 assembled for her concert. In the vast hall in Chicago, where I heard her perform, she seemed to be in a sad, lonely world of her own. She may have lived in a "no-man's-land," trained as a concert singer in the White world but, as a result, cut off from her roots. It was significant that she sang "My Country, 'Tis of Thee" at the great civil rights rally in Washington on 28 August 1963 but, otherwise, played little role in the movement. In January 1955, she sang the role of Ulrika in *The Masked Ball*, the first Black woman to appear in a performance at the Metropolitan Opera.

Although the University had at one time been a proud, and even dominant, member of the Big Ten (Chicago, Illinois, Indiana, Iowa, Michigan, Minnesota, Northwestern, Ohio, Pennsylvania, and Wisconsin), those days were numbered in 1930 with the arrival of President Robert Hutchins, the twenty-nine-year-old *Wunderkind*. He came from Yale, where he had been dean of Law, and his purpose was to make Chicago the pre-eminent centre for the study of the humanities. Initially, he attempted to downplay science, regarding it as too utilitarian, but he found that branch of knowledge too entrenched and, thereafter, left it pretty much alone. But there was no excuse for a place of learning to encourage gladiators from the University of Chicago to wrestle on Saturday afternoons with gladiators from other universities. As he explained, "Football has the same relation to education as bull-fighting has to agriculture." Thus, in 1936, Chicago withdrew from Big Ten football, notwithstanding that the team's celebrated back, Jay Berwanger, had been named first winner of the Heisman Trophy (best football player of the year) only the year before. Basketball and tennis were allowed to continue, perhaps because they were less physical, but they weren't promoted. Hutchins's callous treatment of football enraged an influential segment of the alumni, but he was not fazed, as he was usually under attack for one reason or another anyway.

Students organized some intercollegiate contests on their own. I answered the call for soccer practice and we had an occasional match. The most far afield was with Oberlin College in Ohio. This institution was founded in 1833 as the first in America to offer co-education and, two years later, admitted students "without respect to color." It was also one of the stops on the "underground railway" to Canada. The soccer match involved an overnight car drive, and I don't remember who paid for the gas. We also played Wheaton College, whose staff and students accepted the Bible literally. Some of their players were very skillful. I later learned that they were children of missionaries who had been posted to parts of the world where British influence prevailed. They were likely good at cricket as well, but we had no cricket team.

One of Dempster's students, Chalmers Sherman, was a graduate of Wheaton, and he spent many a lunch hour trying to persuade me that the world was created in October 4,004 B.C. He was a clever man who later became science advisor to the secretary of Commerce. In 1968, he spoke at a computer conference at the University of Manitoba, and we had a bit of a reunion. I casually mentioned to others present at lunch that he had come from Wheaton and that I had played against his college soccer team. He dismissed the mention of Wheaton almost derisively, which suggested to me that he had embraced the geologists' version of the age of the earth.

One night in the fall of 1941, I was called upon by two representatives of the hockey team. They had heard that I was from Canada which, ipso facto, made me an accomplished hockey player. Under pressure, I agreed to bring my skates when I returned to Chicago after Christmas. This was unwise, because I had always been a poor skater, although I was good at stick-handling in street and back-lane games. In the first game, against Drexler Institute (now Illinois Institute of Technology), we won by a score of six to three, and the student newspaper proclaimed that Duckworth had scored four goals. I then realized that a prophet is not without honour, save in his own country. It was absurd that I, who had difficulty making the *Free Press* carriers' team for the St. James district, should have found a team with which to star.

The Chicago White Sox baseball team was the team for the south side of Chicago, the blue-collar side, as opposed to the haughty Chicago Cubs, who played on the north side and had ivy growing on their fences. The star of the White Sox was Luke Appling, the third baseman and always amongst the leading batters in the American League. I was startled that he was booed when he came to bat, but I had misheard the cry: it was "Lu-u-u-ke, Lu-u-u-ke." Everyone knew that he would hit the ball to right field, as was later the case with Ted Williams. But, before doing so, he would foul several balls down the first base line. It was not uncommon for him to draw fifteen or twenty pitches, and the crowd rejoiced in every one that he sent foul.

I went to Comisky Park, the home of the White Sox, with Ritcey and with Clayton Opp, a Coast Guard officer who was at the University of Chicago for a summer quarter. We had not known that it was "ladies' day," which meant that women accompanying men were admitted free. Two female vultures saw that we were unaccompanied and asked if they could *go in* with us, a request to which we courteously acceded. Once in, they stayed with us, attaching themselves to Ritcey and Opp, the two married men, and paying little attention to me, the only eligible bachelor. Once the game began, however, I was content with my lot, as they were raucous in the remarks they directed at the players of the opposing team. For example, Jimmy Fox, the Boston Red Sox home-run hitter, was a "big bag of hay," a fact of which he was frequently reminded during the game.

On another occasion, rain interrupted the second game of a double-header before completion of the seventh inning. This entitled spectators to a rain check, which I used on the next day. In those three games, White Sox pitchers were not at their best and were frequently replaced, with the result that I saw in action all but one of their pitching staff.

The City of Organized Crime

Our experience with the taxi drivers at the bus terminal had led me to expect the worst of Chicago, but the promise of the start was not fulfilled. The University and the area immediately to the south of it were peaceful and, although they were separated from one another by the midway, a 200-yard strip of boulevard and parkway now known as the Midway Plaisance, I regularly crossed it alone at midnight or later. This section of land had housed the midway at the Columbian Exhibition of 1893, one of the early world fairs. It was there that Little Egypt performed the "hoochi-coochi," said to have been a depraved dance.

One night, however, as I was about to cross the parkway leading towards Lake Michigan, I paused to allow a decelerating automobile to pass. As it came to a stop, a man tumbled from it, regained his balance, and fired several shots after the now-receding car. Next day, the *Chicago Tribune* reported the event as a variation of a standard type of robbery in which unsuspecting pedestrians were pulled into cars, removed of their valuables and then unceremoniously dumped. In this instance, the victim was an off-duty policeman and, as it proved, was an excellent marksman, inasmuch as one of the men in the fleeing car had been killed by one of his shots. His kindly companions had then driven to the dead man's dwelling, where they left his body on the boulevard. Although the denouement had taken place on the midway, I was reassured that the grabbing of the victim had taken place somewhere else.

I did not learn until later that one of my professors had been the victim of an attempted robbery whilst crossing the midway at night. This was Robert Mulliken, who taught the course in atomic spectra and was subsequently awarded the Nobel Prize for chemistry in 1966. He was a somewhat dreamy type, whose mind could easily have been elsewhere when he was called upon to stand and deliver. Not wishing to resist, Mulliken began searching through his pockets, but with a growing expression of perplexity. Finally, empty-handed, he said apologetically, "I'm sorry, I was sure I had ten dollars."

Perhaps my closest encounter with the underworld occurred when my regular barber was on vacation and I tried a new one near the corner of Sixty-third Street and Cottage Grove Avenue. It appeared to be a combination cigar store and barber shop, but the barber was not in sight. I asked the man at the cigar counter, "Where's the barber?" He replied, "Go to the corner and get into the black taxi, and he'll take you." I said, "Do you mean that if I go to the corner and get into the black taxi, I'll be able to get a hair-cut?" "You want a hair-cut?" he said. "Forget it!" I had accidentally hit upon a password but will never know what I missed.

Some years later, I was discussing Chicago with one of the toolmakers in the McMaster University machine shop who had worked in Chicago at the same time I was there. In his car one day, he was angered when a large car cut in front of him. In retaliation, he speeded up and cut in front of the large car. Scarcely was he in position when two bullets passed through his rear window and out the windshield. Although he was a tough character himself, Larry said that he pulled meekly to the curb and allowed his rival to pass.

Alberto de Marco: Enemy Alien?

My German fellow lodger did his best to lie low, even before Pearl Harbor, but particularly so after that event. Amongst other things, he registered for courses in theology, which should have assured others of his innocuousness. Even so, he was decidedly edgy, as his response to two actions of mine revealed.

I returned one Sunday from Rockefeller Memorial Chapel whistling the tune of the final hymn, "Saviour, if of Zion's City, I through Grace a Member Am." Albert rushed from his room and demanded why I was whistling that tune. I was unaware that it was the tune for "Deutschland, Deutschland, ueber Alles," which he was careful never to whistle. He apparently thought that one of his compatriots had come to call and was being dangerously indiscreet.

He used to heat canned beans with hot water in the bathroom. One day, finding a can with its label soaked off, I called out jokingly, "There's a U-boat in the wash basin," which also brought him charging from his room, in this case to provide anti-submarine assistance.

When he finally came under official suspicion, it was through his girl-friend, who refused to stand for the national anthem at the close of a movie. Unfortunately, Albert was with her at the time. This led to a search of his room and the startling discovery in his trunk of a German army greatcoat, a relic from a period of compulsory military service. In my view, it was an innocent artifact, saved because he never discarded anything. Nevertheless, it was deemed sufficient evidence of seditious intent, and he spent the remainder of the war in a camp for enemy aliens in North Dakota.

The *Chicago Tribune*

During most of my time in Chicago, there were two newspapers, the *Chicago Tribune* and the *Chicago Daily News*. Shortly before I left, a new one appeared with much fanfare and with a competition to select its name. Hundreds of prizes were offered, so I knew that my suggestion of the *Chicago Guardian* would at least win a prize, even if it didn't win the grand award. The winning entry was the *Chicago Sun* (it was to be a morning newspaper) and I won no prize.

The *Daily News* was a junior version of the *New York Times*, that is, balanced in its reporting, but no fun to read.

The *Tribune* also operated a radio station, with call letters WGN. These letters stood for "world's greatest newspaper," which said much about the publication. It was bombastic, opinionated, one-sided, self-righteous and had by far the best comics and sports in the city. The most gripping comic was "Dick Tracy," the true-blue city detective who battled organized crime in all its embodiments. A typical episode would last several weeks, would be directed against some particularly revolting villain, would threaten the reputation and very life of Dick Tracy, and would end dramatically with the law triumphant. During a recent visit to Chicago, I was relieved to find that Dick Tracy is still on guard, in this case pursuing a recently paroled child molester whom he suspects of abducting Timmy and Kimmy Bush. Two other venerable strips – Moon Mullins and Smilin Jack – have been re-placed by trendy ephemera.

The publisher of the *Tribune* was Colonel McCormack, a fanatical isola-tionist and deep-seated hater of Britain. We were exposed to daily tirades against entering the war until, of course, the attack on Pearl Harbor. Shortly prior to that event, and fearing that Roosevelt was intentionally moving the country to support the Allies, McCormack revealed a British perfidy that had hitherto escaped public notice. It appeared that, following World War I, the British had planned to invade the United States by way of Canada. At the last moment, someone (it may have been Colonel McCormack himself) had blown the whistle, and this attempt to reverse the American Revolution had been thwarted. It was significant that no other paper pur-sued this startling exposé.

Despite its irritating biases and misrepresentations, there was always ex-citement, and the *Tribune* remained for most the paper of choice.

In order to get a different view, as well as some news from home, James Dingwall, a Ph.D. student in economics from McMaster University, solic-ited contributions from Canadian graduate students to subscribe to a Ca-nadian newspaper. To my surprise, the paper chosen was the *Winnipeg Free Press*, so chosen because of its editor, John Dafoe who, as chancellor of the University of Manitoba, had conferred the B.A. upon me in 1935.

Last Days in Chicago

According to Dempster's instructions, the Ph.D. thesis was written in the form of an article for the *Physical Review*, published by the American Physi-cal Society. He forwarded it with his recommendation to publish, and it occupied ten pages in the 1-15 July issue of that journal, under the title "New Packing Fractions and the Packing Fraction Curve." The thesis requirement was then met by ordering fifty reprints with special covers stating that they were being submitted to the University of Chicago "in partial fulfillment of the requirements for the Ph.D."

Nothing remained but the final oral, which at that time was not a defence of the thesis but a searching examination on the whole of physics. Apparently, the university saw the Ph.D. as an abbreviation for "PhilleD," as in "Philled to the brim," and wanted no future employer to complain of short measure. I studied assiduously for several weeks – one of the most pleasant periods in my life – and faced my inquisitors with confidence in mid-August 1942. Although the examination was interrupted briefly by a ferocious thunderstorm, I emerged relatively unscathed and, soon after, packed my effects for Winnipeg and home.

Wartime Service: 1942 to 1945

5

The Signal Corps

When I returned to Winnipeg in August 1942, requirements for the Ph.D. completed, I consulted Major Argue, of the Royal Canadian Corps of Signals and a family friend, as to which branch of the armed services should be bolstered by my enlistment. He suggested the Signal Corps. This had a certain attraction to me, as my eldest cousin, Harry Pickard, had served with Signals during World War I, having enlisted underage and without the knowledge of his parents. Family legend has it that he and only one other in his unit of ninety men escaped wound or death, and that he had been known as "Lucky" Pickard. Having decided to follow this family tradition, I presented myself at Fort Osborne Barracks in Winnipeg and made known my intention. First, however, I was obliged to take an aptitude test.

It soon emerged that the test was not specific to the Signal Corps. Some fifty to 100 of us, varying greatly in appearance and confidence, were herded into a room and seated at tables. There, the obliging supervising officer told us not to be discouraged if we could not read, as several of the questions involved drawings only and could be answered even by the illiterate. This assurance brought smiles of relief to many of us as we prepared to deal with several pages of brief questions. Some of the questions were of the type found on contemporaneous intelligence tests: meanings of words, the next two terms in sequences of numbers, and so on. Also, there was an extensive section in which we were asked to identify various hand tools. As luck would have it, most of these were familiar to me from a shop course I had been obliged to take at the University of Chicago in preparation for a career in experimental physics.

In due course, Major Argue informed me that I had passed the test, and he escorted me to the flag-bedecked quarters of Brigadier General

Rockington, where, in a solemn ceremony, I "accepted the King's shilling" and was sworn in as a second lieutenant in the Royal Canadian Corps of Signals. I was not issued my semaphore flags immediately but was sent home to await further orders. Without Major Argue, I might have chosen the air force or the navy, both of which held a curious fascination for boys from the prairies.

The telephone call to action, when it did come, came not from Fort Osborne Barracks, but from Ottawa. It appeared that a "technical personnel" department had reviewed my test results and other qualifications and had decreed that I should proceed to Ottawa to discuss possibilities other than that of signalman. It was with some sadness that I received these instructions, as I had been looking forward to the social advantages of wearing a uniform. But, as the wisdom of the decision was later borne out by the fact that we won the war, I've had no long-term regrets.

Radar

In Ottawa I was interviewed by David Keyes, who seemed to be a one-man department, having abandoned for the time being his regular post as professor of physics at McGill University. Keyes, acting for the Government of Canada, dispatched me to the National Research Council (NRC), then housed in its splendid Sussex Street building, which it had occupied since 1932 and where I was to be assigned appropriate wartime work.

Following instructions, I reported to the office of Robert W. Boyle, head of the Physics Division, who, I later learned, was a man of consequence. He had come from the Faculty of Applied Science at the University of Alberta, which he had organized, to be the founding director of physics and engineering. Subsequently, in 1935, he had aspired to the presidency of NRC when General A.G.L. McNaughton succeeded H.M.Tory in that position. When I was ushered into Boyle's presence, he was reading a document with such concentration that he failed to notice my presence for what seemed an unreasonably long time. After all, I was not a nobody; I was a doctor of philosophy from the University of Chicago, and, furthermore, I was hot from walking down Sussex Drive. After he had created the desired effect, he was agreeable enough and described the several sections within his division. Also, he arranged for me to meet Donald C. Rose (head of General Physics), George Laurence (head of Radioactivity and X-Rays) and Brigadier Wallace (head of Radar).

I hit it off with Rose and Laurence, and with Donald Hurst (who worked with Rose), all of whom became major figures in Canadian science and whose friendship I long enjoyed. Wallace was from the United Kingdom

Katherine McPherson has just accepted an offer of marriage, 1942.

and had an air of mystery about him, an air of understated authority. Using the adage that the English carry their caste marks in their mouths, I concluded that Wallace stood pretty high in that regard. I later learned that he was not a regular NRC employee but had been especially imported to animate Canada's contribution to this crucial activity. Although Hurst and Laurence had work that was relevant, Wallace's project seemed more urgent, and I ended up as a junior scientist in the radar section at a salary of $2,100 per annum. This was all I needed to propose to Katherine McPherson, who came to Ottawa a few weeks later, and we were married in the home of my great-uncle William Lunam on 21 November 1942. Our first child, Henry William, was born within a year.

Before taking up my duties as a junior scientist, I was obliged to call at the East Block and swear on the Bible a solemn oath of secrecy, by which, I suppose, I am still bound. As it turned out, some of my new colleagues did not feel bound by that same oath.

In all the discussions about my future work, no allusion was ever made to the fact that, only a few days earlier, I had been commissioned second lieutenant in the Royal Canadian Corps of Signals. I may still be listed as a deserter.

RADAR, or *Radio Detection and Ranging*, began in 1924 when the British physicist, Edward V. Appleton, determined the height of the ionosphere, an ionized layer in the upper atmosphere, by measuring the time for electromagnetic waves to be reflected from it. It was eleven years, however, before another Brit, Robert Watson-Watt, developed a workable device for detecting objects on or near the surface of the earth. By the time of the outbreak of war, efficient systems were in operation using wavelengths of the order of one metre. Their value was dramatically demonstrated in the late summer of 1940, when Germany began systematic bombing of Britain as a presumed prelude to invasion. Guided by this locating equipment, Royal Air Force spitfires were able to intercept bombers as they approached the coast and to destroy hundreds of them in the space of a few desperate days. This was the Battle of Britain, in which, according to Churchill, "Never was so much owed by so many to so few." The technology used in this exercise was generally available and not a monopoly of the British.

In 1940, however, the British began developing the means of generating much shorter wavelengths (microwaves), with sufficient power for the purpose. The key was the invention of the resonant cavity magnetron, and, by 1942, ten-centimetre (S Band) radar units were in operation and three-centimetre (X Band) units were in the making. The shorter the wavelength, of course, the better the definition. It was believed that this technology was not known to the enemy and, on that account, it was extremely hush-hush.

The radar work was done at the Radio Field Station, some ten miles south of Ottawa, just off the Metcalfe Road. We were taken there in station wagons driven by volunteer women who wore a somewhat stylish khaki uniform. Mrs. Crerar, the wife of the general, was a regular driver, as was Patricia Collard, whom I came later to know as Pat Condo, the wife of the vice-president (Administration) at the University of Manitoba. I caught the station wagon at the side entrance to the Chateau Laurier Hotel and was delivered back to that area at the end of the day. A few of the employees needed no transportation, as they lived in a small colony of wartime houses located adjacent to the field station. Their families could ride the station wagons for trips to Ottawa.

We numbered in all about 100 persons, classified as "professionals" (having degrees) and "non-professionals." To my knowledge, the only non-degree man to cross the barrier was an electronic wizard named Harold McRae, whose special skills had earned him quasi-degree status. Amongst other things, this exempted him from the indignity of having to sign in and out.

About half the work was in support of metre-wavelength equipment, that is, improving antennas and displays and increasing the power of transmission sets. A smaller group was preoccupied with a ten-centimetre unit designed to provide artillery with range information. This "GL" (gun-laying) was operational and was the showpiece of the station. A smaller group was developing other ten-centimetre applications and was starting three-centimetre developments. I was assigned to this group.

Amongst those working in other groups were Norman Alcock (founder of the post-war Peace Research Institute), Robert Bell (later principal of McGill), Donald Brunton (founder of Isotopes Limited), Arthur Covington (later a distinguished radio astronomer), Harold Ferris, William Haney (who died prematurely), Ned Mazerall (jailed for selling secrets to the Russians), Geoffrey Miller (later with the Department of Communications), the Naismith brothers, Thomas Pepper (later director of the Saskatchewan Research Council) and Ross Smythe. Operating more or less on his own, but having an interest in everything, was the eccentric but brilliant Hugh Le Caine (1914-1977). He lived alone in an adjacent farm house and did most of his own work at night. He then arrived with a flourish about noon and, in effect, kept office hours until the rest of us quit work. During this period, we were free to consult him about our problems or ideas, and he invariably gave useful counsel. I have no idea how this modus operandi came to be accepted by the management but, by the time of my arrival, he was firmly installed as a priceless, genial oracle who chose his own problems and kept his own hours. He it was who suggested the principle of the microtron, a particle accelerator based on microwaves, and after the war it was he who gave Canada a name for electronic music. Brigadier Wallace was in overall charge of the field station, but we seldom saw him unless he had important visitors in tow. His deputy on the ground appeared to be Donald McKinley, a tall, somewhat impenetrable graduate of the University of Toronto, but obviously knowledgeable and smart. I once beat him at chess by sacrificing my queen, which gave me fifteen minutes of fame.

Our three- and ten-centimetre waves were carried by metallic wave guides. Those who envied our high calling referred to us as "plumbers." Fred Sanders directed the group, and William Henderson was assistant director. Other members of the group were Harold Cave, on loan from Queen's University, where he was professor of physics, Durnford Smith and John Ferguson from McGill, Gordon Retallack from the University of British Columbia, and Charles Millar from Bishop's University in Lennoxville. The war had interrupted the graduate work or plans of these last four, but all completed their Ph.D.s later.

Sanders was courteous and conciliatory and, I believe, had been with the NRC before the war. After I had performed a few mundane chores, he assigned me the task of designing a three-centimetre antenna for use on motor torpedo boats in their battle with submarines in the English Channel. About this time, I discovered that some others were being paid more than $2,100 per annum and, when I pointed this out to him, Sanders arranged for me to rise to $2,560, which helped to buy clothes for our firstborn, Henry William. Otherwise, except for encouragement, I was left pretty much on my own.

Henderson (a Canadian) had studied at Cambridge University and had come to the NRC from Purdue University, where he had made a name for himself in nuclear physics. He was gruff but agreeable enough once the ice had been broken. His equanimity was quite destroyed one day when I told him that I had just read his obituary in the *Journal of Applied Physics*. Apparently, two Hendersons had belonged to the Physics Department at Purdue, and when the head, K. Lark-Horowitz, was told that one had died, he mistakenly assumed that it was our man. The least he could do was send off a glowing account of his career to the *JAP*. Thus, Henderson had the dubious privilege of seeing himself as Lark-Horowitz saw him. The rest of us viewed the incident as a huge joke, but Henderson's amusement was muted. I suppose it must have caused some embarrassment, but I understand that his wife stood by him, dead or alive.

Harold Cave was a confirmed bachelor. One day he told me the astonishing fact that his grandfather had fought at the Battle of Trafalgar. He, himself, had been born in 1900 when his father was seventy-two. Thus, he could comfortably account for a grandfather who had been a powder monkey in 1805. Many years after the war, I learned that Cave had married, and I envisaged this remarkable dynasty extending into a new generation, but, to his eternal shame, he had married a woman who was past the child-bearing age. I mentioned these facts to Chancellor Mitchener when I received an honorary degree from Queen's in 1977, expecting him to erect a cairn at least, but he seemed to have more pressing matters on his mind. Harold Cave, a gentle, generous man, died in the early 1990s, about two centuries after his grandfather's birth.

Durnford Smith, who has also passed to his reward, was clever but somewhat mischievous and unpredictable. He turned out to be a "spy." When the Russian cipher clerk Igor Gouzenko defected on 5 September 1945, he provided the names of several Canadians who had been selling classified documents to Russian agents. No action was taken at the time but, on the early morning of 15 February 1946, following a leak in the American press, Smith and Ned Mazerall, another field-station scientist, were arrested. They subsequently spent significant periods of time incarcerated. I believe that both felt that Russia was an ally and should be aided in whatever way possible, even if the Canadian government thought otherwise. In any event, they passed the documents on and, as part of the protocol, received payment in return. The sums involved were trivial, but acceptance of them transformed what were possibly idealistic acts into sordid transactions. Allan Nunn May, who sold documents relating to the atomic bomb, was arrested at the same time but was tried and convicted in Britain. Smith later completed his Ph.D. at McGill, although J.S. Foster, the senior professor, refused to supervise his thesis. He then taught at Memorial University, at that time regarded as the end of the world. Mazerall later found work as a technician in the Faculty of Medicine at the University of Manitoba and died in 1991. Neither man's marriage survived his imprisonment.

Ferguson and Millar, the one as reserved as the other was boisterous, later took their Ph.D.s at McGill with Professor J.S. Foster and went on to honourable careers with Atomic Energy of Canada at Chalk River.

Retallack took his Ph.D. in cosmic rays at the University of California and was hired as an assistant professor at the University of Indiana, hoping (as all did) to obtain tenure. It was a cruel but common practice at leading American universities to hire several staff on a temporary basis, with a view to selecting one or two for permanent positions. Thus, there was intense pressure on those under scrutiny to produce research results. Undoubtedly with the object of improving his chances for tenure, Retallack submitted an abstract to a Chicago meeting of the American Physical Society, reporting evidence for the negative proton. This was an electrifying result, and the room assigned for the presentation of the paper proved much too small. I listened to snatches of his talk and the subsequent discussion through the open door to the hall. Following the presentation, his evidence was brutally criticized, and his prospects for tenure evaporated. It was a tragic happening to a good man, but he went on to an important career in the defence laboratory in Dartmouth, Nova Scotia.

Meanwhile, what about the antennae for the motor torpedo boats in the English Channel? Although I had never seen these craft, I was told that they were fairly steady from side to side but pitched violently from stern to prow. These conditions called for an antenna with a narrow horizontal beam and a wide vertical one. These desiderata were got with a six-inch section of a four-foot parabolic dish that was enclosed bottom and top with plane metal sheets. Sanders was vastly relieved when I showed him the test patterns for this device, as I think he had given me up for lost. As I was transferred soon after, I don't know whether the antenna was ever operational, but I have since seen, at airports, countless examples of the same design. Who knows?

I was sorry to miss the field trial of the antenna. For one thing, it might have involved a trip to the United Kingdom. Also, it was well known that serving officers were sceptical of the "long-hairs," and any demonstration of new equipment had to be more than convincing; this presented a challenge. In a Halifax trial of a sea-borne ten-centimetre unit, a plywood cover had been constructed for protection from the weather. For the test itself, a target vessel pretending to be an enemy approached from a distance and came into view on the display screen, as was hoped for and expected. Before the champagne could be uncorked, however, the screen showed three targets, then five, then seven. Clearly the enemy was attacking from all sides, although those on deck who were relying on their eyesight could discern only one. It was soon realized that nails used to build the cover were causing false echoes, but for a time the worst expectations of the service officers was being fulfilled. There was some basis to their scepticism: radar operators, weary of watching a screen on which no signal appeared, were sometimes wont to conclude that the set was out of adjustment and to begin fiddling with it to the point where it could detect nothing.

It was just outside Halifax harbour, near the end of the war, that a German U-boat evaded all forms of detection and sank several vessels. On news of the Armistice, the U-boat's captain took his boat to Lunenburg to surrender. Harry Welsh, later head of Physics at Toronto and who had studied in Germany in the early 1930s, was in the navy and was sent to Lunenburg to receive the surrender. When the formalities were over, Welsh asked the captain how he had eluded the minefield that guarded the approaches to Halifax harbour. He answered that when studying the charts he had noticed a similarity to the harbour at Kiel and had proceeded on the assumption that Halifax would be mined in the same way.

The Montreal Laboratory

In the summer of 1944, I was summoned to the office of E.W.R. Steacie, a distinguished chemist who was serving as second-in-command at the NRC. He explained that a secret major project had been developing in Montreal and that Professor H.G. Thode of McMaster University, a mass spectroscopist, was operating a satellite laboratory in Hamilton. As I had done my Ph.D. in mass spectroscopy, would I care to join Thode's group? I jumped at the chance.

The secret project was a joint British-Canadian one aimed at contributing to the development of the atomic bomb. I was aware of the American project but, because of the high security surrounding it, had no knowledge of developments since I'd been a student in Chicago. I now learned that the Montreal Laboratory had been established in 1942 when the British decided to transfer most of their related work to North America but wished to have partial independence from the American Manhattan Project. A few key Brits were seconded to the Manhattan Project, but a goodly number came to Montreal, along with a mixed bag of exiles from the continent. Although the new laboratory worked closely with the Americans, the latter were nervous about security, in particular the trustworthiness of those who had come from Europe. The fear was not of Nazi spies but of Communist sympathizers. Subsequent events justified this concern: Klaus Fuchs gave vital information to Russia, and Bruno Pontecorvo later defected to that country. Allan Nunn May, who also sold precious secrets, was about as British as they come.

The Montreal Laboratory had been established in one of the six wings of the impressive new building of the University of Montreal, located on the back slope of Mount Royal. The shell of this huge edifice, surely the largest building in Canada at the time, had been erected, but the interiors were mostly unfinished. The necessary services were quickly installed in the wing in question, and soon a variety of foreign accents were heard in its halls. H. von Halban, who had been working in Paris with Madame Curie's daughter Irene and Irene's husband, F. Joliot, and who had escaped from that city prior to its fall in 1940 with the bulk of the world's supply of heavy water, had been named director. This was a task for which von Halban had no flair, as he was primarily interested in pursuing his own research. It was said that he had used his heavy water to bargain for the job. George Laurence of the NRC and Bernard Sargent of Queen's were the senior Canadian physicists. Laurence had moved from Ottawa to Montreal, and, I suppose, I might have been transferred to the Montreal Laboratory much sooner had I opted for his x-ray section in 1942.

By 1944, under von Halban's directorship, the administration of the Laboratory was in a shambles, and he was replaced by John D. Cockcroft, who had been a professor of physics at Cambridge prior to the war and who was to share the Nobel Prize in 1951. Cockcroft was a man of few words and soon had matters under control. I had an example of his "few words." Shortly after my arrival in Hamilton, Thode wrote a two-page letter to Cockcroft giving reasons for my making a trip to Chicago. Cockcroft replied, "I think Duckworth should go." I never met von Halban, who was rumoured to have withdrawn to his Montreal residence and to have continued some of his experiments in the basement. I visited the Montreal Laboratory on only two occasions: a two-day period during desperately cold weather in January 1945, when the wait for the Côtes-des-Neiges streetcar *n'était pas un cadeau*, and a one-day visit in the following July.

The radioactivity section of the Montreal Laboratory was directed between 1943 and 1945 by an old-time radio-chemist, Friedrich A. Paneth, a Jewish refugee from the Continent. In his pre-war career, he had never dealt with any but minute quantities of radioactive material. On that account, he was unaccustomed to taking the precautions required for more active samples. The consequence of this lack of foresight had struck the laboratory immediately prior to my two-day visit. It had just been realized that two of Paneth's younger staff, Heal and Morgan, had been exposed to fatal doses of radiation. They would not die instantly, but it was inevitable, and a pall hung over the entire place. Colleagues rushed to open doors for the doomed pair and, in other ways, tried to make their lives more bearable. I never heard how long they lived, but, in 1955, when I was invited to lecture at the Atomic Weapons Research Establishment at Aldermaston (near Oxford), I was startled to discover that Morgan was chairing the colloquium. I asked how Heal was and was told that he was well at last hearing. Thus, the two had defied predictions and, rather like Bill Henderson, had received their death tributes long before their actual demises.

As part of wartime security measures, certain key individuals were given *noms de guerre* for use when travelling. Thus, in the United States, Enrico Fermi was known as "Mr. Farmer," and E.U. Condon, who did much transcontinental travel, was given two names: one for the east coast and one for the west. On one flight he was awakened by the attendant and asked his name. He responded, "Where am I?"

In the same spirit, when Niels Bohr was flown secretly to North America, he was given the pseudonym "Mr. Baker." His itinerary included a visit to the Montreal Laboratory. Present at a small social gathering in his honour was a woman who had recently divorced her husband and married

Dr. G. Placzek, a Czech theorist in the laboratory. When she was introduced to "Mr. Baker," she said, "But you are Mr. Bohr." "No," he replied, "I am Mr. Baker, but you are Mrs. X (calling her by her former name)." "No," she responded. "I am Mrs. Placzek," a riposte that caused much innocent merriment.

Harry Thode, a chemistry graduate from the University of Saskatchewan, had taken his Ph.D. in 1934 at Columbia University. In that same year, his thesis supervisor, H.G. Urey (1893-1981), received the Nobel Prize for his discovery, two years earlier, of heavy hydrogen (or deuterium). After five further years in the United States, Thode had accepted a position at McMaster University, in Hamilton, Ontario, then a small Baptist institution. He began a research program on isotope enrichment and constructed a mass spectrometer to monitor his success. Thus, when the new Montreal Laboratory sought the means to analyze minute quantities of fission products krypton and xenon, Thode was able to provide them. Further, in the analysis, he found remarkable deviations from the isotopic patterns found in nature. Almost overnight, he and his students became celebrities in the Montreal Lab, although they were operating at a distance therefrom. I was charged with the construction of an instrument for the analysis of solids, to complement Thode's gaseous analysis capability.

Working with Thode were five students – Gordon Dean, Robert Graham, Lee Harkness, Robert Hawkings, and Ruven Smith – all of whom had been undergraduates at McMaster. Graham and Hawkings later became key figures at Chalk River. An additional staff member arrived shortly after I did, in the person of Denys Roberts. The Montreal Laboratory had requested from the United Kingdom a metallurgist by the name of Roberts, and the wrong Roberts had been sent out. As Denys had had some experience with isotopes, he was shipped off to Hamilton and became my colleague. This unsettled things a bit, as the rest of us were slow to recognize the natural superiority of the English, as personified in Denys Roberts. And the situation was not helped by the fact that he received, in addition to his regular salary, a per diem allowance to compensate for living abroad. Following the war, he joined the Physics Department at Queen's University.

To expedite the task of constructing the mass spectrograph for solid analysis, I was sent to Chicago in November 1944 (with Cockcroft's terse endorsement) where my former professor, Arthur Dempster, provided me with plans from which an instrument with the desired characteristics had just been constructed. Involved in the construction, and now in the use of this mass spectrograph, was Ralph Lapp, who had been a graduate student when I was at Chicago and later became prominent as a self-appointed spokesman for physics. With these two friends at court, I had a good reception and returned not only with the plans, but also with a variety of accessories that would have been difficult to obtain from Hamilton.

Two special events marked my second visit (in February 1945). First, aware of a meat shortage in the United States, I had taken four choice tenderloin steaks to Professor and Mrs. Dempster. These were packed in dry ice and were regarded with suspicion by the representative of the United States Customs Service with whom I dealt. Eventually, he compromised his principles, and the gift reached its appreciative destination. Second, at Dempster's insistence, I was taken to the Argonne Forest, near Chicago, where a primitive nuclear reactor, the first in the world, was in operation behind great barrels of water that served as a shield. Tom Brill, another former graduate-student friend, was a member of this research group. The now-famous Argonne National Laboratory was subsequently built on this site.

The four trips (two to Montreal and two to Chicago) were a considerable drain on the federal Treasury, totalling, as they did, $203.24. The second trip to Chicago exemplifies the lavish style in which we travelled. My expense account showed:

FE 22	Left Hamilton for Chicago 10:58 PM	
	Train fare Hamilton to Chicago	
	and return	35.19
	Lower (!) berth	5.13
FE 23	Porter	0.25
	Taxi to Windemere Hotel – shared with	
	D T Roberts and R L Graham $US0.65	
	Meals (B -0.65, L-0.80, D-1.15) $US2.60	
FE 24	Hotel East Windemere $US3.00	
	Meals (B-0.60, L-0.90, D-1.20) $US2.70	
	Taxi-Windemere Hotel to Dearborn Stn	
	– shared with Roberts and Graham	
	$US0.65	10.93
FE 25	Berth Chicago to Hamilton	5.52
	Porter	0.25
	Street car fare to and from station	0.15

Total 57.42

Although possession of the plans for the mass spectrograph simplified the task, there was much work yet to be done, and the instrument was barely functioning when the war came to an end in August 1945. On 13 August, the Honourable C.D. Howe, Minister of Reconstruction, released the names of Canadians associated in experimental and development work in the field of atomic energy. Terming the whole party "the largest and most distinguished group of scientists ever assembled for a single investigation in any British country," Howe disclosed that eight of the number had been engaged in experiments at McMaster University. Thus, despite my zero-contribution to the atomic bomb, my picture appeared in several papers along with those who had played significant roles, and I did little to correct the record. In another six months I might have had some claim to fame. As it was, I accepted a position as assistant professor of physics at the University of Manitoba, commencing 1 September 1945, and was allowed by Dr. Steacie to take the recently completed instrument with me. In addition, he arranged for a small NRC grant in aid of research to support my work. Thus ended my wartime service.

The author's parents, Henry Bruce Duckworth and Ann Hutton Edmison.

Author with paternal grandfather, Henry Duckworth, and father, Henry Bruce Duckworth.

Author's maternal grandfather, Henry Edmison, third from right, with Queen's University graduating class of 1863.

Winnipeg Free Press carriers, Depot No. 5, winners of the fall 1930 competition for new subscribers. Author stands in back row, beneath the letter T.

Broadway buildings of the University of Manitoba, partly under construction, 1909, as seen from the dome of the Legislative Building. At the right is the first science building, built in 1901, and in the distance Wesley College, built in 1896, with its huge playing field in the rear (courtesy WCPI).

Wesley College, about 1932 (courtesy WCPI).

Wesley College faculty, 1924–25. Those still teaching between 1932 and 1935 are highlighted. Front row, left to right: Watson Kirkconnell (English and Latin), Eleanor Bowes (French and dean of Women), Edna Cragg (secretary); middle row, left to right: O.T. Anderson (Mathematics and dean of Arts), J.H. Riddell (president), C.N. Halstead (dean of the Collegiate); back row, left to right: L.W. Moffit (Economics); A.S. Cummings (comptroller); A.C. Longman (English and dean of Men); A.E. Cragg (Psychology); A.L. Phelps (English) (courtesy WCPI).

Principal W.C. Graham teaching Old Testament seminar (courtesy WCP1).

From top: University of Manitoba senior basketball team, 1937; United College golf champion, 1934; Winnipeg Scottish football team member, 1938.

University of Chicago Physics Department, 1940: highlighted front row, left to right: A.J. Dempster, Enrico Fermi (Nobel Prize, 1938), S.K. Allison, A.H. Compton (chair and Nobel Prize, 1927), Karl Eckart, Barton Hoag, Robert Mulliken (Nobel Prize, 1966); back row, author.

Visit of John D. Cockcroft (Nobel Laureate, 1951) to McMaster University in 1944, left to right (standing): Robert Hawkings, Denys Roberts, Harry Duckworth, Robert Graham, Gordon Dean; (seated): H.G. Thode, J.D. Cockcroft.

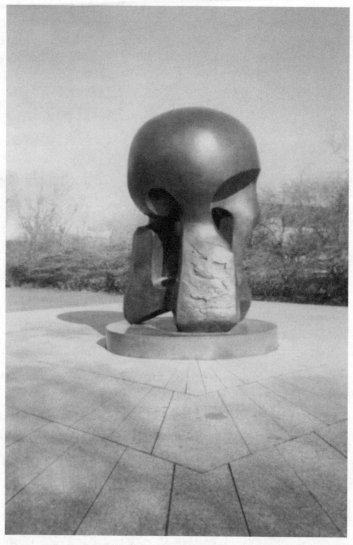

Henry Moore sculpture on site of west stands of Stagg Field, which housed the first chain reactor, 2 December 1942.

The University of Manitoba: 1945–46

6

In September 1945, I arrived at the University of Manitoba, along with the veterans of World War II. I had been hired to instruct them and any others who happened to be around, and they were there courtesy of a grateful nation.

My teaching duties were limited to third-, fourth-, and fifth-year students; thus, I seldom set foot in the Junior Division (in the so-called Broadway buildings). On the Fort Garry campus, little had changed since my departure in 1937. The Buller (senior science) and Tier (senior arts plus library) buildings, in their limestone grandeur, were beginning to look at ease amongst the brick neo-classical buildings of the former Agriculture College. Only one new edifice had appeared: a splendid Georgian house in which home-economics students from modest homes could learn how to manage mansions.

As in 1937, most scholars reached the Fort Garry campus courtesy of the number 97 streetcar, which traversed the full length of Osborne Street before turning north on Jubilee Avenue, south on Pembina Highway, and finally east so as to bisect the Southwood Golf Course. The penultimate stop was behind the Buller building, and the terminus lay behind Tier. Students and staff jostled for seats or standing room with little account taken of academic precedence.

As housing in Winnipeg was at a premium, my wife, two-year old son, and I stayed with my parents in what is now known as the Wolseley area. Frequently, I was allowed to use the family car, which reduced travelling time dramatically; to purchase a car was impossible.

Returning veterans were eligible for gratuities, whose amounts were determined by length and type of service. Amongst the gratuity options was that of a university education. In this option the federal government paid the tuition and living costs of the veterans and also made grants of $150 per student to the host institutions for costs not covered by tuition. This latter subvention was sold to the provinces as being in the *national* interest. Some such rationale was needed because the $150-per-student grant represented federal support for education, which, by the terms of the *British North America Act*, was a provincial jurisdiction.

Only once before had "national interest" been invoked as a basis for federal support of education. This was in World War I, when the National Research Council (NRC) was established, and it made grants to universities to support research relating to the war effort. After that war, research continued to be seen as in the national interest, and the provinces accepted that type of university support as not infringing on their prerogatives. The $150-per-student grant was quite a different matter, but fears of federal interference that the provinces might have harboured were allayed by assurances that veterans could choose their own universities and the federal government would remain uninvolved in university policy. It was the thin edge of a wedge, however, which later met opposition in the province of Quebec, as the wedge penetrated deeper and, much later, caused distress to the rest of the provinces when the deeply entrenched wedge was withdrawn. But, in 1945-46, all the provinces and their universities appeared happy to get whatever help they could.

Although the universities were expecting a rush of veterans, the size and suddenness of it caught them off guard. In the first year after the war, the enrollment doubled from 38,000 to 76,000, and institutions scrambled for facilities and instructors. The University of Manitoba was no different from the rest: enrollment in 1945-46 had doubled from the year before. In the general excitement, United College found itself renting space in a nearby Canadian Legion hall, and even the University compromised its principles by hiring qualified women. Douglas Chevrier, registrar at the University of Manitoba, typified the university officers who were overwhelmed by the incoming horde. After reviewing applications for admission late into the night, he went home exhausted and overslept, apologizing to a colleague for his late arrival at the office. "That's all right, Doug," said the other, "but where were you yesterday?" However, as the deluge was seen as temporary, the trying conditions were tolerated. Little did the Canadian university community know that the enrollment would never again be less than it was in 1945-46.

The veterans were serious students. They had lost several years of their lives and were determined to lose no more. Their urgency was in contrast to the indolence of some of their younger classmates who were enjoying a college loaf prior to earning their daily bread. And their dedication also clashed with the attitude of those professors who were inclined to dilate on topics only marginally related to the curriculum. More than one professor was told, by students who had seen more of life and death than he, to get on with the course.

The president of the University of Manitoba was Albert Trueman, who had succeeded Sidney Smith in 1945 when the latter moved to a similar position at the University of Toronto. Trueman was an English scholar from New Brunswick, where he had been superintendent of Education for the City of St. John. He was an intelligent, personable man with a fine singing voice, but he had arrived not knowing who was boss at the University of Manitoba.

The boss, of course, was Walter Crawford, the comptroller hired following the Machray defalcation to re-establish fiscal stability. Crawford's strategy, which was effective, was to contain expenditures, even those authorized by the president. For example, Trueman's successor, A.H.S. Gillson, began his administration with a trip to Wilson's Furniture Store with a view to smartening up his office. When that establishment telephoned the comptroller for a purchase order and it was refused, the President's Office remained as it was. I've been told that Gillson never asked why the furniture failed to arrive.

But, to return to Trueman: at the close of one meeting of the Board of Governors, before calling for a motion for adjournment, the chairman invited other business. Trueman said that he had a request: the path to the president's residence (which was on campus) was dangerously dark at night. Could a couple of lights be placed to illumine the way? The chairman turned to the comptroller: "Is it true, Mr. Crawford, that you are in charge of the physical plant?" When Crawford acknowledged this to be true, the chairman asked, "Is there any other business?"

The fact that Crawford reported directly to the Board, and had virtually veto power over anything with financial implications, was intolerable to Trueman. In 1948, he accepted the presidency of the University of New Brunswick, where he had to deal with another infuriating character in the person of its chancellor, Lord Beaverbrook.

Late in the morning of one Encaenia (the degree day), Beaverbrook mentioned to Trueman that a woman was present to whom he had promised an honorary degree. Would Trueman make the necessary arrangements? The mind boggles at the difficulty of calling an emergency meeting of Senate, of preparing a citation, and of completing the other necessaries within a two-hour period.

The dean of the Faculty of Arts and Science at the University of Manitoba during 1945-46 was Hugh H. Saunderson, a professor of chemistry and member of a well-known Winnipeg family. He knew the university and the community well and could be trusted to do nothing foolish. Astute, conscientious, honest, and hard-working, he soon joined the NRC in Ottawa and, ultimately, in 1955, returned to the University of Manitoba as its sixth president.

The Department of Physics dated from 1904 when it and other science departments were established. The founding professor was Frank Allen, a New Brunswicker, who had his Ph.D. from Cornell. A quiet, dignified man, he was always a leading member of the University and was known internationally for his studies on the physics of the eye. He told me that he had once received a letter from a German physicist with similar research interests inviting him to engage in a controversy in the British scientific journal *Nature*.

I had been hired by the new head of the Department of Physics, Dr. J.F.T. Young, a gruff sort who had some of the attributes of a sergeant major. He had been head-in-waiting for several years, pending Professor Allen's retirement, which had been delayed because of the war. Now that Young's turn had come, he was intent on making his mark by strengthening the physics Honours Program. In the light of developments in the subject in the late 1930s and during the war, the curriculum was decidedly old-fashioned, but Young's solution was to add an extra lecture to each honours course, that is, to intensify much that was already archaic. Reform of the curriculum had to await Young's death in 1953 and the arrival of Robert W. Pringle as head.

Four others joined the Department at the same time as I: Harold Feeney, William Petrie, John Abrams, and Peter Stewart. Feeney, Petrie, and Abrams had their Ph.D.s; Stewart was younger and had just been demobilized from the navy. The strongest members of the Department, Harold Batho and D.O. Langstroth, had just departed, Batho to the west coast to serve as physicist in a cancer clinic and Langstroth to the Defense Research Laboratory at Suffield, Alberta.

The departments in the Faculty of Arts and Science offered pass (four years) and honours (five years) programs. The first two years were still taught in the old Broadway buildings, located downtown near the provincial legislature. My courses were all taught on the Fort Garry site: a course in electricity and magnetism to second-year engineers, the same to third-year science students, a laboratory that ran every afternoon for all these courses, a fourth-year honours course in electromagnetic theory, and a fifth-year

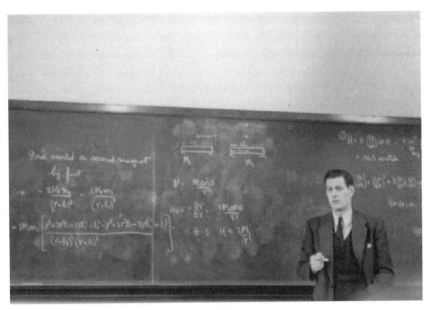

Author lecturing at University of Manitoba, 1945.

honours course plus laboratory in electronics. A group of responsible senior students pretty much ran the electricity and magnetism laboratory, but I had responsibility for it, and I was the sole proprietor of the rest, including whatever marking was involved. In addition, I was assembling the mass spectrograph that Dr. Steacie had allowed me to bring from McMaster University. I often went to class with the ink not yet dry on my notes but managed always to report for duty. Inexplicably, some students from that year, with memories now mellowed by time, claim to have enjoyed the experience. Perhaps they were getting equally ad hoc instruction from their other instructors.

Early in the fall term, I was asked to give a public lecture on atomic energy, to be held in Theatre B, a large lecture hall on the Broadway site. To ensure some audience, I took my wife and mother with me. This was unnecessary, as I had quite underestimated the public interest in the subject. In the lecture, I made a simple calculation of the energy released in uranium fission, showed why the fission products emitted neutrons, and 300 listeners went home happy in the knowledge that they could build an atom bomb if they put their minds to it.

Professor Meredith Jones, a French scholar and director of Extension, heard of my successful lecture and persuaded me to give an evening course on atomic physics in the second term. I tried to illustrate the principles with inadequate experiments and was not very successful. I should have stopped with atomic energy.

My duties were so demanding, or seemed to be, that I saw little of those who were in other departments. True, all the science departments were housed in one building (since named in honour of Reginald Buller, the celebrated mycologist), but there was no staff room in which to socialize, and, anyway, we were all too busy.

We did meet occasionally with our unseen colleagues at faculty meetings. At one such meeting, the subject of admission to medicine came up. Aware that the number of Jewish students in medicine had been purposely limited, I naïvely asked if the Jewish quota could not be abolished. A hush fell over the room as if I had defiled the king, and more than one declared no knowledge of such a quota. My reply, that it was common knowledge, only deepened the mystery. Fred Duval, the prominent Winnipeg surgeon, who entered Medicine in the fall of 1947, has told me that that year was the first year that no quota existed. Apparently, the non-existent quota had been withdrawn in the session following.

My wife had pleasure from the Faculty Wives' Club and from a book group that must have been associated with it. Also, certain of the older faculty wives made a point of entertaining newcomers. I remember Mrs. George Brownell (Geology), Mrs. A.E. Macdonald (Engineering), Mrs. Skuli Johnson (Classics), and Mrs. William Hugill (Classics) in this connection.

Apart from these few contacts, the rest of the University was obliged to operate without my help.

Lewis Slotin: Hero of the Atomic Age

Lewis Slotin was a graduate in chemistry from the University of Manitoba who later obtained his Ph.D. from the University of London (King's College). When I was in Chicago, he was associated with the University of Chicago cyclotron. Although we had not known one another in Winnipeg, because of our common Manitoba background, we became more than nodding acquaintances. Later, he joined the Manhattan Project and was sent to Los Alamos, where the atom bomb was being developed.

On 30 May 1946, he and others were "twisting the dragon's tail," or determining by cautious experiment the critical mass of ^{235}U. This was done by bringing together, physically and just for an instant, two sub-critical portions of this fissile material so as to form the critical value. On the day in question, the screw driver with which the two sub-critical portions were being manipulated suddenly slipped, and they came together in an uncontrolled way. Slotin pulled them apart with his hands, saving the lives of his colleagues but receiving, himself, a fatal dose of radiation. Although he lived for nine days, the certainty of death was never in doubt.

On Sunday, 12 June 1946, in the north end of Winnipeg, and along with hundreds of others, I attended Slotin's funeral service. It was an unlikely place to honour one of the genuine heroes of the Atomic Age.

One of those saved by Slotin's prompt action was Alvin Graves, a former student of Arthur Dempster's and, I later learned, a candidate for the position I was later offered at Wesleyan University. He lost his hair in the accident but, when I saw him a few months later, it was beginning to reappear.

The Future

Although my wife and I had returned to Winnipeg with high hopes and with the intention of spending the rest of our lives in that familiar city, the prospect for a teaching-cum-research career seemed bleak, at least as far as the research side was concerned. By spring, the mass spectrograph that I had brought from McMaster was functioning well, and a modest experiment had been started with the aid of an eager member of the fifth-year class, Benjamin G. Hogg, but the spirit in the Department was apathetic, and the teaching load was punishing. Although the family ties were strong, I began to feel that I should go elsewhere before it was too late.

I shared my unease with Dean Saunderson, for whom I had served one summer as a laboratory assistant, and he took me to see President Trueman. Both were sympathetic, and we discussed ways by which my teaching load might be reduced, all of which would have marked me as a sort of teacher's pet. Salary was not a consideration, as Crawford had sanctioned an increase from $3,300 to $3,400. He was losing his grip!

In this unsettled state, I received a telephone call from a Professor Karl S. Van Dyke of Wesleyan University in Connecticut, asking if he could come to Winnipeg to see me. Van Dyke had his Ph.D. from Chicago and had asked Professor Dempster to suggest names for a vacancy in Wesleyan's Physics Department. As I knew that Dempster had my interests in mind, I told Van Dyke to come. At the end of two days, I had agreed to visit Wesleyan, but with no commitment on either side. Wesleyan had much to offer, but before it was prepared to do so, I was to be interviewed by the president and a number of the senior professors. I passed muster and shortly after my return to Winnipeg was offered an appointment as associate professor of physics, at a salary of $4,000 per annum, the rental of an apartment adjacent to the campus, full moving expenses, $10,000 to construct a new and larger mass spectrograph, and a graduate assistantship for Ben Hogg to work towards a master's degree. After much personal soul-searching, my wife and I agreed that I should accept the offer. The prospect of the apartment was an important consideration, as the post-war housing shortage in Winnipeg showed little sign of abating. At Wesleyan, with an apartment guaranteed, we could live again as a self-contained family.

Before leaving for Wesleyan, Ben Hogg and I determined the relative abundances of the copper isotopes, dismantled and sent the mass spectrograph back to McMaster, and devised an experiment that Ben could complete in one year whilst the new mass spectrograph was under construction. By 1 September, all were in Middletown, we in the two-bedroom apartment and Ben in a back room in the president's house, no less!

Wesleyan University: 1946 to 1951

7

Wesleyan University dates from 1831, one of several men's colleges founded in the first half century after the American Revolution to supplement the nine pre-revolutionary institutions: Harvard, Dartmouth, Yale, Princeton, Brown, Rutgers, Columbia, Pennsylvania, and William and Mary. Wesleyan had been a church college to begin with, as had all the others, but long before 1946 the formal church connection had disappeared. There was, however, a Sunday evening chapel service that was compulsory for all students.

The opening hymn at chapel was always the stirring "Hymn of St. Francis":

> All creatures of our God and King,
> Lift up your voice and let us sing,
> Hallelujah, hallelujah!
> Bright burning sun with burning beam,
> Soft shining moon with silver gleam,
> Sing praises, sing praises,
> Hallelujah, hallelujah!

Led by a splendid choir, and knowing all the words by heart (because they had sung them so often), several hundred young men sang with gusto and created a stunning effect.

Wesleyan and two similar colleges, Williams and Amherst, called themselves "The Little Three," in contrast to "The Big Three," that is, Harvard, Princeton, and Yale. There were sporting events among The Little Three and a certain amount of academic interaction, although Wesleyan felt that it was academically superior to the other two. Williams had been founded in Williamstown, Massachusetts, in 1785 and Amherst in Amherst, Massachusetts, in 1821. Wesleyan itself was located in Middletown, Connecticut.

Middletown is situated on the Connecticut River, about midway between Hartford and New Haven. At one time, at the height of the tea trade, it had been an important port, and many mansions dating from that time were crowned with "widow's walks," from which captains' wives could look for their husbands' return. In 1946, the population was 30,000, and the principal industry was Wesleyan University. This was rather large for a typical college town, but it was sufficiently isolated from the larger world. Students lived in fraternity houses or dormitories under somewhat relaxed *in loco parentis* supervision.

The college experience was still seen as a period of withdrawal from the pressures of society to allow students to discipline and furnish their minds. The intellectual furniture was that of a liberal education, and few colleges could have done it better. No professional training here: that was to come later and somewhere else.

Wesleyan undergraduates, all of whom were men, came mainly from the New England and New York areas or were sons of alumni living further afield. Family loyalty was romanticized and found place in the College song:

> O ivied walls; O storied halls,
> O shrine of long ago,
> The altar fires our fathers lit,
> Shall still more brightly glow.

Most of the students came from prosperous middle-class families, but recruiting was widespread and alumni were expected to bring outstanding students to the attention of the admissions office. Scholarships were available for bright boys who needed help, and the G.I. Bill brought many students who would otherwise have gone to state universities, if at all.

Chuck Stone, a bright, personable young man from a nearby town, was the only Black student in the college in 1946-47 and was a popular member of the freshman class. He was not rushed by the national fraternities but was invited to join the Eclectic House, which was essentially a local fraternity. He became a journalist, and I later saw his byline occasionally in American newspapers. Later, two or three Black students came from Africa under some special arrangement, but during my five years at Wesleyan, I never saw an American Black student other than Stone.

The G.I. Bill of Rights

Some 1,200 men were in attendance during the fall term of 1946, a number somewhat larger than in pre-war times, but augmented in deference to returning veterans. As in Canada, provision had been made to reward veterans for their war service. One of the options under the G.I. Bill of Rights was a day at college for every day in uniform. Because the war against Japan did not end until August 1945, most American veterans did not reach college until a year after their Canadian counterparts. But, when they did arrive, it was en masse: in the fall of 1947, half the students at college were there under the G.I. Bill. As in Canada, they were determined to do what was necessary to get on with their lives. They refused to tolerate the puerile rites of initiation, and they did not take kindly to unreasonable regulations. The president of Harvard had opposed the idea of swinging wide the doors to higher education but later declared that his veteran students were the most mature and promising his institution had ever had. I had my share of the good ones, as Wesleyan had a strong tradition in science.

New Faculty

The new faculty members hired in 1946 outnumbered those who were there before, and many of them had just returned from war service of some type. Three of the new recruits came from Manitoba, the other two having applied for positions after hearing of my appointment. John Abrams, my Manitoba colleague in physics, was appointed assistant professor of astronomy, and Meredith Thompson, who had taught me English at United College, was appointed assistant professor of English. He was too experienced for that status and was unhappy on that account, leaving after one year to a more senior position at the University of Southern California. He ended up as professor at the University of British Columbia, but I don't think he ever regarded his going to Wesleyan as having been a good career move.

The University had purchased the apartment in which we lived in order to provide housing for new staff. Thus, we were under the same roof as assistant professors of anthropology, economics, biology, psychology, government, and English, and many other young staff were stashed in University-owned houses nearby. Early in the semester, we met them all at an ingeniously arranged reception at the president's house. President and Mrs. Butterfield stood inside the front door and greeted the first couple to arrive. Those two then stood next to the Butterfields and the four of them greeted the second couple, who then took their places in the expanding reception line and helped to greet the third couple, and so on until the last couple was greeted by all those present. Thus, in the process, everyone met and talked briefly with everyone else. I never found an occasion to utilize the scheme, but I was impressed by it at the time.

A few days prior to the reception, my wife answered the door to a Mrs. Butterworth. Recognizing the name as that of the president's wife, she invited her in and served her tea. The grateful Mrs. Butterworth then gave my wife the gifts she had brought as representative of the "Welcome Wagon." Thus, Kay was in no doubt as to Mrs. Butter*field's* name on the night of the reception.

The social interaction with this cosmopolitan group of contemporaries was enormously stimulating. All were intent on building successful academic careers either at Wesleyan or using Wesleyan as a stepping stone to something else. It would have been woefully indiscreet, however, to admit to the latter plan, as a friend of Professor Frank Allen's had once done. This candidate had his Ph.D. from Cornell in 1905 and was interviewed for a position at Wesleyan. Following the interview, he was taken to the hill on which the observatory stood. There, as he and his host looked down on the pleasant campus, he was asked his opinion of the university. "I think it would be an ideal place to spend a few years," he naïvely replied. He was not granted his wish.

Amongst those of my contemporaries who achieved greatness elsewhere were: David McLelland (a Quaker), who became a professor of psychology at Harvard; Jack Everett (an aggressive philosopher), who became president of New York University; Norman Brown (a clever Englishman) who was the author of the scholarly best-seller (100,000 copies) *Life against Death: The Psychoanalytic Meaning of History* (Wesleyan University Press, 1959); and Steven Bailey (a Rhodes scholar), who became a congressman. Others failed to get tenure and passed sadly to less green pastures, whilst a happy few found the place entirely to their liking and were allowed to remain.

The Humanities Program

President Butterfield, or "Vic," as he preferred to be called, had recently come from the presidency of Lawrence College in Appleton, Wisconsin, the same institution that provided President Nathan Pusey to Harvard University in 1953. At Lawrence, Butterfield and Pusey had developed a freshman course based on the study of great writings of the past. It was similar in purpose to the Hutchins-Adler Great Books Program but had been developed independently at Lawrence. Butterfield brought the idea with him to Wesleyan.

Once a week, all freshmen were exposed to a lecture on the writing in
r the other two periods, they met in small groups of about
e, under the guidance of the new faculty members bolstered
rans, they tried to winnow meaning out of Plato and Pascal.
f the week was the subject of endless discussion, especially
instructors who were to provide the key to understanding,

and some of whom were as unprepared for the task as were their students. Vic was counting on me to inject some science into these proceedings, but I managed to extricate myself before having to reveal how uncivilized was the young physicist from western Canada. The chair of the Physics Department, K.S. Van Dyke, who was dubious of the Humanities Program, explained to Vic that I must concentrate on building the new mass spectrograph. I had nothing but admiration for the program and wished that I had been knowledgeable enough to pull my weight in it. It typified a program that became very popular after the war, often under the title Western Civilization, and which has recently been labelled "Dead White Males."

The Honour System

Examinations at Wesleyan, and in a number of similar private colleges, were not supervised, as the students were on "the honour system." At the conclusion of an examination, each student wrote, "No help given or received," and signed his name. I never saw evidence of cheating, but the system put pressure on the students, as they were expected to report infractions.

Tenure

The idea of tenure was unknown in Canadian universities, and I had never heard of it, but it was a big topic amongst the younger faculty members at Wesleyan. For them, it spelled security and the privilege of pursuing their academic careers in this suburb of Paradise. Normally, tenure is granted when one is promoted to associate professor. Hence, the many new staff at Wesleyan who had come as assistant professors were hoping for eventual promotion. I was an exception, as I had come as an associate professor, but I still had to earn my tenure stripes, which I did after three years. The assistant professors hoped to be promoted within five years. If not, they would be obliged to leave. In the vernacular, this was the "up-or-out" rule.

I came gradually to understand the rationale for tenure, the circumstances under which it had been introduced into the university system, and the manner in which it functioned (or malfunctioned). I also learned that Wesleyan had played an inadvertent role in its early history.

Academic freedom is supposed to allow those who know what they're talking about to say what they think. It doesn't guarantee an audience to the uninformed or the crank. For that matter, it doesn't guarantee an audience to anyone, but it does ensure the right of professors to express opinions in their fields of expertise. This right to speak freely is, of course, a benefit to individual professors but, more important, it's a benefit to society, for without exposure to criticism society would be slow to improve.

The importance of academic freedom is generally accepted until some indiscreet professor criticizes university authorities, the government, or some powerful vested interest. Then, despite earlier institutional claims to freedom of speech, pressure may be brought on the professor to recant or resign.

Such was the case at Stanford University in 1900. This celebrated institution, which now ranks second only to Harvard in acceptances from admitted students, was founded in 1891 by Leland Stanford and his wife, Jane, as a memorial to their son, Leland Stanford Jr. It is said, and I expect it's true, that the couple first thought that Harvard might provide the vehicle for the memorial, but they were put off by the suggestions made. These discussions ended with Mrs. Stanford rising as she said, "Come, Leland, we can do better than that." And so they did, in Palo Alto, California.

Mr. Stanford's business career, in which he gained great wealth, represented free enterprise at its best, or worst. Much of this wealth was dedicated to the new university, of which he and his wife were joint trustees. Unfortunately, he did not live to see the opening of his son's memorial. Thus, Jane Lathrop Stanford continued as the sole trustee and, under her patronage, all appeared to be going well. That is, until Edward A. Ross, professor of economics, began advocating a number of causes, including municipal ownership of utilities and a public inquiry into the Southern Pacific Railway. Since much of the Stanfords' wealth had derived from municipal utilities and the Southern Pacific, the sole trustee decreed that Professor Ross had no place in her university. The president of the University was instructed to do the necessary and, to his immense relief, succeeded in persuading Ross to resign for the good of the institution. Unfortunately, Ross explained his resignation to the press, the chairman of the History Department protested and was fired, and six others resigned in sympathy.

Indignation amongst academics was widespread, especially at Johns Hopkins University, where research and its free publication had pride of place. But, although there was much talk of action, including the boycott of Stanford by academics, the matter was allowed to fester until 1913, when Wesleyan University, which was much nearer home, fired Willard C. Fisher, professor of economics, for failing to attend church when he was visiting another city. This second event, combined with Stanford's earlier offence, precipitated the founding – in 1915 at Johns Hopkins – of the American Association of University Professors (AAUP), with John Dewey as its first president. The AAUP was dedicated to the protection of free speech for academics and, in time, persuaded universities to adopt appropriate codes for the hiring and firing of professors. Principal amongst these codes is the tenure system.

Tenure is an academic appointment without term and is normally offered after a probationary appointment of several years. Once granted tenure, the incumbent has a secure position until retirement or until dismissal for just cause and after due process. Understandably, the receiving of tenure is the cause of family celebration, as even children have overheard the fateful word discussed. But every joy has its cloud: the son of Walter Bodnar, the distinguished geneticist, overhearing that his father had been given tenure at Stanford, asked with concern, "But what happens after the ten years?"

It's little wonder that tenure was the default topic of conversation amongst the junior faculty at Wesleyan University.

Athletics

I had grown up believing that Babe Ruth was a hero, as were Jack Dempsey, Bill Tilden, Bobby Jones, and the other giants of sport. I had not perceived that only Bobby Jones was a true hero, as the others had been paid to perform their extraordinary feats. And so it happened in September 1946 that I encountered S.A. Callisen, the assistant dean, and asked the innocent question, "Who's going to win the World Series?" Callisen, who had recently come from top-secret army intelligence, snorted, "I have no interest in professional sport." Although I later went to see Jackie Robinson (New York), Ted Williams (Boston), and Larry Dobie (Cleveland) perform, I never confessed my weakness to Callisen; in fact, we may never have spoken again. I soon discovered that there were plenty of local heroes amongst the college teams, and, as the years have passed, I have an increasing sympathy with Callisen's view, although not with his arrogance.

Football launched the fall semester and was the most popular intercollegiate sport, with basketball (winter) and baseball (spring) following, in that order. In our first three years at Wesleyan, the football team had unbeaten seasons, and we came to believe that the team was invincible. In 1949, however, the spell was broken, and we witnessed the heart-rending sight of the students singing the "Alma Mater," which was only sung at a football game if the team lost. We were told that one of the members of the unbeaten team had been seriously considered for all-American, although the honour was usually reserved for players from major universities.

Wesleyan's natural rivals, of course, were the two other members of The Little Three – Amherst and Williams – who were played once a season. The schedule of seven or eight games was fleshed out by contests with Trinity,

Tufts, University of Connecticut, Bowdoin, Bates, and other schools within driving distance.

At the start of the basketball season, the director of Athletics thought that it might add credibility if a professor of physics presided over the scoring. I should have practised with the electronic scoreboard in advance. Early on, and flushed with excitement, I credited a Wesleyan basket to the enemy, which was poorly received by those in attendance. Unfortunately, the scoring device had no reverse gear; in order to reduce the enemy score from eight to six, I had to run up to 100 and start over again. All this had to be done whilst other baskets were being scored and were being jotted down on a piece of paper. The director of Athletics was understanding and forgiving until I repeated the error. I was not asked to keep score again.

Visitors to Campus

The university saw a succession of distinguished visitors as chapel speakers and special lecturers or performers. Some have stuck in my memory.

Roland Hayes, the renowned Black tenor, was in his early sixties when he gave a moving concert at Wesleyan. He had attended Fisk University, a pioneer Black college founded in Nashville, Tennessee, in 1866 by the American Missionary Society. It was one of the institutions for Blacks founded by northern Whites after the Civil War as an act of atonement. It was at Fisk that the potential of Hayes's voice was recognized. Much of his training and early acceptance took place in Europe (he sang before George V when he was thirty-four) but ultimately his voice won him universal recognition. As with Marian Anderson, he stood on the stage as in a world apart, which gave special poignancy to his performance. As was his custom, he finished his performance with a set of spirituals.

Burl Ives, the famous folk singer, caused a stir during his visit and after he had left. It was considered somewhat avant-garde to invite him, but student enthusiasm quite silenced any overt objection. He and his wife were lodged in the University's finest guest quarters, they were entertained by the president, the concert was a success, and many were charmed by the youthful Mrs. Ives. Only after the couple had departed was it learned that Mr. Ives was not married.

Of special interest to me was the visit of George Gamow, an expatriate Russian physicist who had earlier been at the centre of an international cause célèbre. A child of the Russian Revolution and promising young theoretician, Gamow had been allowed to visit Goettingen, Copenhagen, and Cambridge. At Cambridge he announced his defection. The furious Soviets retaliated by preventing Peter Kapitza, a Russian who had been at

Cambridge since 1921, and who was on a periodic visit (in 1934) to his homeland, from returning to England. When indignation at the hijacking had subsided at Cambridge, generous arrangements were made to ship Kapitza's equipment to Russia, where a new institute had been created for him, and he became the country's leading physicist. But that is not the end of the story.

In 1946, Kapitza was suspected of disloyalty and dismissed from his institute. His fate might have been worse had certain incriminating documents fallen into the wrong hands. These his wife had entrusted to her friend, the wife of the chemist Nicolai Semenov. On Stalin's death in 1953, Kapitza was rehabilitated and became again the doyen of Russian physics. Meanwhile, Semenov, who in 1956 became the first Russian to receive the Nobel Prize for chemistry, was blissfully unaware that material inimical to Kapitza's career, and by association to his own, had been sequestered in his bedroom. The details of this feminine intrigue came to me in 1992 from Semenov's daughter; Semenov may never have known.

During Gamow's visit to Wesleyan, he was guest of honour at a dinner given by Mrs. Stearns, wife of the chairman of Astonomy. Gamow was a large man and drank whatever he could find at the preprandial reception. Then, when dinner was announced, he led the way into the dining room, where he chose a congenial seat and occupied it. The fact that it was not the place that Mrs. Stearns had intended caused some confusion, of which Gamow appeared unaware. As the dinner progressed, there were other indications that he had not studied Emily Post.

In 1959, the Canadian Association of Physicists invited Gamow, then at Washington University in St. Louis, to speak at its 1960 congress. His office replied that he was in India. Because I was going to the Indian Science Congress, I jokingly offered to keep my eye out for him. Soon after arriving in Bombay, I entered the dining room of the Taj Mahal Hotel and saw a bulky man devouring his food in a manner reminiscent of Mrs. Stearns's guest of honour. I had found a large needle in a very large haystack.

Three Canadians came to Wesleyan as visiting lecturers: Harry Thode (at my initiative); Arthur Lower (at Meredith Thompson's initiative); and M.J. Coldwell. Thode's talk overlapped a bit with my research and was well received. Lower, who had taught at United College but was now at Queen's, chose to compare the political systems of the United States and Canada. The students had little interest in Canada but knew the American system backwards. Coldwell, then the leader of the CCF Party, tried to bring socialism to a temple of capitalism and was surprisingly well received. His gentle, courtly manner, his clarity of expression, and his obvious sincerity earned him attention, but no one came forward to announce that he'd been saved. I had the chance to spend much time in his agreeable company.

The Seven Sisters

I soon came to know that The Big Three, The Little Three, and the rest had no monopoly on prestige. Operating inconspicuously, but well known to all the best people, were seven women's colleges whose admission and other standards were scarcely inferior to those of their older counterparts for men. Four of these were in New England (Mount Holyoke, Radcliffe, Smith, and Wellesley), two in New York State (Barnard and Vassar), and one in the outskirts of Philadelphia (Bryn Mawr).

Representatives of these institutions first gleamed upon my sight during the autumn house-party weekend, when most of the Wesleyan students imported young women for an orgy of social events. The affair was so significant that an advance list was published, naming the women and their college affiliations or hometowns. In order to make the list complete, the men who had no dates were assigned fictitious names from Long Lane School, a nearby reformatory for wayward girls. To prepare for this female deluge was no trivial matter, as billets had to be found, chaperones had to be arranged, entertainment had to be laid on, and the tiniest wishes of the guests had to be anticipated. As Sunday evening approached and the phantoms of delight prepared to depart, many an exhausted young man breathed a deep sigh of relief. The women were a hardier lot, as many of them also reported for duty at Williams and Amherst, whose house parties were scheduled for other weekends. The second semester saw a similar weekend obsession with those of the opposite gender. My wife and I agreed to chaperone a party at the Eclectic House, with the understanding that activities should be seemly and should end at 1:00 a.m. I was not told that chaperones did not inspect the upper floors! We were not asked to be chaperones again.

Later, I had opportunity to see the women's colleges as academic institutions and to learn something of their origins and ethos. These institutions emerged when thoughtful women, and men who were sympathetic to their aspirations, came to realize that higher education for women was essential for their advancement. They considered two alternatives: to attempt entry to the established men's colleges (as their English sisters chose to do) or to establish special colleges for women alone. Approaches to men's colleges were so soundly rebuffed that the second course was embarked upon, and with a determination not to settle for second best. They had a rough time at the start but, by 1946, they had long since established their place in the firmament. They comprise the so-called Seven Sisters:

Vassar College, Poughkeepsie, N.Y., 1861; Wellesley College, Wellesley, Massachusetts, 1870; Smith College, Northampton, Massachusetts, 1871; Radcliffe College, Cambridge, Massachusetts, 1879; Bryn Mawr College, Bryn Mawr, Pennsylvania, 1880; Mount Holyoke College, South Hadley, Massachusetts, 1888; Barnard College, New York City, N.Y., 1889.

By 1946, when college education was everywhere available to women, the Seven Sisters were attended mainly by students who valued their social cachet. A distinctive character had emerged for each place or, at least, was seen to have emerged. Elaine Kendall (*Peculiar Institutions,* Putnam and Sons, 1975) has put things in a nutshell: "Radcliffe, intellectually rigorous; Bryn Mawr, intense; Smith, athletic; Barnard, sophisticated; Wellesley, blond and literary; Vassar, radical; and Mount Holyoke, refreshingly wholesome." Smith, Wellesley, and Mount Holyoke were well represented at Wesleyan house parties, as was Connecticut College, another nearby women's school.

Of special interest to Canadians is the woman who was head of physics at Mount Holyoke College in 1946. Elizabeth R. Laird, a graduate of the University of Toronto, had obtained her Ph.D. from Bryn Mawr after study at Cambridge and in Germany. On her retirement from Mount Holyoke, she moved to London, Ontario, and presented herself to the head of Physics at the University of Western Ontario with an offer to help. Coming, as she did, unannounced and looking older than her years, she was assumed to be some sort of crank. But she broke through the barrier and did useful work for several years. She published her last research paper at age seventy-eight. After I had moved to McMaster University in 1951, I renewed the friendship we had begun in New England. At her death, four Canadian universities learned that they were beneficiaries of her will. At the University of Winnipeg, the annual Elizabeth Laird Lecture brings natural and social scientists to the campus.

Wesleyan College (Georgia)

Several other colleges bear the surname of John Wesley, the founder of Methodism, and each has its own claim to fame, for example, Ohio Wesleyan and Illinois Wesleyan. The simple Wesleyan College, however, established in 1836 in Macon, Georgia, has the distinction of having awarded the first degree to a woman in the English-speaking world (to a Miss Brewer). This institution still exists and is relatively modest about its place in history. At least, when I visited in 1990, the officers appeared more interested in whether I had a daughter or granddaughter who had yet to select a college than in recalling the unique contribution that their college had made to the liberation of women.

Incidentally, Miss Brewer's degree – the "Testimonial of the Georgia Female College" – was ingeniously different from the masculine bachelor of arts, but not as catchy as the "sister of arts," "mistress of arts," or "maid of philosophy," used elsewhere before reverting to the prosaic B.A.

Committee on the Education of Scientists

Shortly after my arrival in Middletown, I found myself lunching weekly with other members of the Committee on the Education of Scientists. The purpose was to improve the science curriculum. The meetings were chaired by Hubert B. Goodrich, chairman of biology and longtime member of the University, and were somewhat desultory in nature. Sometimes a visitor from another college told us his views, whilst at other meetings we talked in general terms amongst ourselves.

When I returned to my office after a particularly unfocussed meeting, I began using *American Men of Science* (*AMS*) to tabulate undergraduate colleges from which Ph.D.-holders had come. This was a big job; the *AMS* contained some 20,000 names, but very soon the findings provided their own incentive. First, it emerged that relatively few scientists came from the East Coast; rather, they came mostly from the Mid-West. Second, a few liberal-arts colleges produced disproportionate numbers of scientists. It took me some time to work through the *AMS,* but, when I took my rough sheets to the meeting, they were seized upon as a method of studying why scientists had chosen their vocations.

The Committee rationalized that young men raised in the urban East were more interested in careers in business or corporate law than in science. In the Mid-West, however, young men knew nothing of corporate law but had read of the wonders of science and saw it as a route to escape from the small town or the farm. As for the colleges with disproportionate numbers of science graduates, it was assumed that some particularly effective teachers were at work.

Excited that the *AMS* held the key to science motivation, the Committee arranged for Robert Knapp, an assistant professor of psychology, to be granted a year's leave to visit selected institutions and to be aided in data tabulation and analysis by research assistants. It became a big operation, culminating in the publication in 1952, by the University of Chicago Press, and supported by the Carnegie Corporation of New York, of *Origins of American Men of Science,* by Robert H. Knapp and H.B. Goodrich. Complete with innumerable graphs and tables, the study had become a social-science project from which every drop of blood had been wrung. But it gave Knapp a distinctive status in psychology and tenure at Wesleyan. Alas, he died prematurely, perhaps at his zenith. And my early work was not forgotten: the preface acknowledged "H.E. Duckworth, who made some of the preliminary statistical explorations."

The main conclusions were not unlike those suggested when the first rough data had been discussed six years earlier: that scientists "are drawn from the 'grass roots' of America, more frequently from non-industrialized regions, more frequently from institutions of modest attendance costs, more rarely from expensive eastern institutions." Additionally, a number of "high-productivity" schools were examined in detail and reasons for their success described.

Some of the anecdotal evidence that emerged was unexpected. For example, from one small physics department, one student graduated each year to proceed to the Ph.D. It emerged that the physics professor was a lazy fellow who hired the best student in the first-year class to supervise the first-year laboratory the following year, whilst the professor himself took virtually no part in it. These neophytes, with full responsibility thrust upon them, would often become engrossed in the subject and would choose it as a career. Until Knapp visited the campus, this professor had been tentatively tagged by the Committee as inspirational.

One table was of particular interest to the small college community. It listed the leading institutions, in order of scientific productivity, that is, scientists per 1,000 graduates. Leading the list were: Reed College, Oregon, 131.8; California Institute of Technology, 79.1; Kalamazoo College, Michigan, 66.3; Earlham College, Indiana, 57.5; Oberlin College, Ohio, 55.8; University of Massachusetts, 55.6; Hope College, Michigan, 51.1; DePauw University, Indiana, 47.6; Nebraska Western University; 47.4; Iowa Wesleyan College, 45.5. Reed is a remarkable college that excels in every aspect of study, including number of Rhodes Scholars. The reason for Cal Tech's position is self-evident but, apart from it, the first major institution to appear on the list was the University of Chicago, sixteenth (39.9). Wesleyan weighed in at twenty-second (34.3) of the 490 institutions studied.

Department of Physics

The Department of Physics was a three-man department: Karl S. Van Dyke, Vernet Eaton, and myself. The former chairman, Willoubey Cady, of ancient New England lineage and co-inventor of the use of quartz crystals to stabilize the frequency of oscillators, had just retired, and I had replaced him, but at the bottom of the totem pole. Van Dyke, an electronics expert, had returned from defence research to assume the chair. He was a Wesleyan "old boy." Eaton was a Hoosier (from Indiana) with a flair for teaching first-year physics but had been held at associate-professor level because he had done no research beyond the Ph.D. At my coming and, I believe, because of it, he was promoted to full professor and was clearly relishing his new status.

Van Dyke had brought a research contract back from the war, which employed three professionals and provided thesis topics for several master's students. Ben Hogg had come with me from Manitoba. Thus, including master's students, there was a community of about fifteen who were serious about physics, sufficient (Ben and I thought) to warrant a weekly colloquium.

We made two physical arrangements, both of which had initial defects. We found in the attic a large copper vat with a tap at the bottom. When this had been scoured and placed on a trolley, it could be wheeled out and tea could be made with a minimum of effort. In addition, we found a small blackboard, which was placed in the main hall and on which the week's colloquium topic was written. The tea was very popular to begin with, but, after a few weeks, it was obvious that only Ben and I were drinking it, and I was only doing so out of loyalty. At my wife's suggestion, we examined the vat and found that a layer of copper oxide had built up and was poisoning the tea. Scouring the vat became part of the routine, and former partakers were eventually persuaded to give it a second try. The other false start was embarrassing in the extreme. I engaged a sign painter to paint the word "Colloqium" on the blackboard. It was scarcely in position when someone pointed out that that Q is always followed by U. Hastily, I instructed the painter to replace "Colloqium" with "Colloquim" and, after being corrected again, finally got it right. There must have been much snickering behind the scenes. The colloquium continued for the five years I was at Wesleyan and was often attended by senior students and by members of other departments, depending upon the topic. When the popular young philosopher Jack Everett gave a lecture entitled "The Nature of Physical Knowledge," more than 150 were in attendance. Usually the number was fifteen or twenty.

The first two years of the Physics Major Program were offered each year, but courses in the two senior years were alternated. Students emerged from this major with the equivalent of the Canadian penultimate year of honours physics and were accepted directly into graduate school. No wonder the Canadian honours degree is so well respected by American graduate schools.

When Eaton was promoted, it was a pragmatic decision but was taken in grudging recognition of his outstanding teaching ability. Thereafter, he began to receive recognition elsewhere and was eventually elected president of the American Association of Physics Teachers (AAPT). As a result of his influence, the AAPT met in Toronto in 1956 and held one session at McMaster, at which I gave a demonstration lecture entitled "Weighing Atoms." This featured a bogus mass spectrograph with certain amusing features.

The graduate students at Wesleyan, whose duties were mostly confined to the first-year laboratory, came from small institutions in New England, the Maritimes, and the Mid-West to obtain master's degrees. Frequently, they were women, which gave life to the place between house-party weekends. One with the surname Riley was of the family that manufactured Fletcher's "castoria," a patent medicine for which children were said to cry. She was good-looking and from Smith College, and she attracted a lot of attention. Special graduate courses were laid on for these master's candidates, as and when needed.

Van Dyke was insistent that theses be written in a certain form. One of his students, Sam Humphries, spent long hours with him, getting the wording just right. At the end, I overheard another student ask Humphries if Van Dyke was satisfied with his thesis. "He should be," Sam replied. "He dictated it."

Students who worked with me for senior or master's theses, in addition to Ben Hogg, included Richard Woodcock (Bates College), Bertram Calhoun (Manitoba), Robert Stearns (Wesleyan), Richard Preston (Wesleyan), John Handloser, Donald Little (Wesleyan), Cort Kegley (Franklin), Howard Johnson (Franklin), George Stanford (Acadia), G.S. Coutu, and John Olsen (Wesleyan). They were excellent research colleagues but, of course, they continued at Wesleyan only to the bachelor's or master's degree.

The Wesleyan Endowment

For a graduate to revisit his campus, either in mind or in the flesh, is to relive those innocent days when friendships were unreserved, when ideals were untarnished, when enthusiasms ran high, when pleasure carried no burden of care, and when professors were seen as giants of intellect. To set foot once more on that hallowed ground is to recapture briefly the joys of long ago, especially when emotions are aroused by haunting refrains:

> Come all be boys again together,
> Life's short – then fill with joy its span,
> The house of joy is *Alma Mater*,
> Then hail, all hail to Wesleyan!

As it was in every private American university and college, this kind of nostalgia was carefully cultivated by Wesleyan, and few of its graduates came home to an empty mailbox. Until recently, this solicitude was in striking contrast to the attitude of British and Canadian universities. Thus, I have read of an American graduate who later studied at Oxford. When elected to the U.S. Senate, he received a congratulatory note from his alma mater with an invitation to contribute to the current fundraising campaign. Soon thereafter, he had a communication from his Oxford college reminding him of an unpaid laundry bill of seven shillings, six pence.

For private American universities and colleges, the financial support of their graduates is absolutely essential. And Wesleyan graduates had not been found wanting: by 1946 the institution had accumulated more than a nest egg, and it was earning the modest interest associated with conservative investments of the time.

Shortly thereafter, a graduate who had become an investment whiz on Wall Street was elected to the Board of Trustees and, at an early meeting, was dismayed to learn how staid the investment policy was. Some of the other trustees were reluctant to risk hard-got funds on anything that smacked of speculation, but, having chosen the new trustee for his investment skills, they felt obliged to ask him for suggestions. The new trustee made two suggestions: to buy a spaghetti factory in New York City or a Mid-West publisher of newspapers for use in the public schools. The spaghetti factory seemed out of character, so by default it was agreed in 1949 to buy the publisher of *The Weekly Reader*.

This was the period when the children of World War II veterans – "baby boomers" – were making their way through the school system, and enrollments were escalating. Furthermore, in-school discussions of current affairs were becoming popular amongst educators. As a result, *The Weekly Reader* prospered to the point where Internal Revenue questioned its operation by a non-profit institution. This awkwardness was solved by selling the enterprise to Xerox Corporation in return for 400,000 shares of common stock in that company. Xerox then took off on its own flight to glory. This two-stage bonanza brought so much wealth to the University that, by 1962, it had the largest endowment per student of any institution in the country. By 1966, the figure stood at $150 million, a staggering figure for an institution of the size and character of Wesleyan. Some have questioned whether these financial resources have since been put to their best use, but that does not detract from the miracle of their accumulation.

Research Program

My research program at Wesleyan University began with optimism, it encountered disaster, and it ended in triumph.

The initial project was to design and construct a new mass spectrograph
(see Figure 1), using the $10,000 grant that the trustees of the University
had made as part of my appointment agreement. I had every reason to be

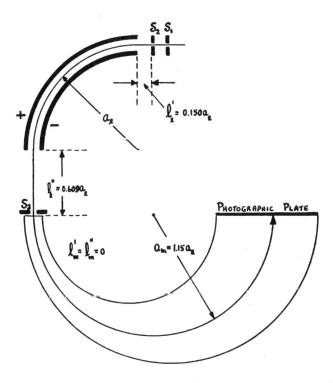

Figure 1: Scheme of mass spectrograph constructed at Wesleyan University for
the accurate determination of atomic masses, 1949.

optimistic, as I had already constructed such an instrument, albeit only
one-third the size of the new version. Also, I was reassured by the fact that
the Physics Department had a good machine shop with a strong, confident
man in charge by the name of Smith. I never knew his first name and I
suspected that his surname had begun life as Schmidt. Smith hired an

assistant for the project, and work began on the electrostatic and magnetic analyzers. Meanwhile, machining of the large magnet was entrusted to a firm in Hartford.

In the early fall of 1947, all parts came together and an attempt was made to detect ions at the collector end. No ions were observed, and the news of this disaster quickly spread through the Department. Not only could the Canadian not•spell "colloquium," but it also now appeared that he couldn't build a mass spectrograph. It was the lowest point in my scientific career!

By testing the parts separately, I was driven to conclude that the electrostatic analyzer was misaligned, probably because it had been constructed with too flimsy material. This was a point on which Smith and I had argued, and I had deferred to his better judgement.

With Van Dyke's agreement, I hired a skilled toolmaker, Clifford Gieselbreth, who reported directly to me and who began to reconstruct the electrostatic analyzer, probably using materials that were more robust than necessary. Early in 1949, the instrument was ready for a second test, and, to my intense relief, ions were detected by a photographic plate at the collector end. On 22 March 1949, a letter was dispatched to *The Physical Review* announcing the discovery of a rare isotope of platinum at mass 190 (^{190}Pt). On 8 April, a follow-up letter reported the non–existence of the hypothetical stable isotopes ^{100}Pd, ^{178}W, and ^{202}Pb. This information helped to locate the line of atomic stability. On 15 July we reported in the *Physical Review* the first result in our long-range atomic mass determination program in an article entitled "A New Measurement of the ^{195}Pt-^{65}Cu Packing Fraction Difference." We were now firmly in the period of triumph.

The discovery of ^{190}Pt occurred during the testing of the reconstructed instrument, for which platinum was a convenient test element. It was not an earth-shaking result, but it was of more than trivial interest, inasmuch as the list of stable isotopes had been assumed to be complete. As it turned out, ^{190}Pt was the last stable isotope to be discovered. When the news made the front page of *The New York Times*, I found myself *persona grata* again, and tenure soon followed.

The purpose in determining atomic masses was to study trends in nuclear stability. The atomic constituents – electrons, protons, and neutrons – have well-defined masses, but, when they come together to form an atom, this atom weighs less than the sum of its constituents. The missing mass disappeared at the time of formation in the form of energy. Conversely, before the process can be reversed, the mass that disappeared at the time of the atom's creation must be restored. Hence, the missing mass is a measure of the stability of the atom, in particular, the stability of its nucleus. Thus, the nuclear components are bound to the nucleus by missing energy in the same way that a man is bound to his home if his wife hides his wooden leg.

The mass spectrograph could not have come into operation at a more favourable time. Maria Goeppert-Mayer (1908-1972), Hans Jensen (1907-1973), and others predicted in that same year (1949) that 28, 50, 82, and 126 proton or neutron configurations (in the nucleus of an atom) would be particularly stable. We were able quickly to examine the region around $N = 50$ and show that the nuclear stability deteriorates dramatically when the fifty-neutron configuration is exceeded. Within the next eighteen months, we had eight publications providing atomic mass evidence for the stability of nuclei containing twenty-eight and fifty protons, and those containing fifty and eighty-two neutrons. These results were shown on a large wall chart, on which new results were immediately entered with coloured pins. The students working with me were drunk with excitement and would have toiled around the clock if encouraged to do so. Van Dyke and Eaton were continually bringing visitors to look at the chart, and I was in active scientific discussion and correspondence with a wide range of scientists, including Charles Townes, Eugene Wigner, Maria Goeppert-Mayer, Emelio Segré, and Glenn Seaborg, each of whom was destined to receive the Nobel Prize. This period was not the only high point in my scientific career, but none was higher. And it was particularly welcome, coming as it did after the debacle of the misconstructed electrostatic analyzer.

The cost of reconstructing the electrostatic analyzer had exhausted the $10,000 grant from the trustees, and I had to seek additional funds. In this respect also, the time was propitious, as various federal agencies were assembling scientific "stables." Physicists were especially desired, because they were deemed to have won the war. The Office of Naval Research (ONR) had been quick off the mark, and numerous research publications in *The Physical Review* acknowledged the support of the ONR. Accordingly, in April 1948, I went to Washington and presented myself at the office of the director of the ONR. His was a palatial office, and he was clearly unaccustomed to people dropping in unannounced. But he was courteous enough and explained that his stable was now full; also, he understood that the Army was in the same situation. Since the Air Force Office of Scientific Research was forty miles away in Baltimore, I proceeded instead to the Atomic Energy Commission (AEC), which was based in Washington and had been entering into major contracts with distinguished scientists; perhaps they had a place for novitiates. I didn't get to see the director this time, but I was given an application form, and by 1949 I was a proud member of

AEC's stable. This allowed me to retain Clifford Gieselbreth, to hire part-time help during the winter, and to support master's students in the summer. From the AEC contract the University received a significant overhead payment, and I, as principal investigator, received two-ninths of my University salary for pursuing research during the summer, which I would have been doing anyhow. At that time, my University salary was about $5,500 per annum, sharply up from the $4,000 figure at which I had started at Wesleyan. When I returned to Canada in 1951 and the AEC funding ceased, I was able to secure a comparable contract with the Air Force Office of Scientific Research, which continued for a further ten years. Thus, for a period of twelve years, I enjoyed a summer research stipend. I never drew more than $2,000 per summer, although two-ninths of my later university salary would have entitled me to much larger amounts.

The Research Corporation of America operated with royalties from certain patents that had been assigned to it. Its grants were modest, and preference was given to professors in small institutions. I applied for, and received, a grant to construct a mass spectrograph for the chemical analysis of solids. With Clifford Gieselbreth on hand, and with senior students wishing to do senior theses, this small instrument was completed in 1949, and some unmemorable work was done with it. Then, in the spring of 1950, Bell Laboratories, that major player in electronic research located in Murray Hill, asked if one of its scientists could use the device for a few weeks. I was somewhat indifferent to the request, but Van Dyke was ecstatic that Bell Laboratories would come to Wesleyan. Accordingly, a clever and person-able chemist, Bruce Hannay, spent a month with us, testing the instrument's usefulness for the detection of impurities in certain crystals, with emphasis on silicon. He returned to Murray Hill with encouraging reports and there pursued the method much further. In the mid-1950s he moved on to other things, eventually becoming a vice-president of Bell Laboratories and a member of the National Academy of Science.

In gratitude for my cooperation, Bell Laboratories invited me to a state luncheon, where I met the top brass, including John Bardeen, who was soon to receive the Nobel Prize for physics for the second time.

Hannay was a graduate of Swarthmore College and had been a member of its golf team. One afternoon, we knocked off and played the public golf course in nearby Meriden. He had seventy-nine and I had eighty-one. He was satisfied and so was I, that being my first and possibly last game for that year.

Arthur D. Little, a major consulting company based in Cambridge, Massachusetts, was chaired in 1950 by Earl Stevenson, an alumnus of Wesleyan and a contemporary of Van Dyke's, at whose home Stevenson always stayed when attending meetings of the Wesleyan trustees. The company specialized in technological projects and the economics relating thereto. During the war, it had prospered, particularly in physics-related projects, and now looked for a way to express its gratitude to the scientific community. Realizing that low-temperature physics would become a popular field of research and that the existing facilities were temperamental, it proceeded to develop a nitrogen liquefier that would operate at the flick of a switch. This unit sold for $10,000 and was bought by universities in unexpectedly large numbers. Thus, what began as a semi-charitable project ended as a commercial success. This led A.D. Little to consider doing another favour for the world of science.

In this context, I was invited to describe the operation of the mass spectrograph to a room full of senior A.D. Little staff members. The spark source that we were using could produce ions from any solid material and, on the face of it, was a solution to many problems of chemical analysis, including that of crystals, as Bruce Hannay was proposing to investigate. I took some photographic plates to Cambridge that showed convincingly the versatility of the spark source, but I expressed some reservations about the accuracy achievable, based on our experiments with the Research Corporation mass spectrograph. In the end, A.D. Little took no action, and the nitrogen liquefier may have been its first and last gift to science.

Using the mass spectrograph for solid analysis remained tantalizingly attractive. In addition to Bell Laboratories' in-house work, several university and commercial laboratories have developed units, and our own laboratory revisited the subject in 1962, when B. Chakravarty wrote a Ph.D. dissertation on the sensitivity and discrimination of the method. Also, I have been consulted several times by companies concerned with specific problems.

K.T. Bainbridge and A.O.C. Nier: Scientific Friends

It was during these Wesleyan years that I formed friendships with two men who encouraged my scientific career and whose friendships I enjoyed for half a century.

Kenneth T. Bainbridge (1904-1996), of Harvard University, whom I came to know in 1946, was a major figure in mass spectroscopy (and in other branches of physics). In 1933, he had gone to Cambridge University on a Guggenheim Fellowship with the intention of working with Francis Aston who, with Arthur Dempster of Chicago, had pioneered the subject.

Aston had supported Bainbridge's application for the Guggenheim, but, when the young American presented himself at the Cavendish Laboratory, he found Aston socially hospitable but scientifically inhospitable. He was allowed to view Aston's mass spectrograph, but that was as far as it went. During the ensuing fifteen months, Bainbridge was frequently Aston's dinner guest at Trinity College, he was often invited to join Aston's Sunday golf foursome, and he was taken to Kent to follow the 1934 British Open, held that year at Royal St. George's in Sandwich. The fact that the victor was the Englishman Henry Cotton, breaking a string of eight American victories (including three by Bobby Jones) may have gladdened Aston's heart. But, whatever else they did together, Aston never raised the subject of mass spectroscopy. Fortunately, Lord Rutherford, director of the Cavendish, was apprised of the situation and provided Bainbridge with research space and modest funds. The main result of his period in the U.K. was the design of a double-focussing mass spectrograph that he assembled at Harvard University on his return to America in 1934, and that yielded the most accurate mass values to date for several of the light atoms.

Perhaps the social highlight of Bainbridge's period in the U.K. was an invitation from Sir J.J. Thomson to dinner at the Master's Lodge of Trinity College. Bainbridge and his wife walked to the gate of Trinity, where they were met by a carriage, drawn by two men, to transport them across the main quadrangle to the Lodge.

During World War II, Bainbridge worked first at the Radiation Laboratory of the Massachusetts Institute of Technology (MIT) and subsequently at Los Alamos. In fact, he was the director of the first atom-bomb test at Alamogordo on 16 July 1945. In the awe-inspiring silence following the test, this gentle, sensitive man turned to Robert Oppenheimer and said, "Now we're all sons of bitches!"

I first met Bainbridge in the fall of 1946 at a meeting of the New England Section of the American Physical Society, which was held at Wesleyan. I presented plans for the new mass spectrograph, and he generously discussed them with me; I believe he came for that specific purpose, as physicists from the major universities rarely attended the New England sectional meetings.

Alfred O.C. Nier (1911-1994), an engineering graduate of the University of Minnesota, had his Ph.D. in physics from that institution and proceeded to Harvard in 1936 on a United States National Research Council fellowship where, with Bainbridge's encouragement, he constructed a mass spectrometer for isotopic analysis. He displayed a remarkable ability to invent apparatus and to implement ideas. At the end of two years at Harvard, when he returned to Minnesota, he had established the isotopic abundances for twenty elements, had observed that the isotopic composition of lead depended upon its provenance, and was about to discover the same fact for oxygen. When Otto Hahn and Fritz Strassmann announced their discovery of fission in early 1939, Nier was in immediate demand to separate minute amounts of ^{235}U. Subsequently, he developed mass spectrometers for determining the effectiveness of the various techniques that the Manhattan Project was exploring for the isotopic enrichment of that isotope. Following the war, he developed instruments for the accurate determination of atomic masses and, later, became the most important contributor to the mass spectrometric study of the earth's upper atmosphere and of the atmosphere of other planets.

I first met Nier in Chicago in 1942, when there was some discussion of my joining the Manhattan Project in a laboratory that he had established at Columbia University. The Canadian authorities vetoed that idea, but our scientific paths crossed again in 1949 when he was slightly chagrined that he had not observed ^{190}Pt during his earlier study of that element at Harvard. By 1950, we were both engaged in the determination of atomic masses and began a friendly rivalry that continued until his interest shifted to lunar samples and instruments to be carried by rockets and satellites. I was privileged to speak at his seventy-fifth birthday celebration and, later, at his memorial service in 1994.

At this time, the standard of atomic mass was still the abundant isotope of oxygen, ^{16}O, but the most useful secondary standard was ^{12}C, the abundant isotope of carbon. Thus, the mass difference between these two atoms (^{16}O − ^{12}C) was crucially important. Nier had set himself the task of determining this quantity with high precision and had published what appeared to be a definitive value. Meanwhile, those who were determining the energy balance in nuclear reactions had studied the reactions needed to connect these two atoms and were reporting an independent, but discordant, value for this important mass difference.

Bainbridge had been following this discordancy and brought two of the (friendly) combatants − Nier and William Buechner (head of Physics at MIT) − together at Harvard in the spring of 1951. I was also invited to the meeting and, although I was running a high fever, was determined not to miss the excitement. The values in question were the following:

^{16}O − ^{12}C (Collins, Nier and Johnson) = 3.996158 (error of 4)
^{16}O − ^{12}C (from reaction experiments) = 3.996196 (error of 17)

The difference between these two values (0.000038) was very small but lay clearly outside the stated errors, and the meeting was unable to suggest a reason for the discrepancy. It remained a mystery for several years until Nier revisited the subject and discovered that an impurity had vitiated slightly his earlier result. In the meantime, the discrepancy furnished a motive for adopting ^{12}C as the standard of atomic mass, an action that was taken in 1960 at the Tenth General Assembly of the International Union of Pure and Applied Physics.

The Monday Club

In the post–World War II period, most institutions had a Faculty Wives Club. At Wesleyan, this group met weekly on Mondays, and members were invited to present papers. For new members, these occasions were command performances on which reputations were to rest, and both spouses lost sleep in the paper preparations. Kay chose to introduce Wesleyan to the Canadian Group of Seven painters and wrote to the National Gallery of Canada for help. In response, the Gallery sent a box of slides, dispatched by diplomatic pouch to the Canadian Consul in Boston, who sent it on to Middletown. I operated the slide projector whilst Kay gave an inspired commentary, which helped to mitigate the "colloquium" fiasco.

The meetings of the Monday Club were listed on the Weekly Calendar of the University. I overheard one student ask another, "What's the Monday Club?" The other replied, "That's where the wives of the professors read the *Encyclopaedia Britannica* to one another." He wasn't so far from the truth.

My Wife's Life Saved by Penicillin

Our second child, Jane Edmison, was born in Middletown. During the event, my wife became infected and seemed destined to die until someone remembered hearing of a new drug that was being experimented with at Yale Medical School. Through a personal contact, her doctor, Dr. Crampton, obtained a sample of penicillin, administered it to my wife, and she made a dramatic recovery. It was one of the first non–laboratory uses of the drug in the United States. Years later, whilst on a lecture tour in India, I met Howard Walter Florey (1898–1968), the Australian who was one of the discoverers of penicillin, and was able to express my thanks in person. He was a genial, modest individual, quite unmoved by his fame.

The *Middletown Press*

Although its population was but 30,000, Middletown had its own daily newspaper. In the spring of 1950, it shared the concern of the world for the victims of the Winnipeg flood, and daily accounts appeared on the front page. The tension rose until one day we read, "Natives Take to the Hills!" Knowing that a native would need to put his face to the ground to see the Winnipeg Hills, we knew that the situation was serious.

Proofreading of the paper could have been improved, and typographic and other errors were a source of merriment or embarrassment. When I mentioned in a public lecture that the earth was 10^9 years old, it was reported that Professor Duckworth believed the earth to be 109 years old. Only shortly before, the First Church (Congregational), which we attended, had celebrated its tercentenary. Once again, my credibility was clearly in doubt.

Perhaps even more discomfitted was the president of the University, whose picture appeared on the front page on the same day as a story of a pig that had died after becoming entangled in a guy wire. Captions for the two photographs were interchanged, with that for the president reading, "Hog Hangs Self."

Departure from Wesleyan

In the summer of 1950, I began to realize that if I were to maintain or enhance the modest place I was establishing in the world of nuclear physics, it would have to be done elsewhere. The present mass spectrograph would continue to be competitive for a few years but would then have to be replaced by a larger and more sophisticated version. This could hardly be done with master's students. In addition, even if the next step could be taken at Wesleyan, there was the threat of complacency. The entire environment was so caressing, and so many of the full professors were basking in the glow of past achievements, that I feared the fate of the lotus eaters, living an idyllic, but unchallenged, life. For the next thirty years, I might be pointed out as the man who had discovered ^{190}Pt!

Although Gerhard Herzberg (head of Physics at the National Research Council of Canada) and I had discussed in 1950 the possibility of my joining his division, I decided to take no other initiatives for the time being.

But, during the following winter, others made approaches to me, including W. W. Watson, the head of Physics at nearby Yale, whom I had first met when he was the American liaison officer at the Montreal Laboratory. My wife and I were mulling over these possibilities when Harry Thode paid me a visit from McMaster, having been told by Malcolm Correll of MIT that our work was attracting attention.

As a result of his wartime work, Thode had status in the world of science and had influence in the upper reaches of McMaster. He had persuaded that university to establish a Ph.D. program in chemistry and that, if I were to join him, a Ph.D. program in physics would be assured as well. My old friend Martin Johns, whom I had known from the time he was at Brandon College, and who had spent a period at Chalk River, was already at McMaster. Thode would arrange the purchase of the mass spectrograph on which my current research at Wesleyan was being done, ensuring little interruption in the research program.

We weighed the McMaster option against others that existed or might be solicited and decided to return to Canada. There was the excitement of a new enterprise, there was the possibility of contributing to Canadian science, and there was the prospect that our two children would be educated in Canada. Thus, motivated more by heart than mind, and certainly not by purse, I accepted the offer of full professor of Physics at McMaster University at an annual salary of $6,600. I had just been promoted to full professor at Wesleyan, at a salary of $7,500 (not including the summer stipend). My colleagues and friends at Wesleyan were dumbfounded that I would depart from Paradise for an unproven graduate program in a small Baptist university. As I look back over the intervening decades, I have no reservations about the decision, but I can understand their disbelief. Despite our decision, the five years spent in the civilizing atmosphere of Wesleyan, the friendships we enjoyed there, and the many kindnesses we received constitute a treasured period in our lives.

The last experiment done at Wesleyan was the mass comparison between ^{234}U (the lightest naturally occurring isotope of uranium) and ^{117}Sn (one of the ten stable isotopes of tin). This led to a useful series of experiments completed later at McMaster.

McMaster University: 1951 to 1965

8

McMaster University and the City of Hamilton were not unfamiliar to us, as we had spent twelve months during 1944 and 1945 in their hospitable environs. But that had been temporary, and this new residence was to be permanent.

McMaster University, a Baptist institution, had been established initially in Toronto in 1887, but by the late 1920s its financial future seemed in doubt. In 1930, hoping to attract a wider clientele, McMaster abandoned its Bloor Street home and moved to Hamilton, where it was given a warm welcome, a generous grant of land, and significant community support towards the cost of two handsome academic buildings. In 1951, it was still small (about 1,200 students), it was still under Baptist governance, and it was still a liberal arts college, with one exception: Harry Thode had recently persuaded President Gilmour that the science departments needed access to full public funds, which were not available to a church institution.

Hamilton College

To qualify for full funding, the science departments had been transferred to a new institution, Hamilton College, with its own governing board and financing but affiliated academically with McMaster. In this arrangement, the university admitted all students to the college, approved all the programs, conducted all the examinations, awarded all the degrees, but bore no financial responsibility for its affiliate.

Although this arrangement was novel for McMaster, in principle it was not novel to Ontario, inasmuch as the University of Toronto had within its academic ambit a number of independently governed and financed colleges, such as Victoria University (United Church), Trinity College (Anglican), and St. Michael's College (Roman Catholic). There was the novel twist, however, that Hamilton College was a secular institution affiliated with a church university, whereas in Toronto it was the other way around. Harry Thode had sold the idea not only to President Gilmour, and through him to the Baptist Convention, but also to the business and industrial leaders of Hamilton, much as had been done when McMaster itself came to Hamilton in 1930. Civic pride had been crucial at that time and was now called upon again to develop a major centre for science and technology.

What was the potential for private support? Hamilton was a major industrial city with large corporations such as Stelco, Dofasco, Studebaker, Otis Elevator, and Canadian Westinghouse amongst its industries. These and others provided board members for the new college and funding for its first building, the Nuclear Research Building. The two most powerful personalities put aside their competitive interests to unite behind the new enterprise. These were Hugh G. Hilton, the small-but-tough boss of Stelco, and Frank A. Sherman, the large-but-urbane head of Dofasco. Incidentally, their steel empires were run in vastly different styles: Stelco was unionized to the hilt and experienced periodic strikes, whilst Dofasco had no union, had a profit-sharing agreement with its employees, and adopted whatever wage settlements were reached between Stelco and its militant unions.

Graduate Study in Canada Prior to 1951

Where had Canadian graduate students gone before Hamilton College opened its doors to them in 1951? When the Ph.D. became available in the United States, aspiring Canadians were quick to enroll. For example, between 1881 and 1890, fifteen Canadians obtained their doctorates from Johns Hopkins University in Baltimore, and eight were in the first class at Chicago: few went to Europe. Many never returned from the United States, giving rise, even before the end of the nineteenth century, to fear of a "brain drain," although that catch phrase had not yet been coined.

Partly for that reason, and partly because they had reached that stage of development, Toronto instituted the Ph.D. in 1894, and McGill did in 1906. These programs were modelled after the American version of the German Ph.D. By 1920, Toronto had awarded twenty-seven doctorates and McGill fifteen; this was clearly not a growth industry. There were few fellowships and few eminent professors. Most professors were obliged to teach a wide range of courses with the result that they were unable to become authorities in any one branch of their subject. Sir William Osler (1849-1919), the distinguished Canadian-born physician, whose career led him from McGill through Philadelphia and Johns Hopkins to a Regius professorship at Oxford, alluded to their broad responsibilities by saying that Canadian professors did not occupy "chairs" but, rather, "settees."

Because of this state of affairs, most Canadians continued their trek to the United States for graduate work, a circumstance that disturbed those who feared a weakening of the ties to Britain. As a result, the Canadian universities collectively made a plea to British academic authorities for a British doctorate that would provide Canadians with an alternative to the American Ph.D. This plea was a material factor in the British decision in 1918 to take such a step. As a result, after World War I, there was an increased flow of Canadians to the United Kingdom, attracted by figures such as Rutherford at Cambridge, and supported by 1851 Exhibition, Rhodes, and other scholarships.

Within Canada, in the period between the two world wars, Toronto and McGill continued to dominate the graduate scene, although the number of degrees awarded was still modest. Thus, the degrees awarded in 1920 numbered twenty, in 1930 forty-eight, and in 1940 seventy-five. Of this last group, thirty-three were awarded by Toronto, thirty-two by McGill, and the remainder by Alberta, Laval, Manitoba, and Queen's. But after World War II, this situation changed quickly when the scientists who had been engaged in war research returned to their universities or took up academic posts for the first time. They had been engaged in stimulating investigations, some of which had affected the course of the war, and they wished now to pursue research of their own choosing with the help of graduate students. And undergraduates who were dazzled by the part played by science in the victory were eager to work for higher degrees. The upshot of this ferment was that several universities that had hitherto offered only a modest master's program were persuaded by their chemists and physicists to offer the Ph.D. Thus, Thode's desire to establish McMaster as a leading graduate school in science was in phase with the times, although he was starting from farther back than most of the others.

The Department of Physics

In 1951, Thode had just persuaded the University to offer the Ph.D. in chemistry and physics. The Chemistry Department may have been the stronger of the two; in addition to Thode, it comprised Arthur Bourns (organic chemistry), Lawrence Cragg (physical chemistry), Ronald Graham (analytical chemistry), and Richard Tomlinson (radiochemistry). Physics had Francis Gulbis (an academic refugee from Estonia), Martin Johns (nuclear physics), Boyd McLay (spectroscopy), Gerald Tauber (theory of relativity), and Henry Duckworth (mass spectroscopy). In addition, on the research side, we could count Thode himself, because much of his work could easily qualify as physics. McLay, a graduate of McMaster in Toronto, and with a Ph.D. from Toronto, was chair of the department. Johns, Thode, and I thought we were competent to direct doctoral dissertations, but we needed to attract students, and we needed to provide them with a proper course program.

Fortunately for me, my former student Ben Hogg, who had accompanied me to Wesleyan and who was working at the Defence Research Board Establishment at Suffield, Alberta, decided to come to McMaster for the Ph.D. In addition, Carman McMullen, with an M.Sc. in physics from McMaster, threw his lot in with Thode, and two years later Hogg and McMullen were the first graduates in what has since become one of the strongest physics programs in Canada. But in 1951 it had a long way to go.

The biggest gap was in nuclear theory. We were doing research in aspects of nuclear physics, and we were working in the Nuclear Research Building, but we were not providing our students adequately with the grand theoretical context in which their research should be viewed. As an emergency measure, I arranged for an acquaintance, Maurice Goldhaber, then a leading figure at the Brookhaven National Laboratory on Long Island, to give a series of lectures in the summer of 1952. Then, for the academic year 1952-53, we persuaded a young theoretician at the University of Toronto to lecture once a week at McMaster. This was Melvin A. Preston, a Toronto graduate with a recent Ph.D. from Birmingham (with R. Peierls) who, in my view, was somewhat isolated and under-appreciated at Toronto. He agreed to join us on a full-time basis in 1953, and it was his coming that gave creditability to the program. For Ph.D. students, we no longer needed to depend on family friends or McMaster graduates.

Accordingly, we began advertising our wares, with offers of fellowships, in the British publication *Nature* and were soon corresponding with students who had read about us in that prestigious journal and were unaware that we were mere upstarts. In the first year, these advertisements brought four students from the United Kingdom and brought us a recognition that, at that time, was scarcely deserved. But, from that point, we gradually became accepted by Canadian universities as a destination for their good students. I well remember the day when John Cameron, an excellent student from the University of Toronto, decided to come to McMaster for his Ph.D.

It's sometimes tricky to select graduate students. The problem does not arise for Canadian graduates, as the standards amongst universities are remarkably uniform, and a first-class degree is a sufficient guarantee, whether from Acadia, Toronto, or Alberta. In the United Kingdom, the system is also clear. There are four classes of degree: First, Upper Second, Lower Second, and Third. At that time, British universities accepted First and Upper Second for graduate work. We followed the same practice, although no First-Class student ever made it to Hamilton. Applications from the Indian sub-continent were numerous and had to be evaluated with care. There were three to four million students enrolled in the Indian universities. Textbooks were scarce, and laboratory equipment was antiquated, with the result that undergraduate degrees were inferior to Canadian ones. A limited number of students, however, proceeded to the master's degree, with the major universities graduating ten to fifteen in physics per year. Moreover, these students were always ranked; thus, students holding master's degrees from major Indian universities who stood first, second, or third in their master's classes were considered good bets. Applications from the United States were virtually non-existent at that time, and very few came from continental Europe.

As the undergraduate enrollment increased and the graduate program grew, new staff were added and post-doctoral fellows made their appearance. New staff included Robert Summers-Gill (with an undergraduate degree from Saskatchewan and a Ph.D. from California), Rudolph Haering (originally from Switzerland and with a Ph.D. from British Columbia), Howard Petch (with an undergraduate degree from McMaster and a Ph.D. from British Columbia), and Paul Zilsel (with an undergraduate degree from Wisconsin and a Ph.D. from Yale).

The first three post-doctoral fellows were Howard Petch in 1952-53 (prior to spending 1953-54 as a Rutherford memorial fellow at Cambridge and returning to the Department in 1954), Ben Hogg, and Carman McMullen, who stayed on following their Ph.D.s in 1953. Petch and Hogg worked in my laboratory.

McCarthyism

I had certain second-hand contacts with Senator McCarthy and his crusade to save America from communism, a crusade that others had launched in the 1930s. With so many unemployed because of the depression during the 1930s, federal and state governments were obsessed with the fear that the Russian Revolution would be replicated in the United States. To combat this deadly menace, jurisdictions began to demand loyalty oaths from their employees, including those teaching in state-supported universities and colleges. By 1936, twenty-one states plus the District of Columbia had climbed on this bandwagon, and there was much resentment amongst academics that their loyalty was under question. The outbreak of World War II took the steam out of this controversy, when the fear of fascism supplanted in part the fear of communism.

Following World War II, however, the nation became alarmed that Russia would develop the atom bomb and use it in an unprovoked attack. It was in this atmosphere in 1947 that Senator Joseph Raymond McCarthy (1907-1957) entered the scene and quickly began seeing communists behind every desk. As the most vindictive member of the House Un-American Activities Committee (HUAC) and later as chair of his own Senate Internal Security Sub Committee (SISS), he at first denounced communism in the government and in the motion-picture industry. When these centres of infection had been purged, McCarthy turned his attention to the world of higher education. Suspects were called to appear as "witnesses" before these committees, where they were invited to reveal their involvement with the Communist Party and to name others who had been involved. Those who invoked the Fifth Amendment to the Constitution (the right to refuse to answer on the ground that it might be incriminating) were assumed to have something to hide and won little sympathy from the academic community, especially from deans and presidents. The assumption that the witnesses were innocent until proven guilty was disregarded. Some of my friends were victims of McCarthy and his colleagues.

Paul Zilsel was a particularly ironic victim. Whilst an undergraduate at Wisconsin, and as a member of an active student organization, he had worked in 1947 for the defeat of Senator La Follette, an arch-isolationist. Zilsel believed that the United States had a lead role to play in the post-war world and, on that account, supported La Follette's opponent, who was none other than Joseph McCarthy. In due course, Zilsel's student organization at Wisconsin was retroactively declared to have been communist, and Zilsel was forced to resign from his position at the University of Connecticut. Thus, he was a victim of his erstwhile hero. He lived as an exile in Israel before bringing his considerable theory skills to McMaster in 1956. Later, after McCarthy's fall from grace and subsequent death, Zilsel returned to the United States to accept a position at Case Western Reserve University in Cleveland.

Leon Kamin was a teaching fellow in psychology at Harvard and was known to have leftist views. Harvard, in a noble tribute to academic freedom, did not fire him but simply did not renew his contract. Blacklisted in the United States, he came to McMaster, where he taught for several years until the American academic world came to its senses. Ultimately, he returned to the United States and became chair of the Department of Psychology at Princeton.

Others not guilty themselves were deemed guilty by association, and their careers were mysteriously made difficult, although they were unaware that they were under suspicion. One such victim eventually learned that his offence had been to have lived next door to a communist when he was a child. Another victim was my friend Katherine Way, who kept an apartment in Washington but was working elsewhere. She received a call from a friend asking if a visiting scientist from Canada could use the apartment for a couple of nights, as no hotel room was available. Her offence emerged much later when the visitor, whose identity she had never known, was the subject of a security investigation. He was none other than Bruno Pontecorvo, a one-time colleague of Enrico Fermi's in Rome, who defected to Russia in 1950. When Kay Way was eventually allowed to see her FBI dossier, the illogical difficulties that had complicated her life were finally explained. By the way, when Pontecorvo and his family first disappeared from sight, there was no proof that they had gone to Russia, as the Russians claimed ignorance of the whole affair. Some time later, Professor Dee of the University of Glasgow was sitting beside a Russian delegate to an international meeting. Suddenly, and mischievously, he asked, "How's Pontecorvo?" Without thinking, the Russian answered, "Fine," before realizing that he had let slip a closely guarded secret.

McCarthy's effectiveness as a communist hunter came to an abrupt end in 1954, when he made the mistake of attacking the United States Army. This led to his censure by the Senate and to the end of his meteoric political career.

Research Activities

Thorium and Uranium

In July 1950, whilst still at Wesleyan, I had received a letter from Glenn Seaborg, the chemist who established the chemical properties of plutonium, asking if we could provide data on the total energy released in the three radioactive decay chains: $^{232}Th \rightarrow ^{208}Pb$, $^{235}U \rightarrow ^{207}Pb$ and $^{238}U \rightarrow ^{206}Pb$. His group and many before them had studied the individual steps in the chain, but he wondered if we could provide overall values, against which the totals of individual values could be checked. Accordingly, George S. Standford, who had his undergraduate degree from Acadia University, undertook to study the isotopes ^{207}Pb, ^{232}Th, and ^{238}U for his master's thesis, and we made a request to the Atomic Energy Commission for a sample of uranium enriched in ^{235}U, the fissile isotope. Our interest lay in the very rare ^{234}U, but we reasoned that whatever process had been used to enrich the ^{235}U would have enriched the ^{234}U even more.

At that time, a request from an associate professor of physics at Wesleyan University for a sample of enriched ^{235}U was no trivial request. However, we had a research contract with the Atomic Energy Commission and, much more important, we were responding to a request from Glenn Seaborg. He later won the Nobel Prize for chemistry in 1951 and became the chair of the Atomic Energy Commission. Whatever the reason for our success, we received the requested sample in May 1951, just as we were completing the last planned experiment before dismantling the mass spectrograph for shipment to McMaster. On Saturday, 19 May, shaking with excitement, we inserted the new sample and discovered that ^{234}U, which is normally present to six parts in 100,000, could be clearly seen on the photographic plate after five minutes' exposure. That weekend and the next three days were devoted to this elusive isotope and, when the instrument was finally dismantled, we had a good value for its atomic mass, in this case relative to ^{117}Sn (doubly charged ions of ^{234}U appeared in the same region of the photographic plate as singly charged ions of the Sn [tin] isotope at mass 117).

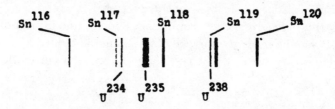

Figure 2: Mass spectrum formed by singly charged ions of tin (Sn) and doubly charged ions of uranium enriched in ^{235}U, 1952.

Other determinations had to be done to comply with the Seaborg request. Thus, in November 1951, with the instrument now re-assembled at McMaster, Ben Hogg and James Geiger (who later had a fine career at Chalk River), completed the work by studying ^{204}Pb and ^{208}Pb and verifying some of the earlier values. Finally, a letter entitled "Masses of ^{208}Pb, ^{232}Th, ^{234}U, ^{235}U and ^{238}U" appeared in the *Physical Review* in the spring of 1952.

Mass Evidence for Nuclear Shells

During my time at Wesleyan, we had reported many data relating to the "magic numbers," believed by theorists to indicate the existence of particularly stable configurations in the nucleus. Kenneth Bainbridge said to me that if I were to publish results as they were obtained, I should ensure that the overall picture was also presented soon. Accordingly, on 25 April 1952, I submitted to the venerable British journal, *Nature*, a letter entitled "Evidence for Nuclear Shells from Atomic Mass Measurements." This was published in the 26 July 1952 issue and included the graph shown in Figure 3, which included our binding-energy-per-nucleon values for 115 of the stable nuclides with atomic number greater than 21, most of the data for which had been published in a series of communications to the *Physical Review*. In the graph (shown in Figure 3), a sudden decline indicates that a stable configuration had been exceeded. Thus, the graph provided evidence for extra stability associated with twenty-eight, fifty, and eighty-two protons, and with fifty, eighty-two, and 126 neutrons. At that time, almost a half century ago, it was an impressive body of data, providing, as it did, the magnitude of closed-shell contributions to the stability of nuclei.

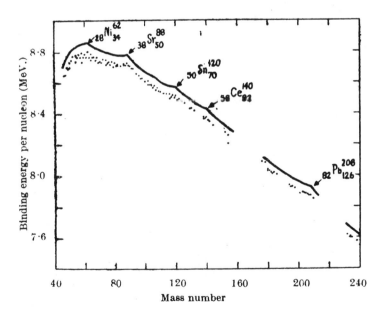

Figure 3: Curve of binding energy per nucleon for atoms with atomic number greater than 21, 1952.

The Rare-Earth Elements

When Ben Hogg and I were discussing possible topics for his Ph.D. dissertation, we were aware that the "rare-earth" elements were crying for attention (they lie in the first gap shown in Figure 3). This curious group of elements, extending from praseodymium (atomic weight = 140.92) to hafnium (atomic weight = 178.6), had recently been purified by Frank H. Spedding at Iowa State University using ion-exchange techniques. Thus, metallic samples were in existence that could be used in our spark source. When I had written to him from Wesleyan requesting small amounts, he had replied, "Young man, do you know how valuable this material is?" and had denied the request. I should have asked Seaborg to intervene, or mentioned that I was a Canadian, inasmuch as Spedding was born in Hamilton, Ontario, in 1902.

The circumstances were now different: I was in Canada and had the support of friends at Atomic Energy of Canada. In short order, we received pure metallic samples of the elements desired, for which someone had paid Spedding several hundred dollars per gram. Hogg's work revealed a broad region of nuclear stability in the rare-earth region, which intrigued Goldhaber during his lecture visit in the summer of 1952, but which had no theoretical explanation at the time. The results were published in 1953 in the *Physical Review* as "Evidence for a Region of Extra Stability between the 82- and 126-Neutron Shells."

Twelve years later, in 1964, when a new, large mass spectrometer had been directed against the rare-earth elements, we were able to shed light on this curious observation. The mills of the gods grind slowly.

Double Beta-Decay

The most common form of radioactive decay is the emission of a negative or positive electron, thus changing the atomic number of the atom by +/- 1. We had heard vaguely of "double beta-decay," in which two electrons were hypothetically emitted, but it seemed unrelated to our work until a visit from Willard F. Libby (inventor of the carbon-dating method) in 1952, who suggested that we might determine the energy available for the hypothetical $^{124}Sn \rightarrow {}^{124}Te$ double beta-decay. Accordingly, in 1952, Hogg and I reported "The Energy Available for Double Beta-Decay of ^{124}Sn," a value that was useful at the time. In the intervening years, my younger colleagues (Barber and Sharma) have provided increasingly accurate values for various double-beta-decay possibilities, which are useful in predicting half-lives.

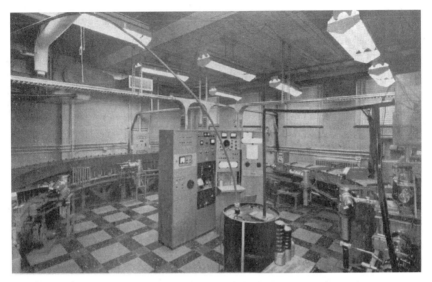

Wide-angle view of "the world's largest mass spectrometer," 1960.

The Large Mass Spectrometer

Even before arriving at McMaster, I had known that the mass spectrograph that I was bringing from Wesleyan, and that rendered good service at both places, would not be competitive for more than a few years. It was essential that plans be made to build a much more accurate instrument. I had two major improvements in mind: to increase the size and to be able to detect the ions electrically rather than photographically. A.O.C. Nier of the University of Minnesota had demonstrated the efficacy of electrical detection and, if it could be done with a much larger instrument, the combination would be potent, indeed.

As with the earlier instrument, the new one would comprise an electrostatic analyzer followed by a magnetic analyzer. The dimensions of these two components were determined by the size of the largest room in the Nuclear Research Building. Thus, the radii of the two units would be nine feet, to create an instrument far larger than any in existence or proposed. By coincidence, the scaling factor was twelve, that is, everything that had been measured in inches in the old instrument would now be measured in feet.

I did not expect financing to be a problem, although a careful monitoring of expenses would be necessary. The NRC had made a generous research grant on my return to Canada, and part of this could be used for construction. Additionally, Joseph Wilhelm, the director of the Ontario Research Foundation, arranged a substantial one-time grant from his organization. Finally, I had recently negotiated a research contract with the Office of Scientific Research of the United States Air Force.

To realize physically the grand design required much technical assistance. My chief advisor on structural matters was Tom Brydon, head of the machine shop, who had been hired originally in 1944 to produce the machined parts needed for the small mass spectrograph that I was constructing at that time, and that was a pigmy by comparison to the new one. Brydon was a clever man, conscious of his own abilities, whose respect I had somehow earned during that earlier encounter. He now fixed his fertile mind on methods for fabricating the massive components needed for the instrument.

The magnetic analyzer comprised thirty separate magnets, aligned cheek by jowl, and each consisting of five iron components. The poles of these magnets (sixty components) were made of special magnetic ingot iron, a superb material but very expensive. The other components, ninety in number, were made of silicon iron that was regularly produced by Dofasco for use in transformers. In the normal course of production, this material began as an ingot thirty-six inches in thickness, which was then hot-rolled in several stages to a final thickness of one-sixteenth of an inch. We required a thickness of ten inches, which Dofasco agreed to produce, at no cost, by interrupting the rolling process at that stage. There was no guarantee of the condition of such iron, as the rolling process had never been interrupted at that stage before.

Brydon hired a skilled toolmaker to machine these forbidding-looking silicon iron ingots to their proper size but, try as gingerly as he could, that skilled machinist never succeeded in penetrating the tough skin of the ingot. After two fruitless days, he resigned in frustration and humiliation, went home, and within days died from a heart attack. I'm sure that his experience with the silicon iron contributed to his tragic death. He was succeeded by a man named Larry, who was unshaven and appeared to have steel whiskers. Instead of attempting to remove thin slivers of iron, Larry took aim at a thick slice and at once broke through the crust. Thereafter, for weeks on end, Larry's corner of the machine shop was a terrifying combination of violent sound and red-hot shavings. Thus was the magnet problem solved, but at the unforgivable cost of one human life.

The vacuum chamber for the magnetic analyzer was a rectangular copper tube especially drawn for us by the Anaconda Copper Company: this tube was later bent at McMaster to form a semicircle. Anaconda's only charge for the tube was the cost of the copper.

The plates of the electrostatic analyzer were formed of segments of the high-quality magnetic iron plated with gold. Its vacuum chamber comprised a flat iron base plus a welded aluminum cover. This base and the analyzer plates themselves were machined for us by Canadian Westinghouse (using a huge vertical milling machine) and the aluminum cover was fabricated by the Aluminum Company of Canada in Kingston. As with the components for the magnetic analyzer, these operations were done wholly or largely as a contribution to the University. At no time were we treated as commercial customers.

Although the ultimate instrument required both components, the magnetic analyzer by itself could be used for experiments whilst the rest of the instrument was being constructed. Thus, its construction was begun first with Ben Hogg taking the lead in its assembly and Howard Petch developing a current supply that could simultaneously vary the magnetic field and determine its value. In this way, we were able to obtain some experimental results while the electrostatic analyzer was under construction. This was desirable because visitors to the University were constantly being brought in to view the "world's largest mass spectrometer," and it was reassuring for them to see that at least part of it was functioning. The first atomic mass determinations obtained with the magnetic analyzer alone were reported to the International Mass Spectrometry Conference held in London in 1958, five years after construction had begun. The theses of Jack Kerr and John Dewdney were based on the work to this point.

Meanwhile, Neil Isenor (Acadia), Philip Eastman (McMaster), and Robert Barber (McMaster) proceeded with the assembly of the electrostatic analyzer, and the first results using the combined instrument were reported to the First International Conference on Atomic Masses and Related Constants held at McMaster in 1960. This work formed the basis of Isenor's thesis. We were now seven years into the project, and frequently at 2:00 a.m. I questioned the wisdom of ever having begun such a foolhardy enterprise. Two years later, by careful adjustment of the two major components, Barber, Alan Cambey (a post-doctoral fellow from the University of New South Wales), John Ormrod, and Roy Bishop brought the instrument to its peak performance, and we were determining, with high precision, the energy with which the last two neutrons were bound to the nucleus (double-neutron separation energy) for a wide range of nuclei. These results proved to be much more significant than any we had originally envisaged. It was

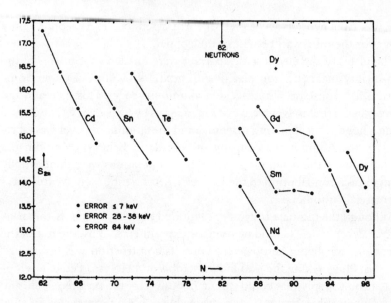

Figure 4: Double-neutron separation energies for even-A nuclides plotted as a function of neutron number,1964.

proof again that improving the accuracy of measurement inevitably leads to unexpected insights.

In the next four years, the instrument provided data for the theses of Barber, Bishop, William McLatchie (McMaster), John Macdougall (New Brunswick), and Scott Whineray (Auckland). The remarkable uniformity of the double-neutron separation energy curves for a large number of elements was presented in 1963 to the Second International Conference on Atomic Masses and Related Constants in Vienna and, in 1964, the dislocation in these curves at ninety neutrons was presented to the *Congrès International de Physique Nucléaire* in Paris, as shown in Figure 4. The value of the instrument had now been recognized internationally, and the results to date had amply justified its construction. The instrument was moved to the University of Manitoba in 1966, where it continued in fruitful service for several additional years and was used by John Barnard (McMaster) and Roy Bishop in their Ph.D. work and by Peter Williams in his post-doctoral studies.

Stopping Power Determinations

This study of the energy lost by ions in their passage through matter was begun by Clifford Eve, one of our first graduate students from the United Kingdom. En route to Canada, he had a shipboard romance with a young woman from Westchester County, New York, which culminated in marriage. The account of the wedding dealt mostly with the dress of the bride and her attendants, but it ended with: "The groom is a student of unclear physics at McMaster University." Eve's thesis (1958) dealt with the luminescence produced when low energy ions impinge on phosphorescent materials. This study was carried a major step further by Arie van Wijngaarden, who had come from Holland to be a technician in botany, and whom I had allowed to take second-year Electricity and Magnetism unofficially. Van Wijngaarden used a magnetic-sector mass spectrometer as an ion gun to make quantitative determinations of stopping powers for ^{1}H and ^{4}He. Then, in the hands of John Ormrod (Manitoba), the study was extended to much heavier ions and, equally important, was correlated with predictions from theory. Finally, James Macdonald (Toronto), following Ormrod's lead, completed the envisaged investigation.

German Physics

Through our work in atomic masses and stopping powers and my participation in various international activities, I came to know a number of German physicists, some of them well enough to speak of the *Nazizeit*.

During the period between 1933 and 1946, German physics went through three convulsions: the expulsion of the Jewish professors, the subjugation of the universities by the National Socialists and, following the war, the de-Nazification of those who had collaborated with the Nazi regime. I was witness to none of these traumatic events, but I have heard tell by several who were, and I saw something of their aftermath.

Harry Welsh, later head of Physics at Toronto, studied at the University of Goettingen between 1931 and 1933 and was aware of Hitler's absurd promises and posturing. With two other students, one a German, he attended a Hitler rally for the express purpose of enjoying the fun. And they were not disappointed: Hitler's performance was fully as extravagant and overstated as they had hoped. At one point, however, Welsh and the other foreign student realized that their companion was no longer derisive but was becoming mesmerized by Hitler's vision of Germany's future. Many other students, and even professors, may have been similarly seduced. But, whether seduced, co-opted or compelled, they offered little resistance to the rules that were imposed on the universities following Hitler's accession to power on 30 January 1933. By these rules, they were obliged to dismiss their Jewish staff, and they were compelled to teach the principles of National Socialism.

In the spring of 1933, 10 percent of all professors were removed from their posts because of their Jewish blood. The scientists most affected were physicists and mathematicians: 26 percent of all physicists and 20 percent of all mathematicians. This led to the exodus of Jewish physicists that so enriched Britain and, especially, the United States. Their loss and the other disruptions caused by the Nazi regime impoverished German science for decades. This is shown, for example, in the Nobel Prizes for physics and chemistry awarded in the thirty-two-year periods before and after 1932 (see Table 1).

The devastation in chemistry was less than in physics because there were fewer Jewish professors in chemistry.

Table 1: Nobel Prizes in Physics and Chemistry

	Won or Shared in Physics		Won or Shared in Chemistry	
	German	Total	German	Total
1901–1932	10	38	13	32
1933–1964	3	46	7	39

The German universities emerged from World War II in a demoralized state. Some professors had actively supported Hitler, some had acquiesced in the Nazi takeover, whilst a minority had spoken out against the treatment of the Jewish academics and the loss of academic freedom. A few lucky scientists had spent the period between 1933 and 1945 in the relative shelter of independent research laboratories, and, although engaged in war-related research, they had been under less pressure to identify with the Nazi Party and its policies. But, after the war, all were obliged to answer to themselves, to their colleagues, and to the outside world for their actions during the *Hitlerzeit*. Some were charged and convicted of war crimes. Most who had acquiesced lay low, quietly adapting to new circumstances as they emerged. The minority, who had not compromised themselves, were in short supply and, as in the parable of the virtuous woman, their price was far above rubies, as the new Germany tried to jettison the baggage from its recent infamous past.

Attention focussed on six mighty German figures – Philipp Lenard, Johannes Stark, Max Planck, Max von Laue, Werner Heisenberg, and Otto

Hahn – Nobel Laureates all. Lenard and Stark had supported Hitler fervently, whilst Planck, von Laue, Heisenberg, and Hahn, the non-Jewish giants of the "new physics," had remained neutral or had opposed his regime to varying degrees. They had decided to weather it out in Hitler's Germany, hoping that better times would come.

Lenard – Nobel Laureate for physics in 1905 and vitriolic anti-Semite – had earned the title "chief of Aryan physics," which had entitled him to advise Hitler on that elusive subject. He was now in disgrace, but what could be done to an eighty-three-year old man?

Stark – Nobel Laureate for physics in 1919 and Lenard's comrade in anti-Semitism - had been named by Hitler to the presidency of the German Research Society. He was examined by a de-Nazification court and, at age seventy-one, was sentenced to four years in a labour camp. The sentence was later suspended.

Planck – originator of the quantum theory and winner of the Nobel Prize for 1918 – was president of the Kaiser Wilhelm Society, a prestigious private research organization. He occupied the most powerful non-government position in German science. He had publicly opposed the persecution of the Jews and had intervened to assist many who were driven from their positions. At the same time, he was intensely patriotic and had continued to serve in scientific societies as a duty to the Fatherland against the day when the *Hitlerzeit* would pass. Until he retired in 1937, at the age of seventy-nine, he did much to hold German science together and to insulate it from the pressures of the Party. His son was executed in 1944 for participating in the abortive attempt to assassinate Hitler. Following the war, the Kaiser Wilhelm Society was renamed the Max Planck Society (Max Planck Gesellschaft) in his honour.

Von Laue – winner of the Nobel Prize in 1914 for the diffraction of x-rays, was enraged at the treatment of his Jewish colleagues and made no secret of his opposition to the Party. His age and fame apparently had secured his immunity, which he had used to assist many who were the victims of persecution.

Heisenberg – thirty-two in 1933, the year of Hitler's accession to power, and winner the Nobel Prize in 1932 for his work in theoretical physics. Stark and other "Aryans" had blocked his appointment to the chair of theoretical physics at Munich because his theories were "un-German," and in 1936 he had been prevented by "military service" from being honoured at Harvard University's tercentenary. Following Hahn's discovery of uranium fission in 1939, the potential weapons value of physics had come slowly to be recognized, and, in 1941, Heisenberg was placed in charge of the atomic research program. That this program never led to an atom bomb has been attributed both to lack of resources and to the disinclination of Heisenberg and others to strive for that lethal result. He had sedulously avoided political alignment but emerged from the war with a slightly ambiguous reputation.

Hahn – like von Laue, although not as vocal, an opponent of the regime and did what he could to assist Jewish colleagues. In 1941, he had become part of Heisenberg's research team. In 1946, when the Max Planck Society emerged from the Kaiser Wilhelm Society, he was named its first president, in recognition of his scientific achievements (Nobel Prize for chemistry, 1944) and his deportment during the *Hitlerzeit*. Immediately following the war, Hahn, Heisenberg, von Laue, and certain other scientists were interned briefly in England to ensure that their "intellectual property" did not find its way to Moscow.

A particularly sad victim of the senseless turmoil in Germany was Lise Meitner (1878-1968), a woman who had studied physics in Vienna before joining the Kaiser Wilhelm Institute in 1907 to work with Otto Hahn, then a young radio-chemist. They collaborated with much success until 1938 when Meitner (a converted Jew, but still a Jew in the eyes of the authorities) was obliged to seek refuge in Stockholm. Although she had been a full collaborator who had probably suggested the final crucial experiment in the discovery of uranium fission and (with her nephew Otto Frisch) had correctly recognized fission for what it was, she did not share the Nobel Prize with Hahn in 1944. Hahn – not to his credit – later rationalized her exclusion, which intensified her disappointment and added a sense of betrayal. The award of the United States Fermi Prize in 1966 to her, together with Hahn and Strassmann, provided some vindication, but the recognition came in her eighty-eighth year and after decades in the wilderness.

I first had personal contact with German physicists in 1951 at a conference on mass spectroscopy in Washington, organized by John Hipple to celebrate the fiftieth anniversary of the U.S. Bureau of Standards. It was there that I met Josef Mattauch for the first time, and also H. Ewald (Mainz), R. F.K. Herzog (Vienna), H.H. Hintenberger (Mainz), W. Paul (Goettingen), and W. Walcher (Marburg). Like others, I was uncertain how to treat these men. Had they collaborated with Hitler? Had they worked feverishly to develop an atomic bomb? Should they be forgiven as if nothing had happened? Hipple assured me that their escutcheons were clean, and, on the strength of that assurance, I invited Mattauch and his wife to visit us in Hamilton. Following the conference, they were to go to Pittsburgh, and I offered to drive there to pick them up. At that time, Mattauch was living in Switzerland but had been appointed director of the new Max Planck Institute for Chemistry in Mainz.

At Niagara, I grandly informed the immigration inspector that I was taking an important German scientist to Canada for a couple of days, and I asked whether he would have any difficulty re-entering the United States. Before the question could be answered, the important German scientist was obliged to answer whether or not he had belonged to a long list of proscribed organizations. One by one, Mattauch denied membership until the German equivalent of Social Security came up; Mattauch explained that everyone living in Germany had been required to belong. When the inspector was unaffected by this explanation, I made the mistake of asking to speak to his superior officer. This dignitary, whom I never saw, called to me over a partition that I must deal with the inspector at the counter. It was then that I learned that United States immigration inspectors hold plenipotentiary powers and resent any suggestion to the contrary. The end result was that, if Mattauch were to leave the United States temporarily and attempt to return, this particular inspector would deny admittance to him as a suspected Nazi war criminal.

As we conferred sadly outside the immigration office, Mattauch suggested that I might have erred in emphasizing his importance. Moreover, he was still living in Switzerland. With these insights, we decided to make a second try at Lewiston. Leaving Mattauch in the car, I told the inspector that I had a Swiss scientist in the car and asked whether he would have any difficulty re-entering the United States. "None whatever," was the reply and, in the event, none there was.

Heinz Ewald, one of Mattauch's former research students and later (1966) called to a chair in Geissen University, had belonged to the Hitler Youth when he was a teenager. Frau Mattauch always held this against him, and it may have been the reason why his call to a professorial chair was delayed until more than two decades after he had earned his Ph.D. degree. If so, it would seem harsh punishment for doing what all the other teenagers were doing. Shortly after he had taken up his new duties at Giessen, he invited me to visit and to stay in a new visitor bedroom, which he had had constructed in the basement of the Institute. I was to be the first guest, and he proudly led me down the stairs, only to discover that the Institute housekeeper had blocked our way with a clothesline of personal laundry.

W. Walcher, professor of experimental physics at Marburg University, spent the *Hitlerzeit* successively as student, assistant, and *Privatdozent* without ever aligning himself with the Party. Within a short period after the war, he received seven *rufen,* or calls to professorial chairs. Subsequent events showed him to be a physicist of substance, but he, himself, attributed much of his early advancement to a form of affirmative action aimed at identifying and exploiting those whose reputations carried no stigma.

Monograph on Mass Spectroscopy

In the summer of 1954, I sent to Norman Feather, professor of natural philosophy at the University of Edinburgh and general editor of the highly respected series *Cambridge Monographs on Physics,* an outline and the first chapter for a monograph on mass spectroscopy. This he promptly accepted, and the manuscript ultimately appeared as the eighteenth volume in the series. It was the first publication in English that purported to describe all aspects of the subject – physics, chemistry, and geology – and it found its place in many university libraries and not a few research laboratories and private bookshelves. The first chapter was introductory and easy to write; in fact, it was written whilst I was on summer holiday on Lake of Bays in Haliburton County. I had begun it with the catchy sentence, "The first mass spectroscopist to inhabit the earth was Goldstein," but Feather toned this down to "Positive rays were discovered by Goldstein (1886)." The remaining ten chapters called for extensive literature searches and the coherent synthesis of much disparate material. I needed a period of time that I could devote exclusively to this project. Accordingly, I began making plans to spend the fall term of 1955 in the United Kingdom. The whole family would go, of course, and they were all keen to do so.

If I were making an academic expedition today, it would be on sabbatical leave, but that type of arrangement was still unknown in Canada. It had been a standard feature in academic appointments to remote parts of the old British Empire, as a necessary period of re-contact with the scholarly world and/or with family. Thus, the universities in Australia and New Zealand offered a year's leave after six years' service, as did most of the institutions in the colonies. This practice continued after World War II and gradually spread elsewhere, now justified less as an antidote for intellectual isolation and more by the need for periodic immersion in research or other scholarly activity. But, as this practice had not yet reached Canadian shores in 1955 (except for Memorial University in Newfoundland), my leave was to be a do-it-yourself version. This involved finding a substitute to give my lectures and a patron to assist in the travel costs. Ronald Bainbridge, a postdoctoral fellow in my research group from the University of Durham, agreed to give my lectures, and the Nuffield Foundation obligingly named me a travelling fellow.

On Monday, 15 August 1955, we sailed from Montreal on the *Empress of Australia* and enjoyed a calm sea to Liverpool. Following a quick automobile trip to the Lake District, Ayr, Loch Lomond, Edinburgh, Durham, and York, we settled in a ground-floor flat at 37 Gloucester Road, South Kensington, which my cousin June (Edmison) Taylor had booked for us. It was an ideal location for me, as it was only a few hundred yards from the Science Museum Library, which had excellent holdings. The rent for the flat was eleven guineas per week, and heat was provided by a single fireplace and hot water in the bathtub. Our two children were enrolled in private schools, Jane in Victoria House School (five minutes away by foot) and Harry in Eaton House School (fifteen minutes away by underground plus foot), and both were attired in the uniforms prescribed by their schools. By early September, we were well settled, and I made my first visit to the Science Museum Library.

I had assumed that the Library would have an open-shelf system and that I would be able to browse through journals of my own choosing, and at my own pace. This was not to be the case. The protocol required a filled-out form for each volume and a wait whilst a septuagenarian climbed a rickety ladder to fetch the requested item. Browsing was almost impossible, and, in addition, I was endangering the life of someone's grandfather with each request. After only one day, I abandoned the conveniently located Science Museum Library in favour of the Patent Office Library, located far away in Chancery Lane. This had an open-shelf system and excellent holdings and boasted central heating. It was forty-five minutes distant but, in every other respect, was ideal for my purpose.

At Chancery Lane I would make notes on the subject under study, eat a sandwich from a nearby shop, and then return home to write up that topic. The day would not be complete until I had 600 words on paper. This proved a demanding daily quota, as the literature searches were time consuming, and usually I did not put down my pen until the late afternoon. Week by week, the words accumulated and, when we boarded the *Queen Mary* on 28 December at Southampton, en route to New York, I had completed 45,000 words, or two-thirds of the final manuscript.

When I was back in Hamilton, the project reverted to lower priority, and the completed manuscript was not in the mail until August 1957. It was published the following year and had good sales over many years. In

1986, a second edition appeared, written with two colleagues, Robert C. Barber and V.S. Venkatasubramanian.

Life in London: 1955

My wife quickly adapted to the etiquette of English shopping. The main point was that she not take items from a shelf and put them in her basket. Rather, she must stand in front of a respectful clerk and request the items, one by one, which he would then fetch, one by one. Initially, she tried to call out a second item as he was departing for the first, but this was against the rules. Also, of course, she was obliged to visit many shops before acquiring all the items she would normally get at one swoop at Loblaw's. She came to enjoy the daily routine of setting forth with her shopping basket to visit the butcher, the greengrocer, and the rest, all of whom were close to our doorstep.

I took responsibility for the newspapers and for heat. The former was easy: before starting work, I walked Jane to her school and then called at the newsagent for the *Times*, the *Daily Express,* and whatever children's comics had come in that day. (Harry made his own way to school.) Slower than Kay to grasp the etiquette, I picked up the newspapers and comics and took them to the cash register. Later, when I was to be on the Continent for a few days, I delegated the task to Kay. "Go to the back of the shop," I said, "where you will find the comics, and then pick up the newspapers near the cash desk." She followed these instructions to the letter and, at the cash desk was told, "You must be Mrs. Duckworth, because he's the only one who serves himself."

When I took responsibility for the heat, I did not know that it would be a major preoccupation. Long before fuel was needed, the housekeeper, Mrs. Hayes, told me that a man was at the door selling coal and that I should buy some. I took her advice and gave her two half crowns as a tip for the coal man. I never spent a better two half-crowns in my life. It was a bitter fall, and coal became scarce, but our coal man came regularly to the door to ask if Mr. Duckworth needed any coal. Incidentally, the fall of 1955 saw a prolonged period of smog (coal fumes trapped in fog), which numerous sufferers from bronchial weakness failed to survive. This fatal event was the last straw for Londoners and led directly to the complete ban on coal fireplaces within the metropolis.

Fortunately, our flat was compact – a large bed-sitting room with kitchen plus a children's bedroom containing a bathtub. Further, the fireplace was equipped with a gas poker which, for six pence, would burn for about fifteen minutes. The gas poker was a device for starting a coal fire but, in the cold weather, I fed six-penny pieces continuously to the gas meter. In this way, even on the coldest of days, I could achieve 70 degrees F. By December, the gas poker had a sad, tormented look, but we had been kept warm. Two other families from McMaster were spending the entire year in the United Kingdom: Jack and Kay Graham (economics) and Arthur and Marion Bourns (chemistry). They lived in commodious houses in the suburbs, which dwarfed our city quarters, but they were cold. Whenever they visited us, they left for home with the greatest reluctance and with their children begging to stay longer. Graham was doing his research at Chatham House, and Bourns was at University College.

In the 1950s, opera and the theatre were relatively affordable, and many attended without reservations, as one would attend the cinema. And programs cost six pence, instead of the two or three pounds prevailing in 1998. Even this professor on leave could afford to take his wife, and sometimes his children(*), to the following: *Much Ado about Nothing* (Peggy Ashcroft and John Gielgud); *Festival Ballet (Natalie Krassovska and Nicolai Polajenko); *Spider's Web* (Margaret Lockwood); *Salad Days;* *Titus Andronicus* (Laurence Olivier and Vivian Leigh); Eby and Bedford; *Painting the Town* (Norman Wisdom); *The Merry Wives of Windsor* (Wendy Hiller); *The Remarkable Mr. Pennypacker* (Nigel Patrick); *The Boy Friend* (Patricia Webb); *As Long as They're Happy;* *Tommy Trinder; *Madama Butterfly* (July Imai and Andrea Mineo); *Tannhäuser;* *The Edinburgh Tattoo; the Oxford-Cambridge soccer match; the Oxford-Blackheath rugby match; Tottenham Hotspur versus Newcastle United.

The ballet program included Act 2 of *Swan Lake*, one of the first performances in its revival. *Titus Andronicus* was performed at Stratford-on-Avon. We had thought we were taking the children to *Twelfth Night* and were dismayed to discover what our tickets admitted us to. However, they survived seeing Vivian Leigh, without arms or a tongue, being fed parts of her children. Responsible parents in the audience literally abused us for exposing young children to such depravity. Eby and Bedford were duo-pianists from Hamilton making their London debut in Wigmore Hall. We were given tickets and with the few others in attendance enjoyed the program but looked in vain for the reviews in the morning papers. Norman Wisdom was the funniest Englishman of his time and didn't disappoint us. Tommy Trinder was one of the most vulgar Englishmen of his time and didn't disappoint us. *Madama Butterfly* was advertised as having a genuine Japanese Cio-Cio-San. She played her role to heartrending effect but didn't have much of a voice. We attended the 159th performance of *Tannhäuser* at the Royal Opera with the Grahams. Jack felt obliged to cover his eyes during the orgy in Act 1, and I understood why Jon Vickers later refused to sing that role, although on another occasion (also at Covent Garden) I saw Delilah (Shirley Verret) take questionable liberties with him before he lost his hair.

On the sporting side, Harry and I went to Wembley Stadium for the Oxford-Cambridge soccer match, expecting its 100,000 seats to be filled. A few school groups, in their uniforms, were present, and possibly 500 others. If I had taken my son instead to Twickenham (southwest London) for the University Rugby Match, we'd have found ourselves in the vast caravanserai of 40,000 old boys, dons, students, spouses, children, and grandchildren, which invariably paralyzes traffic in the entire area. We later learned that the distinction is one of class: "Soccer is a gentleman's game played by hooligans, whilst rugby is a hooligan's game played by gentlemen." We witnessed the gentlemen's version at Blackheath, in the course of which one of the Oxford players was knocked unconscious. His solicitous comrades carried him to the sidelines and checked on him periodically in the hope that he could return to the game. Kay saw him as some mother's son who deserved better treatment. Tottenham versus Newcastle was a proper First Division soccer match played by hooligans, alias professionals. After ninety minutes on the seatless terraces, plus the interval time, Harry and I came to know the true meaning of the word *grandstand*. As the public houses were not allowed to open until after the Saturday afternoon matches, there was no rowdiness. The hooliganism that now mars soccer matches began when the pubs were allowed to open before games.

A required adventure was a family trip to the Continent. With high hopes, we consulted Thomas Cook at the foot of The Haymarket about arrangements to visit France, Switzerland, and Italy, and stipulated what money was available for the trip. "At that price," he said, "forget Italy, but I can give you a long weekend in Paris and Switzerland." Accordingly, we departed London by plane on Friday, 4 November for Orly Airport and were settled in the Hotel St. Petersbourg, rue Caumartin, by 4:00 p.m. In the gathering dusk, we located the neighbourhood store, Au Printemps, to be visited on the morrow. The morrow also included a bus tour of the city and an evening expedition to the Cirque Medrano, where an unhappy elephant played a bugle. The next morning, en route to the airport, the taxi driver drove the length of the Champs Elysées, with a later stop at the Eiffel Tower. Arriving at the Hotel Angleterre in Geneva at 4:00 p.m., we immediately took a taxi tour of that city. Next morning (Monday, 7 November) the train took us to Lausanne, where we had lunch before proceeding to

Berne for the arcades, the bears, and supper. A short evening ride found us in Basel, where we boarded a third-class carriage on the night train to Calais. On the ferry from Calais to Folkestone, again third class, we were the only Whites in a large crowd of West Indians who were immigrating to the United Kingdom and, for some reason, were entering through France. We were instructed to proceed to the first-class section of the ship. Shortly after midday, we had checked into the White Cliffs Hotel in Dover, giving us ample time to explore Dover Castle and purchase tickets for Tommy Trinder's vulgar performance at the Granada Theatre. We returned to London on the morning of 9 November, well satisfied with what Thomas Cook had devised for us.

In mid-September, I attended a conference on isotope separators at Harwell. We stayed at the posh Randolph Hotel in Oxford and were taken by bus to the conference, where I renewed acquaintance with J. Kistemaker (Amsterdam), J. Koch (Copenhagen), J. Mattauch (Mainz), and others from the Continent. Attending the conference led to an invitation to Aldermaston, where I used my perennial topic, "The Present Status of Atomic Mass Determinations."

Mattauch's sixtieth birthday was being celebrated on 21 November with a scientific session, a *Festschrift,* and a feast. I attended as his special guest and gave my standard lecture, "The Present Status . . ." En route to Mainz, I visited Kistemaker's laboratory, gave the same lecture there, and spent St. Nicholas's Eve with him and his family. It was the Dutch equivalent of Christmas Eve, and his two daughters placed their shoes to receive overnight gifts and then had trouble getting to sleep. Part of the trouble may have been fear that Black Peter, who punishes naughty children, might come instead of St. Nicholas.

In Mainz, the cream of German physics had come to honour Mattauch, who now was director of the Max Planck Institute for Chemistry. That Mattauch's institute was for chemistry rather than for physics was a technicality: when he was appointed, there already was a physics institute but no chemistry. Once appointed, a director could implement his own program which, in Mattauch's case, was primarily physics.

Principal amongst the guests was Otto Hahn, now president of the Max Planck Society. Others included Walcher (Marburg), Clusius (Zurich), Haxel (Heidelberg), and others whom I never identified but were obviously "somebodies." The feast had wine, food, wine, speeches, wine, and a lantern slide account of Mattauch's life, followed by wine. Mattauch's colleague, Heinrich Hintenberger, normally a grave individual, presented the slides. He showed Mattauch as a sad private in a World War I Austrian army uniform with the comment, "He joined the army, we lost the war." A series of slides showed Mattauch's encounter with a bear in Yellowstone National Park. At the first telling, the bear and Mattauch were of comparable size but, in subsequent tellings, Mattauch grew steadily smaller, and the bear became steadily more massive. The show convulsed the party, which was in a giggly mood anyhow and had not expected such irreverences from Hintenberger.

The birthday (*Geburtstag*) was to be further celebrated in July 1956 with a landmark conference on atomic masses, and Hintenberger took the occasion of the feast to secure a promise of financial support for the conference from a wealthy industrialist who was present and had raised one too many glasses during the evening. On the basis of this promise, Hintenberger committed certain travel funds, later to discover that the generous donor had no recollection of his promised gift. Hintenberger had promised me 5,000 marks (at that time the mark was worth twenty-five cents), but fortuitously, he was able to find some other sponsor.

The 1956 Conference on Atomic Masses

The 1956 Conference on Atomic Masses, the first of its kind, organized by Hintenberger to Mattauch's specifications and held in belated honour of his birthday, took place in July. The plan was to invite mass spectroscopists, of course, but also experts in other branches of physics who had a knowledge of atomic mass differences. As Mattauch had been engaged in combining and reconciling data from different sources, this conference was a natural extension of his own work. It brought into the fold some who operated cyclotrons and other particle accelerators, some who studied the energy released in radioactive decay, and some who studied molecular spectra. It was the first time that such a disparate group of experimentalists, concerned with this common subject but viewing it from different angles, had assembled in the same hall. And the excitement was heightened by the presence of theorists who were attempting to develop formulae for the calculation of atomic masses.

Otto Hahn again made his appearance, as did his long-time collaborator, Lise Meitner. Amongst the fifty-odd delegates were Kenneth Bainbridge (Harvard), Al Nier (Minnesota), and K. Ogata (Osaka), in addition to many from the Continent, including Aaldert Wapstra (Amsterdam). I presented three papers on various aspects of our work and learned much from the contributions of others and the discussion stemming therefrom. Hintenberger edited the proceedings, which were published in 1957 by the Pergamon Press under the title *Nuclear Masses and their Determination*.

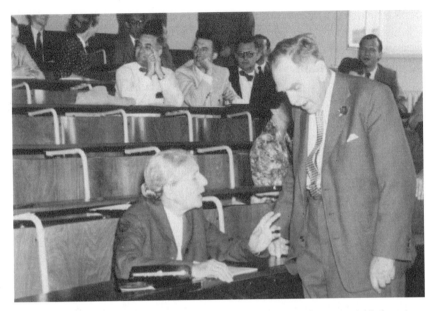

Otto Hahn (Nobel Laureate 1944), who discovered uranium fission, and his longtime collaborator Lise Meitner who first recognized it as such at 1956 Atomic Mass Conference in Mainz.

The scientific interaction was so stimulating that ten similar conferences have since been convened.

As with all good conferences, the 1956 conference had its social aspect. The major event was an evening buffet at a villa in Eltville, a village downstream from Mainz but on the right bank of the Rhine. This luxurious establishment had four levels of wine cellars, at one time stocked appropriately but now almost bereft of those treasures that, in the spring of 1945, had assisted allied troops to celebrate their crossing of the Rhine. On that occasion, the Napoleonic brandy had escaped, but only because of the massive iron bars that still guarded it in 1956. On the evening of our party, the supply of post-war wine was more than adequate.

On another evening, we had a buffet at Mattauch's ample apartment, located on *auf der Bastei* and close to the place where Kupferberg Gold, a premium German sekt, was manufactured. This product flowed freely at the party, and Mattauch assured my credulous wife that his home and the factory were connected by a pipeline. Ogata, who was a teetotaller, was told that the *Sekt* was a form of apple juice. Frequently during the evening he commented on the excellence of the apple juice as he reached for a refill. The next day he was more inscrutable than normal but otherwise not visibly affected.

Everyone brought flowers to the party, as Frau Mattauch knew they would, for she had provided a large vase into which the students' single roses were placed, along with the bouquets of their seniors.

In opening the conference, Otto Hahn referred to the fact that it was occurring long after the actual birthday: "It was not possible to implement the original plan as speedily as the calendar and his birth certificate required without sacrificing the attendance of some essential participants." This was typical of Hahn's excellent English, acquired in 1904 and 1905 in Sir William Ramsay's laboratory (University College, London) and in 1905 and 1906 in Ernest Rutherford's laboratory (McGill), although he admitted to me that he had committed some *gaucheries* in the process. In London, he had been invited to a weekend party in the country, at which they danced on the carpet. Thinking of the bare floor, he explained to his hostess that, in Germany, "We dance on the naked bottom."

Following the conference, my wife and I drove through the Black Forest en route to the Tyrol before returning to Frankfurt via Bavaria. The Four Powers (Britain, France, Russia, and the United States) had lifted their occupation of Austria only a few months earlier, and connections with the Western world were just being re-established. As a result, the Austrian *Schilling* had little international value, and food and lodging were absurdly cheap. At our first Austrian hotel, in Dornbirn, I was quoted a price for a two-bed room plus breakfast that I calculated to be $2.65 Canadian. Disbelieving the result, I recalculated, but I always came to the same answer. In Innsbruck and Salzburg, the prices rose to $3.95 and $5.40, respectively, but, in the intervening pastoral village of Lofer, the overnight cost hit a low of $2.40. On my several subsequent visits to their country, the Austrians have evened the score.

The McMaster Nuclear Reactor

Although I was not a prime mover in building a nuclear reactor on the McMaster campus, I was more than an observer. The idea came, I believe, from Harry Thode himself. If not, he championed it with enthusiasm. Such a device would provide not only radioactive atoms for medical and other applications but, by its very nature, also a beam of neutrons that could provoke nuclear and other effects of great scientific interest. These considerations, plus the desire to acquire something spectacular for McMaster University, constituted a strong motive.

The idea was a bold one, as the safety aspects were both real and imagined. The real aspects would be negotiated with the Atomic Energy Control Board, but the imagined aspects had to be negotiated with the citizens of Hamilton, particularly those living near the university. The nearest similar research reactor was located in Cincinnati at the Battelle Institute. Thus, in 1954, seven or eight of us, including the potential architects, drove in two cars to assess that installation. Its size and protective armour bore no resemblance to the pioneer unit I had seen in the Argonne Forest in the fall of 1944, but it did not appear impossible to replicate in Hamilton.

Richard Tomlinson accepted interim responsibility for safety and endeavoured to allay fears. For example, the reactor was to be water cooled and, as any non-scientist knows, it would carry radioactive materials into the Dundas Marsh. Tomlinson was able to rebut this and other misconceptions, and, ultimately, the City of Hamilton gave its approval to the unholy contraption. The concern for the environment, which has since become a major social cause, would (I believe) prevent such approval from being given today. Tomlinson also answered the less frivolous, and more demanding, questions raised by the Atomic Energy Control Board.

To aid the public relations cause, I arranged a two-week course called Nuclear Physics for Engineers in the summer of 1955, intended for senior members of the Hamilton industrial community. Some forty individuals accepted the invitation, including some chief executives. Classes were held from 8:00 to 10:00 a.m., with most of the lectures given by Johns, Petch, Preston, Thode, Tomlinson, and me. Significantly, and encouragingly for the project, the drop-out rate was close to zero. Later, in 1957, when construction was well under way, I arranged a series of seven lectures on nuclear engineering, which were also well attended; speakers with special expertise were imported for these lectures.

The McMaster Research Reactor was opened on 10 April 1959 and proved a useful research tool until the early 1990s. In 1996, for financial reasons and because of declining research interest, the university decided to cease its operation, but Tomlinson secured a temporary reprieve by proposing that it be dedicated to the production of certain high value radioisotopes. Whether or not this program is fiscally viable remains (in 1998) to be seen.

The American Physical Society

Although we could ill afford it when we were first married, my wife accepted my assertion that I *had* to belong to the American Physical Society.

This brought *The Physical Review* to the mailbox and the pleasure of seeing not-infrequent accounts of our own work in its pages. Also, I attended regularly the January meeting of the Society (in New York) and the spring meeting (in Washington), more often than not presenting a "contributed paper." In this way, although living in Canada, I kept in touch with the scientific friends I had made whilst at Wesleyan and made many new ones. I was never an officer in the American Physical Society, but, in 1954, I was elected to fellowship, and was later asked, from time to time, to give an "invited paper," the sure sign that one had come of age.

Martin Johns sometimes went with me to the New York meeting, although I dreaded his encounter with the United States immigration inspector at Buffalo. Martin had been born in China of missionary parents and felt obliged to admit his place of birth, even at a time when the Americans took a jaundiced view of anything Chinese. I tried to distance myself during the inevitable awkwardness, but he always managed to gain entry. On one occasion, when I had not deserted him, we were asked the standard question, "Why are you entering the United States?" When told that we were attending a meeting of the American Physical Society, the inspector said, "You don't look very strong."

The Canadian Association of Physicists

In the fall of 1945, a number of physicists who had worked side by side with engineers at Research Enterprises Limited, a radar manufacturer in Leaside, Ontario, and who envied the "professional" status that engineers enjoyed, founded the Canadian Association of Professional Physicists (CAPP). Their object was to secure similar legal recognition of the physicist as a professional, a recognition that could be advantageous to those working in industry. This was of little interest to those in universities, but we joined the new association anyway because we welcomed what we saw as a potential Canadian equivalent of the American Physical Society. It was not long before the academics far outnumbered the industrialists and the professional aspect declined; the organization then became the Canadian Association of Physicists (CAP). I joined during the 1945-46 academic year; my membership number is fifty-two and is slowly rising towards the head of the list.

About the same time, Raymond Boyer, a tall, personable chemist from McGill, organized the Canadian Association of Scientific Workers (CASW), which was seen by some as complementary to the CAPP and the other single-discipline associations. I held back from joining the CASW, as there was some ambiguity as to Boyer's motives. It was subsequently discovered that he had sold information to the Soviets, and the CASW vanished from sight, at least from my sight.

I remained a member of the CAP during my time at Wesleyan and, on my return to Canada in 1951, became involved in the Association's affairs. The CAP was still a young organization and was trying to improve its effectiveness and its image. Of its various new ventures, two were taken at my initiative.

The first initiative was the establishment of the CAP examination for undergraduate students. I chaired the first examination committee, and (as I explained at the award ceremony in the Chateau Laurier Hotel), after reading a few of the examination papers, the examiners came to know the correct answers and were able to grade the papers. During the early years there were two to four entries from each of the major universities, with those from Queen's always at or near the top. The rest of us attributed their success to the emphasis that that department then placed on good teaching; it was not a leading research department at that time.

The second initiative was the introduction of the CAP lectures, which are given annually at most Canadian universities by individuals chosen from the membership. These lectures have taken scores of professors from one part of the country to another, not only to lecture but also to make scientific and other contacts. In the first year of the lectures (1958) I did a tour of Maritime universities, lecturing on five successive days, all during a period of wet, heavy snowfall. At the University of New Brunswick (Monday), about a dozen attended; at Dalhousie (Tuesday), about twenty-five; at Acadia (Wednesday), about 200; at St. Francis Xavier (Thursday), about six; and at Mount Allison (Friday), about 200.

The feature of the 1958 CAP Congress, held at McMaster, was a symposium on the futuristic topic, "Canadian Physics in 1967," organized by Harry Gove and held on 17 June. Participants were E.W.R. ("Ned") Steacie (president of the NRC), Lloyd Elliot (head of Physics at AECL), Louis Voyvodic (National Research Council), Philip Wallace (McGill) and me. There was much discussion at the time about establishing in Canada a national science foundation (similar to the one in the United States) to support scientific research in the universities. As the final speaker in the symposium, I enumerated the elements that would be required for such a foundation and concluded that the NRC currently provided them all. In addition, the NRC's management of the university program ensured both high standards in the adjudication of grant applications and a continuing connection between the universities and government laboratories. Although not said with Steacie's presence in mind, I expect that this remark was partly responsible for my appointment to the Honorary Advisory Council of the NRC in 1961.

I also made a plea to international companies to locate research laboratories in Canada:

> The research physicist in industry is almost as rare a bird in this country as the whooping crane. Unlike the whooping crane, the crop that flies south is much larger than the one that returns. One might naïvely suppose, because the population of Canada is one-third that of the United Kingdom and one-tenth that of the United States, that the industrial research activities in the three countries would be roughly in that proportion. . . . If this [could be achieved], we might discover by 1967 that the cranes are not only nesting in Canada but are doing their whooping here as well.

I was elected president of the CAP in 1960 and received its Medal of Achievement in 1964 during the course of its annual congress in Halifax. David Keyes, who had plucked me from the Signal Corps during the war, was honoured at the same congress, and I sat beside Mrs. Keyes at the banquet. She told me that she and her husband had recently represented Atomic Energy of Canada at some event in Egypt. Well past their normal bedtime, they had been taken to a night club in the desert. I asked if they had seen belly dancers. She replied, "They were not *ballet* dancers."

In 1967, the centennial year of Confederation, the CAP arranged a joint meeting in Toronto of the American Physical Society, the Mexican Physical Society, and the Canadian Association of Physicists. John Robson, president of the CAP, asked me to speak at the banquet, which was held in the Great Hall of Hart House on 22 June 1967. My topic was, "How to Live with the Philistines (a.k.a. Non-Physicists)," and I concluded my remarks with the following:

> Before closing, I should like to depart from my main theme to say that Canadian physicists are pleased that so many of our physicist neighbours have come to Canada to share in the celebration of our centenary. We recognize, however, that you are also commemorating important national centenaries. One hundred years ago last Monday (19 June), Emperor Maximilian, the titular head of the French puppet government in Mexico, was executed, thereby emphasizing the end of foreign domination of that country. Also 100 years ago, the United States purchased Alaska from Russia for the price of two Emperor Van de Graaffs [charged particle accelerators]. On 17 March 1867, Charles Summer remarked to the United States Senate, apropos the Alaska Purchase: "The present treaty is a visible step in the occupation of the whole North American continent. . . . By it

we dismiss one more monarch from this continent. One by one they have retired: first France, then Spain, then France again, and now Russia. ...."As things have turned out, Canada has not yet been occupied, or even been *completely* purchased, and thus we have been able to serve as hosts to this very satisfying international meeting.

The CAP is now well established and, in the hands of younger, energetic officers, is playing a major role in Canadian science.

Editor, *Canadian Journal of Physics*

The *Canadian Journal of Physics* was published by the National Research Council and appeared monthly. In 1956, I agreed to succeed Lloyd Elliot of AECL as editor and served in that position for the next six years. Samuel Goudsmit, the editor of the *Physical Review,* encountered me soon after my appointment and gave me what he regarded as essential advice: "Always remember that your readers are your authors." I took this to mean that I should be charitable to the authors; I decided to try to be fair to both authors and readers. For the authors, I would select informed referees and, once their manuscripts had been accepted, would publish them as rapidly as possible. For the readers, I would publish only manuscripts that were both sound and significant.

The success of the operation turned on the proper selection of referees. Thus, each week, the editor would consult colleagues, make telephone calls, and search the literature to identify five to ten persons who were authorities in the subjects of the manuscripts that had been submitted that week. Those who were known to me were sent the manuscripts without further ado, but those who were unknown were written to ask if they would serve as referees. I had virtually no refusals, although one replied that he would read the manuscript for a fee. No one was ever paid a fee. Goudsmit might have said, "Remember that your referees are also your authors." Doubtless, the referees accepted their tasks in the knowledge that someone else was agreeing to referee their manuscripts.

As most authors do not take kindly to criticism, the editor was often cast in the role of mediator and, in the end, had to decide which of the referee's criticisms were non-negotiable. After six years on the job, I felt competent to be a labour conciliator. I made surprisingly few enemies. Also, I was lucky not to have published phony manuscripts. My successor received a good manuscript from an offshore source, which he was proud to publish. Subsequently, he had a letter from a different individual claiming that he was the author and that the manuscript had already been published in another journal, which was true. The forger had chosen an article from a recent journal, re-typed it under his own name, and dispatched it quickly to the *Canadian Journal of Physics*, where it appeared in due course. It was the twelfth paper that the forger had published in the same way in various journals, and they must have contributed to an impressive curriculum vitae to be read by unsuspecting employers.

Incidentally, I knew Goudsmit through common research interests: he had developed at Brookhaven National Laboratory a helical-path mass spectrometer to determine the masses of ^{208}Pb and ^{209}Bi, which overlapped some of our work in the Pb-U region. Years before, he and George Uhlenbeck (both Dutchmen) had postulated electron spin, which revolutionized the interpretation of atomic spectra. Many felt that the failure of the Nobel committee to recognize their contribution was one of the great injustices in modern physics. Goudsmit, a convivial type, was one of the group that followed the Allied advance into Germany to evaluate the scientific developments that had been made in Germany during the war. His account, given in the book entitled *ALSOS,* was leavened with experiences of a bibulous character.

Other Attempts at Writing

After I had been teaching second-year electricity and magnetism for several years, I decided to prepare a text that would be more suitable to my own class (and possibly to others) than the ones currently available. I was emboldened in this venture by the apparent success of the monograph *Mass Spectroscopy.* I revealed this decision to write *Electricity and Magnetism* to my friend Robin Strachan of Macmillan Canada and set about completing the manuscript. For two years, the class used copies of the typed manuscript and, in so doing, revealed many sections that needed clarification or other forms of improvement. Meanwhile, Strachan had struck a deal with the New York publisher Holt, Rinehart and Winston to publish an American edition and print a Macmillan version for distribution in Canada. These editions appeared in the spring of 1960, and some copies were in use in the academic year 1960-61.

At McMaster and many other universities, this course in electricity and magnetism introduced the calculus to physics and, on that account, many problems illustrated the use of the calculus, some of them difficult. As a guide to students and instructors, the problems were graded E (for easy), M (for medium), and H (for hard), with the further explanation that the easy ones should be done by all students, even those intending to fail the course.

By 1968, the publishers were urging me to revise the text because it was still selling well, but I was too committed to other matters to comply. At that time, 15,514 copies had been sold in the United States and 9,535 copies in Canada but, thereafter, the sales declined as the printings sold out. For several years I had occasional letters from professors asking if I knew where they could obtain additional copies.

Holt, Rinehart and Winston were sufficiently well satisfied with the sale and other matters relating to *Electricity and Magnetism* that, in 1961, they asked me to review physics manuscripts that had been submitted and to assist them in the solicitation of desired titles. I was called advisory editor for physics. The terms of this arrangement may be of interest: for each book developed during my term of service, I was to receive $500, and for each revised edition, $300. In addition, for all books published, I was to receive a royalty of 2% of the wholesale price. The agreement continued for five years and was terminated at my request, again because of other commitments. During my tenure, thirteen titles were published and the 2-percent royalty payments continued until these were revised or discontinued.

In 1963, Macmillan and Co. Ltd. published *Little Men in the Unseen World*, which grew out of a lecture I gave to the Hamilton Association. This venerable organization had connected its members to the outside world before the advent of radio and television. In 1958, the Association celebrated its centenary and I was asked by its president, Laurence Cragg (professor of chemistry), to give a talk entitled "A Century of Atomic Physics." I spent most of the Christmas vacation preparing the lecture, aiming at fifty minutes of talk with a joke every five minutes. It was well received, and the next year I repeated the performance at the Royal Canadian Institute, Toronto's version of the Hamilton Association. That meeting was held in Convocation Hall at the University of Toronto, and 900 were in the audience. I got off to a good start (reading my speech), but, when I turned to page two it was page three, and I explained that I was looking for page two. This was treated as a joke, but it was no joke to me, because it's difficult suddenly to switch from the mode of reading to the mode of extemporizing. As I continued to fumble for page two, a reporter who had asked for an advance copy of my speech came running to the platform with his copy of page two – to the thunderous applause of the crowd. My classmate Jack Sword, who was in the audience, accused me of staging the incident, but I could not have planned it that well.

The lecture having enjoyed two successful outings, I spoke with Robin Strachan about expanding the text to provide a lay version of what physicists had been doing during the previous 100 years. My son, Harry, who could have made his living as a cartoonist, drew the illustrations, and the small, 150-page book was published by Macmillan and Co. The "little men" in the title came from an incident shortly after World War II, when a Hollywood studio made plans for a film about the atom bomb. The first idea was to have leading scientific figures play themselves in the movie, and a luncheon meeting was held in Chicago to discuss this possibility. The producer was unimpressed, however, and in parting said to Enrico Fermi and Samuel Allison, "Isn't it strange how important you little men have become?" The book sold 1,516 copies in Canada; I have misplaced the figures for the United Kingdom, but it was not a bestseller. It was sold as a package to a publisher in Japan where, for all I know, it may have topped the lists in translation.

The Demonstration Mass Spectrograph

In the summer of 1956, the American Association of Physics Teachers met at the University of Toronto. Its president was Vernet E. Eaton, my former colleague at Wesleyan University, and he asked if the attendees could make a pilgrimage to McMaster to listen to a talk by me. Preparing this talk was a challenge, as spouses would be in the audience and even some children. Donald Brodie (a summer student who later became a professor at the University of Waterloo) and I constructed a device to illustrate the topic, "Weighing Atoms." This demonstration mass spectrograph was a Rube Goldberg device, but it delivered a not-misleading explanation of the real thing. After making the proper electrical connections, I explained:

> This is a very expensive piece of equipment; in fact, I am rather embarrassed to admit that it is not yet paid for. However, it was felt that it was important for the University to possess this research tool and we are, consequently, purchasing it on what is known as the "installment plan." This is a scheme by which the customer may purchase an object without initially paying very much money. The customer is permitted to take the object home and use it, and is under no obligation other than that of paying so much a month until the object is worn out – and for a period of time thereafter. In short, it's a scheme by which you "pay as you play." The scheme has been in operation for a long time, and was actually mentioned by a celebrated American poet in words which you undoubtedly recall:
>
> > The lives of great men all remind us
> > We can make our lives divine
> > And, in passing, leave behind us
> > Things unpaid for, bought on time.
>
> In our case the financial arrangements are very simple. There is a slot in the mass spectrograph into which we put some money whenever we

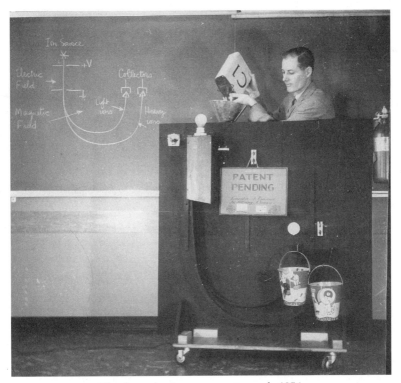

The demonstration mass spectrograph, 1956.

wish to use the instrument. Now if someone will give me a nickel, I shall proceed with the demonstration.

The demonstration itself was arresting as the two chlorine isotopes sped to their respective collectors (sand pails), and, at the end, I was able to obtain an accurate value for their relative abundances. Thereafter, the instrument performed faultlessly on dozens of occasions and always to enthusiastic applause.

The 1960 Indian Science Congress

I was asked to represent Canada at the 1960 Indian Science Congress that was held in Bombay in early January and, thereafter, to visit a number of universities and research institutions. I was to learn that 0.20 percent of all Indians were university students, understandably lower than the corresponding figures for Canada (0.67 percent) and the United States (1.1 percent), but surprisingly higher than that for the United Kingdom (0.12 percent). Except for the four Indian Institutes of Technology, recently established by the United States, the United Kingdom, Germany, and Russia, the major universities comprised central campuses plus numerous academic appendages. The largest and most complicated was the University of Calcutta, which, in 1985, had a central teaching university plus eight constituent colleges and 197 affiliated colleges. The constituent and affiliated colleges prepared students for examinations set and graded by the central university. This system did much to ensure common standards but, in some respects, it was almost paralyzed by inertia. Curriculum changes sent shudders through the entire assemblage, particularly if they required equipment changes or novel teaching expertise that the affiliated colleges found difficult to provide. As a result, many of the science laboratory courses were seldom revised and almost became courses in museology or the history of science.

The Congress, which began on 3 January, was a huge annual reunion attended by several thousand Indian scientists and some thirty foreign delegates. It opened with an impressive ceremony graced by the presence of Prime Minister Nehru himself. The setting was a bandstand opening onto a large grassy area. The Indian delegates sat on chairs facing the bandstand with their backs to the sun. The foreign delegates were seated in the bandstand in such a way as to be shaded from the sun. At the front of the bandstand, in the place of honour, but not in the shade, stood an ornate chair reserved for the prime minister. When we were all in our places, he arrived and immediately sized up the situation, that he would be the only one exposed to the full glare of the sun. He turned furiously to his entourage and demanded, "Who is responsible for these atrocious arrangements?" In the consternation that ensued, frantic organizers rushed forward with parasols, but Nehru literally beat them off with his fists, determined to be a martyr to the situation. And he reiterated his rage in his opening remarks as he mused whether or not he would ever come again to Bombay, when they thought so little of his comfort as to expose him to the midday sun. Thereafter, he greeted each of the foreign delegates personally, and we were all invited to partake of the refreshments that had been laid out on tables next to the seats of the Indian delegates. A stampede ensued and, by the time the foreign delegates had descended from the bandstand, no morsel was left.

That evening, the governor of the State of Bombay entertained the foreign delegates at a reception at Raj Bhavan, a palace within sight of the burying ground for the Parsees, that small, but most influential sect. The bodies of the dead were simply placed on platforms and the resident vultures did the rest. As I approached the reception, I was unaware that I had been careless of my diet but, just before the arrival of the governor, I became deathly ill. When I emerged from the washroom, the governor passed me on the stairs, and, instantly recognizing the symptoms of Delhi Belly, he instructed his driver to return me to the Ritz Hotel. Prior to this event, I had been a relative nobody at the hotel, but, when I emerged from a limousine bearing the armorial licence plate of the governor, I was instantly reclassified as a person of importance. And a good thing it was, because I was confined to my room for three days and needed all the attention I could get.

The Physics Section of the Congress included 165 contributed papers plus a few invited ones, my own included, which was scheduled for noon on 7 January. I arrived early and was appalled to find the audience paying no attention whatsoever to the speakers but engaging in boisterous conversation. I dreaded the approach of my turn, but, when it came, because I was a foreign delegate their mood changed as if on signal: they gave me their full attention, only to revert to form before the poor soul who followed me had uttered his first word.

I was taken to see the Canada-India nuclear reactor, then under construction at Trombay, near Bombay, and designed to deliver forty megawatts of thermal power. Construction was under the supervision of a Canadian engineer named Gray. Concrete was delivered to its destination by an endless chain of closely packed women carrying wash basins on their heads. Locations that would have been inaccessible to machines offered no problem to the women: they simply twisted, turned, climbed, or did whatever else the terrain demanded. The week before, one of the women had dropped out to give birth, and a few links in the chain gang had joined her briefly to provide privacy.

On another expedition, I was flown to Aurangabad, where I shared a room with an intelligent young man named Abdus Salam (who, sixteen years later, won the Nobel Prize for physics), before viewing the Ellora and Agenta caves. These holy places, located in two desolate valleys, had been hewn from the solid rock, in some cases so as to reveal delicate images of gods. The Ellora group of caves numbered thirty-four: seventeen done by Hindu monks about 700 A.D., twelve by Buddhists about 400 A.D., and the remaining five by Jains at a later time. A member of our party was Professor W. Sucksmith, head of physics at Sheffield University. At one time he had served in the British Indian Service where, he declared, he had acquired immunity to the bacteria that were causing distress to the rest of us. He and I were walking together at the Ellora caves when we encountered Niels Bohr, the Dane who had won the Nobel Prize for physics in 1922. I suggested that Sucksmith stand with Bohr for a picture. Scarcely

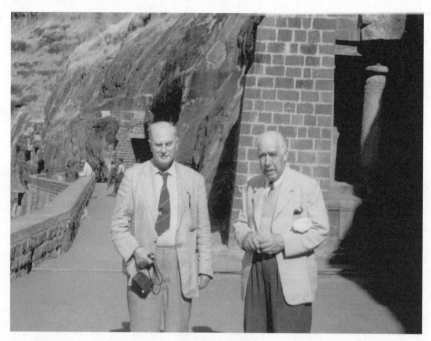

Niels Bohr and W. Sucksmith at Ellora Caves, India, 1960

had the shutter closed when Sucksmith's immunity to bacteria expired and he was leaning helplessly over the parapet.

Following the congress, I was dispatched on a lecture tour of various universities and research institutes in Calcutta, Bangalore, Aligarh, and New Delhi. I was scheduled to lecture at Lucknow, but the students there were in revolt. I was told that Allahabad would be safe, but, when I learned that the vice-chancellor had been dragged downstairs by his ankles, I limited my visit to the Taj Mahal. I also visited Mysore and Madras, but as a tourist.

In Bangalore, I visited the Raman Institute, in which the principal, and possibly only, scientist was Sir Chandrasekhara V. Raman himself. In the 1920s, working at the University of Calcutta, he had observed that scattered light increases in wave length, an observation for which he received the Nobel Prize for physics in 1930. He greeted me formally and showed me the trophy room that housed fifteen medals (including the Nobel medal and others from prestigious national academies) plus numerous scrolls, honorary degrees, and beribboned documents. Finally, we entered a lecture hall where I sat in the front row and received a formal lecture on the theory of colour vision. I have no idea whether his theory was orthodox or balmy, but he treated me as a worshipper, and I was happy to pay him homage, even if he were in his dotage.

In Calcutta, I spent a day with the Ghoshals; S.N. Ghoshal was head of Physics at Presidency College and had spent the 1957–58 academic year in my laboratory at McMaster. Presidency College was one of the constituent colleges of the University of Calcutta, and it was there that Raman had obtained his first degree. When Mrs. Ghoshal was briefly out of the room, I remarked to Ghoshal how agreeable his wife was, and he replied that his brother had made sure of that. They showed me the Victoria Monument in central Calcutta, which is surrounded by a small park. It is there, hiding behind a tree, that many a prospective husband has his one and only chance to view his prospective bride, and possibly bail out at the eleventh hour. Ghoshal was too delicate to say whether or not he had taken that precaution. The *Times of India* carried pages of advertisements describing daughters on offer, with clinical details of family background, education, body dimensions, appearance, personality, and facial blemishes.

It was in Calcutta that a pickpocket stole my fountain pen by bumping against me and removing it in the confusion. When I realized my loss, he was fast disappearing down the street, and I could think of nothing better to do than follow him. At the first corner, passersby pointed to where he had gone, and I continued my futile pursuit. But after the next corner I came upon a policeman holding the young thief in one hand and my fountain pen in the other. A large crowd soon gathered, hurling imprecations at the villain who had stolen from a visitor. The frightened thief turned to me with clasped hands and pleaded, "Please, Papa." I was inclined to forgive and forget, but the matter was now in the hands of the law. Accordingly, we set off for the District Police Station, accompanied by some fifty citizens of Calcutta who were not otherwise engaged. In the quarter-mile to the station, some dropped out, but others took their place, with the result that we were still at full strength on arrival. There, however, only the arresting officer, the thief, and I were allowed to enter the station. After those of us who were not in custody had been served tea in the company of the district chief, I signed a form and was given back my pen, and I was allowed to take a photograph of the thief, together with the arresting officer and the district chief. Finally, the district chief suggested that we visit the chief of all Calcutta, which we did with me riding in the sidecar of his motorcycle. That somewhat bemused high functionary complimented me on my heroism and may have noted a commendation for the district chief, which I realized was the object of the exercise. When the motorcycle and its sidecar deposited me back at the Grand Hotel, my

Pickpocket in the arms of the law, Calcutta, 1960

status became ambiguous: was I a "person of some importance," or had I been "recently released from jail"? Whichever it was, it did not produce the electric effect as when the governor's limousine had delivered me to the Ritz Hotel in Bombay. Incidentally, I was assured that the thief would not be incarcerated as I was unable to stay in Calcutta to testify against him.

The University of Waterloo

In 1957 the major universities in Ontario were surprised to learn that a new university was being established in the city of Waterloo. Waterloo Lutheran University was already there, a faith-related institution, but there would be little overlap, as the new institution was to emphasize engineering. Moreover, it would differ from conventional engineering programs by following a "co-op," or "sandwich," schedule, that is, a schedule in which the students would alternate between study and work. This plan had been tried to a limited extent in the United Kingdom (e.g., at Aston University) and in the United States (e.g., at Antioch College), but never before in Canada.

To my knowledge, the instigator of this enterprise was J. Gerald Hagey, an enthusiastic and personable individual who had worked either in public relations or in personnel. He was fully supported by the Kitchener-Waterloo business community and was named the new university's first president. To the other engineering schools in Ontario, news of the launching of such a university, and in Waterloo, was foolish enough, but to choose its first academic head from the world of business bureaucracy only added to the lunacy. Their attitude was a mixture of disdain and annoyance.

Hagey quietly arranged for space and proceeded to hire staff. His key appointment was the dean of Engineering, Douglas Wright, who later became an influential figure in Canadian higher education. As head of Physics, Hagey hired Arthur Cowan, who was hard-working and more than competent. C.A. Pollock, the president of Electrohome, was the founding chancellor. In due course, students were enrolled, and the essential task of recruiting employers for the four-month work segments was accomplished. This work program involved hundreds of employers across Canada, who reserved full-time positions for the program, knowing that they would be filled (four months at a time) by successive cohorts of students. Students were paid for their labour, they gained experience in a variety of companies, and many were ultimately hired by one of their four-month employers. These remarkable developments took place without fanfare and, of course, without encouragement from the other universities.

In the fall of 1958, Cowan invited me to speak to the physics students. I took with me the well-travelled demonstration mass spectrograph, which guaranteed that the lecture would be a success, and was struck by the enthusiasm that pervaded the department of physics. Then, in February 1960, I attended the opening of the new physics and mathematics building and was again impressed by the esprit de corps. In May 1960, Cowan asked if I would consider joining Waterloo and, not receiving no for an answer, passed the word on to Hagey, who invited me to meet with him, the chair of the Board, I.G. Needles, and a Mr. Hilborn to discuss the position of vice-president (academic). Despite the university's success, Hagey was aware that he was the object of some academic resentment and considerable condescension. Perhaps, in the light of what I had been able to contribute to the rapid development of McMaster, my presence could help to strengthen the young institution's academic respectability. At any rate, I visited Waterloo and talked to all powers-that-be except Douglas Wright. A few days later, he visited me at McMaster and apparently did not veto the idea, as I was given a formal offer of the position. Much torn as I was,

I ultimately declined the offer but retained much respect for the members of the university and their accomplishments.

McMaster becomes Secularized

When Hamilton College was formed in 1950, the rest of the university remained a Baptist institution. This proved a serious financial disadvantage when the Province developed a clear policy for the support of church-related institutions, namely, that they would receive only 50 percent of the support accorded secular institutions. It was not feasible for the church institutions to continue on that basis. Thus, Assumption (in Windsor), McMaster, Ottawa, and Waterloo Lutheran took steps to de-denominationalize. I was not privy to the machinations at those other places, but the decision at McMaster was not easy. Fortunately, President George Gilmour had the confidence of the Baptist community and was able to persuade that proud group that the change of command was not only inevitable but would also strengthen the Baptist Seminary, which would remain affiliated with the university.

Gilmour was a man of many parts; he was clever, personable, handsome, and a brilliant speaker. On one occasion, whilst welcoming the Royal Society to McMaster, he explained its physical layout: "A ravine runs through the campus. The women's residence is located on one side of the ravine and the men's residence on the other. The ravine itself is reserved for wild life." For many years he taught a required first-year course on the New Testament, which may have been the most popular course in the University. It was taken even by Jewish students, who could have obtained exemption.

In 1951 and 1952, Gilmour served as president of the National Conference of Canadian Universities (NCCU), which later became the Association of Universities and Colleges of Canada (AUCC). He retired as president of McMaster in 1961 because of ill health and was succeeded by Harry Thode. He died prematurely in 1963, in part from overwork.

Dean of Graduate Studies: 1962 to 1965

Arthur Bourns, the founding dean of the Faculty of Graduate Studies, stepped down in 1962, and Harry Thode asked me to take over. This I was happy to do, in the knowledge that the Faculty was well run by its efficient secretary, Eugene Shearer, who later married my successor, Mel Preston. Also, I was able to hire Manny Zack as executive assistant. Manny had a master's degree in history from McMaster and was of an intellectual bent but had been trapped in a family retail business. He brought enthusiasm and knowledge of business methods and joined what continued to be a happy and congenial group.

I had assumed that the enthusiasm for Ph.D. programs that had imbued the science departments would be shared by the arts departments. To my surprise, however, several of the senior professors on the arts side were not much interested in directing Ph.D. students. They were active scholars who spent their summers in distant archives or libraries and their winters collating and editing their summer findings. Thus, Roy Wiles (chair of English), Togo Salmon (chair of Classics), and others were reluctant to be distracted by graduate students. Amongst other things, they feared that the presence of Ph.D. students might require them to be land-locked in Hamilton during the summer months.

Clearly, I had been slow to recognize the essential difference between graduate work in science and graduate work in arts. Although, in theory, all graduate students choose their own thesis topics, in science it is usually the thesis advisor who suggests the topic. After all, the science student is expected to be a participant in a well-defined, and ongoing research program. As a member of such a research team, the candidate has ready access to the advisor for advice, because the thesis work is part of the advisor's own work, and the advisor is almost as anxious to have it completed and published as is the candidate.

The other pattern, in which the candidate chooses the thesis topic without assistance, and does the necessary work independently, is common in the humanities and social sciences, and is more likely to lead to delay or even disappointment. Chosen by an overly ambitious student, the topic is apt to be vague and/or grandiose. Further, the candidate is obliged to shop around, thesis topic in hand, to find a professor who is willing to serve as advisor. The advisor may have little personal interest in the topic, hence, whenever the student comes seeking advice, it represents an interruption in the professor's own work.

Notwithstanding some lack of enthusiasm on the arts side, we advertised in the United Kingdom, and several interesting students responded, who gave an international flavour to what had hitherto been a rather parochial group of arts graduate students. Then, in 1964, the government of Ontario took an action that transformed the picture.

The Province of Ontario Graduate Fellowships

It was obvious to everyone that the war veterans had done their part to perpetuate the race. But few in the universities, except for their demographers, took much interest in that domestic matter. Then, in 1955, a statistician at the Dominion Bureau of Statistics, E.F. Sheffield by name, realized that the progeny of the veterans constituted a tidal wave that was moving through the school system and, in the fullness of time, would inundate the universities. He brought these glad tidings to the attention of university presidents, giving them a few years to prepare for the onslaught. In Ontario, this impending crisis was eventually drawn to the attention of the government.

I had not heard of the high-level discussions that took place and was taken by surprise by the announcement in the spring of 1964 that the government would fund graduate students who intended to become university teachers. These fellowships, which came to be known as Province of Ontario Graduate Fellowships (POGS), were aimed primarily at students on the arts side, because graduate work in that area had lagged behind that in science. McMaster was given a small quota for science and little or no limit for arts.

Our first response to the POGS program was one of despair that our well-developed graduate program in science was being discriminated against. No graduate program in the province would benefit as little from POGS as McMaster would. After the initial weeping, we undertook to make the best of it by trying to recruit additional students on the arts side, although the time was short. We wrote individual letters to the heads of all arts departments in the United Kingdom, describing the new initiative and inviting them to recommend eligible students who had not yet made plans for the coming year. In the days before word-processing, this was a mammoth undertaking, but we had a secretary in the office (Mrs. Price) who could type quickly and accurately and who entered into the project with gusto. Over 500 letters were dispatched, which led to endless correspondence and numerous telephone calls. On one occasion, an overseas operator who was determined to connect me to the professor of sociology at the University of Leicester finally brought him to the phone in a barber shop. For thirty minutes the operator had kept me apprised of the progress of her pursuit.

In the end, on 8 May 1964, we submitted to the office of Deputy Minister of Education McCarthy a more than respectable list of arts nominees and, on spec, included all our science students who had no other support, a very long list in total. Our arts nominees were accepted in their entirety, but the authorities in Toronto held the line on our tiny quota in science. But we had surprised everyone, including ourselves, at the success of our desperate effort. Graduate work at McMaster on the arts side was never the same again.

University of Toronto Imperialism

In general, the University of Toronto took a dim view of other Ontario universities offering Ph.D. programs. This was never spelled out in a declaration, but it was obvious to those who were attempting new programs. We had the feeling that an ideal arrangement, from Toronto's viewpoint, would be a family of satellite institutions (McMaster, Ottawa, Queen's, Waterloo, and Western, for example) offering master's work, and feeding their best master's graduates to Toronto for the Ph.D.

The magnificent Robarts Library that was later built on the University of Toronto campus was also a reflection of this attitude. Ernest Sirluck, a distinguished Milton scholar, and at that time dean of the Graduate Faculty at Toronto, had much to do with selling this major facility to the government and, in part, justified it as a resource that would be available to all provincial universities. As far as I know, letters of support from these alleged beneficiaries were never sought. McMaster would not have provided one, nor, I believe, would have many of the others.

The dean of Graduate Studies at Waterloo was Ralph Stanton, a mathematician who had been recruited from Toronto and had set out to make Waterloo the mathematics capital of Canada. With little fanfare and wearing a gaudy yellow tie, he visited practically every secondary school in the province, and, in no time, Waterloo was receiving far more than its fair share of bright young mathematicians. These were mostly got at the expense of Toronto, and Stanton took malicious delight in his accomplishment, as he had not received much of a benediction at the time of his leaving. Incidentally, before he was finished, Stanton had made Waterloo the strongest mathematics school in Canada. The various branches of the subject are there combined in a single faculty of mathematics, and its members are known internationally. His work at Waterloo accomplished, Stanton moved to the University of Manitoba in 1970, and he is primarily responsible for Manitoba's special strength in computer science.

Stanton and I were compatible and found we had the same interest in opposing Toronto's imperialism. Along with others, we sat with Sirluck on the Committee of Ontario Graduate Deans, where we tried to interest him in the welfare of the new institutions, but he was primarily concerned with maintaining Toronto's pre-eminence. This is not to say that a hierarchy of graduate schools, with Toronto at the top, might not have been desirable. But the time for that ideal was past: the government had allowed fourteen independent universities to come into existence, and none of them was now prepared to accept colonial status. A decade later, Sirluck and I found ourselves on opposite sides of another similar issue, he as president of the University of Manitoba and I as president of the University of Winnipeg.

Apropos the hierarchical idea, John Spinks, president of the University of Saskatchewan, was brought to Ontario to advise on its complex university system. At home, he had been resisting pressure from Regina College (a part of the University of Saskatchewan) to become a separate university. True to this doctrine, he recommended in 1966 that one vast university of Ontario be created, with Toronto at its centre and with as many satellite campuses as were needed. The idea was so unrealistic that it was never seriously discussed.

The International Union of Pure and Applied Physics

The International Union of Pure and Applied Physics (IUPAP) is a federation of member countries that guides (by consensus) the world of physics. Thus, it arrives at recommendations with respect to terminology, standards, symbols, and the like. Canada has played a major role in IUPAP: Gerhard Herzberg was vice-president from 1957 to 1963; Larkin Kerwin was president from 1987 to 1990; and my colleague, Robert Barber, is vice-president for the period between 1999 and 2002. IUPAP also sponsors international meetings on topics of current relevance. The General Assembly of IUPAP meets every three years, but, in between, a number of commissions carry IUPAP's work forward in specific areas. In chemistry, a parallel federation exists, The International Union of Pure and Applied Chemistry (IUPAC).

The Commission on Atomic Masses

One of the fundamental constants of chemistry is the atomic weight of an element. Indeed, many of the great chemists in history achieved their fame by determining the atomic weights of various elements. For decades, they were the crown princes of their discipline, and lesser chemists genuflected as they passed. Accordingly, IUPAC early on established a commission on atomic weights, which periodically recommends best values for the quantities in question.

By the 1950s, and even earlier, physicists were determining the mass of an individual atom with much greater accuracy than chemists could determine atomic weight. In fact, many of the recommended best values for atomic weights were derived from atomic mass data obtained in physics laboratories, including our own. In these circumstances, in early 1958, I wrote to a number of colleagues to ask if they would support a proposal for a commission on atomic masses in IUPAP. I also sent a copy of the letter to Dr. Steacie, then president of the NRC, and a well-known chemist. The replies were encouraging, and the Canadian committee for IUPAP agreed to sponsor the proposal. As a result, in 1959, the executive of IUPAP established the Study Commission on Atomic Masses with Josef Mattauch (Mainz) as president, Henry Duckworth (McMaster) as secretary, and other members: William W. Buechner (Massachusetts Institute of Technology), Jesse W.N. DuMond (California Institute of Technology), A.O. Nier (Minnesota), R. Rick (Leningrad), and Aaldert Wapstra (Amsterdam). Although the commission was accorded probationary, rather than permanent, status, we were pleased at the result and undertook our program of work.

Unification of Scales of Atomic Weight and Atomic Mass

The chemist determines the atomic weight of an element by conducting measurements on a large assemblage of atoms. The result is the *average* weight of all the atoms involved. The physicist determines the atomic mass of an individual atom; there is nothing *average* about this result. Until 1929, both thought they were using the same standard, namely, ^{16}O. As oxygen existed only in this one form, its individual atoms weighed the same as their average.

In 1929, however, it was discovered that oxygen possesses three stable isotopes – ^{16}O, ^{17}O, and ^{18}O – with abundances of 99.76 percent, 0.04 percent, and 0.20 percent, respectively. Thus, the two standards were no longer identical, the chemical one being larger than the physical one by a factor of 1.000275. This inconsistency might have been tolerable had it not been found in 1935 that the oxygen isotopic abundances are not constant in nature but vary according to their provenance. Thus, to convert from one scale to the other, it was necessary to use a conversion factor, and the factor itself was not constant, varying as it did between 1.000268 and 1.000278.

By 1956, the accuracy of measurement (particularly in physics) had reached a point where these small differences had become significant, and the Commission on Atomic Weights was uncomfortable with the prevailing situation. At its request, the Chemistry Union approached the Physics Union, suggesting that they jointly seek a solution to the inconsistency. At the 1957 General Assembly of IUPAP, it was agreed to take no action for a year, and it was clear that the Union was uncertain how to handle the suggestion. In the meantime, the proposal for the Commission on Atomic

Masses, which I had submitted on 24 June 1958, and which carried the signatures of twenty-five prominent physicists, had included the statement, "If the matter is not decided in the near future, the [proposed] Commission might help to solve the dual-scale ($^{16}O = 16$ versus O = 16) problem." This offer could not have come at a more propitious moment: the executive of IUPAP seized upon it and, in establishing the Study Commission, asked us to give first priority to the means of unifying the two scales.

The members of the Study Commission soon convinced themselves that the two scales should be unified via ^{12}C. This suggestion had come independently from Nier and from A. Olander of Stockholm; and, in 1957 and 1958, Mattauch had pursued the case for $^{12}C = 12$ with the fervour of a crusader. His principal activities had included a closely reasoned paper in the *Zeitschrift fuer Naturforschung*, a seven-week visit to North America during which he met with numerous interested individuals and groups (including the U.S. National Committee of IUPAP), and a successful effort to secure the support of the West Germany Committee of IUPAP. Accordingly, I prepared a recommendation that both chemistry and physics adopt $^{12}C = 12$ as the basis of their atomic weight/mass scales. This suggestion was a compromise which, although requiring both sides to change, offered advantages to both sides: the essence of successful compromise. On the chemistry side, because carbon has two stable isotopes (^{12}C-99 percent and ^{13}C-1 percent), the new standard would not be found in pure form in nature, a distinct disadvantage. On the other hand, unification of the two scales would make available to the chemist many virtual standards established by physicists. And the changes to relevant chemical quantities would be only forty-three parts per million, much less than the accuracy of commonly used chemical data, and would require no change in the thousands of tabulated values in chemistry textbooks and handbooks. On the physics side, all atomic masses would have to be changed, but only once, and Mattauch and Wapstra were prepared to calculate a new table of atomic masses based on the new scale. Further, for reasons too detailed to include here, ^{12}C would be a more useful standard than ^{16}O had been. The Chemistry Union accepted the recommendation in 1959, on condition that the Physics Union would do the same at its General Assembly in Ottawa in 1960, which it did. And so, despite the inertia inherent in the vast transnational worlds of chemistry and physics, which are not without their politics and their national prides, the two fundamental scales of atomic weight/mass were brought into harmony within a period of two years, an achievement perhaps without precedent in the world of international science.

General Assemblies of IUPAP: 1960 to 1969

I attended the tenth General Assembly of IUPAP in Ottawa, from 7 to 9 September 1960, as a member of the Canadian delegation and, therefore, participated in the unanimous vote (moved by Mattauch) to unify the physical/chemical scales of atomic mass/weight. It was further agreed that the unit of mass would be the *u*. I also voted on the applications for admission from Taiwan and Mainland China. These nations were not friends, and it was feared that, given the opportunity, they would vote against one another. Taiwan was believed to be the less intransigent, so it was arranged that it would be admitted first, although there was latent fear that it might spoil the party. However, like a good sport, its representative then abstained when the vote for Mainland China was taken.

Five years earlier, writer Nancy Mitford had written a best-seller describing the vocabulary of the upper, or *U*, classes in the United Kingdom. Thus, napkin was *U*, whilst serviette was non-*U*, false teeth were *U*, but dentures were non-*U*, and so on. This last was before the ultra-euphemism "oral rearmament" had been invented. In my announcement of the unified scale, made to the world of physics as secretary of the Commission on Atomic Masses, I stated, "The new unit of mass is to be designated by the symbol "u": thus, $^{12}C = 12u$. Readers are urged to be "u" rather then "non-u."

In connection with the Assembly, three international conferences were held in August and September of 1960: Nuclear Physics in Kingston, Low Temperature Physics in Toronto, and Atomic Masses in Hamilton. The Kingston conference was organized by the Chalk River Laboratory and attracted a galaxy of distinguished visitors. I attended the conference banquet at the Royal Military College but was not able to visit the also well-attended event in Toronto.

Erich Vogt of Chalk River was determined that the proceedings of his conference be published promptly, and not appear (as was common) until a couple of years after the delegates had gone home and the news was no longer hot. Hollis Hallett, who was organizing the Toronto conference, and I were taken with the idea, and we three met with Frances Halpenny, then director of the University of Toronto Press. It was agreed that if speakers could bring their papers typed in a standard format, the editing could take place immediately, and the Press would produce the bound copies of the proceedings before the end of the year. This procedure has since become standard, but, I believe, it was Vogt's idea and was the first time that it was used. All schedules were met and the proceedings were in the mail before the start of 1961, to the surprise and pleasure of those who had attended.

The eleventh general assembly of IUPAP was held in Warsaw, from 19 to 23 September 1963. The Canadian delegation comprised Herzberg, Leon Katz (Saskatchewan), George Volkoff (British Columbia), and me. The Assembly was held in Warsaw as an encouragement to Polish physicists and not as a recognition of the high quality of their work. Prominent among them was Leopold Infeld, a gifted mathematical physicist and one-time professor at the University of Toronto who had returned to Poland in 1955. I reported to the Assembly on the work of the Commission on Atomic Masses and was congratulated on the universal acceptance of the unified scale of atomic weight/mass.

Official hospitality was a bit thin, suggesting that physicists were not high on the totem pole. There was, however, a splendid banquet in a country palace, and we were taken to Chopin's birthplace at Zelazowa Wola, not far from Warsaw, where an accomplished pianist played the composer's music.

English speakers were rare in Warsaw. When asking directions on the street, I fell back on my meagre German, but only after asking first in English. I had been told that the Poles spoke and hated German, but would use it to assist a desperate anglophone. Katz had been born in a Ukrainian village that had been subject to Polish overlords. Remarkably, he remembered enough Polish to serve as our interpreter in restaurants and night clubs. We visited only one night club, and that because we were at loose ends and in the bad company of the delegate from Finland. He led Katz, Volkoff, and me to the Palace of Culture, a large, ugly building that Russia had given to the Polish people and, on that account, was despised by the Poles. At the far side of the Palace, we came upon a discreet neon sign reading "Cabaret" which, it emerged, had attracted about thirty patrons. Alcohol was served and the floor show consisted of young women in modest bathing suits hanging washing on a clothesline whilst singing folk songs. Next to us sat a group of Russians, and Volkoff, who was good at their language, asked one of them if they had anything like this in Moscow. From his reply, we gathered that even better establishments could be found at every street corner. Before we left, however, and after much vodka, the Russian turned sadly to Volkoff and said, "We have nothing like this in Moscow."

On three of the other evenings, I attended performances of *Carmen*, *Julius Caesar* (Handel), and *Aida* at the Warsaw State Opera. Not having seen *Julius Caesar* before, I was surprised at the lack of action: the chorus moved onstage to sing, then yielded place to soloists and duetists, with only those who were performing onstage at any one time. Finally, the chorus returned to end the act. *Aida* was another matter: never have I seen such a lengthy victory march and so many ecstatic dancers participating in it.

We were in Warsaw over a Sunday, and I witnessed the streets laden with worshippers on their way to Mass. It was strikingly reminiscent of the Sunday morning scene in Lower Town, Ottawa, during the war, when the Roman Catholic Church still held the French-Canadians in its thrall.

Herzberg, Robert Bell (McGill), John Robson (Ottawa), and I formed the delegation to the twelfth general assembly in Basel, from 25 to 27 September 1966. The meetings were unexceptional, but we had a gala dinner in the Town Hall (Rathaus), which came to an end with the night still young. Bell, Robson, Robson's wife (Nora), and I searched for amusement until bedtime at a neon sign reading "Eve." This proved to be a nightclub at which we were the first customers, thereby enabling us to secure a table next to the dance floor. Bell and I had been unaware that Robson did not dance, or that his wife was crazy about it. We ordered a bottle of wine and, in due course, the band began to play. Bell and I took turns dancing with Mrs. Robson, whilst Robson stayed at the table drinking wine. During the long evening, Mrs. Robson was seldom at the table, Bell and I were there half the time, and Robson was always there. As we consumed a total of four bottles of wine, it follows that Robson drank two bottles and Bell and I consumed one bottle each. Mrs. Robson's lips had scarcely been touched, as she was always in action on the dance floor. Fortunately Robson, although barely mobile, remained in good spirits, and Mrs. Robson remembered the location of their hotel. Bell and I, rather like the blind leading the blind, succeeded in assisting our colleague to his overnight abode.

The Basel Museum of Art (*Oeffentliche Kunstsammlung*) was nearby, and I discovered its unusual holdings of Hans Holbein (1497-1543) and Paul Klee (1879-1940). The presence of the Holbein examples dated from the time he lived in Basel, but Klee was Swiss by birth and an entire room was devoted to some twenty of his whimsical paintings.

Following the General Assembly, I visited Hintenberger in Mainz but, although I was expected, it proved to be bad timing. The institute was in a panic at the arrival of Rudolf L. Mossbauer, who had been offered the directorship, in succession to Mattauch. In 1958, whilst still a graduate student at the *Technische Hochschule* in Munich, Mossbauer had discovered the Mossbauer Effect. Then, in 1961, at the unprecedented early age of thirty-one, he had been awarded the Nobel Prize for physics. As it turned out, he declined the offer, preferring to remain at the *Technische Hochschule*, where he had been a professor for two years, following three years at tho California Institute of Technology.

His early discovery was reminiscent of E.H. Hall's discovery of the Hall Effect in 1879, when he was still a graduate student at Johns Hopkins University. Hall became a professor at Harvard, lived to be eighty-two or eighty-three and could often be seen at meetings of the American Physical Society. On one occasion, a young man saw his name tag and asked, "Are you any relation to old Hall?" Hall replied, "I *am* old Hall!"

Leaving Hintenberger and the rest to deal with Mossbauer, I spent the weekend in Bacharach, a town on the Rhine that was holding its annual wine festival. This was one of a series of festivals organized by the wine towns in the Mittelrhein, so that an inveterate imbiber could spend every weekend during September and October in this pleasant pastime. Crowds had descended on Bacharach, and local vintners staffed booths where a glass could be bought for fifty *Pfennigs*, or fifteen cents Canadian. On another occasion, I attended a similar event at Boppard, a larger town downstream from Bacharach. In both places the visitors had brought many *Pfennigs*, perhaps too many, but the mood was joyous, and there were several days for recovery before the next baccanale.

During these and other visits to the Mittelrhein, I've recorded the traffic on that major commercial artery. In the 1960s, during daylight hours, a substantial ship passed every two minutes, and a train every five minutes. By 1998, the ships had declined to one every four minutes, whilst the trains now passed every four minutes. In 1998, however, the ships were mostly tankers and were much larger than the 1960s' versions. I recommend this census activity to those who have nothing better to do.

The thirteenth General Assembly was held in Dubrovnik, from 10 to 13 September 1969. Dubrovnik was a peculiar site for the meeting, because it had no resident physicists. It must have been chosen for its charm, which was considerable. Herzberg, Bell, and I were the Canadian delegates. Bell brought his wife, Jean, and their daughter. I had left Winnipeg on 5 September, en route to a mass spectrometry conference in Kyoto before pushing on to Dubrovnik. I was back in Winnipeg on the evening of 13 September, having circumnavigated the globe in eight days and having slept in Tokyo (one night), Kyoto (two nights), Hong Kong (one night), Rome (one afternoon), Dubrovnik (three nights), and whenever else I could get comfortable. I had hoped to slide unnoticed into Winnipeg time, but my body ordained otherwise. Needless to say, I was not at my best in Dubrovnik, but I was able to give the report of the Commission on Atomic Masses and Related Constants, of which I was now the president.

Josef Mattauch: Distinguished Physicist and Friend

Josef Mattauch, my friend, and to some extent my scientific mentor, was born in 1895 in Ostrau, Moravia, the son of a teacher. He had his Ph.D. under Professor Felix Ehrenhaft at the University of Vienna.

During Ehrenhaft's long career, he announced two startling discoveries that were subsequently to be proven wrong. The first – in the 1920s – was his discovery of the "sub-electron," a charge smaller than that determined by Robert Millikan at the University of Chicago in 1911 in his celebrated Oil-Drop Experiment. The sub-electron was eventually debunked, but not before several of Ehrenhaft's Ph.D. students had provided experimental evidence for its existence. The second arresting discovery was made in 1948, whilst Ehrenhaft was in exile at the Brooklyn Polytechnic Institute. Here he observed "free magnetic poles," that is, south magnetic poles unaccompanied by north magnetic poles (and vice versa), contrary to the accepted view that the two were part and parcel of the same thing. Ehrenhaft's discovery and its subsequent rebuttal enlivened the *Physical Review* in 1948-49 but, in the end, Ehrenhaft's observations were seen as artifacts, and older physicists sadly recalled the almost-forgotten sub-electron fiasco. Notwithstanding, following World War II, Ehrenhaft was reinstated as professor at the University of Vienna, as part of the compensatory action taken by the Austrian government towards Jews who had lost their positions as a result of the *Anschluss* of 1938. Thereafter, until his retirement, he exercised traditional German professorial authority, although his very presence cast doubt on the credibility of work reported by students in his institute. I once had some contact with R.F.K. Herzog, who became a mass spectroscopist but who had been a post-war doctoral student with Ehrenhaft. I had great difficulty extracting from him the name of his thesis supervisor.

Mattauch was the first of Ehrenhaft's students to fail to observe the sub-electron. Try as he would, he always ended up with Millikan's value, which did not please Ehrenhaft. When Mattauch presented his findings to a meeting of the German Physical Society, he was disappointed that they provoked no discussion. Later, meeting a distinguished professor in the hall, he asked his opinion of the results. The professor confessed that he no longer listened when Ehrenhaft's students spoke. "But," said Mattauch, "I was unable to find the sub-electron. I only found Millikan's value." "In that case," said the professor, "would you be interested in working with Millikan?" And through this notable's efforts, Mattauch spent 1926 and 1927 at the California Institute of Technology on a Rockefeller fellowship, where he worked with W.R. Smythe on an early time-of-flight mass spectrometer.

Shortly after Mattauch's departure from Vienna, a visitor to Ehrenhaft's institute asked where young Mattauch was. Ehrenhaft, who had been furious at Mattauch's desertion to the enemy, but who was nothing if not resilient, replied that he had sent Mattauch to Pasadena to find out what Millikan had been doing wrong.

On his arrival in Pasadena, Mattauch was taken in tow by a young Swiss physicist, Fritz Zwicky (1898-1974), who later became one of Cal Tech's characters. Whilst standing at a street corner with Zwicky and some others, Mattauch felt the urge to practise his English. During a pause in the conversation, he observed, "How many cars there be!" After a brief period to allow that thunderbolt to settle, he added, "How fast they go!" Zwicky quickly took him to one side and told him not to take part in the conversation until he could say more interesting things. Later, however, Mattauch developed a fluency and elegance in English that many a native speaker could envy.

On another occasion, Zwicky took Mattauch skiing in Glacier National Park and proposed that they set foot in Canada. When Mattauch expressed fear that they might not be allowed re-entry to the United States, Zwicky assured him that there would be no problem. "When they ask if you're an American, just say, 'You're goddamned right I am!'"

After his stint at Cal Tech, Mattauch returned to Vienna, where he and R. Herzog constructed a remarkable double-focussing mass spectrograph before he joined Otto Hahn in 1939 at the Kaiser Wilhelm Institute in Berlin. There, he was largely sheltered from Nazi pressure, as the Kaiser Wilhelm Society was a private body, and its non-political character was maintained by its president, Max Planck. After the war, he spent some time in Switzerland but had little opportunity for normal research until 1951, when he assumed the directorship of the newly established Max Planck Institute for Chemistry in Mainz. There, he built a strong mass spectrometry group, which included H.H. Hintenberger, and also became a leader in tabulating and evaluating atomic mass data. He was the first chair of the IUPAP Commission on Atomic Masses and Related Constants and, more than any other, was responsible for unifying the chemical and physical scales of atomic weight/mass via the medium of $^{12}C = 12$. He retired as director in 1966 and died in Klosterneuburg, near Vienna, on 10 August 1976.

Mattauch's sixtieth birthday had been fittingly celebrated in 1955. As his seventieth approached, I was asked to speak at the formal ceremony marking the event. I prepared suitable remarks, which I took to Professor Karl Maurer, head of German at the University of Manitoba, with the request that he translate them into German. I had referred (in English) to Mattauch's "charm," and this proved a challenge, not only to Maurer but to the entire German Department. Eventually, they came up with the word used to describe the attractive power of a magnet – *die Anziehungskraft* – which seemed particularly suitable, inasmuch as magnets were central to Mattauch's mass spectrometers. Armed with the elegantly translated text, my wife and I set off for the *Geburtstag*. When called upon to speak, I claimed that Mattauch's charm was so great that my wife had insisted on coming, which led to the punch line: "*Seine Anziehungskraft hat mir fünftausend Mark gekostet.*"

The evening before the celebration, my wife and I were invited to a small dinner party at the home of the Austrian consul in Mainz. Such an honorary appointment is much sought after for reasons of prestige, and also because the holder is entitled to special consular licence plates, which allow him to flout parking restrictions. The consul was a wealthy industrialist who had known Mattauch for fourteen years on his seventieth birthday. In addition to Mattauch and his wife, the other guests were Otto Hahn and his care-giver, Adolf and Frau Butenandt, and Henry and Katherine Duckworth. Butenandt, a biochemist, had won the Nobel Prize for chemistry in 1939, but had been prevented by Hitler from accepting it (Hitler was infuriated at the award of the 1935 Nobel Peace Prize to Carl von Ossietzky, a pacifist and ardent anti-Nazi). Butenandt was now president of the Max Planck Society, having succeeded Hahn to that prestigious post. My wife and I were there because Mattauch had asked that we be included. There were three remarkable features to the evening: the walls of the room in which we gathered prior to dinner were bedecked with the heads of deer, each labelled as the largest of its type to have been shot in a particular year; the white wine that was served was fourteen years old (very old for white wine; many bottles must have been tested); and hanging in the dining room was a painting by Pieter Breughel the Elder, which the consul's wife had recently purchased, perhaps the last in private hands.

Atomic Mass Conferences: 1960 to 1992

The Atomic Mass Conference held in Mainz in the summer of 1956, in belated celebration of Mattauch's sixtieth birthday, was so successful in bringing together the several branches of physics that contribute to our knowledge of atomic masses that a follow-up conference was inevitable. Ten such conferences have since taken place; I have attended all but the last two.

The first of these conferences was held in Hamilton and was timed to adjoin the IUPAP General Assembly meeting in Ottawa, in the knowledge that some of the IUPAP delegates would choose to attend. In addition, many others came from various parts of the world. Modest financial support came from IUPAP and major support from the NRC. The Study Commission had since been given full commission status, and the new commission provided guidance in the preparation of the program. The conference itself was held at McMaster University between 12 and 15 September. Some twenty-five papers were presented to an audience of about sixty. Scientific business came to a halt on the Wednesday afternoon, when all embarked by bus for *Much Ado about Nothing* at Stratford, Ontario. The conference banquet was held at the Royal Connaught Hotel in downtown Hamilton. The proceedings were published by late December.

M.J. Higatsberger, head of the Austrian Nuclear Energy Authority, organized the second Atomic Mass Conference, which was held from 15 to 19 July 1963 in the imposing confines of the Hofburg Palace in Vienna. Higatsberger also gave some of us a splendid luncheon elsewhere in the Palace, and all attended an evening reception in a Palace garden. Unfortunately, mosquitoes had advance notice of this last event. More exciting was a trip to Grinzing, on a height of ground northwest of Vienna, to taste the new wine. Three of the Russian delegates spurned the wine and took a taxi back to their hotel to fetch vodka. Hans Staub, a corresponding member of the Commission from Zurich, over-compensated for the Russians and, in his enthusiasm, bought a bouquet of roses for my wife, an act that did not please *his* wife. On another evening, we attended the Theater an der Wien for a performance of *Eine Nacht in Venedig.*

The third conference was to have been organized in Utrecht, Holland, by Aaldert Wapstra, a member of the Commission, but he had moved to Amsterdam and felt unable to honour his commitment. In the circumstances, Ben Hogg, Bob Barber, Robin Connor, Max Kettner, and other colleagues cooperated with me to hold it at the University of Manitoba from 28 August to 1 September 1967. We had a grand supper on a paddle-wheel riverboat, and the university convened a special convocation to award honorary degrees to Josef Mattauch and Jesse W.M. DuMond. The latter was an authority on fundamental constants from the California Institute of Technology and a member of the Commission. DuMond was married to a French woman and spent part of his time in Paris. He was a man of strong principle, and during the American presidential election of 1968, he made a special trip back to the United States to vote *against* Nixon.

The 1971 conference, the fourth, was organized by Brian Petley at the National Physical Laboratory in Teddington, England, some twenty miles west of London. We stayed in London and commuted daily to Teddington. The conference banquet was held at the Rembrandt Hotel in South Kensington, and the delegates enjoyed a cruise on the Thames. Their attention was especially drawn by the guide to Lady Astor's former villa, Cliveden, where Profumo first set eyes on Christine Keeler in the buff.

The French know how to do things with style. The fifth conference, held in Paris in 1975, was opened by the band of the Republican Guard playing *La Marseillaise* at full volume, an auditory experience that puts bagpipes to shame. The conference banquet was held on the first level of the Eiffel Tower. One of the Russian delegates, Vitali Goldanskii, was being monitored by a Russian agent who had the good grace to remain at the foot of the elevator and allow Goldanskii to eat his meal unobserved. By now, Frau Staub had forgiven my wife for accepting flowers from her inebriated husband, and they spent pleasant days together in the art museums of Paris.

Walter Benenson of Michigan State University in East Lansing organized the sixth conference in 1979. I was so preoccupied with domestic matters that I attended for one day only, and that was to chair a session.

The seventh conference was held in 1984 in a Lufthansa centre for the training of flight attendants located south of Darmstadt. The conference banquet was held at Kloster Erbach, an ancient monastery north of Mainz on the right bank of the Rhine. Prior to the meal, the present members of a choir that had been singing Gregorian chant for several centuries gave us a taste of their authentic renderings.

The eighth conference was cancelled because of the Gulf War, but I reported for duty at the ninth, which was held in 1992 in the wine town of Bernkastel, celebrated for its *Doktor* vineyards. One afternoon, we were taken by riverboat to the neighbouring town of Traben-Trarbach and challenged to walk back to Bernkastel, a very demanding exercise. I may have been the oldest human ever to have accomplished the feat. At the conference banquet, held in a former monastery in Wehlen (now owned by a winery), I was presented with the SUN-AMCO medal of IUPAP for my contribution to the precise determination of atomic masses. My old friend Aaldert Wapstra gave the citation, and another old friend from antedeluvian times, Richard Cohen, was in attendance, as were my younger colleagues Robert Barber and Kumar Sharma from the University of Manitoba. It was a satisfying swan song to my lengthy association with this long-running, and significant, series of conferences.

The National Research Council of Canada

The NRC was established in 1916 to advise the government on scientific matters and to stimulate research. The immediate concern was to catalyze university research in support of secondary industries, particularly those suffering from wartime shortages. But other scientific research was also encouraged, and a modest number of scholarships and fellowships was provided for young scientists. Most of the members of the Honorary Advisory Council (the body that dispersed the funds) came from the university hierarchy of the time. The Council had no laboratories of its own. In the late 1920s, the need for its own laboratory became apparent, and the splendid structure on Sussex Drive in Ottawa was completed in 1932 to house three types of research: that needed for a bureau of standards; that which would solve problems identified by industry; and long-term research thought to be beneficial to Canada.

The establishment of the laboratory was the achievement of Henry Marshall Tory, president of NRC from 1927 to 1935. He had come from the presidency of the University of Alberta but became *persona non grata* with the Bennett government of 1930. He was allowed to continue in office for five years, however, albeit with constant hectoring from his political masters. He was succeeded by General A.G.L. McNaughton, who had been parachuted into the position, but rapidly gained the respect of the staff, especially when it was seen that he had influence with the government. As a military man, he saw the signs of approaching war and set out to prepare the laboratory to support the war effort, as and when such support was needed. At the outbreak of war, McNaughton was granted leave to command the Canadian Forces Overseas, and the newspapers frequently featured his resolute visage. The direction of the NRC reverted to his deputy, Charles Jack Mackenzie, who, in 1944, became president in name, as well as in fact.

During World War II, all wartime research was conducted under the auspices of the NRC. Radar was not a pre-war division but became a wartime one, as did the Canadian participation in the atomic bomb project. Thus, I had been a temporary employee of NRC for the three-year period 1942 to 1945 and had had a worm's eye view of its operation. After the war, Mackenzie hived off the defence-related work to the Defence Research Board (established in 1947) and the atomic work to the Atomic Energy of Canada Ltd. (established in 1952), whilst managing to retain most of the other huge gains in staff entitlement that had occurred during the war. Mackenzie was succeeded by E.W.R. Steacie in 1952.

The NRC was governed by the Honorary Advisory Council. Despite the word *advisory* in its title, the Council dispensed the funds that the government had allocated for the support of university research and also oversaw NRC's own laboratories. It was not involved, however, in negotiations with the government with respect to the level of funding for these activities.

When I was appointed to the Honorary Advisory Council in 1961 it was chaired by Steacie, and the members were: B.G. Ballard, vice-president (scientific), NRC; H.E. Duckworth, chair of Physics, McMaster University; R.F. Farquharson, chair, Medical Research Council; P.R. Gendron, dean of Science, University of Ottawa; P.A. Giguère, director of Chemistry, Laval University; H.E. Gunning, head of Chemistry, University of Alberta; F.R. Hayes, head of Biology, Dalhousie University; Claude Jodoin, president, Canadian Labour Congress; Paul Lorrain, head of Physics, University of Montreal; C.J.MacKenzie, past president, NRC; I. McTaggart-Cowan, head of Zoology, University of British Columbia; A.D. Misener, director, Ontario Research Foundation; F.T. Rosser, vice-president (administration), NRC; B.W. Sargent, head of Physics, Queen's University; L.H.J. Shebeski, professor of plant science, University of Manitoba; J.H. Shipley, vice-president (research), Canadian Industries Ltd.; J.W.T. Spinks, president, University of Saskatchewan; E.W.R. Steacie, president, NRC; D.L. Thompson, dean of Graduate Studies, McGill University; F.J. Toole, head of Chemistry, University of New Brunswick; J.Tuzo Wilson, professor of geophysics University of Toronto. Except for me, these men were giants, with enormous influence in universities and technologically based industries. I was in awe of them.

At my first meeting, Steacie announced that he wished to discuss a special matter before addressing the regular agenda. This concerned Paul Gagnon, a professor of chemistry at Laval University. It appeared that Gagnon had just completed a stint in Paris as science advisor to the Canadian ambassador. Prior to this, he had served on the Honorary Advisory Council and on the Defence Research Board, and he had come regularly to Ottawa in other scientific capacities. This was at a time when there were few senior scientists in French Canada, and Gagnon had been obliged to do more than his share of advising the government. Now he was back in Canada, which he had served well, but his position at Laval had long since been filled. Steacie stated that Ottawa owed Gagnon a living and that the NRC was the body to provide it. Accordingly, we voted to appoint Paul Gagnon, late of Paris, to the position of official host to visiting delegations, to continue in office until he reached the age of retirement. I occasionally saw him in the performance of his duties, which he discharged with incomparable Gallic panache. This was my introduction to Steacie's candour and decisiveness.

E. W.R. Steacie: President of NRC

Ned Steacie exercised a greater influence for good on Canadian science than any other individual before or since. He was smart, he was confident, he was charming, and he was well connected. A native of Montreal and graduate of McGill, he had studied at Frankfurt, Leipzig, and King's College, London, before returning to McGill in 1928 to begin the slow progress through the academic ranks that that conservative institution felt was good for the souls of young academics. He was well established as an associate professor of chemistry by 1939, when McNaughton called him to direct the division of chemistry at NRC, a position he held until his appointment as president in 1952. Whatever his title at the time, it was he who built NRC into a laboratory of international repute and into an agent for the vigorous stimulation of scientific research in the universities. Following his premature death from kidney disease on 28 August 1962 and the subsequent infiltration of science by politicians, the wail was often heard, "If Steacie were only alive!"

Steacie's predecessor, C.J. Mackenzie, had at one time been dean of Engineering at the University of Saskatchewan. He was intelligent, agreeable, and filled to the brim with common sense, but he had no personal experience in research. Thus, in the university grants program and in the laboratory's own research program, he had been guided by Steacie who, as a distinguished photochemist, had the complete respect and confidence of all researchers. Further, he had the confidence of C.D. Howe, who was powerful in the Cabinet. During Mackenzie's presidency and the first half of Steacie's, I shouldn't be surprised if what later came to be known as "science policy" was decided once a year by Howe and the president of NRC during an agreeable lunch. After the election of Diefenbaker's Conservatives in 1957, Steacie had to deal with Gordon Churchill, who (fortunately) came to be convinced of the need to expand scientific research, although fiscal restraint had been a major plank in Diefenbaker's platform.

An American by birth, Howe was a visionary for his adopted country, and his mind was centred on matters of national concern. So, it was not surprising, whilst officiating at the opening of Howe Hall, a new men's residence at Dalhousie University, that he fervently declared, "Canada has long needed a new men's residence." It was Howe, of course, who initiated and forced through Parliament the legislation for the trans-Canada pipeline.

Steacie's funeral service was held in a small Anglican Church in the Ottawa district of New Edinburgh, across the Rideau River from the NRC Building. Many, if not most, of the members of the Honorary Advisory

Council attended the service and were seated at the front of the church. It was a glorious summer day but a sombre occasion. We all mourned Steacie as a friend and leader but, selfishly, we all wondered who would succeed him.

Following the service, we repaired to the Steacie home for a reception. Mrs. Steacie was gracious, as always, and had a word with each of us. She drew me aside and said that her husband had wished that I had been old enough to succeed him.

Steacie's most spectacular innovation was NRC's Post-Doctoral Program. On the one hand, it enabled new Canadian Ph.D.s to spend two or three years in research laboratories abroad, particularly in the United Kingdom and Europe. Thus, I had one student (William McLatchie, now at Queen's) who held the award at Oxford and two others (Scott Whineray, now at University of Auckland; and James Macdonald, tragically deceased) who held their awards at the Bohr Institute in Copenhagen. On the other hand, the Program brought recent Ph.D. graduates to Canada, especially to the NRC laboratories. This infusion of young talent from abroad, attracted by the outstanding staff that Steacie and others had recruited, created in Ottawa a ferment of energy and creativity that, I expect, exceeded even Steacie's hopes and, even more, his expectations. The atmosphere became so rife with speculation and fervour, and was so bereft of bureaucracy, that the place was hard to recognize as a government laboratory.

On the completion of their terms, some post-doctoral fellows joined the permanent staff of NRC, whilst many others took up permanent posts in Canadian universities. John Polanyi of the University of Toronto (Nobel Prize for chemistry in 1986) and Michael Smith of the University of British Columbia (Nobel Prize for chemistry in 1993) came to Canada in this way. Others returned to their natural habitats with warm feelings for Canada and served as valuable contacts for all of us in all parts of the world.

Central to the success of the Program was its scope. *Many* awards were offered each year. The Division of Chemistry alone, during the period of operation of the scheme (1948-1975), played host to 900 post-doctoral fellows. (Characteristic of the times, only sixteen of these were women.) Thus, there was the force of numbers as well as the force of quality.

The Grant-Screening Committee

Prior to my appointment to the Advisory Council itself, I was asked to participate in the test of a new procedure for evaluating grant applications from university professors. Prior to this trial, all such applications had been reviewed by the directors of the relevant divisions, who made recommendations to the entire council, where the individual applications were discussed and the final decisions were made. For example, the applications for physics were reviewed by Gerhard Herzberg, assisted by his right-hand man, Alex Douglas, before presentation to the Council. These were outstanding physicists (Herzberg later received the Nobel Prize), which ensured that high standards were imposed. This system had been workable as long as the number of applications was small, but it was becoming quite unworkable with the rapid growth of universities and the consequent increase in grant applications for research grants.

In the trial of a new system, an informal grant-screening committee was established for applications in physics. This was chaired by William ("Willie") Watson, head of Physics at Toronto and member of the Honorary Advisory Council. Herzberg and Douglas were members of the new committee, and two others were added who had no previous experience with the process. These were Larkin Kerwin of Laval University and Henry Duckworth (McMaster). Our recommendations were taken to the Advisory Council by Watson where, I understand, they received virtually blanket approval.

This informal committee continued for two years, and we had very frank meetings. Kerwin and I had visited most of the departments in the country in other capacities, and our knowledge supplemented that of Herzberg and Douglas. Watson was not as well informed, but his opinions were well formed, a factor that enlivened our meetings. For two or three days in March we discussed the merits of 150 to 200 applicants. We examined the feasibility of each application, to be sure, but mostly we focussed on the ability of the applicant. If the applicant was a new, young assistant professor, we recommended that he (there were no shes in those days) be given $5,000 for each of two years, to see what he could do with it. Thereafter, he would be judged on performance. The other applicants – good, bad and indifferent – were discussed in a circumstantial way, as we pooled our knowledge of past performances and present needs. Attempts were made to give modest assistance to those in small institutions and to those in larger ones who were not hotshots but could benefit from the supervision of an occasional graduate student. The hotshots were supported as strongly as the purse would permit, with little reference to their detailed proposals. If they were good men, whatever they did would be worthwhile. Incidentally, the application forms comprised four sheets and could be filled out by an applicant during a leisurely afternoon or evening.

Following the successful test in physics, grant-screening committees were established in all subjects. Subsequently, applicants were required to provide much more information about themselves and their projects. Also, the research proposals were scrutinized carefully with the help of referees. These measures were dictated by the increasing number of applications, but I doubt if the end result was any fairer than our rough justice. When I was appointed to the Honorary Council in 1961, I became chair of the Physics Grant-Screening Committee and presented its report to the council.

Ballard becomes President of NRC

B. Guy Ballard, vice-president (scientific), was appointed to succeed Steacie. He, himself, heard the news of his appointment whilst shaving one morning with an ear to the radio. It was not an auspicious beginning.

I felt that Ballard entered upon his presidency with some trepidation. In the past, he had dealt primarily with in-house matters and with persons with generally similar points of view, not with professors who took pride in thinking differently. Further, he was not well known in government circles and, by nature, was somewhat stiff in his manner towards those whom he did not know well. Finally, he had a severe hearing problem, which cut him off from many of the asides and much of the banter that accompany a meeting. But he was a man of pride and determination and he strove conscientiously to discharge his task. As I was re-appointed to the Council for a second three-year term, I sat under his gavel for a total of five years. After some initial frostiness, we came to respect one another and, within the limits of his natural aloofness, became good friends.

When Ballard left office in 1967, he had completed five years of a difficult mandate. It was bad enough to have succeeded Steacie and to have been compared constantly to him. But, in addition, critics of NRC who would have found little audience in the face of Steacie's persona had since emerged from the woodwork and voiced their criticisms in circles to which Ballard did not have easy access. Under his mandate, and mostly for reasons beyond his control, the NRC began slowly to unravel. His successor, William Schneider, did not inherit a comfortable mantle.

At that time, the research support for university professors and their students came principally through the NRC, in the form of a special vote approved by the Treasury Board. The case for this university support was made annually to the Treasury Board by the president of NRC; hence, it was crucial to the Universities that the president be sympathetic to the cause.

When Ballard was appointed, he was an unknown quantity, as he had had little contact with the university grants program. In the spring of 1963, however, he was speaking in Toronto and was reported in the *Globe and Mail* as saying that he believed that research in Canadian universities was adequately supported. As the officer formerly responsible for the NRC laboratories, he may have felt that Steacie had overemphasized the university needs. Whatever the reason, it was an incorrect and alarming statement, and I resolved to take whatever action lay within my power.

Fortunately, the Canadian Association of Physicists was scheduled to meet at Laval University in early June, prior to the June meeting in Ottawa of the Honorary Advisory Council, and practically all heads of physics departments would be at the Laval meeting. I prepared a rough, handwritten sheet calling for the following information: Name of university; number of $20,000 staff; number of $10,000 staff; number of $5,000 staff; number of "dead ducks." The best researchers were assumed to merit research grants of $20,000, the "dead ducks" deserved nothing, and the rest fell into the other two categories.

A meeting with the heads was arranged, and they agreed, on a strictly confidential basis and with no names used, to rate their departmental colleagues in the manner suggested and return the forms to me before leaving Quebec City. Thus, as a special-agenda item at the NRC meeting a few days later, I was able to present for physics a rough-and-ready estimate of operating-grant needs, an estimate that was well above the currently available funds. I don't think Ballard cared much for my approach, but others joined the refrain, and Ballard never repeated his assertion about adequate funding. Instead, he established a forecasting committee with John Spinks (president of the University of Saskatchewan) as chair and me as one of the members. The committee met on 24 October 1963 and made an interim report to the Honorary Advisory Council three weeks later. The report was consistent with my emergency survey, and it must have convinced Ballard because he was able to announce with pride at the 19 March 1964 meeting of the Council that the allocation for university research had been increased *by more than 35 percent*.

Spinks's term on the NRC Council expired in June 1964, and he was replaced as chair of the Forecasting Committee by Louis-Phillipe Bonneau, dean of Engineering at Laval. I continued on the committee, which, I believe, held only one more meeting. But my main contribution had been made before the committee was established.

Gerhard Herzberg and the Physics Division

Gerhard Herzberg was the director of Physics at NRC when the trial was made of the grant-screening committee. He had been appointed director in 1949 but had come to that position by a winding path. In the academic year 1933-34, he had been an assistant at the *Technische Hochschule* in Darmstadt when a young chemist came from the University of Saskatchewan. John Spinks, the chemist in question, had been asked to take a year off, as a Depression measure, in order that the university might save his salary. He came to know Herzberg, a spectroscopist, and became aware of his concern for the future, inasmuch as Mrs. Herzberg was Jewish. On his return to Saskatoon, Spinks persuaded the physics Department to offer Herzberg a job. Thus, Saskatchewan gained an already-recognized authority on atomic and molecular spectra. Spinks, himself, later became president of the University and served in that office with distinction from 1959 to 1974.

Herzberg remained at Saskatchewan throughout the war and until 1945, when he was appointed professor of spectroscopy at the Yerkes Observatory of the University of Chicago. Three years later, Steacie persuaded him to return to Canada to invigorate NRC's Physics Division and, from that vantage point, to stimulate physics in the universities.

I had known Herzberg through his book *Atomic Spectra,* which Mulliken had used in a course by the same name at Chicago. I first met him personally in June 1950, at the meeting of the Royal Society of Canada at Queen's University. At that time, the professional societies were not well-developed, and most university research was reported at the annual meetings of the Royal Society. In order to maintain my Canadian contacts, I had driven from Connecticut to present our recent atomic mass determinations, which were beginning to attract attention. Herzberg was interested in the work, and we discussed the possibility of moving my laboratory to NRC. This did not go past the discussion stage, but, when I moved to McMaster the next year, he did much to encourage and assist me.

The NRC laboratories had two functions: to serve as a bureau of standards and to conduct research that was in the interest of Canada. In the first category, in physics, there were facilities to calibrate accurate instruments, to provide accurate time, and to discharge other similar functions. In the second category, Herzberg (and Steacie) took the view that whatever was good for the world was good for Canada. Thus, many of the research projects were not directed at Canadian problems but took their place on the world stage. This disinterested view was an intoxicating idea, perhaps Utopian, but it was consistent with the optimism of the times. Later, however, it was to incur the criticism of those who looked for near-term return on research done in government laboratories.

In 1952, work in the bureau of standards and applied research were removed to a new division; called Applied Physics, under the direction of Leslie Howlett. This, I believe, was Herzberg's idea, although it may have originated with Steacie, whose Division of Chemistry was similarly split at the same time. In any event, the new arrangement freed Herzberg of much administrative work, in which he had little professional interest. The new physics division concentrated principally on spectroscopy, low temperature physics, and nuclear magnetic resonance, and attracted post-doctoral students of outstanding quality. It was now a division of "pure" physics.

The Physics Division reached its apogee in 1971 when Herzberg was awarded the Nobel Prize for chemistry for his research on the spectral properties of hydrogen. The fact that the award was in chemistry rather than physics may have indicated that more good physicists existed than good chemists. The award gave Herzberg a pulpit at a time when pure research was coming under attack and needed defenders who were seen to be persons of consequence. He used the platform at every opportunity, but his advocacy had little effect in the corridors of political power. The opposing tide was running too strong. But the Division of Physics has remained a bastion of research that is undertaken for its own sake, and Herzberg was an active participant in its outstanding work until his death in 1999.

Herzberg was extremely thorough in everything he undertook. In 1967, at the end of his term as president of the Royal Society of Canada, he used "Hydrogen" as the title of his presidential address. He spoke for a full hour, using numerous supporting slides. He had begun his address by saying that until we understood hydrogen (the lightest element) we couldn't understand anything. The incoming president, geologist James Harrison, said, in thanking Herzberg, that he believed that if we could understand hydrogen, we could understand anything!

The second most important member of the Physics Division, although he would have been the last to admit it, was Alex Douglas. Douglas was from Saskatchewan, where he had done his M.Sc. with Herzberg before obtaining his Ph.D. from Pennyslvania State College. He joined the NRC soon after the war and devoted himself to Herzberg and to the division, freeing Herzberg of many administrative duties. He was also a superb spectroscopist in his own right, but his modesty and self-sacrifice often hid his scientific excellence from view. He died in 1981.

The Need for a Science Policy?

In 1963, the Royal Commission on Government Organization (the "Glassco" Commission) expressed concern that the scientific activities of the government were fragmented and uncoordinated. To correct this fault, the Commission recommended that a minister be made responsible for science policy and that this minister be supported by a small science secretariat and advised by a national scientific advisory council. This last point was at odds with the original act establishing the NRC, which had specified that the NRC advise the government on scientific matters.

C.J. Mackenzie was asked by the prime minister to advise what action should be taken on the Glassco recommendations. On 19 March 1964, at his last meeting as a member of the Honorary Advisory Council (he had been a member since 1935), Mackenzie reviewed for the council the gist of his report: first, the NRC should continue what it was doing but seek an amendment to its act removing the "advice to government" part, inasmuch as it had not been relevant for many years. Second, he saw no harm in a science secretariat and a science council, as long as they concerned themselves with broad policies and priorities and didn't interfere with the existing government laboratories including, and especially, those of the NRC. His valedictory to us was, "Do not worry, everything will be all right."

In the spring of 1964, the Science Secretariat was established as part of the Privy Council Office, under the directorship of Frank Forward, a professor of engineering from British Columbia. Two years later, the Science Council was established, under the chairmanship of Omand Solandt, the founding president of the Defence Research Board. The Science Council had nine representatives from universities and seven from business and industry. These were leavened, however, by seven full and four associate members from the government sector. To my knowledge, none of the non-government group had ever served on the NRC, and some were known to be critical of its operation.

Two years later, in 1968, a new county was heard from, namely, the Senate of Canada. Senator Maurice Lamontagne, a former professor of economics at the Universities of Laval and Ottawa, a former assistant deputy minister of Northern Affairs and Natural Resources, a former economic advisor to Lester Pearson, and subsequently a member of Pearson's Cabinet, had been summoned to the Senate in 1967, where he lost no time in establishing a senate special committee on science policy, which began holding hearings and inviting briefs. Lamontagne had stated that Canada had no science policy and was careening rudderless in a world that was increasingly dependent upon science and technology, an opinion that he had developed whilst lurking in the shadows of power. His committee provided a forum for scores of individuals and organizations to put forward their often-conflicting views.

There were malcontents, to be sure, amongst those making presentations to the committee, there were those attempting to defend the status quo, and there were all degrees in between. Most of the malcontents were enemies of the NRC for one reason or another. Some were unsuccessful or underfunded applicants for research grants. Some felt that the NRC laboratories were robbing the university program of its fair share and that the program should be entrusted to a new agency with that special mandate. Some who had good opinions of themselves were resentful that they had never been appointed to the Honorary Advisory Council. Still others thought that the NRC laboratories were not dedicated enough to Canadian problems. And still others, it must be said, were motivated by the view that Canada's scientific effort should be better integrated and should be guided by some overall policy.

As the Lamontagne hearings proceeded, and he, himself, seized any opportunity to trumpet the crisis, the scientific community became polarized into pro-NRC and anti-NRC camps. I had been sufficiently involved with NRC to believe that the university program had not suffered from its juxtaposition to the laboratories. On the question whether or not NRC should continue to be entrusted with the university grants program, I found myself firmly on the side of the existing arrangement. The program benefited from the high standards imposed by NRC scientists, it provided an effective link between universities and government, it was well run, and duplication of it would lead to an unnecessary duplication of bureaucracy.

As to the relevance of NRC in-house and grant-supported research, I realize, in retrospect, that I was more impressed by research that was in vogue internationally than by research directed primarily at national problems. My own work on the determination of atomic masses had brought me into contact with others in the United States and Europe, and it was a heady experience. I was not that big a fish, to be sure, but I was swimming in the Atlantic Ocean and not in Lake Winnipeg. If I were given another chance, I would not change my own research career, but I would place more value on physics applied to Canadian problems.

Schneider becomes President

William Schneider, a distinguished chemist and the vice-president of NRC, succeeded Ballard in 1967 and continued in office until 1980. He inherited an organization that was under fire from individual critics and was under scrutiny by the Science Secretariat, the Science Council, and the Lamontagne Committee. Mackenzie had promised that everything would be all right; he should have warned us that Pandora's box was about to be opened.

My second (and last-allowable) term on the Honorary Advisory Council ended as Schneider's presidency began. Shortly thereafter, he asked if I would consider the position of vice-president (university program). I was not able to accept the offer but was much honoured that he had made it.

Although I became preoccupied with other matters, I was aware that the Senate Committee made its report (in three volumes: 1970, 1972, and 1973). It recommended that the Ministry of State for Science and Technology (MOSST), which had been established in the interval (1971), be given more authority and that the university grants program be removed from both the NRC and the Canada Council (which had been the granting agency for the humanities and social sciences). It also quoted at great length the wise sayings of Anthony Wedgwood Benn, hereditary-lord-turned-commoner, who was minister of Technology in the Wilson (Labour) government. For example, special emphasis should be given to the statement, "Science as an arm of economic advance must be demand-oriented and not self-generated." Benn later became known as "the thick edge of the wedge."

The first minister for MOSST was C.M. Drury who, a few years earlier as minister for Industry, had stated: "We must give top priority to scientific and technical endeavours directed toward economic and social goals." Pure research was clearly in the doghouse. In my view, MOSST never amounted to much, for the simple reason that it controlled no money. There was lots of hype, lots of promises, lots of bluster, but no power. Nevertheless, the current was running against the NRC and the university grants programs were removed from it and the Canada Council in 1978. Despite my opposition to this change, I was appointed a charter member of one of the new granting agencies: the Natural Science and Engineering Research Council.

Atomic Energy of Canada Ltd.

The research and development associated with nuclear energy, which had operated under the wing of the National Research Council, was transferred in 1952 to a newly created crown corporation, Atomic Energy of Canada Ltd (AECL). Its laboratories were located at Chalk River, some 100 miles upstream from Ottawa on the Ottawa River. The employees of the Chalk River laboratory lived in a newly created town named Deep

River, which may have housed more brain power per acre than any other spot in Canada. And in a very short time the laboratory became one of the most respected nuclear physics centres in the world.

The first vice-presidnet (scientific) of Chalk River was Wilfred Bennett Lewis. During the period between 1952 and 1965, the scientific staff boasted a remarkable group of physicists, including the director of Physics himself, Lloyd G. Elliott, plus Hugh Carmichael, Geoffrey Hanna, Bernard Kinsey, John Robson, and David Ward from the United Kingdom; and Gil Bartholemew, John Bromley, Bertram Brockhouse, George Ewan, James Geiger, Harry Gove, Robert Graham, Edward Hincks, Donald Hurst, John Kuehner, and Douglas Milton from various Canadian universities. I enjoyed friendship with all these men, and several were most helpful to us in our research program. Occasionally I visited Chalk River, either to lecture or for scientific meetings, and was frequently entertained in private homes.

On one occasion, I was a dinner guest at the Kinseys', and they had obviously gone to some length to ensure an uninterrupted evening. Although they had young children, they were not in sight, and Kinsey began to serve us glasses of sherry, while Mrs. Kinsey looked on approvingly. Before the serving was complete, the door to the kitchen opened slightly and a child's voice called out for attention. Mrs. Kinsey disappeared briefly and returned to sip her drink. Very soon, however, another voice came from the kitchen, and Kinsey left to deal with the new situation. On his return, we tried to pretend that nothing had disturbed the carefully orchestrated sherry hour, but a third interruption soon followed. As Mrs. Kinsey left, Kinsey turned to me and said with feeling, "Duckworth, married life is a sordid affair!"

On another occasion, I dined with Ted and Sarah Hincks. She was operating a small gift shop from their house, but Ted had persuaded her to store the gifts (for the evening) on the stairs leading to the second floor; thus, they were completely out of sight of the dinner guests. Dinner had scarcely begun when a prospective customer knocked on the door, and, to Ted's obvious displeasure, Sarah took her to the stairway where a whispered conversation ensued before she returned to the table. Later, a second customer was similarly dealt with, Sarah showing no indication of unease but avoiding her husband's eye. She was a refreshingly uninhibited woman. Later, when Ted had joined Carleton University, I was a dinner guest again. This time she met us at the door with an open cookbook and her index finger pressed against a recipe. "Are you going to get something good!" was her greeting. As the recipe was being implemented, a daughter asked her mother to sew a ski badge on her jacket but, of course, Sarah was too busy with the meal to oblige. Although my sewing experience was zero, I volunteered to do the job, and I expect the badge is still in its place.

An Accelerator for Everyone?

In the 1960s, physics was still the darling of the sciences, and nuclear physics was still the darling of physics. Unfortunately for the rest of the world, the equipment needed to pursue nuclear physics was complex and expensive. In Canada, most major universities were petitioning the NRC for funds either to enter or to remain in this fashionable field of research. These included British Columbia, Alberta, Saskatchewan, Manitoba, Windsor, Western Ontario, McMaster, Toronto, Queen's, Ottawa, Montreal, Laval, and Dalhousie. And the picture was further cluttered by Atomic Energy of Canada's announcement that it would construct at Chalk River an intense neutron generator (ING), which would dwarf any of the instruments preceding it. If all the aspirations of nuclear physicists were to be fulfilled, the available funds would be so committed that other scientists might just as well enter society or become social scientists.

The Intense Neutron Generator

Chalk River's fame as a research centre owed most to the neutron beam from its research reactor. For example, John Robson determined the half-life of the neutron, Bernard Kinsey and Gil Bartholemew studied the gamma-rays emitted following neutron absorption, and Bertram Brockhouse deduced crystal structure from neutron scattering (for which he won the Nobel Prize in 1994) To remain competitive with other laboratories, the neutron flux would have to be increased. This could be done with a more powerful reactor or, as W.B. Lewis, vice-president (scientific) believed, by accelerating heavy atoms to high energies and then bringing them to an abrupt stop. A cloud of smaller particles (spallation products), including neutrons, would be ejected from the stopping material. This was to be the Intense Neutron Generator (ING).

No major scientific project was ever undertaken with less attention to public relations. The universities, battling with one another for hundreds of thousands of dollars, learned in 1964, by the grapevine, that this device was to be constructed, and at a cost of tens of millions of dollars. Moreover, there was no indication that professors would be involved in the planning of the instrument, or even in its subsequent use. I chaired a meeting of physicists in Ottawa on 4 December 1964 at which the university nuclear physicists vented their spleen and instructed some of us to explain to Lewis and other AECL executives that the universities would oppose the project unless they were admitted as partners. The expenditure of $100 million on a Chalk River facility would inevitably impinge on the funds available for nuclear facilities in the rest of the country.

Somewhat belatedly, Lewis realized his gaffe and moved into overkill in the opposite direction. In April 1965, he invited professors of influence to an ING seminar at Chalk River, where he received us with a warmth that was as close to unctuousness as his reserved personality would permit. We were given details of the project and, at the end, a splendid banquet at which I had been asked to speak. Before making a plea for sharing the use of special large research facilities, I tried to lend a light tone to the evening:

> It is always an exciting experience to visit this laboratory, this major cathedral of Canadian nuclear physics, presided over by Archbishop Lewis and Bishop Elliott, who are assisted in turn by divers deans, deacons, and priests, not counting the apostates who have shifted to reactor physics. It is true that other cathedrals exist in Canada, such as those of Bishop Bell and Bishop Katz, but they can compare with this one neither in splendour nor in number of holy works. Although less splendid, the other cathedrals are more accessible; for example, Bishop Bell's cathedral lies on the direct route of persons travelling from Cornwall to Three Rivers, and that of Bishop Katz is visited easily by those travelling by canoe on the South Saskatchewan River. The very remoteness of *this* cathedral shelters its inmates from the fleshpots of the world, with the result that visitors are either holy men or pilgrims. Despite the difficulty of the pilgrimage, there are many pilgrims who come, as the size of this gathering attests. And with what interest have we learned of the proposed new addition to the cathedral, the Immense New Gargoyle (ING) from which will spout a potent stream of sanctifying rays.

In January 1966, I attended my first meeting of the ING Study Advisory Committee, and, not long after, the universities were sent a list of specific projects that they might undertake under contract with AECL. These actions, plus the news that the project would not be completed until 1973, that most of the cost would be buried in AECL budgets and that professors and their students would be welcomed at Chalk River quite mollified the university community. In due course, the heavy ion accelerator (the pseudonym for ING) was constructed and remained an instrument of international importance until it was shut down in 1997 by the Chrétien government in the name of economy. The closing of the facility was done with a brutality and callousness that shocked the scientific community, and that tarnished the scientific reputation of the once-proud Chalk River Laboratory.

W.B. Lewis, who guided the Canadian scientific research and technical development relating to atomic energy from 1946 to 1973, had been a student with Lord Rutherford at Cambridge, where he developed electronic counting devices. Later, he was a leader in radar development before being recommended by J.D. Cockcroft to head the Atomic Energy Division of NRC, which evolved into Atomic Energy of Canada in 1952. A bachelor, he was a prodigious student of scientific reports and literature and invariably entered a meeting with more relevant knowledge than any other present. I said to Don Hurst before he left for the Atoms for Peace Conference in Geneva in 1955, "That should be a nice holiday." "Holiday nothing," said Don. "I'll have to attend every session and make notes because, at some meeting next winter, Lewis will turn to me and ask, 'Hurst, what was that value given at Geneva?'"

I shouldn't joke about the Atoms for Peace Conference because it was important and necessary to assure the world that atomic energy could be directed at peaceful as well as military targets. As my friend, radio-chemist Leo Yaffé, once said, "To be introduced to atomic energy via the atomic bomb is like being introduced to electricity via the electric chair."

My first significant contact with Lewis was as a member of the Advisory Committee on Electronic Research of the Defence Research Board, which was chaired by Gar(nett) Woonton, then director of the Eaton Electronics Laboratory at McGill. At first, I found Lewis's presence intimidating, and I hesitated to question his opinion, but I got over that difficulty and we had a good relationship. Never, however, did I address him as other than "Dr. Lewis," and, of those who called him Ben, few did so to his face, although I fancy he might have welcomed it. He was no good at small talk but had a documented view on any serious topic. I saw much of him during the ING discussions and later, as a favour to him, served on the AECL Selection Committee. He retired to Kingston where, before he he died, he surrendered his extraordinary mind to Altzeimer's cruel attack.

Rationalization of Nuclear Physics Facilities

The NRC had requests for particle accelerators from many universities. Each request was taken seriously; a visiting committee was established, which made a report on the scientific merit, on the competence of the staff, on the University's commitment, and on proposed sharing arrangements with other universities. This report was made as well to the Atomic Energy Control Board, which, at that time, was also a major supporter of nuclear physics.

(The act establishing the AECB gave It the authority to regulate the use of nuclear energy *and* to encourage research related to nuclear energy, a conflicting pair of mandates. In the 1980s, the act was amended to limit AECB to its regulatory role.)

Lloyd Elliott (Chalk River) and I were perennial members of the visiting committees, and the other two members were drawn from Harry Welsh (Toronto), John Robson (Ottawa), Larkin Kerwin (Laval), Bob Bell (McGill), and Claude Geoffrion (Laval). At the same time, I was chairing an NRC committee, comprising mostly non-physicists, that was discussing how to deal with the demands of nuclear physics.

Aware that I was at the centre of things and overestimating my skill at conflict resolution, I invited the Ontario physics departments to a meeting at McMaster on 23 November 1964 in the hope that we could find some cooperative arrangement within our own province. For example, by agreeing on a single facility, centrally located and open to all, we could obtain a more powerful unit than any could obtain individually. McMaster had a request before the NRC for a tandem accelerator and, since it had the strongest nuclear physics group, would Hamilton not be the logical site for the major unit in Ontario? The others were not averse to the idea, but Harry Welsh, the head of Physics at Toronto, believed that an accelerator more powerful than the McMaster one should form the basis for an institute that would be independent of any one university. Welsh hadn't become a world authority on molecular spectroscopy by capitulating or compromising; we emerged with no consensus and returned to the policy of "every man for himself." The next year, I was able to persuade my colleagues on the Honorary Advisory Council of NRC to grant the McMaster request, and Welsh's grander vision was never realized.

Leaving McMaster: 1965

During the 1964-65 academic session, I was invited to move my laboratory to the University of Toronto, and, at the same time, I was invited to return to the University of Manitoba. My wife and I chose the latter, and arrangements were made for my recent Ph.D. student, Robert C. Barber, to join Manitoba as assistant professor of physics. Our indispensable technician, Paul Van Rookhuyzen, also agreed to join the migration.

Thus, in the fall of 1965, my wife, who was an active volunteer with the Hamilton Art Gallery, reported instead to the Winnipeg Art Gallery; my son, Harry, who had just completed a degree in biochemistry at McMaster, took up a fellowship at Yale University; my daughter, Jane, who had completed Grade 12 at Ontario Ladies' College (in Whitby), registered in the university entrance program at Balmoral Hall School. Meanwhile, I attempted to give good value in my new position as vice-president of my alma mater.

The large mass spectrograph remained at McMaster for a year to allow Bill McLatchie, Scott Whineray, and John Macdougall to complete their Ph.D. theses, and I made monthly trips back to McMaster to keep in touch with their work. The instrument was moved to Winnipeg in the fall of 1966 whilst, in the meantime, Barber had begun construction of a smaller, but in many ways superior, instrument. The work of the laboratory was only briefly interrupted.

Research group at Wesleyan University, 1951, left to right: Cort Kegley, George Standford, author, Clifford Gieselbreth, John Olsen.

Leaning on the magnet of the large mass spectrometer, left to right: a technician; John Dewdney, Jack Kerr, Howard Petch, author, Benjamin Hogg, 1954.

Vacuum cover for the electrostatic analyzer with, left to right: Clifford Eve, Jack Kerr, R.E. Fox, author, Neil Isenor, Philip Eastman, 1956.

The first nuclear reactor as portrayed by author's son, Harry W. Duckworth, in *Little Men in the Unseen World* (1963).

Prime Minister Nehru welcoming author to Indian Science Congress, Bombay, 1960.

Atomic Mass Conference, Winnipeg, 1967.

Special convocation at University of Manitoba, 29 August 1967, left to right: President H.H. Saunderson, Jesse DuMond, J.H.E. Mattauch, Chancellor Samuel Freedman.

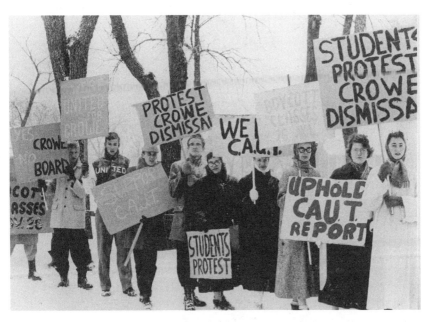

Student protest on behalf of Harry Crowe, 1958 (courtesy (WCP1).

Laval University Convocation, 5 June 1971. Left to right: Pierre Grenier, author, S.E. le Cardinal Maurice Roy, Armand Frappier, Jean Beaudoin, Mgr. Louis-Albert Vachon, Alfred Pellan, Mgr. Elzéar Fortier.

Author arriving at the University of Winnipeg, 1971. According to *VOX*, the student yearbook, "Now everything is just ducky."

Author with Wilfred C. Lockhart, first president of the University of Winnipeg.

Manitoba College, 1912, whose centenary was celebrated in 1971, was located on the north side of Ellice Avenue, between Edmonton and Balmoral Streets (courtesy WCP1).

The Entrance Scholarship Committee, 1972, left to right: Jean (MacKay) Curtis (lady stick, 1946–47); Gail (Pearcey) Hall (lady stick, 1963–64); James Miller (student president, 1970–71; Hugh Murray (president, Alumni Association; Ronald Riddell (assistant to the president); Murdoch MacKay (senior stick, 1950–51); P.H.T. Thorlakson (chancellor); R.O.A. Hunter (senior stick, 1936–37); author; Joy McDiarmid (director, Alumni Affairs); Janet (Clark) Saunders (class of 1936); William Norrie (senior stick, 1949–50). Absent: Donald Bennett (senior stick, 1947–48); Berenice (Warner) Sisler (lady stick, 1944–45).

Pinning proclamation of Manitoba College centenary (1971) to Nisbet Hall, where first classes were held, with Chancellor P.H.T. Thorlakson and Marilou McPhedran, student president, 1971.

The Great Rock Climb

At the University of Winnipeg, 1978: left to right: Chairman of the Board John Bulman, Chancellor Rod Hunter, author.

Family portrait at author's installation as chancellor of the University of Manitoba, 23 October 1986. Back row: Andrew W. Maksymuik, Jane (Duckworth) Maksymuik, author, Mary Lynn (Hollier) Duckworth, Harry W. Duckworth; front row: Catherine Maksymuik, Katherine(McPherson) Duckworth, Michael Maksymuik, Daniel Maksymuik.

Biographical plaque for Frank Allen Building (Physics), 1989, left to right: Thomas H.B. Symons (chair, Historic Sites and Monuments Board of Canada); Lillian Allen (daughter of Frank Allen); Charles Bigelow (dean of Science); Robert C. Barber (head, Physics); the author; Arnold Naimark (president).

Author with second wife, Shirley, in New York on St. Patrick's Day, 1996.

Author with his two children, Harry and Jane, at naming of Duckworth Quadrangle, 25 May 1992.

The University of Manitoba: 1965 to 1970

9

In 1965, I arrived for the fourth time at the University of Manitoba. I had arrived as a freshman in 1931, I had returned in 1935 to obtain a B.Sc. and a teaching certificate, I had come back in 1945 as an assistant professor of physics, and now I appeared as vice-president (development). This is a position normally associated with the raising of money, but it was understood in my case that the mandate was academic development. The following year, with the departure of William Waines to the Association of Universities and Colleges of Canada (AUCC), I succeeded him as vice-president (academic). In this position, whilst the Faculty of Arts and Science and the Faculty of Medicine reported directly to the president, most of the others reported to him through me.

Except for the Faculties of Medicine and Dentistry, the University was now consolidated on the Fort Garry campus, the former site of the Agricultural College. No longer were Junior Division students isolated from their seniors, and no longer did the Fort Garry campus seem so remote. In the nineteen years since we had last lived in Winnipeg, the city had expanded in all directions, but especially to the south, and the University was surrounded by fast-growing subdivisions. The campus itself was dotted with new buildings, either complete or under construction, and the baby boomers were claiming their right to higher education.

In the summer of 1965, Samuel Freedman was chancellor of the University, Hugh H. Saunderson was president and vice-chancellor, and Peter Curry was chair of the Board of Governors.

Freedman, the sixth chancellor of the University, was a justice of the Manitoba Court of Appeal and the most popular public speaker in the province. His style was unhurried, his language was elegant, and he had jokes that no one in Manitoba had heard before. For example, until he told us of it, we had been unaware of the mixed gathering at which hen-pecked husbands were ordered to one side of the hall and those who were not hen-pecked to the other side. Only one man went to the non-hen-pecked side. When asked why he had gone there, he explained that his wife had told him to.

Saunderson came from an old and respected Winnipeg family and had been president since 1954. He was a cautious administrator, cheerful and unflappable in manner, loyal to his associates, and driven by a powerful sense of duty. He was entirely supportive of initiatives that I attempted and, at the personal level, was a valued friend.

Curry, who was soon to become the seventh chancellor, was a prominent Winnipeg businessman who later served as midwife for the takeover of two Winnipeg financial institutions (Investors Syndicate and Great-West Life Assurance Company) by Paul Desmarais of Montreal (Power Corporation). A handsome man with an engaging public persona, he gave the University much of his time but was sometimes baffled by academics.

The Practice House

Our new home in Winnipeg was a house on the University of Manitoba campus that most recently had been occupied by the dean of Agriculture. But my wife and I knew it as the practice house. It had been built in the late 1930s as a place where home economics students could learn to run a household. Thus, the students in their final year of Household Management would spend a month in the practice house, playing the various roles that a splendid house required: first cook, second cook, downstairs maid, upstairs maid, nursemaid, and even mistress of the house. My wife had lived in the house as a student in the spring of 1941, and, on a brief vacation from Chicago, I had arranged to pick her up one evening. She was nursemaid that evening, and the baby would not fall asleep. For thirty agonizing minutes, I sat in the living room under the gaze of nine young women and the house mother, Miss McLaughlin, until the baby lapsed into the land of nod, and Kay was free to pursue other interests.

The baby was a special feature of the house. A new one appeared each September, chosen from amongst those available for adoption. Then, in the following April, it was turned back for adoption, having served as guinea pig for the academic year. The 1940-41 baby had been born to an unwed mother, but the father was a matter of record. To the infinite delight of Kay and her co-residents, the mother and father decided to marry and to reclaim their child at the end of its tour of duty.

The "practice-house baby," in the tender care of Katherine Jane McPherson, 1941.

In 1965, it gave Kay an ironic pleasure to live again in the old practice house, ruling every day as its mistress, but without the corps of servants for which the house had been designed. A housecleaner coming in twice a week was hardly the equivalent. But it was a great place for our daughter, Jane, to bring friends for coffee between university classes, and I was within five minutes of my office. We occupied the house until 31 July 1970, when we left to spend a year's leave at Laval University in Quebec City.

The University and its Affiliated Colleges

In 1965, in addition to its own complex network of faculties, schools, and colleges, the university had five affiliated colleges, which prepared students for university examinations. These were St. Boniface College (le Collège Universitaire de Saint-Boniface), St. John's College, United College, Brandon College, and St. Paul's College. These proud institutions had their own governing boards and were responsible for their own finances, but their professors were subservient, academically, to the heads of the University departments and ultimately to the University Senate. It was an uneasy relationship, as the colleges were treated somewhat as colonies of the University, with the effortless condescension that usually accrues to that status. St. John's and St. Paul's, which had recently moved to desirable sites on the University's Fort Garry campus, seemed to accept the situation, but the other three were increasingly restive at the restrictions on their freedom to initiate new programs. Major changes in the College-University relationships were made in 1967.

St. Boniface, the oldest of the colleges in the Red River Settlement, was one of the three founding colleges that came together in 1877 to form the University of Manitoba (the other two being St. John's College and Manitoba College). All instruction in St. Boniface College was in French, and its curriculum followed that of the classical colleges in Quebec but led, of course, to a University of Manitoba degree. There was little interaction between St. Boniface College and the rest of the University. Father Guy, a jovial priest of small stature, was dean in 1965 and usually represented the College at University meetings and convocations.

In 1969, the year of my daughter's graduation, Guy and I sat together in the front row of the platform party. I had conceived the idea of strewing rose petals in my daughter's path as she came forward to receive her degree and, to that end, had a supply of rose petals under my academic gown. I invited Guy to join in the tribute, and together we provided a copious fragrant carpet which, when tramped upon by subsequent graduands left an ugly stain. I'm sure he was the only dean in captivity to participate in such an unpardonable event.

For some reason, I had little contact with St. John's College, the second oldest of the three founding colleges. Its ties were to the departments in Arts and to the Anglican Church; the Bishop of Rupert's Land was its chancellor and it awarded fellowships and certain theological degrees and certificates at its own convocation.

St. Paul's College, operated by the Jesuits, had achieved affiliation in 1931. It seemed less isolated than St. John's from the rest of the University community. My wife and I were frequently within its walls. Father Burke-Gaffney, a Winnipeg native of urbane manner, was rector and represented the College effectively. Unfortunately for the College and the University, he was later transferred to a lesser post in Saskatchewan. One had the impression, probably erroneous, that he was being brought low deliberately.

The most popular of the teaching priests were Father Plunkett (English) and Father Jensen (history). Plunkett invited my wife to the College for lunch on the first Friday that the Catholic Church allowed meat to be eaten, and he scandalized the sisters by loudly ordering roast beef. It was he who was responsible for the windows (from Chartres) and most of the religious ornaments and utensils in the St. Paul's Chapel. Jensen, a bluff but kindly man, later served as acting rector and then rector. Virtually all instruction, except for science, was offered by the priests. As I write (in 1999), the Jesuits no longer provide rector or teaching priests.

Brandon College, the second-largest of the affiliated colleges, had been established by the Baptist Church in 1899 with the understanding that its students would write University of Manitoba examinations and receive its degrees. This was accepted as an interim arrangement, as the ultimate aim was an independent University charter. When the Manitoba legislature refused to grant this request, Brandon lost patience and turned to McMaster University, the Baptist University in Toronto, and in 1910 became a college affiliated to that institution. Thus, McMaster courses were taught in Brandon, McMaster examinations were sat in Brandon, and McMaster degrees were awarded at a special convocation held in Brandon. This arrangement continued until 1938, when the Baptist Church was no longer able to support the College. It then became affiliated with the University of Manitoba and, for the first time, received funding from the provincial government.

In 1965, the president of Brandon College was John E. Robbins, a thoroughly decent man who had been in office for five years, having just finished a time as editor-in-chief of *Encyclopaedia Canadiana.*

United College, the largest of the colleges affiliated with the University of Manitoba, traced its roots to Manitoba College (founded in 1871 by the Presbyterian Church, and the third of the three founding colleges of the University of Manitoba) and Wesley College (founded in 1888 by the Methodist Church). With the formation of the United Church of Canada in 1925, the two colleges moved under one roof, with Wesley offering an arts program and Manitoba College teaching theology. In 1938, they combined to form United College, which evolved into the University of Winnipeg in 1967.

In 1965, the principal of United College was Wilfred C. Lockhart, an ordained United Church minister who had been a successful pastor and sometime general secretary of the Student Christian Movement at the University of Toronto. He had been in office since 1955, and between 1966 and 1968, whilst president of the University of Winnipeg, he served as moderator of the United Church of Canada. Like Saunderson, he was a cautious administrator and highly principled. Moreover, as I learned in 1971, he had the respect of his staff, and he ran a tight ship.

For many years, the relations between Wesley/United College and the University of Manitoba had been somewhat testy, but, in the decade preceding their final separation in 1967, these became decidedly more so. First, United College did not accept a 1957 invitation from the University to move from downtown to the Fort Garry campus, as St. John's and St. Paul's had done. This led to some bad feeling, both internal and external to the College. Internally, it led to the resignation from the Board of the College of two of its most influential members – Muriel Richardson (head of James Richardson and Sons) and Harry Manning (president of Great-West Life Assurance Company). Externally, it led to some pique on the part of the University that its well-meant invitation had been spurned. Then, in 1958, the "Crowe Case" exacerbated the already-uneasy relationship.

Harry S. Crowe was an outstanding graduate of United College who later returned as a popular, if somewhat iconoclastic member of its Department of History. Whilst on leave in the spring of 1958, he wrote a letter to W.A. Packer of the German Department, which was uncomplimentary towards both Principal Lockhart and the College's Board of Regents. Through the good graces of an unknown agent, this letter was slipped under Lockhart's door. Instead of treating it as an anonymous letter, which he normally would have ignored, Lockhart wrote of his displeasure to Crowe, who told friends that he had been threatened with dismissal. In no time, some of Crowe's colleagues declared their support, portraying Lockhart's action as an infringement of academic freedom and tenure. The upshot was the appointment of a committee of investigation by the officers of the Canadian Association of University Teachers (CAUT), the unconditional firing of Crowe and a scandal nonpareil for the *Winnipeg Free Press*, the *Winnipeg Tribune,* and major newspapers elsewhere in Canada.

At the time of these tumultuous events, the CAUT was a young organization, having been formed in 1951. It was to be the Canadian version of the American Association of University Professors, which by this time was firmly established and played an influential role in American higher education, especially when academic freedom was in peril. But in 1958 the CAUT had little to show in the way of achievement. Four years earlier, in 1954, I had attended its annual general meeting (in Winnipeg), as the McMaster representative. I was to be in Winnipeg anyhow, to be inducted into the Royal Society of Canada. Thus, I could attend the annual general meeting of CAUT at no cost to the McMaster Faculty Association. The president of CAUT at that time was a professor of engineering from McGill who gave us a lengthy harangue on the inadequacy of the salaries in Canadian universities.

Before closing the meeting, and with obvious reluctance, he agreed to invite other business, and I waited expectantly for the salient suggestions that my fellow delegates would bring forward. Two hands were raised. The first suggestion was that the Association encourage its members to return to the wearing of academic gowns, and the second was that members be urged to attend baccalaureate services. There was nary a word about academic freedom.

As another cost-saving device, all the officers of the CAUT were located in the same city, and they served for one year at a time; for the next year, the officers would be from another city. There was no permanent office and, of course, no permanent staff. Coincidentally, for the academic year 1958-59, the officers were located at the University of Manitoba, in a good position to monitor the Crowe case. In the summer of 1958, the CAUT president, Clarence Barber of Economics, appointed a committee of investigation, which ultimately comprised V.C. Fowke (Economics, Saskatchewan) and Bora Laskin (Law, Toronto). This committee descended upon Winnipeg in October 1958, listened to the few witnesses who presented themselves (all supporting Crowe), and reported a month later that Harry Crowe had been mistreated and should be re-appointed. Later, in fact, he was re-appointed but soon resigned. Meanwhile, some of his colleagues – notably Stewart Reid (History), Kenneth McNaught (History), and William Packer (German) – had also resigned in protest. Most of the rest of the teaching staff rallied to Lockhart's defence, and he provided prudent leadership to the institution until I succeeded him in 1971.

Although not in Winnipeg at the time and only learning of events (informally) through friends and (officially) through the McMaster Faculty Association, I felt (as many did) that the officers of the CAUT might have over-reacted in their desire to show that the CAUT was a body to be reckoned with. Whatever the wisdom of that course, it propelled the Association onto the national stage and transformed it from a desultory body preoccupied with salaries to one that took a serious interest in academic freedom. In 1959, Stewart Reid became its first executive director and, on his untimely death in 1964, the J. H. Stewart Reid Medal for contributions to the association was named in his honour. Two of the first recipients of the medal were Harry Crowe and Bora Laskin; evidently, the CAUT felt that it had won its spurs at United College in 1958. But the intervention of the CAUT officers (who were located at the University of Manitoba) created a deep and long-lasting rift between historians and economists at United College and those at the University of Manitoba.

Incidentally, the 1959 annual meeting of the CAUT in Saskatoon, where the events in Winnipeg were still on everyone's mind, was addressed by Frank Underhill of the University of Toronto, who had, himself, tested the limits of academic freedom. Prior to World War II, he and Frank Scott of McGill, both articulate socialists, had rattled the establishment, and it is said that Underhill had almost been dismissed from the University of Toronto in 1940. Crowe had taken a master's degree with Underhill, who took a slap at Winnipeg in his address. He said that he had once thought Winnipeg "a city of the world," but the Crowe case showed "that it was not that kind of city at all." Rather, "it had sunk to the intellectual level of Toronto, [where] togetherness, harmony and Rotarian virtues had replaced intellectual values."

The Baby Boomers

My 1945 arrival at the University of Manitoba had coincided with the coming of the war veterans, and the University had been struggling to accommodate them. In 1965, it was their children who were causing the problems.

Statistician E.F. Sheffield had warned universities of the tidal wave, but, when it arrived in the mid-1960s, it bore two features that had not been part of Sheffield's demographics. First, a larger percentage of high-school graduates chose to attend university than had been the case in the past. That is, the *participation rate* exceeded previous levels. Second, the social sciences and certain of the humanities were unexpectedly popular. This latter feature precipitated severe shortages of teaching staff in some subjects.

Although the booming enrollment caused formidable difficulties for the universities, it could not dispel a pervasive optimism. The economy was booming, jobs were plentiful, and there was a naïve belief amongst students that the social sciences could eradicate the problems of society. Furthermore, governments had been assured by the Economic Council of Canada that, in some undefined way, graduates created wealth. In this blind belief, governments provided generous financial support with few questions asked. During this surreal period, which ended in 1970, the total full-time enrollment in Canada rose to 310,000, ten times the pre-war figure. The character of the universities had changed: no longer the preserve of the privileged, they were now becoming the domain of the proletariat.

As corollary to the above, new buildings were quickly planned and swiftly built. *Time Magazine*, using the analogy to the old British Empire, described universities as "the Empires on which the concrete never sets."

In 1965, the University of Manitoba was experiencing all these developments, the most critical problem being the recruitment of teaching staff.

Shortage of Teaching Staff

Most of the incoming students were intent on studying sociology, psychology, economics, political science, anthropology, and the other social sciences. The necessary professors for these subjects, or at least most of them, should have emerged from the post-war Canadian graduate schools, but these had been emphasizing the natural sciences rather than the social sciences. For example, in 1960, 305 doctorates were awarded in all of Canada, of which 201 were in natural science, fifty-nine in the humanities, and forty-five in social science. Furthermore, more than half the social scientists were in experimental (or "rat") psychology, and none was in anthropology or sociology.

The cry for help went out to all the world, but the response came mostly from the United States and the United Kingdom. In the United States, opposition to the Vietnam War was growing, and many scholars of conscience were happy to accept teaching posts in their neighbour to the north. Some were of draft age and were labelled "draft dodgers" by their compatriots; "peace seekers" might have been a better term. Most of the members of this large contingent were persons of principle, and not a few were political and/or social activists. To those who came from the United Kingdom, Canada had no political allure, but it offered academic careers that were becoming scarce at home. Most of the group from the United Kingdom were first-generation university graduates, and many came from trade-union backgrounds. It was, of course, to redress this professor shortage that the Province of Ontario had established the Graduate Scholarship Program (POGS) in 1964.

At the University of Manitoba in 1969, there were 880 full-time faculty members. Of these, 18 percent had their first degrees in the United States, 11 percent in the U.K., and 15 percent in other countries, but these distributions were quite uneven across departments, with American imports being particularly strong in the arts departments. Thus, eight of nine anthropologists had come from the U.S., twenty-two of thirty-three psychologists, six of seventeen sociologists, ten of twenty-five historians, two of thirteen political scientists, and seven of twenty-five economists. The total figure for foreign imports of 44 percent was almost identical to the 46 percent then prevailing at the University of Toronto. For the newly established York and Simon Fraser Universities, this figure would have been much higher.

Clash of Academic Cultures

With the rapid growth of academic staff, each department at the University became a mixing bowl with at least three academic ingredients: Canadian, American, and British. If the department had been strong and well-established before the influx, the Canadian ingredient was apt to prevail, but, if not, it would begin to veer in the American or British direction. The Americans were accustomed to a four-year degree in which the student majored in one subject, but not to the exclusion of most others. This was the essence of a liberal education. To them, the structure of the honours degree was not only foreign, but it was also excessively specialized, and much of its content should be delayed until graduate school. The British, on the other hand, had invented the honours degree and had exported it to Canada and other parts of the former Empire. Liberal education was important, to be sure, but it was the job of the schools to provide it. The university was the place to "drink deep or taste not the Pierian spring." To them, the American "major" was little better than a gargle. In Manitoba, the Anthropology Department, led by the energetic American import William Mayer-Oakes, was particularly impatient with the honours degree. Notwithstanding such internal attacks, the honours degree survived but was later supplemented by a specialist degree, which demands a strong core of one subject but allows significant study of others. Also, it has more forgiving academic requirements.

Academic marks offered another difficulty. Traditionally at the University of Manitoba, First Class covered the numerical range 75 to 100; Second Class, 67 to 75; Third Class, 60 to 67; and Failure, 0 to 50. This system, or at least the First-, Second-, and Third-Class" terminology, was familiar to the British but was passing strange to the Americans, who had been weaned on a grading scale of A = 90 to 100, B = 80 to 90, C = 70 to 80, D = 60 to 70, E = 50 to 60, F = 0 to 50. Without some sort of adjustment, the "gentleman C" students of the American system could find themselves elevated to First-Class scholar. The adjustment took time but, at the University of Manitoba and at most other Canadian institutions, the grading system has come to resemble the American one.

A potentially more serious clash was not immediately evident, that is, the clash of scholarly interests. Understandably, the imported scholars brought their scholarly interests with them, and precious few of these related to Canada. Thus, the social science departments were flooded with professors who were unfamiliar with Canada's history, political institutions, cultural traditions, and national personalities: all the stuff that constitutes the Canadian ethos. When the implications of this situation were realized, the AUCC established the Commission on Canadian Studies, headed by Thomas H.B. Symons.

Interdisciplinary Research Groups

Recruitment of enough new staff was a perennial problem and was not helped by the impression gained by many that it was not possible to survive the Manitoba winters. Murray Donnelly encapsulated this myth by referring to the publish-or-perish policy that existed at high-power American universities. During the winter in Manitoba, he averred, it was possible to do both. I had the idea of identifying and encouraging certain research themes as a means of attracting desirable new staff, in particular, themes that required the participation of more than one discipline. It was not that interdisciplinary research was novel; indeed, it was becoming popular, but the idea of using it as a recruitment tool may have been novel. To show the power of such research, I cited the collaboration between a professor of physics and a professor of anatomy that led to the law governing the circulation of the blood, namely, that it flows down one leg and up the other.

With President Saunderson's agreement, a start was made with Northern Studies. A committee already existed, chaired by Jack Hildes, a professor of medicine who had spent much time in the North. This seemed a good base on which to expand. Accordingly, advertisements were placed in *Nature*, with the catchy heading, "Have you Scholarly Interests in the Canadian North?" It emerged that many did have such interests, and for a while I was obliged to respond to twenty or thirty inquiries per week. Some of the interests expressed were rather tenuous; for example, one correspondent had no personal knowledge of northern Canada but offered, instead, his experience in northern Bengal. However, a number of qualified individuals responded, and a few were ultimately hired. Further, from this initiative emerged an interest in single-industry towns in the North, which led to the establishment of the Centre for Settlement Studies, a research group that functioned for several years under a grant from the Central Mortgage and Housing Corporation (CMHC). I can't recall whom I contacted at CMHC, but it was an ex-Manitoban. At that time, the federal civil service was riddled with graduates of the University of Manitoba, many of them in positions of influence. Thus, before I went foraging in Ottawa, I sometimes asked John Gordon, the alumni director, if we had any graduates in the target departments, and I chose them as the points of entry. Following the introduction of the federal bilingualism program and the emphasis upon increasing the number of civil servants from the Province of Quebec, fewer Manitobans qualified for the civil service. Thus, that particular old boys' network is now much less effective.

Much of the success of the Centre was due to the administrative skills of Gordon Leckie, followed by Len Siemens, who invited research grant applications from staff, arranged seminars and advisory committee meetings, and oversaw the publications program. Except for Leckie and Siemens, all participants in the Centre were researchers in regular university departments who aligned themselves with the Centre to varying degrees and to the extent that the association benefitted their research. Thus, if and when their interests waned, they resumed full residency in their permanent academic homes. Also, all graduates supported by the Centre obtained degrees in regular University departments. This practice has not been followed everywhere, and the fringes of the academic world are peopled by not a few Ph.D.s in Interdisciplinary Studies who spend much of their time trying to explain to prospective employers what their degrees represent.

Transportation was chosen as a second interdisciplinary theme. This idea was suggested by Clarence Barber, head of Economics, and was followed up by Saunderson and me in a visit to the federal minister of Transport, from whose department a substantial research grant was subsequently received.

This initiative was nearly pre-empted by a meeting called by Premier Roblin to discuss the formation in Winnipeg of a Canadian transportation research institute. Arthur Mauro, then a Winnipeg lawyer who was specializing in transportation issues and who later succeeded me as chancellor of the University, had conceived the idea, and Roblin's invitation had brought representatives from the railways and other organizations based in the East. At that time, both railways were headed by University of Manitoba graduates: Ian Sinclair of the CPR and Norman McMillan of the CNR. Mauro made the general case for Winnipeg, and I was asked to outline the relevant work at the University. The visitors listened without apparent enthusiasm and then poured cold water on the idea. Apparently, an eastern centre would be more suitable, if *anything* were to be done. Robert Bandeen, a vice-president of the CNR, and much later the chancellor of Bishop's University, was particularly unimpressed. Having spent seventeen years in Ontario, I was startled by the indifference with which the West could be treated. Fortunately, the University's own initiative paid off, and the Institute for Transportation Studies has continued for thirty years.

Water resources was the third research theme to be pursued. This suggestion came from Ed Kuiper, a professor of civil engineering who was currently exploring the feasibility of diverting water from the Nelson River system to the thirsty Americans. He described his project with the fervour of an Old Testament prophet, carrying all hearers before him. His compelling style of speech was seen again in 1997, during the Red River "flood of the century." Reporters searched him out for terse, colourful sound bites, which either assured us or alarmed us, as the situation warranted. But, in 1966, there were other interesting, but less grandiose, research proposals as well. Armed with these, I visited James Harrison, a classmate at the University of Manitoba and now assistant deputy minister in the federal Department of Mines and Technical Surveys, who received me warmly and arranged for generous financial support. Things went well for a couple of years but then foundered in the hands of a young engineer in whom we had placed too much confidence.

The fourth research theme was identified following a day-long session (Saturday, 18 June 1966) at which thirty to forty professors from across the campus described their research relating to radiation science. What emerged was the Institute for Cell Biology, which was aimed at drawing medical scientists and pure scientists together. It also offered a point of contact to the University for John Weekes and other health scientists in the Atomic Energy of Canada Laboratory at Whiteshell, some eighty miles northeast of Winnipeg. No money existed to prime this pump, but the needed leadership came from Lyonel Israels, a distinguished cancer specialist, and the Institute celebrated its twenty-fifth anniversary in 1992.

The fifth initiative was the Natural Resources Institute, for which a major grant was obtained from the Ford Foundation. This institute has continued and for many years has offered a master's degree in natural resource management. This is the one exception in which graduate degrees are not offered in one of the regular departments.

These institutes and centres were established after discussions with interested professors, but without prior approval of the university senate, and they reported directly to me as vice-president (academic). It was a way of getting quick action, but it also may have given the impression that I was empire building. After my departure from the campus in 1970, wiser heads arranged for these bodies to report to the Senate, which would have been a desirable practice from the start.

Apart from the disregard for academic protocol – and that is not to be trivialized – I believe these interdisciplinary initiatives added a useful dimension to the University. They highlighted the fact that many of the problems facing society cannot be solved by one discipline alone. Rather, they lie in the spaces between the traditional departments and require, for their solution, the type of collaboration that explained the circulation of the blood. Further, they brought professors from different parts of the campus together and, in some cases, gave lone researchers the satisfaction of working with a team.

The Research Board

In an industrial laboratory, where research is intended to lead to commercial applications, a director of research ensures, or should ensure, that research projects contribute to the mandate of the corporation. There is no such officer in a university, nor should there be, as professors are expected to pursue research of their own choosing. But they can be encouraged in their efforts, they can be informed of research opportunities, and they can be assisted in a variety of other ways. In 1965, the University of Manitoba had no campus-wide agency to serve these functions, although research was becoming a major activity and was being recognized as an obligatory function of the institution, and not simply an element in the training of graduate students. True, the Faculty of Graduate Studies had some nominal responsibility for research, but it was primarily concerned with the regulation of graduate students and graduate programs.

Again with President Saunderson's approval, and also with the blessing of the dean of Graduate Studies, I proposed the creation of a research board, where matters relating to research could be discussed in depth, and not as an afterthought. Each faculty involved in graduate work would be represented on the new board by the dean (or his or her deputy) and a professor elected by the faculty. In addition, any member of the University sitting on one of the national granting agencies (National Research Council, Canada Council, Medical Research Council) would be a member ex officio. These latter would share with the others the current policies and practices of the granting agencies. The more than 200 members of the Faculty of Graduate Studies were reluctant to surrender what had been a nominal responsibility, viewing it as a loss of privilege and power, but they eventually agreed on the condition that the research board make an annual report to them. The research board is still in operation as the much reorganized Research Committee of Senate, but it may be significant that no other university has chosen to follow suit.

The Churchill River Diversion

Manitoba Hydro had been making plans to exploit the Nelson River for hydroelectric purposes. To ensure dependable flow, water was to be diverted from the Churchill River system into the Nelson by damming the outlet of the large Southern Indian Lake.This would allow a portion of the Churchill water to be rerouted into the Burntwood River, a tributary of the Nelson.This was a controversial project: On the one hand, huge amounts of hydroelectric power would be generated, but, on the other hand, the ecology of the whole region would be seriously affected. Stewart Anderson, deputy minister of Mines and Natural Resources for the province, and a far-sighted public servant, persuaded the president of Manitoba Hydro, Donald Stephens, to ask the University to estimate what financial damage would be done to the Southern Indian Lake and to those who lived upon its shores.

Accordingly, on 11 July 1966, a small group flew north and spent two days making a rapid assessment of the potential damage to the Native community and its livelihood. Kuiper was the flood expert, and Harold Welch, head of Biology, was the expert on fish. Also, Mayer-Oakes examined archeological sites that would be flooded, and William Brisbin conjectured whether potential mining sites would be inundated. Gerry Clayton, a professor of engineering and a veteran of the North, arranged for us to be transported, housed, and victualled.

We found what appeared to be a happy Native community, supported by fishing in the summer and trapping in the winter. At the time of our visit, the weather was superb, and the lake was pristine. On one of the nights, and perhaps not coincidentally, a movie was shown in the school hall that depicted the devastation caused in Africa by the building of a dam. As we departed for home from the dock in front of the Hudson's Bay store, we were heavy with the knowledge that most of what we had seen would soon disappear.

In due course, I collated the assessments of the others and wrote a summary statement.Then I added the personal opinion that "it would be unworthy of Manitoba Hydro" to destroy the Southern Indian Lake community.This opinion was not part of the mandate, and Stephens was furious when he read these gratuitous words, which appeared to criticize the whole grand scheme.The work proceeded, the community was effectively destroyed, and public indignation has never completely subsided. A few years later, I flew with Premier Schreyer over the entire area and saw for the first time the price that had been paid for 200 megawatts of electricity.

In the protracted political controversy that followed the diversion of water from the Churchill system, reference was occasionally made to a University of Manitoba report.This was our report, which was never made public; thus, my emotional words never appeared in the newspaper, or in other ways added fuel to the fire.

Stephens and I had been friends before, and before his death we became friends again. He was a no-nonsense type, enormously admired by those who worked for him. For a time, he was one of the three Canadian representatives on the International Joint Commission, and it was he, as a director of Atomic Energy of Canada, who was responsible for the Whiteshell Nuclear Research Laboratory coming to Manitoba.

Council on Higher Learning

In 1965, the Roblin government established the Council on Higher Learning to advise it on the development of the university system. It was chaired by A. Searle Leach, a personable and respected business leader who had attended Dartmouth College as an undergraduate and had later studied at Oxford, where he played on the same ice-hockey team as Lester Pearson. The heads of all colleges sat on the Council, as did representatives of the University of Manitoba and a few citizens-at-large.

I was not a member of the Council, but I came to know Leach, and he was interested to learn that I had some knowledge of Dartmouth from my time at Wesleyan. I told him an anecdote that was new to him.

Dartmouth College, one of the nine pre-Revolutionary colleges, is located in the town of Hanover, New Hampshire, some four miles from the larger town of Lebanon. During the Great Depression, the citizens of Hanover imposed a poll tax as a device for obtaining some revenue from the Dartmouth students, whose presence constituted a significant drain on the town's finances. As it happened, the implications of this somewhat impetuous action had not been fully thought through. The students protested, to no avail, before realizing that the poll tax was not all bad: it carried with it the right to vote. Accordingly, in substantial numbers, they presented themselves at the next town meeting. At an appropriate time, one moved and another seconded that a sidewalk be built to Lebanon. This passed by a wide majority, as did a second motion that a new town hall be built with dimensions three feet by four feet and nine stories high. At this climactic point, just as a pipeline to a brewery in Montreal was about to be proposed, action was taken to adjourn the meeting. In subsequent undercover moves, the poll tax was abolished and the ambitious building program was shelved. I should add that Dartmouth archivist Kenneth C. Cramer once told me that this story is apocryphal. Pity!

A major topic for the Council on Higher Learning was a request from Brandon College for university status. This institution was 140 miles west of the University of Manitoba, an awkward distance to traverse for departmental and other committee meetings. Also, the existing university-college system discouraged Brandon from launching initiatives on its own. The Brandon request raised the status of the two other off-campus colleges, St. Boniface and United. St. Boniface, to the surprise of many, declared itself satisfied with the existing arrangement. United was ambivalent: some were keen on independence, but others, including Principal Lockhart, were not so sure. The wish of the University of Manitoba became the deciding factor. Dean William Sibley, who had presided fairly and diplomatically over the Faculty of Arts and Science, and who knew intimately the strains under which the complicated system operated, recommended devolution. The council advised the government to establish Brandon and United as separate universities, a recommendation that was promptly accepted. Thus, by order-in-council, Brandon University and the University of Winnipeg came into existence on 1 July 1967. Saunderson concurred in the decision – indeed, he was party to it – but he objected to United College's using the name "Winnipeg." However, Lockhart had paid a private visit to Roblin and his minister of Education, George Johnson, and had obtained their agreement in advance.

Accommodating the Two New Universities

There were now four institutions to receive operating grants from the provincial government: Manitoba, Brandon, Winnipeg, and St. Boniface (which had previously received a grant separate from the University of Manitoba). The deputy minister of Education, Scott Bateman, who had driven a MacArthur truck with me in the summer of 1936, suggested that Manitoba follow the example of Alberta and establish a non-political body to recommend on the needs of the four institutions and to divide amongst them the block grant that the government would ultimately make to this new commission. The Universities Grants Commission Act was drafted, and Bateman cleared it with the four institutional heads. One of its provisions would have empowered the Universities Grants Commission (UGC) to order universities to discontinue programs. When the draft legislation was made public, I was alarmed at this provision and sought counsel with Bill Sibley. Together, we decided to seek a change in the legislation when it reached the stage of the Law Amendments Committee. Specifically, we argued that the UGC should not be able to discontinue a program unless it were funding it. Any program financed by the University's own funds should be immune. I spoke with Bateman in advance, he agreed with the point (and a couple of smaller ones), we made our presentation, and the government accepted the changes. Sibley and I saw ourselves as defenders of University independence, but I suspect that some others wondered why we were so exercised. I was prepared to resign if Saunderson had not supported our crusade. Fortunately for the welfare of my wife and children, I was not obliged to take that melodramatic step.

For a period at the start, Bateman chaired the UGC whilst continuing as deputy minister. Douglas Chevrier, registar of the University of Manitoba, joined as executive director, and a sterling group of individuals rounded out the Commission. Two came from the University of Manitoba: Dean Funt of Graduate Studies and Dean Shebeski of Agriculture. They, with Chevrier, brought academic experience to the task, whilst not bringing vested interest, as the other institutions offered neither graduate work nor agriculture. Other founding members of the UGC were James Doak (Virden, vice-chair), Roland Couture (St. Boniface), Roderick Hunter (Winnipeg), Blaine Johnson (Thompson), Searle Leach (Winnipeg), and Wesley Lorimer (Winnipeg).

Now that Winnipeg and Brandon were no longer part of the University of Manitoba family, the heads of the three institutions no longer saw one another in the regular course of business. They agreed to meet informally, on a monthly basis, and asked me to be their secretary. These meetings were mostly held at the University of Winnipeg, as it was the most convenient location, and were completely off the record. When the Inter-Universities North Program was established in 1970, it was decided that its director should report to what came to be known as the Committee of Presidents. Prior to that time, the meetings were not secret, but no one knew about them. They were simply a means of exchanging information and, occasionally, of consoling one another. The discussion was remarkably carefree, as no one was listening, and no one was obliged to report to any other body. The minutes were simply an *aide-memoire* and were as factual as possible. There were occasions when what appeared *between* the lines could have served as the basis for libel.

Much later, the committee came to be seen as an official body. It acquired its own acronymic name – COPUM (Committee of Presidents of Universities of Manitoba) – and had matters referred to it by the UGC and other bodies. The name was probably invented by Lloyd Dulmage, who also held the dubious distinction of inventing COWCUP (Committee of Western Canadian University Presidents).

When I returned to Winnipeg in 1965, I had hoped that I might be a useful mediator between United College and the University of Manitoba. First, I spoke to the United College Senate, describing certain new interdisciplinary research units and inviting participation by United College staff. A couple of professors responded, and the rest, I believe, appreciated the offer. Then, after the establishment of the University of Winnipeg in 1967, when its staff no longer had access to graduate work, I took the initiative of importing from Ontario the adjunct professor idea. This not only allowed qualified University of Winnipeg staff to teach and direct graduate students, but it also provided a useful mechanism for other scholars in the Winnipeg area to participate in the graduate program of the University of Manitoba. From the point of view of Manitoba professors who remembered the Crowe case, arranging for the appointment of adjunct professors from the University of Winnipeg was not the most popular thing I ever did.

Student Unrest

In the 1960s, students in many parts of the world were restive, some to the point of revolt. Many had good cause for unrest, whilst the motives of others were questionable. Canadian students were amongst the last to become exercised and in the end were amongst the least aroused.

The most dramatic events took place in the United States, where some students became flower children and hippies, opting out of society; at least for a while, some fought for civil rights and later pitted themselves against the Vietnam War, and still others attempted to use the universities to transform society. At no time were more than 10 percent of American students involved in these activities, but those were more than enough to keep deans and presidents busy. The unrest spread from America to Europe where, in 1968, it erupted with terrifying intensity. Without question, 1968 was the "international year of student unrest." Local issues may have varied, but all student activists had one unifying theme: they were unhappy with institutional authority, especially as exercised by governments. They saw ordinary individuals as pawns in systems that were said to be democratic but that were, in fact, controlled by relatively few. And they saw the relationship between student and university as analogous: the university was serving as agent for those in power, as it subtly prepared its students to take their places, submissively, in the existing social/economic/political system. And, fortunately for the cause, the campus presented a favourable site for battle since the university, with its tradition of free speech, was unusually tolerant of the activities of student radicals.

The student movement in the United States comprised two main groups, young Blacks and young middle-class Whites. For the Blacks, the motivation was specific: to achieve their civil rights. For the Whites, the motivation was often vague. Their parents had provided them with everything needed for a happy life except a purpose, which they hoped to discover in some form of social action. Some Whites sought to identify themselves with the Black cause, and did so in 1964, when 1,000 of them went south to assist Blacks to register as voters (a total of 1,700 were registered!), but were ultimately squeezed out of that crusade. At this juncture, the Vietnam War emerged as a suitable substitute; indeed, it soon offered more than enough for all. Also, throughout the decade, a number of local issues, some of them contrived, helped to keep the pot boiling.

Prominent in the student movement were the Students for a Democratic Society (SDS) founded at the University of Michigan in 1960 by Thomas Hayden and others who sought to achieve a society in which individuals could share in decisions affecting their lives. It was a noble purpose, preached by personable evangelists, and it appealed enormously to young people who felt they were trapped in a world they never made. The SDS became the most important core group in the student movement. Chapters were established on hundreds of campuses, and action focussed on peace, the Vietnam War, and whatever local issues could be used to embarrass local authorities. During the late 1960s, when university officers were frequently under siege, any mention of SDS caused most of them to tremble, so menacing had the power of that group become in the mythology of the time. But it was not a myth that local student leaders who were engaged in battles with institutional authority could get instant advice from SDS headquarters as to how to exploit local situations to their advantage. For example, what reasonable-sounding demand could be made that the administration would be unlikely to grant? And how could the ante be raised if it appeared that the demand were likely to be granted? Towards the end of the decade, however, the SDS was destroyed from within when militants usurped power, took to the streets, were unprepared to accept the police brutality that their militancy evoked and, in the course of it all, lost the sympathy of the average student, which had been the keynote to its previous success.

A second major initiative was the Berkeley Free Speech Movement. To an outsider, the University of California at Berkeley was an unlikely venue for a social earthquake. Nobel laureates were there, as were scholars of comparable reputation and achievement in other fields of study. Undergraduates had a wide choice from a modern curriculum, and graduate students could engage in well-supported research. Moreover, the administration was known to be tolerant, and the year-round climate in Berkeley was one of the best on offer in the United States. As it happened, the climate had been attractive to the flower children and their evolutionary successors, the hippies, who hung out near the University and regarded it as their neighbourhood recreation centre. The university also became the destination for serious students who had been alienated from families, sur-roundings, or institutions in other parts of the country. These arrived with chips on their shoulders, found the distinguished university they had expected, but discovered that they were small fry in a vast impersonal enterprise, a situation that other students had accepted as part of the deal. Thus, there was imported dissatisfaction, there was latent indigenous unrest, and there were numerous non-students who were ready to join in any excitement. The trouble began when activists set up tables on campus to solicit funds and volunteers for civil-rights initiatives. The solicitation of funds for non-university causes was against the rules, but the cause was so popular amongst students, and so politically sensitive, that the transgression was viewed by the administration with a blind eye. But, when other organizations set up tables, the University belatedly decided to enforce its own regulation. Thus, when non-student Jack Weinberg sat down at his CORE (Congress on Racial Equality) table on 1 October 1964, he was arrested and placed in a police car. Before the car could depart, however, it was surrounded by sitting students. This situation continued for the next thirty hours, whilst the jubilant besiegers played guitars, sang songs, and were stirred by Mario Savio and others who declared that the University had abolished free speech. In this improbable manner was the Free Speech Movement (FSM) born.

A few weeks later, Savio and three others were charged with acts of violence against the campus police during the earlier event. This led, on 2 December, to a rally of several thousand students at which Savio denounced the University, Joan Baez sang "The Lord's Prayer" and "We Shall Overcome," and those assembled marched solemnly to Sproul Hall, the seat of the administration, and took possession of it. When gentle persuasion failed, the governor of California ordered the students to be removed by force. In this action, 635 regular police spent twelve hours removing and arresting 814 limp occupants, 224 of whom were non-students. The police arrest was said to have been the largest such exercise in the history of the United States. It was followed by a student strike and various intermittent ructions over the next few years. This "sit-in" manoeuvre, borrowed, of course, from the black sit-ins of business establishments in the South, had not been employed before on a university campus but quickly became a major stock-in-trade of the student movement. It received unprecedented publicity as television cameras captured graphic images of defenceless students struggling for free speech in the face of bureaucratic cynicism and police brutality.

Most American colleges and universities experienced student protests of some form, often provoked by visiting activists and frequently orchestrated by strategists at SDS headquarters. One of the last events – and certainly the most tragic – was the demonstration at Kent State University in Ohio in the spring of 1970, in which four students were fatally shot by ill-instructed and young National Guardsmen, an event that did much to bring the nation to its senses.

Although Canadian institutions were virtually insulated from these events, every day brought news reports and television images of them. In addition, some of the draft dodgers who had made their way north brought personal accounts of protests in which they had been involved. And so, not surprisingly, Canadian students felt the urge to participate in what had become an international student movement.

It took a while for Canadian students to focus on a serious cause. In the meantime, a few took action against the status quo, for example, a sit-in at the principal's office at McGill. Carl Winkler, a distinguished chemist from the Manitoba Mennonite community, and at the time vice-principal for graduate studies and research at McGill, drifted over to see what was happening. Engaging one of the occupiers in conversation, he asked if any professional activists were in the group. She surveyed the crowd and admitted that there were two or three. "Are you a professional?" he asked. "No," she replied, "but I've had quite a bit of experience in the southern states."

Vancouver's climate seemed to attract more than its share of itinerant malcontents, and these took pleasure in embarrassing the administration at the University of British Columbia. This culminated, in 1968, with the arrival of a new president, Kenneth Hare, formerly dean of Arts and Science at McGill. Perhaps their meanest antic was to appear unannounced at the president's house, with all their belongings, to inform an innocent Mrs. Hare that they had been billeted with her. The more-than-mischievous events were so disturbing that Hare resigned early in the following year. Amongst many other things, he went on to be provost of Trinity College, University of Toronto, and chancellor of Trent University.

Occurrences such as these failed to elicit wide support, but protests against companies known or believed to be complicit in the Vietnam War attracted a wider following. Thus, Dow Chemical, the maker of napalm, became the symbol of immoral warfare and was regularly prevented from interviewing students on campus, a result that infuriated engineering students who were looking for jobs, and often led to scuffles. At the University of Manitoba, for example, on 7 November 1968, thirteen engineering students were forcefully barred from scheduled interviews with the Dow recruiter, whilst one demonstrator held high the sign "Dow Shalt Not Kill." Six weeks later, on 12 December, a group of engineering and commerce students cleared the way for those to be interviewed by Hawker-Siddley (aircraft). At no time did the combatants number more than 250.

The issue that soon united Canadian student leaders was that of participation in university governance. This was a genuine, home-grown issue, which engaged the attention of ordinary students and which provided ample opportunity for student resourcefulness. The experience at the University of Manitoba was not atypical.

Meanwhile, the students of Brandon University were also seeking representation on the University Senate. President Robbins was sympathetic and sought government approval, but not to the extent of equal representation with faculty, as demanded by the student officers, who were led by Harko Bhagat, an East Indian student from Kenya who had come to Brandon as part of a Robbins program to bring students from the Third World. Bhagat and his radical clique chose confrontation and personal invective in preference to rational discussion. In the spring of 1969, having been vilified for months in the student newspaper (*The Quill*), Robbins resigned in a "presidential" protest and, in an article in the 10 May 1969 issue of the *Globe and Mail*, warned that the majority of Canadian students and faculty "sit silent, often in disgust, and allow their leadership to go to those who do not really represent them."

The episode sobered the campus but gave a sad ending to Robbins's otherwise positive reign and disillusioned many Brandon citizens who had contributed to the foreign-student project. Bhagat, himself, moved on to the University of Manitoba, where he failed to make his mark as a demagogue, although he tried his best to do so.

The University of Manitoba Act of 1968

In 1963, the AUCC and the Canadian Association of University Teachers jointly commissioned a study of university governance. The impulse for the study came from the CAUT, who thought that professors should be represented on governing boards. The AUCC must have agreed to the proposal in a weak moment, as there was little other pressure to do so at the time. The two commissioners were Sir James Duff, one-time vice-chancellor of the University of Durham and son of a fellow of Trinity College, Cambridge, and Robert O. Berdahl, a young academic from San Francisco State College. He must have been young then because, after I had delivered a speech in 1983 to the American Society for Education, he came up to speak to me, and he still looked pretty young.

Duff, of course, was completely familiar with the British tradition. Apart from Oxford and Cambridge, which were governed entirely by professors, the supreme university body in the U.K. at that time was the council, comprising a minority of professors and a majority of lay members named by outside bodies. In Scotland, students were represented by a rector, but nowhere else did they have a voice on the council. The council had legal and financial responsibility for the institution as a whole, but it traditionally delegated authority for academic matters to a senate, which determined admissions policy, curricula, and examinations whilst overseeing student progress and academic facilities. Any senate decision with financial implications had to be ratified by the council, but the senate could also make representations to the council on a variety of other financial matters. Membership on the senate was drawn primarily from the teaching staff with a sprinkling of administrators included, but no students. In theory, the senate also served as an academic forum where grass-roots suggestions could begin their tortuous journey towards implementation. In practice, the result often fell short of that ideal: "Along these lines from toe to crown / Ideas flow up and vetoes down."

Berdahl's experience in the United States was completely different. The state universities were governed by regents appointed by the state legislatures, whilst the private universities were also governed by lay boards, heavy with alumni and often self-perpetuating. Professors had no place whatsoever in these supreme bodies. In some cases, even the president had no vote. At Harvard, the governing body was blatantly called the overseers. This prompted irreverent members of the university to suggest that the "overseers" "overlooked" agenda items, and that their decisions were "oversights."

Duff and Berdahl visited universities, listened to all vested interests, and recommended in March 1966 that professors be elected to the governing boards of Canadian universities but that outside members constitute the majority. Despite pleas from students, Duff and Berdahl felt that they should not have seats of their own but should elect a member who would represent their interests. This was a throwback to the practice in the four ancient Scottish universities (St. Andrew's, Glasgow, Aberdeen, and Edinburgh) of electing a rector to serve as student advocate on the university court, as the supreme body in Scotland was called. In Canada, there was precedent for such a representative at Queen's University, a practice obviously traceable to its Presbyterian origin.

If Canadian students had bought into the rectorship idea, which they didn't, it could have made for a lot of fun. The Scottish rectors were elected for three-year terms. Traditionally, the elections were contested, and hundreds of well-known personalities have allowed their names to stand for election. To an outsider, it's remarkable that they (especially politicians) would expose themselves to the embarrassment of defeat, for the results of these elections were not buried in local newspapers but were blazoned across the national press. During the nineteenth century, for example, at Glasgow University, Benjamin Disraeli failed for a second time in 1859, whilst his political nemesis, William Ewart Gladstone, lost the election in 1865 but was successful in 1877. Earlier, Gladstone had been elected at Edinburgh in 1859. At various times, Sir Walter Scott and Alfred Lord Tennyson were unsuccessful candidates at Glasgow. During this period, the rectors were chosen because of their prominence in public life or in literature, and the office was highly regarded and treated seriously. But, with time, candidates also emerged from the world of entertainment, and many of the elections developed into media events. Consider, for example, the result of the Edinburgh election of 1963, just three years before Duff and Berdahl recommended an analogous office for Canada: James Robertson Justice (actor), 1,916 votes; Peter Ustinov (writer and actor), 1,521; Dr. Nyerere (prime minister of Tanganyika), 354; Yehudi Menuhin (violinist), 239; Sean Connery (movie actor), 224.

A few years later, the students at Edinburgh took the unprecedented step of electing one of themselves, an action that had consequences beyond the university.

Following release of the Duff-Berdahl Report, the university established a committee to review the University of Manitoba Act. This committee (on which I served) was broadly representative of the university, including students. After numerous meetings, many of them marked by wrangling over student representation, the following principles were agreed to:

Board: twelve members appointed by the government, three members elected by the graduates, six members elected from the senate, plus the chancellor and vice-chancellor ex officio. Thus, lay members constituted a slight majority, and students had no guaranteed seats.

Senate: all deans plus twice as many professors, the president of the student union and six other students, two representatives of the Board, the deputy minister of education, plus chancellor, president, and vice-presidents ex officio. This made for a very large senate. Senate representatives to the Board were to be elected from the entire Senate membership and not by category.

Senate: given rather vague powers to advise the board on the university budget.

University and Community Council: a new body aimed at providing the University with the views of the community. It was to comprise twenty-five representatives from within the University and twenty-five members from outside.

These were the major points in the new act that was proposed to the provincial government and that was approved by it in the summer of 1968. But, the new act also included an innocent-looking clause that proved to be a "sleeper," namely, that the act would come into effect when all bodies had named their representatives to the Board and the Senate. I believe this clause was introduced by government lawyers at the drafting stage as a standard pro forma provision. But the students, who are always one step ahead of university administrators, seized upon it as a means of blackmail. They could delay naming their representatives to the Senate until certain "non-negotiable" demands were met. The fun had just begun.

The student union demanded that it conduct the elections of students to the senate, that one of the senate representatives on the board be a student, and that meetings of the board and senate be open to the public. Viewed in retrospect, these were pretty tame demands. I had no difficulty with the first and strongly favoured the other three, provided that confidential matters could be discussed in closed session at the Board and Senate. As yet, however, the students were unwilling to settle for anything but full and open meetings. I attempted to broker a compromise but was accused of conspiracy. In the meantime, the university was functioning as of old, with the new Board and Senate sitting unused on the shelf, and the student union and the *Manitoban* (the student newspaper) were calling for the resignation of the Board of Governors.

At this point, I suggested to Saunderson that he might solve the impasse by soliciting the help of the senior sticks, as the presidents of the faculty student societies were called, and who, as a group, were inclined to be conservative in their views. A meeting was called, but each senior stick brought with him or her the representative on the student union of that faculty. Before Saunderson could introduce the subject, all sticks announced that they would be represented by their student union representatives. Thus, in the twinkling of an eye, Saunderson found himself facing the same implacable group that he had been trying to bypass. The meeting was a fiasco, but Saunderson never reproached me for my bad advice.

Gradually, under pressure from its constituents, the student union agreed that certain matters could be decided in camera, and the Senate agreed to

UMSU president Chris Westdal and vice-president Janice Johnson, 1968-69.

open meetings and to reserve one of its places on the board for a student. The student union conducted elections to the Senate, with the six representatives chosen on 29 January 1969 from a total of twenty-six candidates. The Senate elected its representatives to the Board, and the Board agreed to debate the subject of open meetings for itself. I had been elected to the Board from the Senate, as had Lloyd Dulmage, who was now dean of the Faculty of Arts. The Board agreed on the following procedure: to *debate* the subject of open meetings at an open meeting and then move into closed session to reach its decision. Scarcely had the debate begun under the gavel of Frank Meighen of Brandon, the current chair, when Dulmage moved and someone seconded that board meetings be open. The many students in the gallery erupted into cheers, and Meighen had no choice but to put the question. I voted against, because we had agreed to hold the vote in camera but, under pressure of the cheers, the motion passed. Thus, I was perceived as opposing open meetings (which I favoured) and Dulmage became the darling of the gallery by breaking the agreement. The *Manitoban* later reported "that this senior administrator [Duckworth] could not be trusted."

The student leaders who led the campaign included Chris Westdal, later Canadian ambassador to Ukraine, Janice Johnson, who sits in the Senate of Canada, Thomas Traves, currently president of Dalhousie University, and Nelson Wiseman, who became a well-known political scientist. No wonder they outsmarted the rest of us.

In commenting on the effectiveness of the new versions of the Board and the Senate, I do so as a veteran observer with twenty-one years on university boards, at McMaster, Manitoba, and Winnipeg, and well over thirty years on senates.

The new board had six representatives from the Senate, one of them a student. Additionally, the government chose to include two recent students amongst its ten appointees. Thus, the new elements were three present or recent students and five professors; at the start, these new members had a tendency to feel their oats. But things soon settled down, and an agreeable modus operandi developed. As before, the president introduced most of the agenda items, but, if the new members thought that he had missed a point or misrepresented it, they were quick (but courteous) to correct the record. In other words, they kept the president honest, although this was scarcely necessary, as Saunderson was not one to deceive or dissemble. On controversial matters, the students were particularly assiduous in defending student interests. The professors were more inclined to consider the welfare of the institution as a whole. Meetings were longer than before, but matters were discussed more thoroughly and with greater knowledge. Without doubt, the new board was more effective than its predecessor.

Confidentiality was a new concept for the students who, idealistic as they were, felt that all facets of the university should be open to view. In addition to legal and contract matters, it was agreed that individual salaries would be confidential, as they always had been. On this understanding, William Condo, the vice-president (administration) continued to distribute to all Board members a book listing all the salaries in the institution. What a mine of information that was for the curious or the envious! One of the early student members leaked the salary information to the *Winnipeg Free Press*, which earned him reproach but provoked no remorse. He became a local lawyer, and his name appeared again in the *Winnipeg Free Press* a few years ago as owing more traffic tickets than anyone else in the city. He was the exception to a highly responsible group of student members.

The Senate took longer to settle down. For one thing, it was a huge body, with about 100 members. But, in addition, there was the vague clause in the Act that authorized the Senate to "make recommendations to the board with respect to academic planning, campus planning, a building program, budget policies, procedures in respect of appointments, promotions, salaries, tenure and dismissals, *and any other matters considered by the senate to be of interest to the university*" [emphasis mine]. Some saw this clause as a once-in-a-lifetime opportunity to seize power for the Senate, provided they acted quickly and before the lay members of the Board realized what was in the wind. The long-term result of this pre-emptive mood was the Planning and Priorities Committee of Senate (PPC), which reports to Senate on major matters, including financial ones. It has become a useful and integral part of the decision-making process. In addition, the new senate appointed a plethora of committees that gave its members more than enough to chew on. In fact, the students (who initially were so anxious to be involved in everything) soon found that they were unable to provide enough students to fill their allotted committee places. Agitating for participation is a lot more fun than attending dreary meetings.

To expedite what were now very lengthy agenda, a senate executive was established, which reviewed the agenda before Senate meetings and, in most cases, recommended appropriate action. Because I reported for the executive, I had a detailed knowledge of the often-complex matters under consideration. Overweight as it is, the senate has continued to function in much the same fashion. Fortunately, not all members participate in all debates. The student senators have been particularly restrained, but they have been effective when they do intervene.

The university and community council, although splendid in the abstract, never caught on and disappeared unwept, unhonoured, and unsung.

Faculty of Education

When I assumed administrative responsibility for the Faculty of Education in 1966, it was only one year after teacher training at the Teachers' College in Tuxedo had been transferred to the University. This had quadrupled enrollment in the faculty, and Dean John Brown was busy integrating his new students and his new staff. In addition, he had to deal with a new vice-president who thought that the academic qualifications of his staff should be raised. Understandably, the Teachers' College had not demanded doctorates from its staff, but this was now the University, and higher standards were essential.

I entered into my discussions with Brown with the view that education was a somewhat lesser discipline. My own experience in the Faculty of Education during 1936-37 had been disenchanting, and I had since heard that many theses presented for the D.Ed. were below Ph.D. standard. One day, Dean Brown proudly brought to my office for interview a candidate who had a Ph.D. in mathematics. I asked which branch of mathematics he had studied, but could find no common thread. Finally, half joking, I said, "But you have studied differential equations?" He had not; rather, his Ph.D. had been on the teaching of Grade 4 mathematics.

With Brown's help, I came to realize that advanced study in education cannot be compared with advanced study in physics. The nature of the classroom is not the nature of the physical world. For a high-school physics teacher, a knowledge of physics is essential, but it is not the task of the Faculty of Education to provide that teacher with it. Rather, the Faculty provides the intending teacher with the techniques and personal understandings that are needed to impart his or her knowledge of physics to high school students.

Two little-known events occurred during this period. The first was a conversation I had with Wesley Lorimer, then deputy minister of Education. I was describing to him the need for additional space for education and the inability of the university to provide it. Lorimer said that he might find the needed funds in his own budget – which he did – and the new facilities appeared as soon as architect and builder could complete their tasks. In 1980, Lorimer became chair of the UGC and presided over that office with a firm, but fair, hand.

On another occasion, I was asked to go to the office of Larry Desjardins, then sitting as a Liberal in the Manitoba legislature. There I found Alfred Monnin, who later became chief justice for Manitoba but, at that time, was closely associated with St. Boniface College. They explained that French-language schools in the province needed teachers whose training had been given in that lanugage. I agreed with their point and offered to speak with Saunderson, who also agreed. This was before the UGC was established; in other words, before decisions on new programs became complicated. I telephoned Desjardins and Monnin to give St. Boniface the green light and informed Dean Brown that St. Boniface would begin to train French-language teachers. He raised neither eyebrow nor objection; he was relatively new to the university and accepted the decision as a fact of life. Participatory democracy had not yet come to the University of Manitoba.

The Defence Research Board

When I was appointed to the Defence Research Board (DRB) in 1965, Hartley Zimmerman was its chairman, a soft-spoken, somewhat reserved individual who seemed in control of the situation. Among the ex officio members were the chief of staff of the Army (General Allard), the deputy minister of Defence (Elgin Armstrong), the deputy minister of Defence Production (Gordon Hunter) and the president of the NRC (Guy Ballard). These were powerful personalities, but I was less awed than when I had joined the Honorary Advisory Council of the NRC four years earlier. Appointed members included Wilfred Bigelow (a native of Brandon), the pioneer heart surgeon who had observed during the war that body functions slow down with cold and had conceived the idea that cooling the heart would give more time for surgeons to perform their work. Another appointed member was A.S. ("Van") Van Cleave, then dean of Graduate Studies at the University of Regina, who had obtained his doctorate in chemistry from Cambridge University whilst being supported by an 1851

London Exhibition scholarship. These awards had been established with the surplus from the great London Exhibition of 1851 to enable science students in the British Empire to pursue advanced study. Because Van Cleave was married, he was not allowed to live in college at Cambridge, and he and his wife stayed in quarters approved by the college. To fulfill the requirements, Mrs. Van Cleave was declared the official "landlady." Each Monday morning, Van Cleave had the humiliation of delivering a letter from his landlady wife to the college administration, attesting that he had been a resident in her establishment during the preceding week.

The DRB had been established after World War II under the founding presidency of Omand Solandt, a wartime expert in operations research and, like myself, a son of the manse. It had several defence research establishments located across the country, for example, at Dartmouth, at Valcartier (north of Quebec City), in Toronto, and at Suffield (Alberta). In addition, it operated an extensive extramural research program in the universities, under the administration of Ronald Low and with the help of advisory committees. I had entered the DRB ambit as a member of the Advisory Committee on Electronic Research, chaired by Garnett Woonton of McGill University. The whole operation was well run but, of course, all research had to be related to defence.

DRE Suffield was the site for defence against biological and chemical warfare, and lurid stories appeared from time to time in the press about the unholy goings-on in that highly secret laboratory. One of those who spoke against the laboratory was Mrs. Muriel Duckworth of Halifax, and she became a regular agenda item at DRB meetings. I kept silent but was the target of hostile looks until I pointed out that she was not a relative of mine. Matters came to a head when Mrs. Duckworth announced in Calgary that she was going to attempt to enter the Suffield laboratory. The superintendent decided to cooperate fully, meeting her at the gate and inviting her to tour the establishment. After a tedious walk through various buildings, the superintendent said there was only one building yet to inspect. According to the DRB version of events, Mrs. Duckworth said, "Forget it," and returned to Calgary, where she told the waiting press that there was one building that she was not allowed to enter.

Zimmerman was succeeded by Robert Uffen (a geophysicist) and he by "Hap" l'Heureux, both of them effective and agreeable chairmen. It was the pleasant custom of the chairmen to invite board members to dinner at their homes. Mrs. Zimmerman was a particularly engaging hostess, because she included members of the Ottawa establishment in these parties and regaled us with unlikely stories. One evening she told Louis Rasminsky (governor of the Bank of Canada) and me that she had been a technician in the laboratory of Frederick Banting at the time insulin was discovered. Sufferers from diabetes flocked to Toronto; at one time, eleven private railway cars were parked in Union Station. She also told of dealing with the securities in her father's estate. The last security to be dealt with was an American one, with a note stating that it had been bought for $540 on the advice of Mr. Snowflake, a friend of her father's. It turned out to be the original stock of Eastman Kodak and was worth $225,000.

I served on the DRB for two terms, from 1965 to 1971. In 1974, the DRB was disbanded, and its functions were subsumed by the Department of Defence. The research establishments still exist, but they are constituents of the Defence Research and Development branch rather than parts of a free-standing research body.

Presidential Search Committees: 1966 to 1971

Shortly after arriving in Winnipeg, I was asked to consider the presidency of the University of Guelph, which had just been created from the Ontario Agricultural College, an affiliate of the University of Toronto. Although I was reluctant to consider moving so soon, Saunderson urged me to meet with their representatives, if only as a courtesy, which I did in the course of another trip East. One of the group was Moffat Woodside of the University of Toronto, who was obviously assisting the institution in its transition. His father had been the minister of St. Stephen's-Broadway United Church in Winnipeg and a friend of my father. Woodside was older than I, but we had that Winnipeg connection in common. In that meeting, I suggested that the background of the institution called for a biologist rather than a physicist. In any event, I indicated that I was not a candidate for the position, *even though the president's house came with a full-time maid*. William Winegard, a metallurgist from Toronto and later minister of state in the Ministry of Industry, Science and Technology in the Mulroney government, was appointed to the position and served the institution well.

In 1967, the prospect of higher office came somewhat closer, when I was invited to address the Vancouver Institute, where unannounced tryouts for the presidency of the University of British Columbia were being held. Several declared or undeclared candidates had already addressed these Saturday-evening meetings, and more were to follow me. And so, on 4 February 1967, as part of the charade, I had dinner at the home of my friend George Volkoff, a professor of physics at UBC, only to discover that Chancellor and Mrs. Nathan Nemetz were among the guests. During the meal, it emerged that Mrs. Nemetz had recently read my effort at popularizing physics, *Little Men in the Unseen World*.

Following dinner, we moved to a well-filled auditorium, where my speech appeared to be well received. On my return to Winnipeg, my wife and I decided that it was still too soon to leave the University of Manitoba, and I asked that my name be removed from consideration. I was later sent a clipping from a Vancouver newspaper reporting that the leading candidate had withdrawn; perhaps I was spared the fate that befell my friend Kenneth Hare.

A year later, in the spring of 1968, Dean Robert Wallace, a physicist, asked me to visit the University of Victoria, which was looking for a new president. This was an intensive visit, as I was passed from one person to another and quizzed about a variety of subjects, in particular whether or not the university should establish a law school. My off-hand view was that it might be premature. I was never a formal candidate and, I suppose for that reason, learned only from the newspaper that the vice-president (administration) of Johns Hopkins University in Baltimore, B.J. Partridge, had been appointed to the post. Amongst his qualifications were two law degrees (LL.B. and J.D.) from Blackstone University. Early in his administration, he alienated the students, who set out to destroy him. Although his curriculum vitae had listed Blackstone as the institution from which he held the law degrees, the students discovered that it was not an accredited university, but one that *sold* degrees for less than normal work. This precipitated his resignation, and many felt that he had been shabbily treated. If the provenance of the law degrees had been so important, the search committee should have satisfied itself on that point. A couple of short presidencies followed at Victoria before my old friend Howard Petch moved there from Waterloo in 1975 to give exemplary leadership for fifteen years. Incidentally, recent assessments by *Maclean's* magazine have rated the Victoria Law School as the best in Canada.

Saunderson was due to retire on 31 August 1970. Accordingly, a search committee was established that was representative of all parts of the University, with chancellor Curry as chair and Maurice Arpin, chair of the Board, as vice-chair. This committee worked in secret, but it ultimately emerged that it had narrowed things down to an internal candidate, me, and an external candidate, Ernest Sirluck of the University of Toronto. Sirluck had taken his Ph.D. at Chicago and had served there as full professor before being invited to Toronto as vice-president for Graduate Studies and Research. He was a recognized scholar, was extremely articulate, had come from the largest university in Canada, and had been an undergraduate at the University of Manitoba. I understand that few members of the search committee failed to support his candidature.

Meanwhile, I had been asked to meet the search committee at the University of Waterloo. This led to a two-day visit to that campus, a public lecture, and a whirlwind of interviews with individuals and groups. My friend Howard Petch was vice-president (academic) but, for some reason, was not a candidate for the presidentcy. Before departing for home, I was asked if I would accept the position if it were offered to me. I answered that I could not give that assurance, as I was a candidate for the presidency of the University of Manitoba. I thought that it was an unfair question. Chancellor Needles phoned me soon thereafter to say that Burt Matthews of Guelph had been appointed.

With Sirluck coming to Manitoba, I thought that we might both be happier if I were to disappear for a year. Accordingly, I asked for, and was granted, one year's leave-of-absence with the proviso that I not be required to return to the University. This enabled me to go to Laval on leave, and to consider other employment options. In the weeks following these events, I received two telephone calls, one from Chancellor Steinkopf of Brandon University and the other from my wartime friend Robert Bell, now dean of Graduate Studies at McGill.

Brandon was seeking a successor to its recently retired president, John Robbins. My wife and I spent a Saturday talking with Steinkopf and the chair of the Board, Milton Holden, president of the Wawanesa Mutual Insurance Company, and on whose company board I later served for fifteen years. It was enticing to return to the city of my birth, but we expressed our thanks and proceeded with our plans to spend the next academic year in Quebec City. Brandon subsequently appointed Lloyd Dulmage, dean of Arts at Manitoba.

Bob Bell was a member of the search committee at McGill. He asked me, as a personal favour, to meet with the committee. Without much enthusiasm, because the arrangements to go to Quebec City were now complete, I made the trip to Montreal and on 26 May reported to Bob's office. He said that he would not be accompanying me to the meeting as he had resigned from the committee to become a candidate. I wished that I had known that before leaving Winnipeg the night before. In the event, I told the committee that I had not known that Bell was a candidate but, now that he was, I supported his candidature. Davidson Dunton, formerly president of Carleton, was the third name on the short list. Bell received the appointment.

In the early fall of 1970, Sirluck asked me to decide by 1 November whether or not I intended to return to Manitoba, an entirely reasonable request. I replied that I would do so by 1 February. I knew that the University of Winnipeg was considering my name, and I had the impression that something attractive might turn up in Ottawa. Late in January, Chancellor Thorlakson phoned to invite me to meet with the Winnipeg search committee, a meeting that led, on 30 January, to the offer of the presidency. It was a close call as, by this time, I had been invited to become executive director of the AUCC and to become the metric commissioner for Canada, both positions with lots of scope. I accepted the offer from my old college and spent the next ten years in its happy employ. The other final candidate was John Clake, dean of Arts and Science, with whom I enjoyed a satisfying relationship. Without doubt, his candidature suffered from being an internal one: distant fields are always greener.

At the time I was considering the offer of metric commissioner, the United States had committed itself to the metric system. Indeed, that was the major factor in Canada's decision to go metric. But soon after I had declined the position, the United States reneged on its commitment, and Canada found itself unaccompanied by its neighbour on what was now a much less popular path. Many times since have I expressed relief that I did not become the metric commissioner for Canada, but who was to know that at the time?

Royal Society Meeting in Winnipeg, 1970

The Royal Society has the tradition of holding its annual meetings at different universities across the country, having received or extracted invitations two or three years in advance. At one time, the arrival of the Society, with its celebrated scholars, was an event to cherish, with no financial obligation other than to lay on a banquet for the fellows. Gradually, however, other scholarly societies were formed and began to hold their meetings before and after the Royal Society's meetings, and at the same university. This moving caravan of savants, which rapidly grew in size, came to be known as the Learned Societies or, as George Gilmour called them, the so-called Learned Societies. Thus, the impending arrival of the Royal Society no longer meant the coming of 200 to 300 individuals but an avalanche of thousands of professors and their graduate students, each of whom expected to receive some form of hospitality from the host institution. Only the larger universities could now afford to invite the Royal Society, and its arrival became less of an honour, more of a burden.

The Royal Society had met at the University of Manitoba in 1954, the year I was inducted, and in 1970 its turn had come around again (it met once more in Winnipeg in 1986). Lloyd Dulmage was placed in charge of arrangements and wisely hired Mary Elizabeth Bayer (who had been a central Manitoba figure in the centennial celebrations of 1967) to be his working second-in-command. As I was the vice president (designate) of the Royal Society, I had special responsibility for its meeting, which took place between 31 May and 3 June. The other Winnipeg-based fellows and their spouses were also involved in the arrangements and the hospitality.

I was hoping, as many previous officers of the Royal Society had done, to discover a useful role for the society to play, in addition to its encouragement and recognition of scholarship. Accordingly, after touching base with a few others, I proposed that the society institute a symposium program for the ventilation of topics of current concern. Further, I suggested that the first symposium deal with mercury pollution, a subject of the greatest concern to the residents of Minamata, Japan, and one that was potentially serious for Canada as well. I expressed the view that symposia of this sort could be supported by outside money and would not be a drain on the meagre resources of the society. Although the society is notoriously reluctant to do anything new, the fellows agreed to the proposal, and an organizing committee for a symposium called *Mercury in Man's Environment* was struck and had its first meeting before the fellows left town. The committee included non-fellows, in particular the energetic Wallace Johnston, then director of the Freshwater Research Laboratory, located on the University of Manitoba campus. The symposium was held in Ottawa on 15 October. Since then, more than thirty symposia have been sponsored by the Royal Society, and in every case the proceedings have been published as a permanent record of the event.

Honorary Degrees

The honorary degree is amongst the highest honours within a university's gift. Furthermore, it is awarded publicly. For these reasons, and also because honorees are often well known in the community, there is unfailing discussion of the merits of those selected for this form of academic beatification.

Prime candidates for honorary degrees are graduates of the institution whose accomplishments are a natural source of familial pride. Also highly acceptable are eminent scholars or persons who have excelled in literature or the arts. Professors can empathize with this sort of achievement, and the honoree can usually be depended upon to give a good convocation address. The honouring of entertainers can easily become a travesty; for example, Bill Cosby is said to have received $25,000 for delivering the commencement address at the University of South Carolina in 1986, and shameless colleges have invented ad hoc degrees for Bob Hope (e.g., he was given the Doctor of Humane Humor at Benedictine College). Nominations from the world of business must be handled carefully: if the individual has made a major gift, the connection between the degree and the gift must be minimized and a decent time allowed to elapse between the cause and the effect. As for politicians, it's best to wait until they leave politics. Perhaps the most publicized example of the danger of not waiting was the refusal of Oxford University to award an honorary degree to Margaret Thatcher, the prime minister of Great Britain and *graduate of Oxford*. Angered at what was regarded as inadequate government funding for higher education and for scientific research, the "congregation" (the parliament of Oxford) assembled in the Sheldonian Theatre on 29 January 1985 to vote 738 to 319 against the motion. Mrs. Thatcher later told an audience that she was a graduate of Oxford but had never let that hold her back.

Sometimes the recognition comes too late. Thus it was in 1961, when the University of Manitoba honoured Fred Varley, one of the Group of Seven, who was then in his eighties At the dinner on the evening before convocation, Varley left his seat to ask the woman who was looking after him, "Why am I here?" And the next day, as the academic procession left the platform, his newly acquired hood began to slip over his shoulders, seemingly destined to trip him. But, just as the hood fell to his ankles, Varley miraculously stepped out of it, and Douglas Chevrier, walking behind him, scooped it up in his arms. Varley died in 1969.

Tom Lamb, a bush pilot and founder of Lambair, was another who was honoured by the University of Manitoba. He also operated a general store in the North. At the dinner prior to his convocation, he told of receiving an order for two pairs of bloomers from a woman who lived in the bush. It closed with the words, "Ask Tom Lamb, he knows the size."

Jack Pickersgill, another recipient, was a 1926 graduate of the University of Manitoba who had lectured in history at Wesley College from 1929 to 1937, and who became secretary to the Privy Council before entering politics himself. He was introduced to convocation by Walter Swayze, professor of English at United College. Walter said that Pickersgill had been so affected by one of Prime Minister King's speeches that he had joined the Liberal Party and, ultimately, wrote King's speeches for him. When Pickersgill rose to address convocation, he said that he had not been converted to liberalism by King's speeches but by those of Arthur Meighen (King's Conservative opponent).

Many years later, in 1989, whilst I was chancellor of the University of Manitoba, I awarded a D.Sc. (*honoris causa*) to Andrei Sackarov, the Russian physicist-turned-activist. He is said to have been the cleverest physicist ever to have attended the University of Moscow. Arriving on the scene too late to contribute to Russia's atomic bomb, he contributed the crucial idea to its hydrogen bomb. Later in life he became inflamed in the cause of human rights, not a popular cause in Russia at the time and, as a consequence, became persona (summa) non grata. He came to Winnipeg to receive the

Humanitarian Award of the St. Boniface Hospital Research Foundation. At the dinner honouring him, the Russian national anthem was sung, although none of us understood the meaning of the words. Before he delivered his speech of acceptance, Sackarov told us that the words were an old version of the anthem and that he was offended by them. That stunned the audience, but I suppose a true activist must never allow anything offensive to slip past. Although he suffered badly from heart disease and was fatigued, he was made to visit the Physics Department, including our mass spectroscopy laboratory. He seemed only slightly impressed by our work, perhaps because he was weary, but I also sensed a touch of arrogance. I guess he had good reason to be arrogant; after all, he had been the cleverest physicist ever to have attended the University of Moscow.

I should like to have been present at Oxford when Sir Rowland Hill, the inventor of the postage stamp, was honoured. The chancellor and Sir Rowland were the final members of the academic procession and, as they mounted the stage at the Sheldonian Theatre, it became apparent to all that only one chair remained for the two of them. In the brief period between the recognition of the problem and its solution, a student called from the gallery, "Stick him in the upper right corner."

Following the degree ceremony, there is often good-natured banter as to whether the new "doctor" can provide medical treatment. This is reminiscent of Stephen Leacock's ocean voyage shortly after receiving the Ph.D. from the University of Chicago. He heard an announcement on the public address system that the ship's nurse had injured her leg and a doctor was needed. Although he ran as quickly as he could, he found that a doctor of divinity had beaten him to it.

Leaving Manitoba

I had been increasingly embarrassed by my lack of knowledge of the French language and hoped that a year at Laval would put me more at ease with the many French Canadians I was meeting through the Royal Society and other national bodies. Further, I had good friends at Laval in the persons of Larkin Kerwin (then *vice-recteur*) and Garnet Woonton (then *directeur* of the *Centre pour Recherche sur les Atomes et les Molecules*). My wife who, as always, supported the adventure, and my daughter, who had majored in French, resolved to do graduate work at Laval. We set off in high spirits and conscious that I might not return to the University of Manitoba.

Laval University: 1970–71

10

Before taking up residence in Quebec City, my wife and daughter and I spent the month of August in Europe, where I was to give the banquet speech at the International Conference on Mass Spectrometry in Brussels. We spent the first week in Deauville at le Nid d'Éte, where the only available accommodation included full *pension*. As veteran travellers know, it's demanding to face a regimen of full-course meals at noon and in the evening, but we needed rooms and had no other choice. As each of the meals had a cheese course, I became overly familiar with the principal cheeses of Normandy (*camembert*, good; *Pont-l'Évêque*, not bad; and *Livarot*, not to my taste), and acquired a taste for lesser-known varieties from other parts of France, such as Savoie and Rondon. As for *chèvre*, the goats should be made to eat it themselves. The Norman apple brandy, *Calvados*, was also used discreetly to create a space in the stomach (the *trou normand*) when further eating seemed desirable but physically impossible. After a few days in Paris, we made our way to Bernkastel, on the Mosel, where we observed the celebrated Doktor vineyards but drank labels we could afford. Finally, after Brussels and in London, we went down to breakfast on 5 September 1970, at the Strand Palace Hotel to find ourselves surrounded by distraught Russian ballet dancers: the day before, their star, Natalia Makarova, had defected to the West, where she subsequently had a distinguished career both in the United States and the United Kingdom. We saw her in 1997 at the Chichester Festival, where she played Lina Szczepanowska, the physical fitness tyrant in Shaw's *Misalliance*. She looked as if she could still dance.

Our abode in Quebec was in Sillery Plaza, a large apartment in St. Foy overlooking the St. Lawrence River, and a mile from Laval University. My friend, Larkin Kerwin, from his position of influence, had secured an appointment for me as *professor visiteur*, had provided me with an office in the

Department of Physics, and had arranged instruction in French for both my wife and myself. Additionally, Monsignor Parent, who had invented the CJEP for the Quebec post-secondary system, sent me a membership in le Cercle Universitaire, located on rue des Ramparts in the Old City. We felt that we were bona fide members of the University. Parent, who was greatly respected, died the following spring, and the huge basilica was quite inadequate to house those who wished to pay him tribute.

The October Crisis

The first major event was the October Crisis, when Prime Minister Trudeau dispatched troops to control the militant FLQ (Front de Libération du Québec). Certain individuals were regarded as possible targets of this revolutionary group and were also deemed important enough to protect. Thus, on my nightly walk with our dog along the rue de la Falaise, I was aware of a silent sentinel guarding a particular house. We were told that to qualify for an armed guard was to zoom to the top of the social register, and wives were known to have castigated their husbands for failing to provide that unique cachet. Otherwise, we were unaffected by the crisis, and life appeared to unfold in its normal way, at least until the murdered body of Pierre Laporte was discovered and the Canadian Broadcasting Corporation drew relentlessly from its record library of dirges.

Life in Quebec City

We took immense pleasure in the ambience of the city. Because it was completely French-speaking, a few English-speaking interlopers, such as we, offered no language threat. Our attempts to communicate in French were indulged as if to a child and, in other ways, we were aided and assisted. In addition, of course, we were living in a city rich in history and of great beauty. That particular winter we enjoyed a special treat – 180 inches of snow – as *tempête* after *tempête* inundated the city. Ottawa suffered the same fate: the *Ottawa Citizen* showed a man shovelling snow from his driveway into his basement, having run out of places to stow it. I put snow tires on *all* wheels in a desperate attempt to secure traction.

Lupita and Larkin Kerwin had adopted us as their special wards, and we enjoyed endless kindnesses at their hands. My wartime colleague, Gar Woonton, had moved from Western Ontario to Laval, via McGill, and we also took pleasure in his company and that of his wife, Isabel. Gar showed me a pile of scribblers, all full, in which he had written French verb forms in his determination to become bilingual. The Kerwins, by the way, were trilingual, as Lupita's father had been the Mexican consul in Quebec.

Mercury in Man's Environment

The Royal Society Symposium on Mercury Pollution was held in Ottawa on 15 October. By courtesy of Guy Sylvestre, the national librarian and a fellow of the Society, we were able to use the auditorium in the National Library, which seated about 300 persons. The place was packed with scientists concerned with, or involved in, the problem and, especially, with public officials who would be responsible for dealing with it. We had an expert from Minamata, who showed us harrowing photographs of the victims of "Minamata disease," and another from Sweden, where the disease (although much milder) had been recognized as a consequence of the pulp-and-paper industry. American and Canadian authorities fleshed out the program. In my introductory remarks, I reminded the audience that mercury had been the traditional treatment for syphilis. This has led to the aphorism "A night in the arms of Venus leads to a lifetime in the clutches of Mercury." Although the Royal Society has since sponsored dozens of symposia, none has been more timely or better received than was this, its inaugural effort.

Governance of Laval University

In the academic year 1970-71, the governance of Laval was still in the hands of the Catholic Church. Cardinal Roy was the chancellor, and Archbishop Vachon was rector and vice-chancellor. In 1972, the University became secularized, and Kerwin was elected its first lay rector, despite the fact that his background was Irish and not *pure laine*. But, after the transition, the institution continued to operate under its two charters – from the Queen in 1852 and from the Pope in 1886 – an academic version of the belt-and-braces policy, and one that is unique in Canada.

Studying French

Of the nine months we spent in Quebec City, I spent fifty-nine working days in other places. Thus, counting travel time, I was elsewhere for almost thirty percent of the time. For thirty-nine days, I was in Ottawa for the National Reseach Council (NRC), the Defence Research Board, the Royal Society, and the Nuffield Foundation. A convenient flight departed Quebec City for Ottawa at 17:25 hours, and the return direct flight left Ottawa at 15:45. I spent the remaining twenty days in Winnipeg, Montreal, Vancouver, and the Arctic. My wife and daughter came to know well the village of Ancien Lorette as they drove me to and from the airport. Because of this excessive travel, my attendance at French class was inevitably erratic. Notwithstanding, I managed to lose my fear of the language and, had I been placed in a

French environment, I would soon have been able to function in the French equivalent of broken English.

In the spring, to compensate for the missed classes, I hired a student named Gagnon to have lunch with me. Each day he would choose a restaurant that offered a "businessman's" lunch, and I would order the food. In this way, we patronized several of the finer dining places in the Old City, including La Réserve, Café de la Paix, Le Beaujolais, Continental, La Seigneurie, Restaurant aux anciens Canadiens, La Chaumière, Chez Guido, and Chez Rabelais. I don't think young Gagnon had ever been so well fed. Driving back to the University one day, I stopped at a corner to be sure the coast was clear. Gagnon said, *"C'est beau a droit."* I turned to see the beautiful view before realizing that I'd been told that no cars were coming.

Of course, idioms work both ways. Paul Giguière, probably the leading chemist at Laval, had spent a sabbatical in California at a time when Madame Giguière's English was rudimentary. During the day, when Paul was at the laboratory, she had difficulty dealing with salesmen who knocked on the apartment door. Paul advised her to say, "I'm not interested." To the next caller, she said, "I'm not interesting," which elicited the reply, "That's what you think, Lady."

French-Canadian Family Names

In hotel rooms, I have often chosen the telephone directory over the Gideon Bible, not only looking for Duckworths but also to ascertain the most common names in those cities. Following the same bent, I discovered that Tremblay was listed 1,400 times in the directory for the City of Quebec, whilst three names followed with 800 entries each: Côté, Gagnon, and Roy. This simple observation has served as a popular conversation topic with numerous French Canadians, whether from Quebec City or elsewhere. Usually they get the Tremblay right but have trouble with the next group of three, even when told the numbers of letters in each name. But most are determined to guess the names without help. I am told that Chicoutimi is the ancestral home of the Tremblays: in that city, one can greet a strange man with, *"Bonjour, Monsieur Tremblay,"* and be correct fifty percent of the time.

Committee on Plasma Research

Bill Schneider, president of the NRC, had asked me to chair a study of the financial support needed for plasma research (Committee on Plasma Science and its Applications). Other members included W.B. Lewis (vice-president for research at Atomic Energy of Canada Ltd.), Morrel M. Bachynski (RCA

Victor, a plasma expert), Don Hurst (president of the Atomic Energy Control Board), William Cheeseman (president of Canadian General Electric), G.G. Cloutier (from Hydro Quebec), and A. John Alcock (NRC) as secretary. We held a one-day symposium in Ottawa in January, at which speakers reviewed for us the applications of plasmas to physics, chemistry, engineering, metallurgy, et cetera. With this knowledge, plus whatever we had had before, we began working on our report. Lewis was a fanatical defender of power from uranium fission and, whenever Bachynski mentioned the potential of nuclear *fusion* as a source of power, Lewis took it as a personal criticism. Conversely, but to a less indignant degree, whenever Lewis spoke favourably about fission power (which he always did), Bachynski took it as a slur on fusion power. This feud led to lengthy meetings. A few years ago, Hurst and I were reminiscing about the committee and he said, "Just as the tension between Lewis and Bachynski reached its peak, you would say, 'Don, will you take the chair: I must catch the 15:35 flight to Quebec City.'" However, we finally cobbled something together, to which Lewis and Bachynski assented. Predictably, it called for increased support for plasma research. In due course, I presented it to the full council. Schneider had invited his minister, Alastair Gillespie, to hear the report, but he seemed quite underwhelmed by it. I wished I could have energized him, because Schneider probably had a tough time getting him to the meeting.

Tour of the Arctic

During the five-day period between 17 and 21 May, as a member of the Defence Research Board, I had a remarkable tour of the Arctic. On the 17th, our party of twelve to fourteen flew from Ottawa to Bagotville, en route to Frobisher Bay. At Bagotville, we were bundled into two Army helicopters and flown over the village of St. Jean Vianney, which had just suffered a horrifying disaster: heavy rainfall had weakened landfill on which a group of houses had been built, and these had slithered into a valley, with considerable loss of life. From the air, the whole tragic scene lay before us.

Back on our military plane, we proceeded to Frobisher Bay on Baffin Island, home to 1,200 Inuit and the largest such community in Canada. There we spent that night, and I purchased a ceramic pot from the local cooperative store. It was made of red clay, unglazed, and of crude workmanship, but on its outside were embossed figures of a man at four stages of a dance that involved jumping into the air. It was about the size of a champagne cooler, it cost $500, and it had come from Baker Lake, which is located northwest of Hudson Bay. I knew what it was and was astonished to find it in Frobisher Bay.

Inuit carving is an indigenous art form, but Inuit printmaking is based on a technique introduced from the south. At the time it was introduced, much care was taken not to suggest subject matter to the printmakers. Buoyed by the commercial success of the Inuit prints, the Department of Northern Affairs looked for other techniques that might provide a livelihood for artistic Inuit. Ceramic making was chosen, large amounts of clay were shipped to Baker Lake, and the residents were invited to have a go. When the promoters of the idea returned to assess the project, they found shelves of red objects, unglazed and of poor workmanship, declared them unfit for sale, and ordered them destroyed. My pot somehow escaped the massacre; perhaps it had been warned in advance and sought sanctuary in the cooperative store in Frobisher Bay. I have protected it from the Philistines ever since.

The next day, the 18th, we flew to Thule, the American Distant Early Warning base in Greenland where the indigenous population was 250 Inuit and 1,000 dogs. There, we inspected the missile-detecting system and stayed the night. We had expected to be received as visiting royalty, but our visit coincided with that of the American secretary for Defence. Although our party included the Canadian deputy minister of Defence, Elgin Armstrong, that cut little ice in Thule. We had dinner in an alcove adjacent to the main dining hall where the garrison was being exhorted to heights of patriotism by the secretary. Armstrong was a little miffed, but the rest of us took it in stride: the food was good. On the 19th, we flew over Alert, the northernmost-occupied place in Canada, waved to its residents from the air, returned to Thule for gasoline, and flew to the western Arctic to Resolute Bay. Before bed, we inspected the Eskimo village, where there were polar-bear skins hanging next to skidoos. The next day, still at Resolute, we met the scientists there, enjoyed a preprandial drink (from which the Inuit were excluded), and then had dinner with community leaders, including Inuit ones. One of the elderly Inuit was invited to speak on behalf of that constituency, and his remarks were well received. This prompted another to share his impressions; he was followed by a third, a fourth, and so on, until all urges to speak had been satisfied. As no stopwatch was in play, it was a lengthy dinner but jovial and enjoyable withal as we watched the ice carvings that graced the table gradually lose their form. Kudloo, a carver from Pond Inlet, had come specially to create them.

Perhaps the most interesting character we met was the northern pilot Weldy Phipps, who had made two innovations in northern flying. First, to deal with soft landing ground, he had replaced normal airplane tires with a balloon version, which spread the weight over a wider area. Second, he took off and landed on steep inclines. Thus, he could take off in a space of three plane lengths followed by a steep cliff. This gave him good speed to the cliff and then enough height to level his plane before hitting the water. One passenger remarked, "They're laughing when they should be praying." Phipps had been a northern pilot since 1950.

On the 21st, we flew to Churchill, inspected the rocket range, saw some polar bears, and flew back to Ottawa. I was given a ride to Montreal on his private plane by Laurent Beaudoin, president of Bombardier (he was another member of the Board), and caught the first flight from there to Quebec City. Never was so much seen by so few in such a short time. We were satisfied to have confirmed that Canada was safe from northern attack, as long as the Americans remained our friends.

Final Days in Quebec City

The sojourn at Laval ended in style on 5 June 1971 when Alfred Pellan (artist), Armand Frappier (medical researcher), and I were awarded honorary doctorates by Laval University. Frappier gave the convocation address and, at the subsequent luncheon, I thanked the university on behalf of the three new graduates. I knew Frappier by reputation, as he was director of the Institut-Frappier at the University of Montreal, and my wife and I were happy owners of a painting (*Jardin Étang*) by Pellan. After the luncheon, Kerwin told me that I had passed my French oral exam. The next day, we proceeded to Ottawa to attend the induction of my first Ph.D. student, Benjamin Hogg, into the Royal Society. Three days later I was elected its president for the year 1971-72 and, shortly thereafter, we set sail for the University of Winnipeg.

The University of Winnipeg: 1971 to 1981

11

My return to the University of Winnipeg in 1971 was not exactly a home-coming, because the home had changed so much. When I left United College in June 1940 to pursue full-time graduate work at the University of Chicago, the institution had comprised the old college building, a women's residence (Sparling Hall), and a small house for Mr. Pye, the potentate in charge of the physical plant. The rest of the large city block had been dedicated to a front lawn, some tennis courts, and a playing field that doubled as an outdoor rink in winter. The playing field and tennis courts had since disappeared under an interconnected complex of academic and other buildings. Except for the front lawn, the large city block was now crammed with structures and parking lots.

The people had also changed. Only Lawrence Swyers in chemistry and Margaret Graham in the library remained from the pre-war staff, three of the other legendary figures having recently retired: Evelyn Mills (instructor in mathematics in the Collegiate), Victor Leathers (professor of French), and David Owen (professor of philosophy). In 1940, I had been the most junior member of staff: now my connection with the past was exceeded only by that of Margaret and Lawrence. I took satisfaction from this primordial link and from the fact that I had once given and received lectures in what was now the president's office in Wesley Hall.

Fortunately, throughout the years, I had come to know a number of the current teaching staff and so did not arrive as a complete stranger.

A Liberal Arts College

The University of Winnipeg was still a liberal arts college, despite its honorific title of "university." In this century, in Canada, it's been felt necessary to be a university in order to award degrees, with the result that many historic colleges, such as Acadia (Wolfville, Nova Scotia), Mount Allison (Sackville, New Brunswick) and Bishop's (Lennoxville, Quebec), which were authorized by charter to award degrees and which were functioning very well on that basis, have since assumed the university title, presumably to gain prestige. But, it was simply a change in name and did not mean that the institution had suddenly begun training for the professions, which is the criterion that normally defines a university. Were it not for this peculiarly Canadian affectation, the University of Winnipeg might have become Winnipeg College or might simply have remained United College, but with degree-granting powers.

In any event, the designation "liberal arts college" is one of honour and is heavy with tradition. Harvard and Yale each began as such, and each still refers to its undergraduate program as the "College." These liberal arts "colleges" within large universities are still dedicated to the disinterested study of the sciences, the humanities, and the social sciences. Moreover, hundreds of other colleges in the United States, including Wesleyan "University" in Connecticut, where I spent the years between 1946 and 1951, also satisfy that definition. And, so it was in 1971 with the University of Winnipeg, whose graduates went elsewhere to qualify as lawyers, medical doctors, and teachers. In most liberal arts colleges the governing boards are conservative: the "liberal" element comes from the curriculum and the professors. Indeed, the latter are often seen as radical by the governors. But students entering college need to have their inherited attitudes challenged, and the professors in the liberal arts colleges are masters at that skill. In that respect, the faculty at the University of Winnipeg took a back seat to no one.

The State of the University

As president, I inherited an institution with many strengths and few weaknesses. It was about to observe its centenary, and none could celebrate a prouder century of service to its constituency. As in the past, its students were well taught by professors who took a personal interest in them and gave high priority to their teaching duties. Consequently, its graduates had grateful memories of their student days and were unusually loyal to their alma mater. President Lockhart and Dean Clake had been prudent managers, and I inherited an accumulated surplus of three percent of the annual budget. At a time when other universities were seeking to be more relevant to society, the University of Winnipeg was securely located in downtown Winnipeg and was clearly a physical part of the real world. It had been an independent university for four years and had made the major administrative adjustments required by that change of status. It had begun to exploit

its new independence by offering new programs, including interdisciplinary ones, but not to the neglect of traditional subjects, for which it was
nationally respected. And, in addition, it was governed by a board of regents
that was unique in composition and unusual in its dedication. In short, the
operation was solvent and trouble free, with a long tradition of high standards and dedicated teaching. No incoming president could have asked for
more favourable conditions.

The new institution, however, did lack some visibility as a university. It
was a member of the Association of Universities and Colleges of Canada
(AUCC) to be sure, and Lockhart had also secured its membership in the
Association of Commonwealth Universities (ACU) and the International
Association of Universities. But, although it had all the right credentials, it
remained slightly self-conscious in its new role. Further, because of its name,
there was frequent and understandable misidentification with the larger
University of Manitoba (also located in Winnipeg), as President Saunderson
had predicted would happen. Finally, persistent memories of the Crowe
case still constituted something of a shadow. Four of my major aims were:
(1) to establish graduate work (as a basic requirement of a true university);
(2) to introduce additional programs with a vocational component; (3) to
improve the name recognition; and (4) to exorcize the place of the Crowe
legacy.

The Board of Regents

Prior to 1967, United College had been an educational arm of the United
Church of Canada. Thus, the members of its board were appointed by the
national Church, from which it received modest operating grants and to
which it reported through the Division of Ministry, Personnel and Education. As a liberal arts college, it had the same status within the Church as
did Mount Allison University in Sackville, Victoria University in Toronto,
and Huntington College in Sudbury. As a theological college, it had the
same status as did the other United Church seminaries across the country.

When the college became a university, Lockhart achieved a remarkable
feat: the continuance of the United Church presence in what was now a
provincially supported institution. His vision of a joint enterprise between
church and state was sold to a receptive Premier Duff Roblin and a sympathetic Education Minister George Johnson. Of course, the United Church
brought to the enterprise the physical assets of the college, which Lockhart
valued at the time at $30 million. Thus, when the University of Winnipeg
was established by order-in-council on 19 June 1967, it emerged that the
joint enterprise was to be that of equal partners: the University would be

governed by a board of regents of twenty-eight members, ten appointed by the provincial government, ten appointed by the United Church of Canada, four elected from the academic staff, two elected by the graduates, plus the chancellor and president, ex officio.

In explaining to me the implications of these arrangements, Lockhart emphasized two points. First, if any provincial government should seek to remove the United Church presence from the Board, it would be obliged to reimburse the Church to the present value of thirty million 1967 dollars. He said that someone in the Schreyer government of 1970 had casually questioned the propriety of Church involvement in a publicly supported institution but did not return to the subject after the $30-million figure had been mentioned. Second, as far as the Church was concerned, the University of Winnipeg was one of its *national* institutions, reporting to its central body, and not to the Manitoba Conference or the Winnipeg Presbytery. Thus, the ten Church appointees to the new board were named by the national Church, ensuring that the institution did not become a pawn to local pressures or disputes. In practice, these appointments were always made by the national Church on the recommendation of the University, thus giving the Board the effective power to name some of its own members. Those so nominated by the Board were not necessarily members of the United Church but were at least sympathetic to its educational aims. This arrangement has proven an enormous advantage when needed legal, financial, or other expertise were not present amongst the government appointees. On the basis of my experience with the arrangement, I'm convinced that every public university should be allowed to choose a number of its own board members.

Pressing Matters

Although Lockhart had left affairs in good shape, a barrage of pressing matters emerged that demanded the attention of the new president. Not all of these had been high on my own preconceived list of priorities.

The Price of Coffee

Students returned to class in September 1971 to discover that the price of a cup of coffee had risen from ten cents to twelve cents. The increase could be viewed in one of two ways: it was only two cents or it was a 20-percent increase. The University of Winnipeg Student Association (UWSA) took the latter view and prepared to fight to the death. High-level negotiations led to a compromise price of eleven cents, which the students hailed as a victory of Olympian proportions and I emerged as a compassionate feudal lord. It was a classic example of a trivial matter being important because some thought that it was important.

The Front Lawn

The front lawn, which was expansive and represented the only green space along two miles of Portage Avenue, was protected from the public by a decaying fence. What type of fence should be used as the replacement? It was agreed not to protect the front lawn from the public at all, but to open it up to them. Thus, the decaying fence was scrapped, a couple of footpaths were built, benches were put in place, and we were commended for providing an amenity to the neighbourhood. The benches were occasionally used by those recovering from a hangover or by those who were in the course of inducing one but, on the whole, the co-existence with our neighbours has been harmonious.

Acquisition of Property

It had been evident for some time that the university needed space for future growth. The old Manitoba College site, most recently occupied by St. Paul's College prior to its move to the University of Manitoba Fort Garry campus, was only 100 yards to the northeast, but the intervening space encompassed a major traffic intersection. Nevertheless, it had been eyed as the natural direction for expansion. In the summer of 1971, however, a gasoline filling station in the block west of the university came on the market, and the Board agreed to purchase the property. This represented a policy decision that future expansion would take place towards the west, and we authorized Peter Rattray of Enderton and Associates to purchase and manage on our behalf whatever properties came up for sale. There were about fifty different owners in the designed area. Every few weeks Peter would report another purchase, and Jack Brown, the comptroller, would colour in the corresponding area on his master plan. This was all done without disclosing that the University was the purchaser. Ten years later, only one property (a good house) remained in private hands, and its owner was approached directly. He held out for an unreasonable sum, which he got, and then offered to move the house, thus saving us the ultimate cost of demolition. He bought a property nearby, replaced its poor house with his excellent one, and is probably still telling strangers how he outwitted the University of Winnipeg.

The total purchase price for the fifty properties was about $1 million, with every property but the last acquired at market price. When the Pawley government agreed in 1981 to fund an athletic centre, the University had more than sufficient space to accommodate it. Halfway through the purchase program (in 1975), and thanks to its chairman, William Condo, the Universities Grants Commission (UGC) reimbursed the University for purchases made prior to 1 April 1974 ($512,000). Until that time, the Board had used the University's own endowment funds in a confident endorsement of its acquisition policy. When the new athletic centre was authorized, the UGC reimbursed the balance remaining; the gamble had paid off.

Student Representation on the Board and Senate

Although student participation in university governance was very much in the air in 1967, no provision for students had been made in the order-in-council establishing the University of Winnipeg, and the students lost no time in raising the matter with me. The chancellor, P.H.T. Thorlakson, chaired a committee that recommended that four students be added to the Board of Regents and seven students to the Senate. Until the order-in-council could be so modified, these bodies agreed to accept student members *as if* they were regular members. The minister of Colleges and Universities Affairs, Saul Miller, endorsed the action and, after some delay, arranged for the order-in-council to be altered accordingly.

As had happened at the University of Manitoba, some of the students were over-zealous at the start and were somewhat disinclined to see other points of view, but they soon came to realize that all members were expected to act for the good of the institution as a whole.

Alcohol Policy

The traditional attitude at United College had been that the consumption of alcohol was a mortal sin, more lethal than the seven deadly ones. Men had been expelled from residence for lesser offences, and any sign of alcohol at student social functions was investigated without mercy. Dr. Lockhart, much to his credit, had maintained this zero-tolerance policy, pointing out that "beer parlours" existed in the neighbourhood where those who were of legal age and wished to endanger their passage to heaven could do so at their peril. The UWSA, perhaps because of the compromise on the price of coffee, may have seen me as a softer touch. At any rate, they requested permission to hold socials on campus, at which beer would be sold.

I was sympathetic to the request, believing in the principle of every-thing in moderation, but I realized that we ran the danger of alienating some members of the United Church who, whilst professing temperance, were actually advocates of abstinence. I recommended to the Board that we authorize use of alcohol at a limited number of campus functions and, in the case of the socials, with adequate police supervision. The initial number would be four per term, two for the use of students and two for the use of the president. Further, the Alcohol Use Committee would consider each request. The Board accepted the recommendation without dissent and, I believe, was relieved that the initiative had come from me.

I named to the committee persons I knew would be tough-minded and not accede to irresponsible requests. In particular, I named Edwin D. Eagle, a former dean of Arts and Science, knowing that he would err on the side of caution. How wrong I was, unaware that beneath that dean-like visage lurked a spirit of permissiveness, but others filled the restrictive role I had envisaged for him.

Shortfall in Enrollment

During the summer of 1971, there was no reason to suspect that the enrollment growth that had marked the preceding decade would not con-tinue, and budgets for the 1971-72 academic year had been based on that premise. Hence, it came as a shock to the University of Winnipeg and to most of the universities in Canada when first-year enrollment actually *de-clined.* The shortfall in budgetted tuition-fee income for the University of Winnipeg was $160,000, which represented two-thirds of the accumulated surplus. I proposed to the Board that we split the difference, taking $80,000 from the accumulated surplus and finding the other $80,000 in budget savings. For example, certain low-enrollment courses were cancelled, which allowed some evening classes (for which professors were to have been paid extra stipends) to be taught as part of the regular teaching load. This was not a popular action with staff, some of whom may already have spent the anticipated extra income, and it was not one aimed at improving the popu-larity of a new administration. But it was a valuable initial lesson for me, not to take enrollment for granted, but persistently to endeavour to attract good students to the institution. Moreover, some long-term action must be taken to prevent the repetition of another such eleventh-hour shock.

Manitoba College Centenary: 1871 to 1971

A century in western Canada is a long time, but it was indeed that long since the Presbyterian Church, meeting in Quebec City in 1871, had acceded to the Rev. John Black's request to establish a college in the Red River Settlement. This college would ensure a supply of ministers for the West and would provide higher education to other students.

A recent ordinand, George Bryce, listening to the debate from the back of the hall and inflamed by the challenge, volunteered to be the first professor. Thus, in the very fall of 1871, Manitoba College began accepting students, at a site in Kildonan, and Bryce began thirty-eight years of remarkable service to the institution. Bryce ultimately specialized in English literature but, in his long stint, taught whatever was needed. In the year of his retirement, he was elected president of the Royal Society of Canada (RSC), an unusual honour for one so far removed from the corridors of academic power.

Six years after its founding, in 1877, Manitoba College became one of the three colleges that taught students in the new University of Manitoba. It continued this role until 1914, when, in concert with the other English-language affiliated colleges, it agreed to withdraw from the teaching of arts and limit itself to theology. At this time, the College occupied a splendid building on the north side of Ellice Avenue at Vaughan Street, where, as a ten-year-old, I was once publicly sick from overeating. By 1910, it had prepared 200 men for the Christian ministry, most destined for service in the expanding West but not a few dispatched as missionaries to India, China, and Japan. These men, like my father (who took his training at Knox College in Toronto), had not chosen the ministry as an occupation but believed they were answering a "call," and "service to others" would be the motivating force in their lives. In recent years, the ministry has become a professional career, but this was not the case in the glory days of Manitoba College.

Following Church union, the Manitoba College property was sold to the Jesuits to house St. Paul's College, and its staff moved into cramped quarters in Wesley College, to take responsibility for the training of ministers for the United Church. Meanwhile, Wesley confined its activities to the teaching of arts and the Collegiate. It was a sad move for the noble institution, whose elaborate Victorian turrets had long adorned the city skyline. Then, in 1938, Manitoba College merged with Wesley College to form United College and became only a memory. But it was a hallowed memory, and the University of Winnipeg took pride in 1971 in celebrating the centenary of its senior founding college and, by the way, in installing its new president.

Under the chairmanship of R.O.A. Hunter, and with the enthusiastic cooperation of the departments, a committee comprising Ronald Riddell (assistant to the president), alumni director Joy McDiarmid, UWSA president Marilou McPhedran, and others arranged a plethora of lectures, displays, demonstrations, performances and children's entertainments which, on an inclement 16 October, brought 5,000 visitors to the crowded campus, most of whom were unaware that another 1,400 were attending an installation ceremony below their feet in the gymnasium.

The standard protocol for the installation of a chancellor or president is to invite sister institutions to send or bring greetings. The greetings, if brought, are presented at the ceremony by representatives. Thus, if the representatives are numerous, it makes for a colourful affair, as their academic gowns draw from all parts of the rainbow. My daughter, Jane, addressed the invitations, and the representatives of other universities and organizations numbered 102, including several personal friends, among them Harry and Sadie Thode (McMaster), Bob and Jean Bell (McGill), Larkin and Lupita Kerwin (Laval), Jack and Connie Sword (Toronto), Robert Hubbard (RSC), and Donald Le Roy (NRC), in addition to numerous Winnipeggers who had been asked by their universities to serve as their emissaries. An additional 186 institutions sent greetings. Ronald Gibson composed a fanfare for the event, Archbishop Boudoux of the diocese of St. Boniface (a large and generous personality) pronounced the invocation, John Spinks of Saskatchewan composed a playful poem on behalf of the AUCC, Leo Kristjanson, who had left the Collegiate because of the Crowe case, represented the Canadian Association of University Teachers (CAUT), Premier Schreyer, who was to have represented the Province, failed to show, and Lawrence Swyers, the senior professor, helped me into the president's gown. My remarks included the following:

> From our inception a century ago, we have sought to provide an environment in which young people may develop along lines appropriate to their own individualities. That is, we have existed for the self-realization of others — that they might serve as intelligent, concerned and useful citizens in a dynamic world. That is still our purpose and I trust it shall so remain.
>
> We began in the countryside, to serve a small segment of a particular denominational group, and at a time when life and work were simple. A

great city is now our campus, the community is our constituency, and life
and work are complex. Thus, although our purpose is constant, the means
of achieving it must reflect these vastly altered circumstances... The (Arts
and Science) curriculum traditionally has been disinterested and liberal,
deriving in part from the ancient view that University students come
from a select social group and deliberately withdraw from society for a
few years – to read, to discuss and to reflect – before returning to assume
positions of privilege. As universities increasingly become egalitarian and
graduates are expected increasingly to work for a living, it is not surprising that our curriculum has been adding a here-and-now component as
an optional supplement to its traditional, timeless core. Thus, students still
take note of the effects of the Industrial Revolution on the poorer classes
of England, but those who are interested in the present plight of Native
peoples in Winnipeg must not be overlooked. Classical French literature
is still studied, of course, but the wish of growing numbers of young
people to converse *en français* with their French-Canadian compatriots is
not to be lost sight of. Molecular orbitals are still studied, of course, but
those who are interested in the chemical aspects of pollution and de-
pollution are not to be ignored. Adam Smith and Jeremy Bentham are
still read, of course, but Edgar Benson [then Minister of Finance] and
John Connally must not be forgotten. The London County Council is
still of interest, of course, but so is the new Unicity Council.

The Great Rock Climb

David Owen, the recently retired professor of philosophy, suggested that
the centenary be marked by the erection of a cairn. That was a bit quaint,
but a large rock might serve the purpose. Accordingly, John McWilliams, a
friend from college days, took me to see two modest boulder monuments
on Portage Avenue, one at Vimy Park (honouring the Canadians who captured Vimy Ridge) and the other at Deer Lodge Place (honouring the
painter Lionel LeMoine FitzGerald). We concluded that the idea was sound,
but it called for a stone that was more arresting than the ones I'd just seen.
Rod Hunter arranged with Duncan Robertson of Winnipeg Supply and
Fuel, for us to visit his gravel pit at Gull Lake, on the shore of ancient
Glacial Lake Agassiz, where we chose and were given a large rock. I asked
the foreman to estimate its weight and was told that it was about ten tons,
a nice round number. The truck bringing it to the campus was required to
stop at a weigh scale, where the rock registered twenty-five tons, an even
better number. This handsome boulder, ten feet high, which some glacier
had prophetically deposited at Gull Lake, was mounted at the Portage

Avenue entrance to the university, and a plaque carrying wording by David
Owen explains its presence:

1871–1971

This granite boulder brought from Glacial Lake Agassiz commemorates
the centenary of the institution which is now the University of
Winnipeg and the following important events in its history:

1871 – Manitoba College founded in Kildonan by the Presbyterian
Church

1877 – Charter for Wesley College granted to the Methodist Church

1926 – Manitoba and Wesley Colleges associated as United Colleges
after establishment of the United Church of Canada

1938 – United Colleges merged into United College

1967 – United College became the University of Winnipeg

This plaque was unveiled October 8, 1971 by the Minister of
Colleges and University Affairs of the Province of Manitoba, the
Honourable Saul A Miller. Paul H T Thorlakson was then Chancellor
and Wilfred Cornett Lockhart had just been succeeded by Henry
Edmison Duckworth as President of the University of Winnipeg.

LUX ET VERITAS FLOREANT

Seeking a function for the boulder other than aesthetic, I asked David
Anderson, director of Athletic Studies, to bring three basketball players
to test its scalability. It proved difficult, but possible, to climb, the climbers
making use of a shallow niche located four feet above ground. Thus, at
the start of the 1972-73 school year, the Great Rock Climb was instituted. In this annual contest, teams of three start from the steps of
Wesley Hall, run seventy-five yards to the rock, where, using no props,
they attempt to seat themselves on its summit. The record for the contest is 9.4 seconds, established by three agile young men who, one by
one, literally ran up the face of the rock, using the niche as the first
step. On one occasion, an even more agile competitor ran up the rock
and over the other side. But most teams heave one member up, who
then attempts to haul up the others. This leads to an elapsed time of

fifteen to twenty seconds. Occasionally, ceremonial attempts have been made
– by Carl Ridd and others wearing gowns and carrying brief cases, by
Elmer (Al) Reimer and others carried in sedan chairs by female slaves –
which have occupied two to three minutes. After the inaugural year of the
Climb, except for one occasion, the craven basketball coaches have not
allowed their players to compete, giving fear of injury a higher place than
glory. It has become an important September media event, as new reporters rediscover its novelty and unpredictability. I regard the prize money of
seventy-five dollars (first), sixty dollars (second) and forty-five dollars (third)
as a bargain and, overall, view the event as one of the great athletic contests
in the history of the world.

The Library Budget

The Library Committee of the Senate was chaired by Vincent Rutherford,
chair of History and a strong believer that the library needed more books.
The librarian, Raymond Wright, shared Rutherford's belief but also knew
that the library had other needs, such as cataloguers, reference librarians,
shelvers, and circulation clerks. All the money couldn't go for books, but
clearly, if there were more money, there could be more books. Rutherford
and Wright came to request a higher allocation for the library. I demurred
and asked for time to study the matter, in particular to study the tables
prepared by the financial officers of Canadian universities. There, I found
that the average library allocation was less than 6 percent of the institutional annual budget, excluding research grants. At the next meeting with
Rutherford and Wright, I proposed that the University of Winnipeg adopt
a figure of 8.5 percent of the annual budget, a figure second only to the
University of Victoria (which was trying rapidly to increase its holdings).
Rutherford, who had initiated the discussion with a club in his hand, gulped
at the offer, and he and Wright left in high spirits.

This proved a brilliant action. Instead of constant wrangling with me
over the need for more books, the library committee wrangled within
itself over the division between acquisitions and services, content in the
knowledge that, overall, the library was being generously treated. Incidentally, I was surprised to discover that the larger the library, the larger the
percentage of budget that is allocated to services. Thus, Harvard spent 25
percent of its budget on acquisitions, whilst the University of Winnipeg
spent about 50 percent.

Towards the end of my term, when money had become tight, I was
forced to reduce the library allocation from 8.5 percent to 8.0 percent, but
it remained one of the highest in Canada.

Courses for Senior Citizens

In January 1973, acting on the suggestion of a young man who was working with Lloyd Axworthy in the Institute for Urban Studies, we announced special free courses for senior citizens. Birth certificates were not checked; it was enough for them to sign a registration form and pay a two-dollar fee. In addition to the five special courses, seniors could enroll in regular courses with the permission of the instructors. This program was an instant success, with 200 registrants and with advice on course offerings from an advisory committee chosen from amongst the users. It was the first offering of its sort in Canada and has continued until the present. Perhaps not surprisingly, instructors have taken special pleasure in teaching these appreciative individuals, who are so rich in life experience.

A small number of the seniors registered for credit courses from the start, with the hope or intention of qualifying for a degree. One of these received her B.A. at the age of 87.

Recruitment of Students

Although universities sometimes forget the fact, their primary function is to teach students. Moreover, students pay tuition fees, which contribute to institutional revenue. Thus, students are needed on principle and are necessary in practice. They were particularly necessary at the University of Winnipeg, where student fees constituted one-third of the total revenue. This was high compared to that at the University of Manitoba (with its expensive professional schools) where tuition represented only one-eighth of the total. Thus, every September, officers and professors at the University of Winnipeg awaited with bated breath to learn the enrollment figures, a condition of suspense that never abated during my ten-year period as president, and that was heightened by the experience of my first year in office.

The Entrance Scholarship Program

In early 1973, Chancellor Thorlakson chaired a committee comprising Donald Bennett (senior stick, 1947-48), Jean (Mackay) Curtis (lady stick, 1946-47), Gail (Pearcey) Hall (lady stick, 1963-64), Roderick Hunter (senior stick, 1936-37), Murdoch MacKay (senior stick, 1950-51), Joy McDiarmid (director, Alumni Affairs), James Miller (student president, 1970-71), Hugh Murray (alumni president), William Norrie (senior stick, 1949-50), Ronald Riddell (assistant to the president), Janet (Clark) Saunders (class of 1936), Berenice (Warne) Sisler (lady stick, 1944-45) to devise an entrance scholarship program (ESP) that might appeal to the graduates. Each class was asked to raise $500 per year to provide an entrance scholarship to the outstanding student in one of the provincial high schools. At that time, tuition fees were $420 and the price of textbooks had not yet skyrocketed, so $500 covered everything but living costs for a student. We believed that if we could get the outstanding student in a school, some of his or her classmates would follow. As Murdoch MacKay said, "The scholarship winner will be the 'bell cow,'" a remark that offended some of the female members of the committee, but I thought it was the perfect analogy. Murdoch recently told me that he would now use the term "queen bee" instead of "bell cow."

The ESP was novel to the province and it brought thirty-three bell cows to the university for the 1973-74 session from the province's 145 high schools. This initiative, supplemented by a flashy and informative brochure for Grade 12 students, with a cover designed by the well-known artist Bruce Head, RCA, reversed the first-year enrollment decline, which had greeted my arrival, and brought students from schools that had not been represented in the institution before. Not all classes were able to raise the $500, but there was no stigma attached to a shortfall; the funds were simply carried forward as a starting point for the next year. In all, more than 1,000 graduates contributed in the first year of the program, with most gifts in the range of five to twenty-five dollars. I wrote a personal letter to the 150 who gave fifty dollars or more. Actually, in the first year, more students accepted the entrance scholarships than the ESP could fund; the extra money needed to fund the other seventeen acceptances was provided by the Board of Regents. The following year, the number of top students who accepted the scholarship offer rose from fifty to fifty-nine, or about 40 percent of the possible total. On the basis of enrollment alone, our share of the bell cows would have been twenty. It appeared that we had turned the corner on enrollment.

Although this scholarship initiative was praiseworthy, I was reluctant to publicize its success, fearing some retaliatory action by the University of Manitoba. Indeed, I was almost furtive about it, down-playing it at Senate meetings or in discussions with professors. Several of our staff had spouses who taught at the University of Manitoba, and I didn't want details of the ESP to be passed to our arch-rival over the dinner table. Our professors noticed that they had more good students in their classes but assumed that their reputation for good teaching had attracted them; little did they know that many had been bought with cold hard cash. By the third year, the University of Manitoba was roused to action and began using its Dr. Hogg bequest to assign an entrance scholarship to every high school in the province, and the number of bell cows at the University of Winnipeg dropped to fifty. We had known that our initiative would not remain unchallenged indefinitely, but, in the meantime, we had diverted more of the current students in our direction.

The coordinators of the ESP were Janet Saunders (wife of my classmate Tom Saunders), Lawrence Swyers (following his retirement) and, finally, Gail Hall (class of 1964 and sometime high school teacher). In their hands, the program was a powerful recruiting tool that, literally, brought hundreds of outstanding students to the university and also provided our graduates with an affordable and satisfying means of supporting their university. There was rivalry amongst classes, of course, particularly between Rod Hunter's class of 1937 and my own class of 1935. At the time of my retirement in 1981, we both claimed victory but, in fact, we were tied, having each endowed two entrance scholarships. At least, they were endowed until interest rates plummeted.

Another Enrollment Decline

As we approached the start of the 1977-78 session, we were complacent about enrollment. And who wouldn't be, on the basis of the recent growth in full-time enrollment, culminating in the previous year's record total. But we were in for a shock, as the enrollment figures in Table 2 indicate.

Table 2: Full-Time Enrollment Figures, 1971-72 to 1981-82

	All Years	First Year
1971-72	2,363	934
1972-73	2,307	870
1973-74	2,377	942
1974-75	2,499	1,011
1975-76	2,702	1,112
1976-77	2,871	1,215
1977-78	2,758	1,029
1978-79	2,579	926
1979-80	2,288	786
1980-81	2,334	940 (+19.6%)
1981-82		991 (+ 5.4%)

The decline in first-year enrollment in 1977-78 took us by surprise, but we were inclined to regard it as an anomaly, with the result that our recruitment program for 1978-79 was little changed. The fact that I was off campus from 15 October to 31 December 1978 (on a mini-sabbatical, at the end of my initial seven-year appointment) did not help the situation. In 1979-80, however, the first-year enrollment was in free fall, and the problem could no longer be disregarded. It was small comfort that the decline coincided with a national disenchantment with general education in favour of training for specific vocations. This disenchantment was actively promoted by the press, which carried accounts of the ease with which students from community colleges obtained jobs whilst B.A. graduates remained jobless. As a liberal arts institution, we felt the full force of this disenchantment. We had tried to stay in the running by introducing paraprofessional options such as business computing, business administration, justice and law enforcement, athletic studies, and art history, which had a core of liberal arts plus a vocational component and which I described at convocation as "programs for today (vocational) and tomorrow (liberal arts)"; however, these options failed to staunch the enrollment bleeding. It was abundantly clear by the fall of 1979 that we needed a new initiative to supplement the ESP.

The 1979-80 Recruitment Blitz

Janet Walker, a former student officer and graduate of 1978 who had been working in the admissions office at Red River Community College, agreed to launch a recruitment blitz for the University of Winnipeg in the Winnipeg high schools. Its secret was to provide "scholarships" to students who had not qualified for the major entrance scholarships. These new awards were to be made according to the following schedule: an average of 90+, $500; 85-90, $400; 80-85, $300; 75-80, $200; 70-75, $100; 65-70, $50. Janet invaded the Winnipeg classrooms with this startling offer, seducing students into applying for admission as part of the scholarship application. By June of 1980, my colleagues Norma Gwizon and Marilyn Lockwood, who staffed the home front, had hundreds of files awaiting the final marks, which would determine the scholarship values. By an arrangement that, although not illegal, is best not revealed, we obtained the marks of these students before the students were informed themselves. Thus, we were able to send prompt letters of congratulation and scholarship offers consistent with the marks. The result was dramatic. Students who had filled out application forms as a favour to Janet Walker now found themselves scholarship winners, beamed upon by their parents and bragged about by their grandparents. The group in the 65- to 80- percent range were particularly exultant, as their names and the term *scholarship* had never before appeared in the same sentence. In the end, the first-year enrollment increased by 20 percent, and we had a great victory luncheon on 10 September 1980. The same tactics were employed during the next (and my final) year, and I had the satisfaction of leaving the institution well stocked with students – and many of them very good ones – and with enrollment again on the rise.

Part-Time Students

Part-time students are so much a part of the current university scene that it's hard to recall that, within living memory, they had no place on the campus, except in non-credit courses. When I was an undergraduate, for example, the standard first-year program was five full courses. If, at the end of the summer supplemental period, *all* of these courses had not been passed, the year was lost. It would count for naught that, say, four had been passed, and perhaps with high marks. The pre-war disdain for part-time students had been inherited from the British universities, which had offered extension lectures, some of them for centuries, but had doctrinaire objections to offering degree programs on other than a full-time basis. The view was strongly held that much of the value of a degree depended upon the student's exclusive dedication to it, upon the interaction between subjects that were being studied simultaneously or in a logical order, and upon the informal contact amongst fellow students and between them and their professors.

When I joined McMaster in 1951, I discovered that students could work part-time towards an extension B.A., that is, they could accumulate course credits, a few at a time, until they reached the required total. True, their degree was less prestigious than a regular B.A., but it was a university degree nonetheless, and a great deal better than what the pre-war University of Manitoba had offered.

When I joined the University of Winnipeg in 1971, things had changed dramatically: part-time students could now accumulate credits towards regular degrees. Because of its downtown location, the University was in an excellent position to provide part-time instruction. Moreover, part-time students could compensate for declines in full-time enrollment. Accordingly, with the full cooperation of Dean Clake and the department heads, a campaign for additional part-time students was begun. I mentioned our philosophy specifically at the 1972 spring convocation: "We have the obligation to provide education to as many as can profit from it, and to develop methods of extending it to those who, by virtue of location, work or other factors, are unable to become full-time students."

Ronald Riddell was a key figure in this campaign, as we offered courses at times and places thought to be convenient for the aimed-at clientele. University at Noon courses were offered twice a week at various commercial locations (Richardson Building, rent $750 per month; Union Centre, rent $192; St. Stephens-Broadway United Church, rent free; Eaton's Store, rent free; CJAY Polo Park, rent free; and Great-West Life Assurance Company, rent free) where working students could eat their lunch and learn during their regular lunch hours. University at Ten and University at Two were intended for mothers who had children at school. Attending classes for an hour and a half twice a week, they could stay at home until their children left for school and be back when they returned. In addition, preschoolers could be left at a special daycare centre for fifty cents an hour. University at Five was designed for those coming directly from work and supplemented the regular evening session, which ran from 7:00 to 10:00 p.m.. Courses were also offered at suburban locations and on Saturday mornings.

This barrage of part-time programs was a shotgun effort that sometimes hit the mark and sometimes missed. But, collectively, it showed us to be an institution determined to serve the part-time constituency, and that component of our enrollment steadily increased, as it was doing in other Canadian universities to varying degrees.

The Open University

Meanwhile, what was happening in the United Kingdom? Consider the figures shown in Table 3. The part-time students were largely, if not all, graduate students.

Table 3: Some United Kingdom Enrollment Figures for 1965 to 1967

	Full-time	Part-time
Cambridge (66–67)	8,182	0
London (65–66)	22,545	1,700
Oxford (66–67)	7,748	0
All universities (65–66)	145,373	4,827

It was this continuing reluctance to accommodate those who could not study full-time that led to the remarkable Open University, which was established in the United Kingdom in July 1969, under royal charter, and only slightly caricatured in the stage play and movie *Educating Rita*. The initiative for the venture came from the Labour government of Harold Wilson, which came to power in 1964. Responsibility for implementing the idea was entrusted to Wilson's undersecretary of state for Education and Science, Jennie Lee, who was the moving force behind it. When the Heath government came to power in 1970, there was fear that the project might be scrapped, but Mrs. Thatcher was assigned the Education portfolio and, after studying the project herself, gave it her full support.

The Open University accepted its first students in January 1971, choosing about 24,000 from 43,000 applicants. Instruction was offered by correspondence, supplemented by radio and television broadcasts, residential summer schools and an extensive counselling and tutorial service. By 1973, when the first graduates emerged, the routine mailings to students had already reached 2.7 million per year. Little wonder that, at the 1973 Congress of the ACU in Edinburgh, the vice-chancellor of the Open University was ogled as an academic celebrity. The fact that he had been recently remarried, to a woman much younger than he, who was constantly seen changing the diapers of a newborn child, only added to his aura of potency.

Emphasis was given to interdisciplinary study, which met with enthusiastic student response. One student reported that he now detested economics, knew something of politics, felt involved in sociology, was entranced by geography, and could spell *psychology*.

Since the early days of the Open University, the curriculum has been expanded in response to demand, some graduate work has been introduced, and many of the regular universities have changed their tune. In 1985, for example, the full-time university enrollment in the United Kingdom was 168,000, and the part-time enrollment was 120,000. The latter figure was only slightly skewed towards men. Obviously, the regular universities had previously been neglecting a vast constituency.

Electronic Instruction in Canada

During the 1970s, delegations from several Canadian provinces made pilgrimages to the Open University with the hope of transplanting it to Canada. But they discovered that a key to its success was its program of local and summer seminars, which brought students together for discussion under the guidance of tutors. These meetings took place at 250 study centres that were within feasible driving distance of all corners of the kingdom. Reluctantly, it was decided that the larger distances and smaller populations in Canada mitigated against the transplant.

In the 1960s, however, Canadian universities had begun flirting with the idea of television instruction; indeed, some saw it as the panacea for shortage of staff. Scarborough College of the University of Toronto was purpose-built as a wired city, with a spellbinding vision of electronic teaching, which ultimately failed to satisfy its users, the students. Similarly, television teaching at the University of Manitoba had limited success. In Introductory Psychology, for example, professors (trained or not in television techniques) would tape their lectures for later playing to large or multiple classes, where graduate assistants would turn the tape on at the start and off at the end. Otherwise, no academic authority made an appearance. Students listened or not, they conversed or not, and they entered and left at will. The whole thing was sterile, uninspiring, and unpopular. On one occasion, when my daughter and I were at the opera, she whispered to me, "I recognize those ears!" They belonged to a man in front of us, and it was the first time she had seen her psychology instructor in the flesh. Perhaps unfairly influenced by anecdotal evidence, I took no steps to initiate television instruction during my tenure as president.

The Universities Grants Commission

By 1971, the UGC was well established under the chairmanship of Scott Bateman, and I was preparing to submit my first operating-grant request on behalf of the University of Winnipeg. Scott and I were friends of long standing, but I knew that friendship would not affect his decisions.

Anxious to demonstrate fiscal responsibility, I submitted a bare-bones request and awaited the result. In early 1972, Scott came to my office with a long face, and I feared the worst. "Harry," he said, "the commission believes that you did not request a large enough grant, and hopes that you will accept an additional $200,000."

Also in early 1972, Bateman made an astonishing suggestion to Donald Tomlin (chair of the Board) and me. Our vast new building (now known as Centennial Hall) was nearing completion, and Bateman thought that we would not fully occupy it. Partly to solve that imagined problem, and partly for pedagogic reasons, he suggested that the Faculty of Pharmacy and the Schools of Nursing and of Social Work be transferred from the University of Manitoba to the University of Winnipeg. Such a move would bring Pharmacy and Nursing much closer to the Medical School, which was downtown, and would place Social Work in the midst of its clients. We did not encourage the idea but expressed an interest in the Faculty of Commerce. Nothing came of this discussion, but I expect that the University of

Manitoba would have been indignant to know that it was a pawn in a hypothetical game of academic chess. As it happened, we had no difficulty in finding uses for all of Centennial Hall; after all, nature abhors a vacuum.

On 1 January 1975, to the astonishment of everyone, the Schreyer government appointed Willard Condo, the vice-president (administration) of the University of Manitoba to succeed Bateman. Condo was not only a Conservative, but also an outspoken one who lost no opportunity to flaunt his political allegiance. He was an American who had come to Canada during World War II to join the Canadian Army whilst his own country was pretending that it could honourably stay out of the war. He and I were good friends, and he had been popular within the University of Manitoba. His appointment to the UGC gave the NDP government reason for virtuous pride in making what was obviously not a patronage appointment. Condo and President Sirluck had not seen eye to eye, and it gave Condo some wicked pleasure to accept a position that, in certain respects, represented a reversal of seniorities. Condo served as chair of the UGC until his sudden death on 19 May 1980 and always did his best to be fair whilst under pressure from many sides, including the political one. He was succeeded by Wesley Lorimer, a member of the UGC and former deputy minister of Education.

During the 1975-76 session, the tuition fees had been $425 per year. By 1976, several other jurisdictions had raised tuition, but we were led to believe that the Schreyer government wished tuition in Manitoba to remain unchanged. Notwithstanding, for 1976-77, the University of Manitoba felt obliged to raise fees to $450 and, for 1977-78, Brandon raised its fees to $475. Out of consideration for our students, and unwisely (as it turned out), we remained at $425. When the Lyon government came to power in 1977, it made it known that tuition fees for 1978-79 should be increased to $540. It was not an order, because the setting of fees was a legal prerogative of the universities, but Manitoba and Brandon adopted the "suggestion." Torn between compassion and financial exigency, Winnipeg stopped short at $525, an increase of 24 percent over the $425 value that had prevailed since 1969. To our consternation, the UGC grants to the three universities were made on the assumption that all had followed the "suggestion" and that those with the largest fee increase could now tolerate the smallest increase in grant. According to this logic, UGC grant increases to Brandon, Manitoba, and Winnipeg were 3.8 percent, 3.1 percent and 1.5 percent, respectively. Thus, Brandon, which had been benefitting from the highest tuition, was seen to require a compensatory grant, since its tuition increase in 1978-79 was only 14 percent. Meanwhile, Winnipeg, wallowing in the largest tuition increase (24 percent), could be fobbed off with a negligible grant increase. Moreover, the tuition value used to implement this logic toward Winnipeg was the suggested $540 (up 27 percent) rather than the actual value of $525! In this classic case of double jeopardy, we were credited with tuition that we did not receive and were penalized for scrimping in the previous two years in order to shelter our students.

This action by the UGC (presumably acting under instructions from the government) was a crippling blow to us and led to the first operating deficit in seven years, that is, since the initial year of my administration. The next year, having learned who was boss, we increased our fees to match those of Brandon and Manitoba, whilst the UGC grants to the three universities increased by roughly equal percentages. But our increase was calculated on the historically low base of the previous year's grant, and this unfairness persisted until 1981-82, when Wesley Lorimer (then chair of the UGC) heroically took the decision to correct the disparity. Previously, Condo had tried to mitigate the situation with small special-purpose grants, but Lorimer's bold action put us on a par again, although we had lost several hundred thousand dollars in the meantime. The $250,000 accumulated surplus that I had inherited from Lockhart, and that had risen to more than one million dollars by 1976, was down to $250,000 again by the time I left office in 1981, but the annual deficits were a thing of the unjust past. In 1982, Lorimer, whilst still serving on an interim basis, was asked by the minister (in the NDP government of Howard Pawley) to reduce the Commission's budget request for the coming year. When he objected that the request reflected the best judgement of the commission, he was removed from office and his long and distinguished service to Manitoba education was never acknowledged.

The UGC comprised eight members plus its chair and its staff. The members, who made their decisions on the basis of information provided by the Universities and the staff of the UGC, were intended to be knowledgeable, respected, representative, and impartial. The founding members (see page 214) met these criteria, and I was content to put our case to them, knowing that, if they could be convinced of our needs, their opinion would carry more weight with the government than anything I could do or say. But, as time wore on, the character of this group changed to reflect explicit political hues. To some extent, money was involved. The original members declined the offer of an honorarium, preferring to work as volunteers, but during the Schreyer administration a modest payment was instituted. For some, this came to be seen as a desirable patronage appointment, which did not improve the competence of the Commission.

Incidentally, no honorarium was ever paid to the government appointees on University governing boards. Shortly after the Schreyer government was returned, a call was received at the University of Manitoba asking the amount of the honorarium and expressing disbelief that such a misguided precedent had been established. By and large, those appointed to university boards were motivated by interest in the task.

Graduate Work

The orders-in-council establishing Brandon University and the University of Winnipeg decreed that these two institutions be limited to undergraduate work. There was logic in concentrating the graduate work at the University of Manitoba, but the new arrangement excluded the University of Winnipeg professors from the training of graduate students, a privilege they had long enjoyed as professors in an affiliated college. Further, there was the ignominy of the University of Winnipeg being declared a university but not with all the rights and privileges thereto appertaining.

Whilst still at the University of Manitoba, I had attempted to mitigate this situation by introducing the "adjunct professor" category, by which scholars from other institutions could participate in graduate work. But appointments to this position were subject to departmental initiative, and were somewhat in the "grace and favour" category. Moreover, the device did little for the prestige of the other institutions. Accordingly, shortly after my appointment to the University of Winnipeg I requested permission from the UGC to offer master's work in history, English, and religious studies, subjects in which we possessed unquestioned strength and, in the case of the first two, a long history of participation.

As expected, this put Ernest Sirluck (president of the University of Manitoba) and me on a collision course. As the University of Toronto was the intellectual mecca for Ontario, Sirluck saw the University of Manitoba as the exclusive graduate centre for this province, and he had the strong argument of "needless duplication" on his side. As for the government, it had appointed the Task Force on Post-Secondary Education and would take no decisions until that body had reported.

The minister of Education announced early in 1972 the membership of the Task Force, which was to study all aspects of post-secondary education in the province. Michael Oliver, chair of the Task Force, was an economist and vice-principal at McGill and had been a national president of the NDP. But, more significant for us, he had taught at United College prior to the Crowe case and had taken the side of Crowe, although he had already resigned to take another position. The task force also included Kay Sigurjonsson, a former teacher in the Collegiate and well-known Crowe supporter. The Task Force seemed to be stacked against us.

Oliver assured me that he harboured no hard feelings, but in early discussions with the Task Force we gained the impression that it would recommend that graduate work be limited to the University of Manitoba. Notwithstanding, we made our case, emphasizing our limited but legitimate aspirations and, to our surprise, in early 1973, the preliminary report of the Task Force recommended that we be allowed to offer a modest M.A. program. This point was bitterly opposed by the University of Manitoba, but the Task Force held its ground and the recommendation appeared in the final report released on 17 January 1974. It remained to be seen whether the government would accept the recommendation. In spite of much lobbying by the University of Manitoba (or perhaps because of it), Minister Ben Hanuschak ordained on 18 December 1974 that the two universities be joint proprietors of the master's programs in English and history.

Implementation of Hanuschak's ordinance was not automatic. We were instructed by the UGC to submit a proposal for joint programs by 15 November 1975. At 15:40 hours on Friday, 14 November, we had received no response to our proposal from the University of Manitoba. In the circumstances, we requested the UGC for permission to offer an independent program. Minutes after this request had been dispatched by courier, we received a copy of a letter from the University of Manitoba to the UGC suggesting that joint programs be administered by its Faculty of Graduate Studies and that joint committees be weighted according to department size. These suggestions were unacceptable to us. Fortunately, the UGC interceded, and these one-sided obstacles were overcome and Manitoba's History Department entered into constructive discussions. The English Department, however, dragged its feet, first suggesting that the joint program be limited to Canadian literature but eventually agreeing that all of English literature be included. We were frustrated enough by the delays, but the chair of the UGC was livid at the obstructive tactics.

The shotgun marriage was finally consummated in the summer of 1976, and the two universities began jointly to share master's programs in history, English, religion, and public administration under the Joint Master's Committee, which reports to both senates. There was some initial personal enmity in English and history, but that gradually subsided and the arrangement has continued, although the English Department at the University of Winnipeg has temporarily withdrawn from the program.

In addition to its pronouncements on graduate studies, the Task Force on Post-Secondary Education made a number of other recommendations. These included the obligatory demands for accessibility, accountability, openness and cooperation between institutions. To our disappointment, there was little acknowledgement of our significant efforts to serve new constituencies. Three of the recommendations, however, were decidedly novel.

One was the recommendation that the United Church be given fewer seats on the Board of Regents, but the government never took such action.

Another was that all post-secondary institutions be overseen by one body, but with the UGC continuing (under the proposed Council on Post-Secondary Education) to fund the universities. The universities assailed this suggestion as adding an additional level of bureaucracy, and it was not implemented. Many years later, in 1996, such an overall authority was established to replace the UGC and to fund all universities and community colleges. The task force was obviously working in that direction but failed to go the whole way.

A third recommendation related to funding categories. The universities had received their grants in five categories: operating grants, first claims, miscellaneous capital, major capital, and reimbursement for municipal taxes. The task force suggested that the number of categories be increased, one of which was to cover salaries. The universities viewed this as an intrusion on their autonomy and condemned it on principle. It was not implemented, but Oliver later told me that he saw the suggestion as a protection for universities against unreasonable salary demands by militant professors. During the period of the Task Force's work, Oliver had been appointed president of Carleton University and may have seen this as a problem looming on the horizon. If the suggestion had been accepted, it would likely have led to salary negotiations between the professors and the government, as is the case in the United Kingdom. It could have saved the universities a lot of grief, but we were too preoccupied with autonomy to realize the full implications.

The Training of Teachers

Teaching was a common destination for the graduates of United College and the University of Winnipeg. Graduates in arts and science took a one-year teaching-training course at the University of Manitoba, as I had done in 1936-37. In 1971, the Faculty of Education at Manitoba announced plans for a four-year integrated program leading to the degree of Bachelor of Education (B.Ed.) as a desirable alternative to the former combination of degree and teaching certificate. As this program was to be offered only at the University of Manitoba, our traditional contribution to the teaching profession would virtually disappear. We naturally assumed that the action was intended to contribute to our demise, and we appealed to the UGC for help. That body promptly ordained that the B.Ed. be offered jointly by the two universities and, by February 1972, we had emerged with a mutually acceptable plan by which our students would take their first three years at the University of Winnipeg, with the necessary education courses taught by itinerant professors from the University of Manitoba. For the final year, all would join hands at Manitoba.

At first, the B.Ed. program was resisted by the minister of Education but was finally approved for introduction in the 1973-74 session of the legislature. We were concerned that the fact that everything culminated in the final year at the University of Manitoba would weaken our chance to attract students. We met with Robert Hedley, a fair-minded professor of education, who saw our point and (apparently on his own authority) agreed that the University of Winnipeg should admit one-third of the incoming students, or 150 of the initial total quota of 450, not a bad saw-off between reasonable individuals. Two decades later, in 1996-97, the teacher training-program was increased from four to five years, but with the compensatory by-product that two degrees, a B.A. or a B.Sc. and a B.Ed., would be awarded at the end of the time. Further, at long last, the University of Winnipeg was also empowered to provide all training needed to instruct the young.

Faculty Certification

Although in theory I had sympathy for the labour movement, I believed that unions were antithetic to the spirit of a university, at least amongst the teaching staff. After all, we were a community of scholars who pretty much governed ourselves. As president, I was a sort of *primus inter pares* who still retained the experience and instincts of a professor. Although I was doing no undergraduate teaching, I still gave an occasional lecture at the University of Winnipeg, still directed an occasional graduate student at the University of Manitoba, sometimes shared in teaching a graduate course in mass spectroscopy, and regularly received research grants and co-authored research papers. Every Friday morning, I went directly to my laboratory at the University of Manitoba, where Bob Barber and I discussed current progress and future plans with his and my research students. From the start,

I expected to establish collegial relations with my new colleagues at the University of Winnipeg and we would work together for the good of the institution.

Canadian Association of University Teachers

At the time of the Crowe case (1958), CAUT had advised persons seeking academic positions to avoid United College, as its administration did not permit free speech. This had little effect on staff recruitment, but it was a somewhat demeaning situation and, when I arrived, there was the feeling that the university was still in the bad books of the CAUT. It was because of this that I had asked the CAUT to bring greetings to my installation. Later that first year, the Faculty Association asked if I would meet with the president of CAUT, who was planning to visit the campus. This, I gathered, would be a significant meeting, and it was hoped that I would make a favourable impression on this important, and somewhat feared, dignitary. On the fateful day, the president who entered my room was none other than Charles Bigelow, who had been a graduate student in chemistry at McMaster when I was there. To the relief of the others, we reminisced about old times and casually established that the University of Winnipeg was no longer *persona non grata* with the CAUT. Charlie later came to Winnipeg as dean of Science at the University of Manitoba, and I have much enjoyed his continued friendship.

Faculty Salaries

Also early in my first year, the Faculty Association met with me to make a case for higher salaries. The discussion was amiable, and I offered to obtain salary data for Canadian universities that were comparable to the University of Winnipeg in size and program. The institutions that we agreed upon, with no knowledge of what would emerge, were Acadia, Mount Allison, Bishop's, Brock (in St. Catharines), and Lethbridge. When we next met, data in hand, the University of Winnipeg was seen to be slightly behind, and I promised to aim for the median of the group. The 1972-73 budget made provision for this action, which showed that my heart was in the right place. The next corrective action took place in March 1974, just before the end of the 1973-74 fiscal year. It emerged that we were facing an operating surplus, and the Board agreed to award an immediate $600 increase to each professor and to calculate 1974-75 increases on that new base. By 1975-76, we had raised our sights and were preparing to play in the major league, that is, we began to compare our salaries with all universities in

Canada (except for Quebec, which was always the "odd-man-out"). To reach our proper place in this larger group, the Board agreed to a two-stage catch-up: 60 percent in 1975-76 and 40 percent in 1976-77. To this end, the average salary increase in 1975-76 was 16.5 percent. I had every reason to feel satisfied, as did the members of the teaching staff. The officers of the Faculty Association were complicit in these actions in the sense that I apprised them in advance but, on principle, they did not always endorse them. I was on good terms with them and, invariably, found them responsible both to their membership and to the institution.

Certification at the University of Manitoba

In 1974, most of the professors at the University of Manitoba voted to apply to the Manitoba Labour Board for certification as a labour union. The president of the Manitoba Faculty Association was Roy Vogt, an economist and a peace-loving Mennonite. He did me the honour of discussing the matter before he submitted the application, and I tried to dissuade him, but he felt that circumstances left him no choice. Murdoch MacKay chaired the Labour Board at the time and rather reluctantly granted the application, regretting that a "master-servant" model was being forced upon what should have been a collegial society. This was the first case of professor unionization in English Canada, and unfortunately (in my view) it has served as a precedent for the many certifications that have followed.

The Anti-Inflation Board

The professors at the University of Winnipeg appeared to take the University of Manitoba's unionization in stride, but their patience was put to the test in 1976 when the anti-inflation measures were put into effect, limiting pay increases for the next three years to 10 percent, 8 percent, and 6 percent, respectively. The only exceptions to this schedule were legal commitments, that is, union-negotiated contracts. I had promised our professors for 1976-77 the second stage of the catch-up, which, if implemented, would lead to an increase of more than the permitted 10 percent. On the strength of the promise I had made, the increase was implemented. This brought the wrath of the Anti-Inflation Board (AIB) upon us. One of its members, William Ladyman, a respected Manitoba labour leader, visited the university, read a copy of the commitment I had made, and reported back to the AIB, which ordered the University to limit the increase to 10 percent. What a travesty of natural justice, that a solemn written promise had less standing in the eyes of the AIB than a labour contract. Because part of the second stage of the catch-up had been paid before the AIB ruling, I had to order certain amounts to be deducted from future paycheques. If I had been the subject of such unfair treatment, I might have sought certification myself, but my colleagues held steady.

Votes on Unionization

In 1978, at the end of my initial seven-year contract, I was offered an extension of an additional three years, which would bring me to the normal retirement age of sixty-five. I accepted the offer on condition that I be granted a "mini-sabbatical" (2.5 months). During my absence, the Faculty Association voted on unionization and decided against it. On my return, I established a budget advisory committee, which included a representative of the Faculty Association and two other professors, in addition to the student president and a representative of the non-academic staff. For the next two years, the budgets that I presented to the board carried the approval of this group. We were still a collegial family.

In the meantime, I had named a committee on academic development under the chairmanship of John Hofley, a well-liked and highly respected professor of sociology. Hofley invited suggestions and complaints and unearthed a wide spectrum of irritants that needed to be resolved. By the time of his final report, most of the problems had been resolved. His direct but amiable approach later served the institution well during his term as dean of Arts and Science.

Finally, in the dying months of my tenure, the Faculty Association voted again, this time in favour of certification, albeit by a slender margin. I was told that it was not because of me, but because they couldn't be sure of my successor. Thus, in preparing my final budget, I was unable to implement the salary increases that the corrective UGC grant of 1981 would have made possible. Instead, I had the unhappy task of naming a negotiating team to hammer out the first union contract, a task that was incomplete when I finally stepped down on 31 August 1981.

Relations with Students

UWSA was the official representative of the student body. Almost without exception, the incoming president of UWSA had a project to be accomplished during his or her regime. On the whole, I was on good terms with the student leaders, although we did not agree on all matters. Even when we were in disagreement, however, it was imperative that the University president not appear unreasonable or intransigent. At the slightest sign of bullying by the president, the students would have rallied to the support of their leaders, even if they were at odds with what they were trying to do. In short, in a public dispute between students and the president, the president could never emerge the winner. Through discussion, however, his view could sometimes prevail.

In my first year, the student president was Marilou McPhedran, who later qualified as a lawyer and in 1985 was named to the Order of Canada for her work on behalf of women, in particular for securing specific mention of women in the 1982 Charter of Rights. On one occasion, early on, I introduced her as president of the UWSA and referred to her as "a good-looking young woman" (which she was). After the event, she quietly said to me, "Dr. Duckworth, the important thing is that I'm the president, and not that I'm good-looking." It was a lesson I needed and never forgot; years later she told me that she had been afraid that she might offend me.

On 3 April 1973, Donald Lidstone, president of the UWSA, requested professors to provide him with book lists, as he intended to establish a student-operated bookstore in time for the 1973-74 session. Under the imprint Pioneer Publishing Company, he would compete with Classics bookstore, which had been operating under the University's patronage for several years. According to the students, Classics bookstore was charging too-high prices. I immediately wrote to the teaching staff, explaining that our contract with Classics (Louis Melzack) was in force until 31 March 1974 and asking them to deny Lidstone's request. This sabotaged his project, but we agreed to name a committee, under the chairmanship of Professor Brian Evans, to advise what should be done for the 1974-75 session. This led to the establishment of the University's own bookstore (to be operated on a non-profit basis) and the withdrawal of a student-run shop that had been selling a variety of supplies and apparel. We were able to entice a superb manager from Brandon University (Wendy Shand), who made a slight profit in the first year, which was used to reduce textbooks prices in the second; the chronic complaints about book prices became a thing of the past. Chalk one up to Lidstone who, even when threatening to bring down confusion, was invariably courteous and respectful!

Chris Guest, the 1974-75 UWSA president, was an engaging psychology major whose main accomplishment, from my point of view, was establishing a daycare centre. It was such a useful project that the University assisted in numerous ways, without taking the credit or the responsibility. It was located in the basement of the library, providentially close to washrooms but, if the University had been the proprietor, it would likely have been criticized for its subterranean location. In the spring of 1975, Guest and his colleagues organized the annual Grads' Farewell, a dinner and dance for which many students acquired new outfits. Whilst waiting for my wife to emerge from the washroom, I stood near two young men who were discussing the event. One said to the other, "I didn't know good pants were so comfortable."

Paul McFadzen, president in 1975–76, was married to another student and was conscious of the cost of food. When coffee in the cafeteria became too pricey (well above eleven cents), he began selling it for less at the cafeteria door. We both knew that he could not lose: if I closed him down, the students would revolt; if I ordered the price of coffee to be reduced, he would make his point. I visited his booth, bought a cup of his bargain coffee, and instructed the cafeteria to lower its price. In celebration, he took me to lunch at McDonald's. It was also McFadzen who introduced the first motion (of many to follow) that Board meetings be open to the public, but the Board chose to limit the open aspect to presentations by interested individuals or groups, rather than going whole hog.

Hart Schwarz, president in 1978–79, concentrated on tuition fees and, with a 1,000-student petition, undoubtedly influenced the Board in its decision to stop short of the Lyon government's "suggested" figure of $540. This was the last stage in our misguided policy of trying to limit tuition increases, for which I must bear responsibility.

The open-meeting question came to a head in 1979–80 during the student presidency of Harvey Thorliefson and the Board chairmanship of Robert Siddall. To observe how open meetings worked, Siddall and I attended a meeting of the Board of Governors at the University of Manitoba, where Siddall rather expected to find a crowd of spectators. We were the only ones, were conspicuous by our presence, and may have been suspected of industrial espionage. Siddall was convinced that it was time for the University of Winnipeg to take similar action. Meanwhile, Thorliefson (who later took a Ph.D. in geology and became the Canadian expert on diamonds in northern Canada) and his constituents were understandably concerned at the cost of tuition and requested that discussion of the budget occur during an open meeting of the Board. Siddall and I agreed to support the request and promised to introduce an open meeting resolution as the first item on the agenda. If it were then approved, as we were sure it would be, the students waiting in the hall would be invited to join the meeting. Before the resolution could be introduced, however, the students burst into the meeting, led by some with whom I had made the bargain. I felt betrayed and moved to adjourn the meeting but to reassemble in Convocation Hall where we could discuss the issues. For the next meeting of the Board, at which the proposal to discuss the budget in public would be debated, I asked the chief of Security to post a guard at the door to prevent students from entering until the Board had taken action. Misinterpreting my level of concern, this officer saw his task as that of quelling a revolution. He doubled security and arranged for two police cars to be on standby in the adjacent street; we were made to look like fascists, and the *Winnipeg Free Press* published a cartoon somehow linking the event to the Crowe case. In the end, however, the Board was permitted to take the necessary action without invasion. Closed meetings were a thing of the past, and soon the number of spectators had dwindled to zero.

Relations with Senate

The Senate is the supreme academic body of the University and, in the main, its decisions are final, the Board having delegated such authority to it. Exceptions to the above are new programs and other actions involving financial expenditures. At the University of Winnipeg, it includes all department chairs, seven students, a few administrative officers, and a number of professors-at-large. The president presides and, during my time, the registrar (Richard Bellhouse) was its secretary. In the 1975-76 session, it voted to admit spectators to its meetings, except for that portion dealing with honorary degrees. For that topic, spectators retired, and a conspiratorial hush fell over the room as the president presented the report of the Honorary Degrees Committee.

Because of the United Church connection with the University, I continued the practice of opening Senate meetings with prayer, and it was the secretary's duty to arrange for a prayee. The prayer settled things down, and no objections to it ever reached my ears. It did not continue, however, into the next administration.

It was a harmonious senate, scrupulous in ventilating all aspects of a subject, but never intemperately and always accepting the majority decision. The monthly meetings began at 15:40 hours and usually ended by 17:00. Those whose opinions were particularly respected included John Clake (dean), Walter Swayze (English), Gerald Bedford (English), Vincent Rutherford (History), Gordon Blake (Economics), Lawrence Swyers (Chemistry), James Duff (Physics), Richard Veatch (Political Science), Carl Ridd (Religious Studies), John Hofley (Sociology), and James Richtik (Geography). I once ruled that a motion to table until the next meeting was non-debatable. Closer students than I of *Robert's Rules of Order* knew that a motion to table is non-debatable only if it carries no conditions. I escaped impeachment, and the matter was settled amicably when we next convened. A major accomplishment of the Senate was the drafting of the Tenure By-Law during the 1972-73 academic session. This was approved by the Board, without modification, and stated clearly the conditions under which permanent academic appointments were to be made.Vincent Rutherford chaired this important committee. No brief to an outside body (and there were several) went forward without Senate approval.

A diverting series of reports ensued when the Senate undertook to design a University coat of arms without incurring the expense of consulting the College of Arms. We were led through these treacherous waters by Gerald Bedford andVincent Rutherford, who showed us an attractive option with a Maltese Cross in the background and featuring the superb motto *Lux et veritas floreant* (Let light and truth flourish). Scarcely had this design been approved when our experts reported new and bad news: according to the rules of heraldry, nothing must be placed in front of the cross. At the next meeting, however, we learned that heraldic elements could be placed in front of the cross, provided the cross was itself in front of something else. A simple shield was made to serve as the background necessity, and we had accomplished our purpose without the help of the Duke of Norfolk, the hereditary earl marshall.

Relations with the Board of Regents

Five men served as chair of the Board of Regents during my ten-year presidency: Donald Tomlin (chartered accountant),T.A.J. (Jack) Cunnings (hospital administrator),William Norrie (former Rhodes Scholar from the College, lawyer and later mayor of Winnipeg), W. John A. Bulman (businessman and later fourth chancellor), and Robert Siddall (corporate secretary).These were experienced, intelligent men who were dedicated to the welfare of the institution; I could not have asked for better.

The ten members named by the United Church were nominated by the University and, by definition, were desirable members.We had no control over the ten appointed by the provincial government. Rather naïvely, I once asked Scott Bateman, chair of the UGC, if we could suggest possible names to the government. In effect, he said, "You have control over the ten United Church appointees, don't push your luck." Thus, as terms of appointments expired (three years), we waited in suspense to learn who the new government appointees would be. Sometimes they were known to us and sometimes they were not, but, almost without exception, they identified quickly with the institution and conspired with the others for the common good. One of the NDP appointees – a prominent lawyer – attended no meeting during his three-year term; to give a charitable interpretation to his absence, I assume that he may have felt that affairs were being so well managed that they did not require his attention.

In 1971, when I arrived, John Bulman was a Board member, having been appointed by the previous Conservative government. His term had expired, however, on 30 June of that year, and the current NDP government had chosen not to replace him, apparently realizing his value as a Board member. For three or four years, he continued in this "serving until replaced" category; it was a clever ploy to continue his membership without the political embarrassment of re-appointing a well-known Conservative. Eventually, however, because the sword of Damocles was always above his head, we transferred him to the United Church slate.

Three of the Board members were elected by the graduates; these were known friends and became strong members. Four of the Board were named by the UWSA: its president and three other students. One year, the student members were drawn largely from political science, and they informed me that they were intending to play the role of "antagonists," presumably as a political exercise. I reminded them that the university was not a playground game, and they dropped the idea. Interventions by the student members were carefully listened to by their elders, with whom they may have enjoyed a better rapport than with some of their own parents. The four representatives of the Senate were drawn from the teaching staff and brought with them an intimate knowledge of the University; more often than not, the Board was swayed by their views.

Board meetings began with a detailed president's report, which usually comprised fifteen to twenty items, with something for everyone, and which had been circulated in advance. If I had misstated something, there was always a professor or a student to correct the record. The report invariably provoked questions and comments and got things off to a good start. Reports from all committees were listed in the agenda, which encouraged committees to meet in order to have something to report.

I sat to the right of the chair, with the chancellor on my right. To the left of the chair sat the secretary, John (Jack) K.A. Brown. Brown was honest to an extreme and would correct me if he thought that I had slurred over some point or had misrepresented it. I was never offended by his rectitude, and his emendations were a source of both reassurance and amusement. The chancellor rarely intervened, but his presence was appreciated and his infrequent remarks were hung upon.

Chancellors of the University of Winnipeg

The first chancellor of the University of Winnipeg had been Richard H.G. Bonnycastle, a well-respected businessman who was fast becoming wealthy as the publisher of Harlequin romances. He died suddenly in 1968 and was succeeded in 1969 by Paul H.T.Thorlakson. Bonnycastle's family has continued to support the University, and his contribution has not been forgotten.

Thorlakson was an eminent surgeon and the founder of the Winnipeg Clinic. Although he had had no prior connection with the University, he had been sought out by Lockhart because of his prominence in the community and the respect in which he was held. When the Order of Canada was established in 1967, Thorlakson was one of the initial group of Companions of the Order.

Thorlakson, of Icelandic descent, was the son of a Lutheran minister. After graduating in medicine from the University of Manitoba in 1919, he had entered into practice with Dr. Brothers in Shoal Lake, Manitoba. Shortly after his arrival in Shoal Lake, the leading citizens of that town were the target of one of the Chautauqua girls, intent upon obtaining guarantors for the annual visit of the Chautauqua troop. She had been told that the town doctor was a hard sell but that it was important to get his signature. Although Brothers was the hard sell, it was the unsuspecting Thorlakson who was exposed to the considerable charms of Gladys Henry of Killarney, Manitoba. She had also graduated in 1919, in home economics. Thorlakson (or "Thor"), never knew what hit him; he signed on the dotted line and they were married the next year.

In 1978, Thor declared his intention not to stand for re-election. We had glowed in his presence and that of his wife and, I believe, they had treasured their association with the University. He had the ability to relate to individuals of all types, and the students, in particular, responded to his friendship.

The third chancellor was Roderick O.A. Hunter, a student of United College in the class of 1937. A lawyer who spent much of his career as secretary of Great-West Life Assurance Company, Hunter had chaired the Board of United College from 1962 to 1964 and had been a member from 1948 to 1967, only resigning to become a founding member of the UGC. He was a popular choice, not only because of his long service to the institution and his intimate knowledge of it, but also because he and his three sons were graduates. He had wide connections in Winnipeg and he and his wife were persons of unusual charm. For the first time, we had not imported a luminary but had selected one of our own.

As Hunter and I had been at the college together and had remained friends, it was a happy association for me. He was beginning his second three-year when I stepped down In 1981, and he was succeeded by W. John A. Bulman (another long-time servant of the University) in 1984. I had had the earlier pleasure of serving under Bulman when he chaired the Board, but never served under his chancellorship.

The President's Secretary

Behind everything the president does stands the president's secretary, anticipating needs, taking initiatives, answering inquiries, dispensing information, accommodating visitors, placating those whom the president has offended, drafting letters and reports, and playing numerous other roles never observed by the public.

Marilyn (Reimer) O'Hara came to the office on 14 February 1972, having served her apprenticeship as recording secretary for the University of Manitoba Senate. She was a University of Winnipeg graduate and scholarship winner in history. She resigned five years later to try her hand as a librarian.

Norma (Bornholdt) Gwizon came on 14 February 1977, having served her apprenticeship in the Premier's Office. After completing first year at the University of Manitoba, she had opted for an immediate career. She continued as secretary to my successor.

Marilyn Lockwood, already a long-time employee of the University, joined the President's Office in 1979 bringing with her a vast knowledge of the institution. She was a "jack of all trades" and master of all, and served the institution for a further eighteen years after my departure. I owe a heavy debt to these three gifted and dedicated women.

Convocations and Honorary Degrees

The Honorary Degrees Committee of the Senate was chaired by the president and was representative of the several University constituencies. In the main, the Committee chose to recognize graduates of the institution or those who had made distinctive contributions to Manitoba rather than to seek out national or world figures who had little or no local connection. That is, we chose *to honour individuals* rather than *ask individuals to honour us.*

Centenary of Winnipeg: 1974

On 1 January 1974, the University inserted newspaper advertisements congratulating the City of Winnipeg on its centenary and announcing that a special convocation would be held later in the year to recognize this important event. Further, the university welcomed suggestions of individuals who might be honoured at the special convocation. Few suggestions were actually received, but the advertisement raised expectations, which was its purpose. That was the easy part. What remained was to select ten individuals who would be seen to have contributed to the many facets of city life. Under the leadership of Chancellor Thorlakson, and with the advice of several friends of the University, the following slate was presented to Senate and approved: Edward Cass, outstanding athlete and sports executive; Arthur Coulter, labour leader; Sister Dorais, Grey Nuns administrator of St. Boniface Hospital; Stephen Juba, mayor since 1957; Gordon Lawson, vice-president of James Richardson and Sons; Leo Mol, sculptor; Nan Murphy, city councillor; Florence Pearce, co-founder of Good Neighbours' Club; Saul Simkin, head of BACM Construction Company; Joseph Zuken, school trustee and city councillor.

The convocation was held on 20 April 1974 in the Manitoba Theatre Centre, which was practically filled for the occasion. Participating were George Richardson, then governor of the Hudson's Bay Company, and John McKeag, then lieutenant governor. Together they represented authority in the Red River Valley before and after the creation of Manitoba in 1870. Perry Nodelman, professor of English, composed an ode for the ceremony, which was set to music by Ronald Gibson and sung by a university choir. The chorus of the original version of the ode contained the words "Jubalation!, Jubalation!," an obvious reference to Steve Juba, the long-time mayor of the city. Like many others, Chancellor Thorlakson was not an unreserved admirer of Mayor Juba, but he had agreed that he should be included in the slate. As he said, "The people of Winnipeg have chosen him." But it was another thing to immortalize Juba in a centennial ode. I explained the problem to Nodelman, who was reluctant to alter the clever wording. As desperate conciliator between two men with strongly held views, I eventually got an agreement that the printed program would read "Jubilation" but the choir would sing "Jubalation," which they did, and perhaps more defiantly than the occasion required. It's a tough job being a defender of academic freedom.

Steve Juba was very effective at courting the ethnic vote; some might have said that he did so cynically. He and I both attended a banquet of the German-Canadian Society, and I was witness to his first action on arrival. He carried four splendid-looking certificates, signed by him but with the names of the honorees left blank. He asked the president for four names, which were entered in the blank spaces, and these individuals, who were chosen almost at random and at the last minute, were more than gratified to be called forward later in the evening to receive what was assumed by them to be a predetermined honour.

The University regarded the special convocation as an important event and prepared a plaque commemorating it, which listed the names of the ten citizens honoured. We gave this plaque to the City with the suggestion that it be mounted in City Hall. To my knowledge this was never done. If we had also listed the names of the current members of City Council, it might have met a better fate.

Centenary of Arrival of First Mennonites

Later in 1974, we recognized the arrival of the first fourteen Mennonite families in Manitoba. They had settled in the Steinbach area, southeast of Winnipeg, and were followed by thousands of others in the ensuing decades, becoming an unusual force for good in the province. The Mennonite members of our faculty were asked to recommend three individuals to be honoured at the fall convocation (28 October). This proved no easy task for the group, as many of their faith had achieved prominence in the community. In making their report, they explained that everyone knew that Mennonites could make money if they put their minds to it. Thus, they decided to recognize success not in business but in three other aspects that showed Mennonites at their best: religion, music, and Third World service. The individuals so chosen were Benjamin Horch (musician), Gerhard Lohrenz (pastor), and Helena Reimer (nurse, who had long served in the Third World). The choice of Nurse Reimer was appropriate in another sense as well: the Klaas R. Reimer (1837-1906) who had come in the first contingent was the most prolific member of it, fathering twenty-four children. By 1974, his descendants numbered well over 800.

International Women's Year: 1975

Numerous events marked International Women's Year, including the honouring of three outstanding women at the University of Winnipeg's fall convocation: Mary Elizabeth Bayer (who had achieved the highest position to date in the provincial civil service), Thelma Forbes (first female cabinet minister in Manitoba), and Annie Moore (president of the University of Winnipeg Women's Auxiliary). The event was well received and passed without untoward incident, unlike a much earlier graduation ceremony at the Winnipeg General Hospital, when the nurses were congratulated on "now entering the world's oldest profession."

Honouring Sir William Stephenson

One world figure we did honour was Sir William Stephenson, the "Intrepid" of World War I fame. One of the student senators, Ian Restall, knew that Sir William had been born in Winnipeg but had pursued his illustrious business career in the United Kingdom before being appointed Churchill's personal wartime representative to President Franklin Roosevelt and head of British Intelligence in North America. Restall's nomination was accepted, and he was asked to read the citation at convocation. As Stephenson was not well enough to travel from his home in Bermuda, an exception was made to the normal rule that recipients must attend the ceremony. Rather, a telephone link was arranged so that Stephenson could hear the proceedings and, in his turn, address convocation, which was to be held on a certain Sunday. The link had been tested on the preceding Friday, but it appears that Bermudian telephone operators slack off on Sundays. As a result, when I called upon Sir William to speak, there was no response. That was anticlimactic, but we were able to gaze upon a blown-up photo of him, and Chancellor Hunter had awarded the degree, so the event was not a complete failure. He later sent me the text of his intended remarks, in which he dwelt on the threat of communism and the watchfulness of the RCMP in protecting us from it. At the time, the RCMP were under fire in the newspapers for illegal wire-tapping, and Sir William's accolades might not have drawn unreserved endorsement.

The University of Manitoba was chagrined that we had honoured Stephenson who, following World War I, had taught briefly at that institution and was arguably its most famous alumnus. Shortly after our convocation, the University of Manitoba's Chancellor Auld and President Campbell journeyed to Bermuda to award him a University of Manitoba degree in person. Subsequently, our Chancellor Hunter and his wife, whilst vacationing in Bermuda, made contact with Stephenson, established a personal friendship with him, and, following their return to Winnipeg, the University of Winnipeg received $100,000 (U.S.), which now provides the endowment for the prestigious Stephenson Awards.

Photographers at Convocation

Media types frequently attended convocation, and we were somewhat flattered to have them. One photographer was invariably present, moving close and blocking the view, as is the wont of her profession. After three years of tolerating her intrusions in the hope of gaining free publicity, we learned that she was a self-appointed photographer and that her camera held no film. But she had a good time while it lasted.

A dependable and welcome figure at all convocations in Winnipeg was the photographer Barney Charach. He took up his position so as to catch students as they were receiving their diplomas, not all students, but those who had contracted with him in advance. At one ceremony, the last student had just crossed the platform and I was rising to bring convocation to a close, when Richard Bellhouse (the registrar, who had been announcing the graduands) asked John Doe to come forward again, as Mr. Charach had missed taking his photograph. Previously, I had imagined that I was in charge of convocation, but I then realized that the ceremony was subject to a higher power than mine. Many years later, when, as chancellor of the University of Manitoba, I was congratulating the graduates of the Agriculture diploma course, I was startled to find that all the students, as they stretched out their hands to shake mine, turned towards Barney Charach and flashed big smiles. The next year at the same event, I explained to the students that this was not Hollywood; they were to look me in the eye when we shook hands, and Mr. Charach would be able to capture a good profile view. Charach has provided excellent photographs to thousands of graduates and, amongst other things, took superb photos of my daughter's wedding.

Installation of Paul Desmarais

Moses ("Mose") Morgan, president of the Memorial University of Newfoundland, had persuaded the Sudbury-born financier Paul Demarais to accept the chancellorship of that university. He also persuaded me to represent the AUCC and the ACU at the installation ceremony, to be held in St. John's in the fall of 1977. Desmarais arrived with an entourage that included Roger Lemelin (who wrote "The Plouffe Family") and Brian Mulroney, the recently named president of the Iron Ore Company of Canada. In my remarks, I mentioned that the chancellor of the exchequer in the United Kingdom had responsibility for all widows, orphans, and idiots in the kingdom but university chancellors had an easier time, as there were few widows or orphans under their care.

Mulroney told two anecdotes that may be self-revelatory: (1) Lloyd Henderson, a minister of the United Church and mayor of Portage la Prairie, ran for the leadership of the Liberal party at the convention that elected Pierre Elliott Trudeau. He received a single vote on the first ballot, and a journalist accused him of voting for himself. Henderson denied the charge, saying he was not a voting delegate, although his wife and mother-in-law were. (2) Having spoken at a Conservative Party gathering, Joe Clark asked an aide to discover why a man in the front row had not applauded. The aide later reported that the man had only one arm.

Intercollegiate Athletics

The academic side of Canadian universities has drawn heavily on both British and American practice. What is the case for athletics?

In the ancient universities of Oxford and Cambridge, the team captain is elected, and it is he who names the members of the team. Coaches may assist in the training and in other preparations for action, but that's the limit to their role. By contrast, in the United States, the coaches are virtual dictators, holding the power of life or death over their charges, many of whose services have been purchased by athletic scholarships. The British tradition is clearly more amateur in its approach, although cracks have appeared recently in the purity of the Oxford-Cambridge boat race.

American intercollegiate sport provides a species of religion for students and alumni, it earns dubious prestige (but often profits) for its institutions, and it gives entrée to professional careers to many of its athletes. Of the several sports, men's football, men's basketball, and men's baseball head the list in order of game attendance.

Except for post-season games (which are multiplying without limit), the football schedule runs from September through November. During this period, millions of Americans devote their Saturdays to the game, first, by attending pre-game festivities, second, by exhorting their heroes to greater effort, and, third, by dissecting the result. The University of Michigan Wolverines, for example, have for twenty-five years played home games before 100,000 spectators, whilst the University of Nebraska Cornhuskers have performed before sellouts (75,000) since 1962.

The oldest rivalry exists between the schools of the Ivy League: Brown, Cornell, Dartmouth, Harvard, Pennsylvania, Princeton, and Yale. Although the standard of play is now inferior to that in other major conferences, some of which have become virtually professional in their operation, the Ivy League rivalries are long-standing and deeply held, particularly that between Harvard and Yale. The most remarkable of these contests took place on 23 November 1968. With forty-eight seconds remaining, and Yale leading twenty-nine to thirteen, the issue was no longer in doubt. But in that morsel of time, Harvard scored two touchdowns plus a pair of two-point conversions, a resurgence that is said to be without precedent in the history of football. And not even Yale begrudged the *Crimson* its headline: "Harvard beats Yale 29 – 29."

The basketball schedule is heavier than football's but, of course, the players are subject to fewer injuries. As with football, players are subsidized to the permissible extent, their coaches arrange dubious academic programs, and every lost game is a tragedy.

It is the American model that Canadian intercollegiate sport has tended to follow, although (thank heaven) it is still a pale image of its mentor. Athletic scholarships exist, but they are modest and fail to prevent Canadian athletes from accepting much larger ones at American schools, particularly in hockey. Further, in my experience, the Canadian coaches give more emphasis to the academic side. And basketball, volleyball, and hockey players line up to shake hands after games.

In 1971, the University Wesmen participated in five intercollegiate sports: men's and women's basketball, men's and women's volleyball, and men's hockey. The hockey program was discontinued, but the other four teams have remained remarkably competitive, considering the size of the school. They reached their zenith in the winter of 1993, when all four teams stood number one in Canada for a period of several weeks. More important, however, they always did their best, they played fairly, and they were good sports. I was proud to support them by voice and, to a modest extent, with institutional funds.

Cooperation with Red River Community College

A post-war development in Canada, as an alternate post-secondary option, was the community college. Its courses were job-oriented, were one to two years in duration, and were inspired, I believe, by the polytechnic colleges in the United Kingdom. Because their programs were less academic, they were looked down upon by the universities, although this disdain was never overtly expressed. But it was evident when a student sought course credit at a university for work taken at a college. It was usually a case of starting over again from scratch.

Manitoba had three community colleges: Red River Community College in Winnipeg, Assiniboine in Brandon, and Keewatin in The Pas. I had sat on the Community Colleges Advisory Board under the chairmanship of John Bulman and, on that account, had some knowledge of their strengths, weaknesses, and aspirations. Many suspected that their ultimate aim was to offer degrees, but I knew that they were proud of their distinctive role and had no desire to become degree granting. But they did have a desire for recognition of their programs by the universities.

Early in my first year at the University of Winnipeg, the dean and I met with the director of Red River Community College and his senior staff to discuss transfer of course credits from the College to the University. Our departments were asked to compare certain College courses with University ones of the same titles in the hope of finding equivalencies. It appeared to be a straightforward exercise, but, when our departments were asked to identify these equivalencies, they all concluded that the university courses were more demanding. This was not flattering to the College and their instructors, and it appeared that we had lost goodwill and gained nothing in return. Another tack was needed.

The solution was to grant university credit for a body of college work, with the stipulation that the corresponding university courses could not be taken for credit. Thus, a college student might receive thirty credits for a two-year college diploma, which could lead to a three-year degree in a further two years, but could not take courses like first-year economics, physics, or psychology to complete the remaining sixty credits needed for the degree. The discussion then turned to the transfer of credits in the opposite direction, a flattering possibility that the College had not contemplated. The College readily agreed to give degree holders one year credit towards a two-year diploma. In this way, a student could obtain a degree plus diploma in four years starting at either end. This led to an agreement on a number of paired programs such as administrative studies/business administration, psychology/child care, and chemistry/chemical technician in time for the 1973-74 session. Modesty prevents me from mentioning who suggested the idea, which was probably more important in principle than it was in practice. It was a long time before the University of Manitoba could bring itself to grant comparable recognition to work done at the colleges.

Association of Commonwealth Universities

The ACU grew out of the first Congress of Universities of the Empire, held in London in 1912. Invitations had been sent to fifty-one universities, all of whom sent representatives: eighteen responded from Canada, including the University of Manitoba. The Congress was famously successful, especially on the social side, and even the British universities, which, in their desire for independence, had never collaborated on anything, were keen to form an association with their colonial sisters. It was agreed that congresses be held every five years and that an office be established in London. Accordingly, the Universities Bureau of the British Empire emerged in 1913 with plans to publish a yearbook and to circulate information on university vacancies and other matters. Large universities were levied fifty pounds and small universities twenty-five pounds towards the cost of these endeavours. Five of the British universities refused initially to pay the levy, but the overseas group, like obedient children, sent cheques by return mail.

The next congress, planned for 1917, was postponed because of the war but, in that year, the Bureau convened a meeting to ask if British universities could supplant German and Austrian ones as the "finishing schools" (that is, Ph.D. universities) for American, British, and colonial scholars. A few months later, and with momentum provided by Lord Balfour, the British foreign secretary, the British universities were urged to offer the Ph.D., which most agreed to do in 1918. Oxford anticipated the momentous event by offering the doctorate in 1917, whilst Cambridge and London delayed action until 1920. Thus, the Bureau, although intended for Empire matters, had provided a forum for the discussion of an internal policy of the highest importance.

Following the war, quinquennial congresses were held regularly, and the Bureau demonstrated its growing usefulness. The Eighth Quinquennial Congress was held in Montreal in 1958, the first to be held outside the British Isles. At that time, the member universities numbered 119, and the chair of the congress was Andrew Stewart, president of the University of Alberta. I had been invited by President Gilmour to be one of the McMaster representatives at this congress but did not fully appreciate the honour and declined it in favour of a mass spectrometry conference in London.

I was not invited to the 1963 congress in London but, in 1968, Saunderson included me and William Fyles, dean of Medicine, in the delegation to the tenth congress in Sydney, Australia.

Sydney: 1968

The 1968 congress was held in Sydney. The Australians were hosting their first congress and were determined to make a good impression. Amongst other things, the organizers approached the Australian wine trade for gifts in kind. "Delegates will be here from all corners of the globe," they said. "It's an incomparable opportunity to bring your product (which was little known outside Australia at the time) to the attention of the world." The wine merchants accepted this challenge with the result that we never sat down to a meal, including breakfast, without a bottle of wine at each place! Most of the papers presented at the congress were earnest and dreary, but, throughout the congress, I realized how much the Commonwealth universities had in common and could see the value of the personal contacts that the congress provided. In the main, the universities were cast in the British mould, with the senate as the supreme academic body. Everyone knew who the registrar was, what constituted an honours course, and was familiar with the rest of the academic lingo. But, most of all, the lingua franca was English, and every delegate could converse with every other one.

I sat one evening at dinner with Lady Cameron, wife of Lord Cameron, the pro-chancellor of Edinburgh University, and naïvely asked if her husband's title indicated that he was head of the Clan Cameron. That was not so, she said; rather, he had been made a "law lord" when he was elevated to the Court of Session (the supreme court of Scotland) and, as was the custom, had been allowed to choose his own title. She further explained that wives of law lords had not always been entitled to the title "lady." Early in the century, Mr. Anderson (let us say) was elevated to the court and chose the title Lord Glengarry (let us say). Taking his wife to London, he announced to the desk clerk at the Savoy Hotel that they were Lord Glengarry and Mrs. Anderson. The clerk replied that the Savoy was not that kind of hotel, which led the irate lord to write to the *Times* and in other ways stir up a fuss, with the result that wives of law lords were allowed thereafter to share their husbands' honorifics.

The Australians arranged elaborate post-congress tours. My wife and I joined the group that went to Canberra, Melbourne, and Tasmania, visiting universities in each place and engaging in discussions with university officials. When we landed in Hobart, Tasmania, it seemed that we had come to the end of the world, but it was there that we received much the warmest welcome, perhaps because visitors from the outside world were infrequent. A few years earlier, to add colour to its tercentennial celebration, the government of Tasmania had decided to invite a descendant of Abel Tasman, the Dutch navigator who had discovered Tasmania in 1642. When advertisements in Holland brought none to light, it was agreed to settle for anyone who carried that name. The choice fell on an acquaintance of mine, a Dutch mass spectroscopist who was somewhat imbued with the grand manner. According to him, he had gone to Tasmania and played the unique role expected of him, but I was relieved to learn in 1968 that the Tasmanians had also been satisfied with his performance.

Edinburgh: 1973

The eleventh congress was held in Edinburgh in 1973, and John Clake and I represented the University of Winnipeg. The environment was a featured topic, and speakers from the Western world railed against the use of DDT. Then we were sobered by a delegate from the tropics who quietly told of the lives saved from malaria by the control of mosquitoes that DDT had made possible.

On the lighter side, a bus bringing spouses back from an excursion to St. Andrew's broke down on the Firth of Forth Bridge. Although it was the height of traffic, these spouses were determined not to be late for an evening banquet and walked the remaining length of the bridge, but not in military order. The incoming lanes of that celebrated bridge have seldom seen such chaos. For that matter, the entire congress barely escaped chaos.

At that time, student organizations against apartheid were targeting the Smith government of Southern Rhodesia and were objecting to the planned attendance at the congress of R. Craig, principal of the University College of Rhodesia, although he and his institution were leaders in providing higher education to Blacks. University of Edinburgh students were amongst those aroused in the cause and, on another front, were concurrently agitating for seats on the University Council. When this latter campaign foundered, it was pointed out that no statute prevented the rector, who was elected to the Council to represent the students, from being himself or herself a student. Accordingly, in the triennial election of 1971, they elected Jonathan Wills, aged twenty-four and a graduate student in social sciences, who had run against John MacKintosh (Labour member of parliament for Berwick and East Lothian), William Rushton (co-founder of the magazine *Private Eye*), Ian Simpson (a student working as a law apprentice), and Paddy Dusser (a third-year history student). As rector, Wills was entitled to chair the Council and to name the vice-rector, both of which he did. Then he threw his weight behind the anti-apartheid campaign. Using his impressive rector's stationery, he wrote to the heads of the other Commonwealth nations in Africa asking if they intended to allow their universities to be represented at a congress attended by Craig. These heads of government had been blissfully unaware that such a congress was to take place but, having had the touchy issue brought to their attention *by the rector of Edinburgh University,* they could hardly turn a blind eye. Consequently, all Commonwealth universities in Black Africa were forbidden to attend the congress if a Rhodesian representative was to be present. In the interest of harmony, and to save the congress from collapse, the excellent Dr. Craig declined to attend, although he was held in the highest regard by the Blacks in his own country. It had also been the practice of the ACU to continue services to the South African universities, although that nation was no longer a member of the Commonwealth. Following the congress, and after a heated debate, these long-enjoyed services were withdrawn.

The twelfth congress was to be held in Canada in 1978, at the University of Western Ontario in London, under the chairmanship of Carl Williams, then president and vice-chancellor of that institution. Western Ontario would be celebrating its centenary in the year of the congress. Whilst we were still together in the United Kingdom, Carl called a meeting of the Canadian presidents to discuss various matters, including the raising of money for the congress. I suggested that the Canadian universities tax themselves for the next five years, the large universities paying $1,500 per year, the medium ones paying $1,000, and the small ones (like the University of Winnipeg) paying $500. The suggestion was embraced and, by 1978, we had amassed $200,000 plus interest, which formed the bulk of the needed funding. Perhaps because of this brilliant suggestion, I was named one of the four Canadian representatives on the ACU Council and, a couple of years later, was asked to serve as vice-chair to Williams for the 1978 congress. This seemed a modest responsibility, as Williams would be organizing the event at his own university.

ACU Council: 1973 to 1979

The ACU was guided by its secretary general, Sir Hugh Springer, who had succeeded John Frederick Foster in 1970. Springer had been registrar of the University of the West Indies, assistant secretary general of the commonwealth secretariat, and was subsequently to become governor general of Barbados. A man of few words but impressive presence, Springer was recognized for his integrity by members from every country. The ACU Council, to which he reported, numbered twenty-seven and was representative of the 190 universities that formed the ACU in 1973.

A major player on the Council during my period of membership and beyond was Tom Symons, the founding president of Trent University. He was influential in moving the perceived centre of gravity of the ACU from the British Isles to somewhere in the Atlantic, Pacific, or Indian Oceans, and in stabilizing its frequently shaky finances. Later, he led a campaign that raised two million pounds for interchange of Commonwealth staff and, at all times, infused the ACU with his enthusiasm for its work.

It was a cardinal doctrine that the ACU was not an arm of governments but a voluntary association of universities. At a meeting of executive heads in Wellington, New Zealand, in February 1976, word of the death of Kenyatta (president of Kenya) reached the meeting, and the Kenyan vice-chancellors departed immediately for home, possibly to protect their positions in the new regime. A motion was proposed by another African delegate that we send our condolences to the government of Kenya. I was chairing the meeting, with Springer at my side, and observed his agitation at the suggestion that we communicate in any way with the Kenyan government. He suspected that the mover of the motion was attempting to draw us into the world of international politics. I ruled that we would consider the motion after coffee. When we reassembled, I reminded the meeting that we had no governmental ties and suggested that we send our condolences to our Kenyan colleagues, the vice-chancellors. The mover had no ulterior motive and was happy to accept the suggestion, never realizing that he had almost precipitated a constitutional crisis, and we moved on to other matters.

One of Springer's right-hand colleagues was Tom Craig, a precise Scot who was responsible for the ACU's publications. These included the *Yearbook,* a massive annual publication that described the history and programs of all member institutions and listed all departmental members. It was and is an indispensable source of reference. Craig, through no fault of his own, was not able to establish rapport with Springer's successor, Anastasios Christadoulou, a Cypriot who had previously been founding secretary of the Open University.

Also prominent in the secretariat was John Whittingham, the financial officer, who paid council members their per-diem expense allowances for attending council meetings. He had a handlebar moustache, had been an auditor in Ghana, Kenya, and the Gambia, and brought the per-diem funds in cash in a brief case. Council members were beckoned in turn to a corner of the room where they were paid off in banknotes. It had all the earmarks of a drug transaction.

Vancouver: 1978

Carl Williams's plans for the 1978 congress, which was to have been held in London, Ontario, were sabotaged by two events. First, his own appointment as president expired in 1977. He had thought that Western Ontario might allow him to retain the title of "vice-chancellor" for an additional year, whilst replacing him as president. Because "vice-chancellor" was the usual title for the heads of Commonwealth universities, this arrangement would have allowed him to serve as official host, as Trent University had done for Tom Symons in 1972 to allow him to host a meeting of the ACU Council. But Western Ontario, which was not kind to Williams in his last days, would have no part of this precedented device, and he was obliged to resign as chair of the 1978 congress, that task now falling to the unsuspecting vice-chair, H.E. Duckworth.

The other event related to venue. When potential delegates from the United Kingdom learned that the congress was to be held in London, they asked that it be held in Vancouver instead, which they understood was a more interesting city. In the circumstances, on 16 April 1977, Larkin Kerwin (then rector of Laval and a former president of the AUCC) and I met with the presidents of the three British Columbia universities (Howard Petch of Victoria, Douglas Kenny of British Columbia, and Pauline Jewett of Simon Fraser). Bold as brass, Kerwin announced to the three that the AUCC had decided that the congress would be held in British Columbia and that the three universities would be responsible for the local arrangements. No one demurred, the congress was held on the University of British Columbia campus, with visits to Victoria and Simon Fraser, and my physicist friend Erich Vogt was placed in charge of local arrangements. I had seen him in action with the International Union of Pure and Applied Physics conferences in Canada in 1960 and knew that matters could not be in better hands.

The 1978 congress was a moveable feast. The council of the ACU met for a couple of days in Quebec City where we were entertained by Laval and by the Parti Québécois government in the person of Claude Morin. In his owl-like way, he told the members of Council that, the next time they met in North America, they would be guests of a sovereign Quebec. A vice-chancellor from Black Africa expressed our thanks for his hospitality and, with masterful diplomacy, expressed the hope that, in the next election, Morin and his colleagues would enjoy the success they deserved. Passing through Montreal, we enjoyed a reception hosted by Paul Lacoste, rector of the University of Montreal, before travelling to London for a two-day meeting of vice-chancellors, hosted by Williams's successor, George Connell. Thus, the vice-chancellors at least were able to compliment Western Ontario on its 100 years of history. A visit was also made to the Stratford Festival.

Next, the vice-chancellors moved to Calgary, to be overnight guests of William Cochrane and the University of Calgary, and to be sworn in as honorary citizens of Calgary. This honour did not come lightly, but at the expense of swearing a demeaning oath, for which we were rewarded with white hats. Despite the ignominious wording of the oath, most felt that it was a fair bargain, particularly the Indian vice-chancellors, who seemed disposed to wear their new hats to bed.

The final stage took us to Vancouver, where we joined the members of the congress who had not been involved in the previous events. My wife and I joined John Bulman (chair of our board), Donald Kydon (dean of Arts and Science), Richard Bellhouse (registrar), and their wives Laureen, Motria, and Margaret, and also Joy McDiarmid, who had been at my side in most planning meetings. The number of participants in the moveable feast had now grown to 1,400. They were housed in University of British Columbia dormitories, they listened to learned papers on "reconciling national, international and local roles of universities with the essential char-acter of a university," they had endless conversations with one another, they ate baked salmon, they watched Native dancers pretending to be birds, they were entertained by Simon Fraser, and they made a charter voyage on the *Princess Marguerite* to be received at the University of Victoria. Then, on the final morning of the congress, they awoke to learn that Air Canada, which had brought most of them to Vancouver, had been shut down by a strike.

At the closing session, normally a festival of mutual congratulation, I had sadly to announce that post-congress visits to other universities had been cancelled. For example, in Winnipeg, a paddle-wheel steamer would make its way empty, the heavenly voices of Mennonite children would be unheard, and bubbly would lighten no heads. Elsewhere, other expectant locals would receive no guests, whilst frustrated visitors would decamp to Los Angeles or San Francisco in a desperate effort to get home. Erich Vogt, almost in tears, bought a case of peaches to console the disconsolate. The British, accustomed to industrial action, took it in stride, and others were inclined to exonerate the organizers, but it was a bitter end to what Sir Hugh Springer has called "a brilliantly successful week."

Birmingham: 1983

The thirteenth congress convened in Birmingham in 1983, and my wife and I were invited to attend as special guests of the ACU, although I was no longer in office. I sat at breakfast one morning with Sir Douglas (Jock) Logan, principal of the University of London and long-time member of the ACU council. I commented to him on the excellence of the congress arrangements, and he replied, "The arrangements would have to be good to get anyone to come to Birmingham." He, himself, had not been to Birmingham for twenty years.

Technology was the theme of this congress, and the current buzz words saw frequent use. I was asked to speak at the closing session to express the thanks of the visiting delegates. Perhaps it was to atone for the dismal news I had brought to the closing session in Vancouver. I found much to praise, including the "golden days" of weather, and noted only one unfortunate incident. At a reception, a nervous waitress, serving cream and sugar to the vice-chancellor, Lord Taylor, for his tea, blurted out, "How many Lords, my Lump?"

Perth: 1988

The fourteenth congress met in Western Australia, and President Naimark thought that the University of Manitoba delegation should include its chancellor (I had been elected in 1986). Thus, I was honoured to attend my fifth successive congress. At the congress banquet, the minister of Education for Australia, who was to propose a toast to the Commonwealth, made derogatory remarks instead, and then ended with an insulting remark about Canada. Tom Symons, who displayed surprising knowledge of Australian history, rose to thank the minister and, in his most benevolent manner, pointed out that Australia was in no position to criticize Canada on whatever point it was that the minister had fastened upon.

It was in Perth that we learned of the new Bond University being established in Brisbane by Perth's most famous son, Alan Bond, the real-estate magnate. This private institution was to cater to students from wealthy Asian families, was to charge high fees, was to pay high salaries, and might even make a profit. The vice-chancellor of the University of Western Australia had already been seduced and was being congratulated by his envious friends. After Bond's real-estate empire unravelled in 1990, his prized painting, *Irises* (Van Gogh), which he had bought for fifty-four million dollars in 1988, found a new home in the Getty Museum (Malibu, California), for an undisclosed price, and Bond University carried on. It has been advertising in Canada for students.

University of South-East Asia

The story of the University of South-East Asia is one of academic seduction. A meeting of Commonwealth vice-chancellors was scheduled for the spring of 1981 in Hong Kong, and some 200 were expected to attend. In 1980, we received notice that the University of Macao was being established and that the grand opening would be timed to allow visitors to the Hong Kong meeting to attend. The Hong Kong organizers were somewhat annoyed at this attempt to piggy-back on their party but grudgingly agreed to schedule time for the unanticipated event. The next mailing from Macao provided specific information: we were to bring our academic regalia and we would join the academic procession at the opening, not of the University of Macao, but of the high-sounding University of South-East Asia.

This was almost too much for the venerable University of Hong Kong and the Chinese University of Hong Kong. They were the leading institutions in southeast Asia, but their regional name had been hijacked by an upstart institution located on a small Portuguese-controlled island a few miles off the coast of China. But fume as they would, the deal was done. At the appointed time, 200 vice-chancellors, carrying suitcases or bulky garment bags, embarked on a hovercraft in Hong Kong harbour destined for Macao. There, in a vast Hai-Jai court, we joined the heads of certain American and

Portuguese universities to pay our respects to the operators who had suc
ceeded in this audacious coup. More university heads may have attended
the opening of the still nonexistent University of South-East Asia than had
attended any other event in academic history. Fittingly enough, we had
lunch in the casino before being shown the site of the future university and
being bundled onto the hovercraft for the return trip to Hong Kong, having played our ignoble part in a magnificent charade.

Federal Support of Higher Education

Amongst the provisions of the British North America Act was the stipulation that education was the responsibility of the provinces. If the federal
government had subsumed this responsibility, the present university system
might, arguably, be better or worse, but, without argument, it would be
simpler. Also, we should have been spared the controversy surrounding
some of the initiatives by which the federal government has attempted to
achieve some influence over higher education.

For seventy-five years after Confederation there was not much to argue
about. The university and college system was little drain on provincial treasuries, as most church colleges existed on the charity of their denomina-
tions, and state institutions were models of frugality.

The federal government had been allowed to intervene in the area of
research. Thus, beginning in World War I and continuing thereafter, the
universities, their professors, and their graduate students were eligible for
research grants from the NRC. This principle of federal support of university research has never been seriously questioned, as such research has been
viewed as a national priority. Such federal support, of course, has never
been the sole support of University research.

A second form of federal support (in the national interest) was the offer
of a university education to World War II veterans as one of their gratuity
options. Whilst many chose a home and furniture, an unexpectedly large
number decided to have a go at higher education, although, in most cases,
there was no such family tradition. In this program, the federal government
paid the tuition and living costs of the veterans, and made grants of $150
per student to the host institutions for costs not covered by tuition. Fears of
interference, which the provinces might have held, were allayed by assur-
ances that veterans could choose their own universities and the federal
government would remain uninvolved in university policy. Thus, although
this was a more direct form of federal support than were the research grants,
considering the special circumstances, the provinces also found this form
of federal subvention acceptable.

Within six years, the matter was carried a step further. In 1951, a royal commission on national development in arts, letters and science (the Massey Commission) recommended that, "in addition to the help already being given for research and other purposes[,] the federal government make annual contributions to support the work of the universities . . . to ensure . . . that their work . . . may be carried on in accordance with the needs of the nation."

This recommendation was accepted by the federal government but, as it turned out, without adequate consultation with the provinces. A grant was established at fifty cents per capita of population; thus, for a total Canadian population of fourteen million, the grant for all of Canada was seven million dollars. This slightly more than offset the $150-per-veteran grant, which, by this time, had largely passed through the system. As was done for the two previous forms of federal support, this grant went directly to the universities and was not routed through provincial treasuries.

The Province of Quebec objected to the arrangement as a constitutional infringement and, after the first year, instructed its universities to refuse the grants. They suffered this deprivation only briefly, however, as the Quebec government arranged in 1959 for a compensatory amount to be paid directly to its treasury, from which it supported universities according to its own priorities. Likewise, when the federal government introduced new social programs, Quebec had its own versions and negotiated the transfer of federal monies.

The other provinces, although irritated at the manner in which the fifty-cent-per-capita subvention had been introduced, found the means to salve their consciences and chose not to interrupt the flow of new-found money. Moreover, their universities were not at all offended, as the idea for such a grant had been suggested by them to the Massey Commission on the basis of the national contribution that they were making.

Five years later, in 1956, the federal grant to universities was doubled to one dollar per provincial capita, and by 1966 it had risen to five dollars, ten times its initial value in 1951. Moreover, certain capital funds had also been provided. As the amounts of these federal payments increased, the provinces (not their universities) became restive at not being part of the arrangement. As a result, beginning in 1967, the federal support was established at half the cost of the post-secondary system. And this now-large sum of money *was remitted directly to the individual provinces rather than to their universities.* The new arrangements struck most as generous and equitable. The provinces were particularly happy because, with the feds covering 50 percent of the cost, and tuition a further 15 to 20 percent, their share was now but 30 to 35 percent. The federal government, although it had lost visibility in the change, had achieved its aim of limiting its contribution to 50 percent. Those negotiating for the federal government, however, had made a massive blunder.

The provinces soon realized, and perhaps had always known, that the arrangement was open-ended: the more they spent, the more they would receive. The province of Ontario, for example, was accused of lavish spending in order to qualify for lavish matching funds. Thus, the federal government had not only lost most of the credit for its munificence, but it had also failed to limit its spending. Moreover, it had become part of a system in which the rich provinces got richer. The whole exercise was a public relations failure and a financial disaster.

The frustrated federal government first limited the costs they would match and then decided to withdraw from the arrangement altogether. The incursion into the direct support of post-secondary education, begun innocently as a post-war benefit to veterans, had become too expensive to maintain.

The AUCC and Federal Support of Universities

The AUCC began life in 1911 as the National Conference of Canadian Universities (NCCU). Its main activity was to provide regular meetings at which university representatives could meet to encourage or console one another. These were pleasant, harmless gatherings from which the future of the world emerged unaffected. Then, in 1957, in order to make its universities subvention appear more hands-off, the federal government asked the NCCU to serve as the conduit through which the federal monies passed. Incidentally, the formula for distribution was that each province received an amount determined by its population and, within the province, each institution received an amount determined by its enrollment. Thus, overnight, the NCCU changed from a combination social-debating club to one that handled vast sums of money. In order to play this role properly, it established a special trust body known as the Canadian Universities Foundation (CUF), hired the personnel needed to execute its new task, and added the word *Colleges* to its own name (now NCCUC); soon after, it became the AUCC. As time passed and (through CUF) it sent increasingly large cheques to its member institutions, the AUCC came to view itself as a major player in the financing of universities, although it simply accepted federal money, took a cut for expenses, and sent the rest forward. And after 1967, when the fifty-fifty cost-sharing arrangement was entered into and federal money went directly to provincial treasuries, the AUCC failed to accept that it was out of the critical loop. Thus, when the government of Canada indicated in 1976 that it would discontinue the fifty-fifty funding arrangement, the AUCC expected to be involved in determining the future arrangements.

The leader in this expectation was Michael Oliver, president of Carleton University and 1975-76 president of the AUCC, who was determined that the AUCC sit at the same table with the federal and provincial representatives. The strategy was to prepare a brief outlining the potential contributions of the AUCC to the upcoming discussions and deliver this brief to federal and provincial governments in turn. This should lead to a tri-partite forum in which the federal and provincial governments would meet with the AUCC to discuss the universities' purposes and needs.

The first problem was with the brief. To achieve credibility, it would need the endorsement of the universities in all provinces, particularly those in the province of Quebec. John O'Brien (rector of Concordia University) was chair of the committee of rectors and principals of Quebec when some of us were in Ottawa attempting to draft the brief. Larkin Kerwin was there as past-president of the AUCC, and I was there as vice-president. We would compose a few crucial lines of the brief, which Oliver would then read to O'Brien on the telephone, to see if they would fly in Quebec. O'Brien was anxious to be helpful but refused to endorse anything that smacked of impingement on Quebec's authority over education. This led to an increasingly watered-down set of words to which not even O'Brien could object. It was not a very persuasive document for Oliver to take to the other members of the hoped-for tripartite forum.

Early in 1976, Oliver's missionary efforts began with the personal presentation of the brief to the prime minister of Canada and to the first minister or his or her representative in each of the ten provinces. This was followed by a pilot tripartite forum, organized by the AUCC on 25 and 26 March 1976 and held in Montreal, to which senior representatives of the federal and provincial governments were invited to ventilate certain timely topics. At this event, which was limited to 125 attendees, the federal government was well represented at the deputy-minister level and was obviously not averse to consulting the universities on matters of common interest (or using any other device that would give them a continuing role in higher education). The provincial governments, on the other hand, sent only token representation and hewed to what was clearly a party line: the arrangements for the support of post-secondary education were purely fiscal, and any discussion relating thereto would take place between ministers of finance.

The 25-26 March forum was followed in May 1976 by an P.SC symposium that provided an opportunity for more intensive discussion and this
led to the initiation of studies on "foreign students and staff," "the international activities of universities," "the development of centres of excellence,"
and "the financing of universities." These topics were representative of those
the AUCC believed should be discussed before new fiscal arrangements
were agreed upon.

The provinces remained cool to the tri-partite-forum idea, on the principle that education is a provincial matter and each province should deal
separately with its own universities.The federal government appeared more
open to the idea but was obviously sensitive to the provincial point of view.
There was also equivocation within the university community itself as to
whether or not the AUCC should be attempting to discuss educational
matters with the federal government. Quebec universities, for example,
saw their government as their primary point of contact and were concerned that any attempt to engage the federal government might be viewed
as disloyalty. It appeared that the tri-partite idea, as a device for ensuring
AUCC involvement in affairs of state, was unlikely to materialize.The new
fiscal agreement between the federal government and the provinces was
arrived at without AUCC input.

The 1977 Federal-Provincial Agreement

In the new accord, announced in 1977, the full financial responsibility for
operating universities and colleges was reassigned to the provinces. The
responsibility for medicare was transferred at the same time, along with
certain tax points and equalization payments.The federal government continued to support research that, since 1957, had included humanities and
the social sciences as well as the natural sciences and medicine.

In general, the provinces welcomed the increase in their own tax revenue and the independence that this afforded, although the poorer provinces faced a less certain future. A comment made at the time seemed
ominous to the universities. A provincial minister explained to the press
that, although the transfer of tax points included monies that had previously been designated for higher education, the province was free to spend
the new money as it pleased.To emphasize the point, he stated that the new
money could be spent on highways, for example.

Canadian Committee on the Financing of University Research

In 1973, the Canadian Council of Ministers of Education (CCME) had
become exercised on the topic of research, in effect demanding that federal

funds for university research be approved by the provinces and pass through the provincial coffers. Alberta, for example, wanted any grant greater than $15,000 to follow this route. The planning secretariat of Manitoba was also concerned but was less rigid in its views.

There were several reasons for this provincial concern. The large sums of federal money that were flowing into the universities in support of research were proving costly to provincial treasuries. For example, although federal grants-in-aid-of-research paid most of the direct costs, the time spent on research by professors was paid for by the universities, as were the costs of research laboratories, research libraries, technical infrastructures, and countless other research necessities. Moreover, there was no guarantee that research performed would help in the solution of provincial problems. And underlying everything, but expressed in loftier terms, was the chronic provincial desire for more control. These concerns were expressed so stridently that the federal government became alarmed. In addition, the topic was vigorously and anxiously discussed at the 1973 annual meeting of the AUCC.

The chair of the CCME rotates amongst the provinces, and the issues that the Council espouses often originate with the chair. In this case, the chair may have come from Alberta. In any event, although the topic of research was not forgotten, the Council received a new chair and turned its main attention to other issues. Manitoba reached a compromise with its universities by requiring that professors be informed of topics that the province hoped some of them would address. As far as I could see, this was a toothless gesture.

The unease about research simmered, however, and led (in 1976) to an agreement between the federal government and the provincial ministers of education to establish the Canadian Committee on the Financing of University Research (CCFUR). This body had twenty members: one from each province and ten from the federal side. Wesley Lorimer, the Manitoba deputy minister of education, asked me to represent Manitoba, as one of the four university members on the committee; the other six provincial representatives were civil servants.

The first meeting of this committee was held on 12 January 1977, when we were called to order by Denis Hudon, deputy minister for the Ministry of State for Science and Technology. I had met Hudon informally and had found him pleasant. But, when he called the meeting to order, his manner changed completely, from geniality to arrogance, at least towards the provincial civil servants. He was especially truculent towards the Alberta representative, a deputy minister by the name of Colesar. I realized that it was a studied transformation, intended to establish who was in charge; after all, from the time of World War I, it had been the federal government that had supported the free-choice research of professors, and much of their sponsored research as well. His manner took me completely by surprise. Many times had I met deputy ministers at both federal and provincial levels, and I was usually impressed by their ability and their likeability, but I had not before attended a meeting between the two groups. From that experience, and a similar later one (when I was consultant to a federal crown corporation), I can understand why federal-provincial relations are often strained. And I would be inclined not to lay the blame entirely on the provincial side.

The mood of the second meeting of CCFUR, held in June 1977, was completely different, largely because a federal paper entitled "Exchange of Information" was placed on the table. This paper summarized the current federal support of university research (against a background of total federal research expenditure) and provided the rationale for each of the components. It revealed that the planned new granting agencies (the Social Sciences and Humanities Research Council [SSHRC] and the Natural Science and Engineering Research Council [NSERC]) were being asked to: (1) achieve greater regional balance in scientific capability; (2) intensify research in areas of national concern; and (3) encourage interdisciplinary research. Also, it stated that "the Committee should be informed of any major changes in policy and programs affecting university research in advance of the changes having been made." Further, the federal government "would expect that similar information would be provided by the other representatives on the Committee." The Committee agreed to study this (to me) handsome offer by the federal government as a basis for developing university research programs which served both provincial and national priorities. As my membership on CCFUR came to an end, I was not able to observe the outcome of this study.

Clarification of Division of Powers

When details of the 1977 fiscal arrangements became known, they seemed to imply that the federal government's interest in the national role of universities had declined. In order to clarify this point, and to ascertain by how much the equilibrium had shifted, a letter was sent to the prime minister, with a copy to the chair of the CCME:

February 28, 1977

Dear Mr Prime Minister

The Universities and Colleges of Canada have followed with the greatest interest the discussions of the proposed new fiscal arrangements for the support of post-secondary education. Now that the legislation is before Parliament, we beg leave to observe that it contains no reference to arrangements: (A) for guaranteeing inter-provincial mobility of university students; (B) for the support of programmes of special importance to Canada as a whole; (C) for observing (over the course of time) the effectiveness of the new system of financial support; (D) for the treatment of foreign students.

Yours sincerely,

H.E.Duckworth
President, AUCC

This letter caused no unease amongst the Quebec universities as it simply identified important specific issues and our willingness to assist the federal government and the CCME in their dealing with them.

The prime minister replied on 25 April 1977, expressing interest in the topics raised but suggesting that they be dealt with through the CCME or CCFUR. Thus, the Canadian universities, which had been wont to regard themselves as national, if not international, institutions were clearly relegated to provincial status. And the hoped-for tri-partite forum, for which Michael Oliver and others had striven so valiantly, had vanished in the wind.

1988 National Forum on Post-Secondary Education

Ten years elapsed before I was involved again in the federal-provincial tussle for influence over post-secondary education. In 1988, under David Crombie, secretary of state, the federal government made a short-lived attempt to regain some influence in higher education. With the support of Roland Penner, minister of Education for Manitoba and chair of the CCME, Crombie convened the National Forum on Post-Secondary Education in Saskatoon, to which most provinces responded willingly, but to which others had to be dragged. Brian Segal, president of the University of Guelph, was the nominal chair of the event, which, without doubt, was the most impressive convocation in the history of Canadian higher education. I attended as one of the twenty-five delegates from Manitoba. Many eloquent and distinguished speakers explored the challenges and opportunities facing Canadian universities and colleges to prepare for the twenty-first century. The subject was ventilated to the edification of several hundred attendees, but the federal government came with no funds to meet the challenges and left with no new role to play. Canadian higher education remained at the tender mercies of provincial governments.

Changes in the AUCC

The executive director of the AUCC during the 1960s was Geoffrey Andrews, an amiable former professor of history at the University of British Columbia. His aim was to expand the influence of the AUCC by bringing other constituencies into its ambit. Thus, although the organization had begun as a tool of university presidents, Andrews was able to infiltrate the Board of Directors with ordinary professors and with students. Further, he created a series of associate committees that reported to the Board but that contained a distinct minority of executive heads. Although the professors had their own association – CAUT – they were now also joint proprietors of what had been an organ of the university administration. Likewise, the students had their national organization(s) but now had their feet in someone else's camp as well. I was once a member of the Associate Committee on Science, but I can't recall that we fed any useful advice into the pipeline. I believe the associate committees were more show than substance.

The weakness of this aggrandizement emerged at the 1971 annual meeting, when the student delegates attempted to usurp the agenda. Fred Carrothers, the president of the University of Calgary and a lawyer by trade, was in the chair, and by brilliant use of *Robert's Rules of Order* was able to frustrate the attempt, but the presidents realized how nearly they had lost control of what they regarded as their own organization. They still had a majority on the Board of Directors, but a determined minority could create a good deal of distraction, and perhaps even destruction. As an interim measure, until something better could be done, the presidents on the Board met on the eve of each Board meeting and decided in advance how each sensitive issue would be handled on the morrow. The subsequent Board meetings were not quite formalities, inasmuch as debate was encouraged, but seldom did the debate affect the decisions taken at that meeting.

This stratagem, which, I must admit, I was sheepish about participating in, continued until 1978, when Moses Morgan, the strong-willed president of Memorial University, pushed through an amendment eliminating all but presidents from the board of directors. The AUCC was back in safe hands again.

The University of Winnipeg delegation to the 1971 annual meeting included our student president, Marilou McPhedran. One of the activists at the meeting was a physics graduate student from the University of Toronto by the name of Spencer, who was smitten by Marilou and followed her back to Winnipeg. At our next Senate meeting, which at that time was closed, he was found sitting beside her. Before calling the meeting to order, I whispered to him that guests were not allowed and was much relieved when he quietly left the room.

In 1973, I was elected to the Board of Directors of the AUCC; Sister Catherine Wallace of Mount Saint Vincent University was president, and Larkin Kerwin of Laval was the vice-president, in line to be president the following year. Michael Oliver of Carleton became president in 1975-76, I did in 1976-77, and Moses Morgan was in office for 1977-78. Claude Thibault had succeeded Colin MacKay as executive director.

I was surprised to be asked to take the presidency of AUCC, as I believed the natural candidate was John Evans, the president of the University of Toronto. I suspect that he was asked but declined on the plea that he was too busy implementing the "unicameral" form of governance that he had inherited from his predecessor, Claude Bissell. I first learned of Evans in 1965 when he agreed to establish the McMaster Medical School and his qualifications were described to the McMaster Senate. As we were told of his M.D. plus a D.Phil., his superb play in football, and his Rhodes Scholarship, Arthur Patrick (associate dean of Arts) whispered to me, "I never thought I'd ever see his like this side of heaven." Evans became president of the University of Toronto in 1972.

The Commission on Canadian Studies

The unnatural situation in which hordes of scholars were brought from the United Kingdom, the United States, and elsewhere to meet the need for professors in the humanities and social sciences led the AUCC in 1972 to invite Thomas H.B. Symons to examine the status of "Canadian studies" in Canadian universities. Symons had recently stepped down as founding president of Trent University, and he entered into this project with characteristic determination to get at the facts. It turned out that the facts were plentiful, but some were hard to get at. Also, many wanted to present briefs to the Commission on Canadian Studies. As a result, meetings of the AUCC directors were told that Symons had missed his latest deadline, and some feared that the Commission might never report. Those who knew Symons, however, were aware that he would do things in his own way and to meet his own standard.

The Commission placed special emphasis on the "culturally sensitive areas of anthropology, art history, literature, economics, geography, history, political science and sociology" and reported in 1975 that the Canadian component was woefully underrepresented in university curricula and research. As one brief to the Commission had declared, "Canadian economic history is more than U.S. economic history with snow on it." Most of the foreign imports, whose coming had enabled Canadian universities to cope with the baby boomers, and who have contributed enormously to Canadian higher education, had brought their research interests with them and, understandably, continued along the same lines, whether it was sheep economy in New Zealand, the United States presidential election of 1948, or the potato famine in Ireland. In addition, some Canadians were sufficiently self-conscious that they thought Canadian topics were not significant enough to pursue.

These and other points, some of them bizarre, were published in 1975 in the Commission's report, under the title *To Know Ourselves,* and did much to stimulate interest in Canadian Studies per se and to infuse existing courses with greater Canadian content. In particular, graduate students were stimulated to choose Canadian thesis topics and to pursue academic careers with research interests in Canadian matters. For rather longer than he wished, Symons acted as a semi-guru as he was invited to present his electrifying findings to educational groups in all parts of the country. In the end, the AUCC forgot about the missed deadlines and took pride in the splendid result.

At one stage in his work, Symons asked me if there was a Canadian aspect to science. I suggested that if biologists had a choice between studying the camel or the polar bear, they could pass on the camel. Symons tried this litmus test on several biologists and was told that my suggestion was simplistic. Subconsciously, I had been influenced in my suggestion by a family proverb: "The thirsty camel fears not the polar bear."

The Royal Society of Canada

Most civilized countries have national academies for the recognition and promotion of scholarship; for example, the National Academy of Science in the United States, the Royal Societies of London and Edinburgh, and the French *Académie*. These are non-governmental organizations, although they often provide disinterested advice to governments, and they receive financial support from governments.

The RSC was founded in 1882 by the Marquess of Lorne, then governor general of Canada. At the same time, he established the Royal Canadian Academy for the Encouragement of the Arts. The RSC was to promote learning in the new dominion and was patterned somewhat after the Royal Society of London (which dates from 1662). The RSC, however, includes all branches of learning rather than just the natural sciences. Membership is by election, and approximately sixty fellows are currently elected each year to one or other of the three academies: *Académie des lettres et des sciences humaines*; Academy of Humanities and Social Sciences; Academy of Science. Currently, about fifty economists are fellows, as are some eighty physicists and 110 geologists (at one time the quota for geologists was overly generous), but only twenty anthropologists and ten students of religion/theology. The society also recognizes scholars (fellows or not) by the award of various medals, and it encourages the presentation of learned papers at its annual meetings.

For decades, the RSC was the only national body dedicated to learning. Professors brought their graduate students to its annual meetings, where their findings were presented and discussed, and subsequently published in the *Transactions of the Royal Society of Canada*. In addition, many national institutions were created at the urging of the society; for example, the National Library, the National Archives, and the National Science Museum. Moreover, its expert advice has been sought by governments on a variety of topics.

By the 1960s, however, the specialized societies (e.g., the Canadian Historical Society, and the Canadian Association of Physicists) were well developed and their members were presenting their learned papers at their own meetings and publishing their results in specialized journals. Thus, the society had ceased to be an important forum for the world of scholarship. As for giving advice, amid the turmoil over science policy, none of the protagonists appeared to be looking to the Society for guidance. Election to fellowship was still highly prized, as was the award of a medal, but many felt that the Society should be playing a greater role in the life of the nation.

I was elected to fellowship in the RSC in 1954 at the tender age of thirty-eight and was awarded its Henry Marshall Tory Medal in 1965. This medal is awarded every second year "for outstanding research in a branch of astronomy, chemistry, mathematics, physics or an allied science carried out mainly in the eight years preceding." The Tory medallists from 1953 to 1977 were: 1953, G. Herzberg★; 1955, E.W.R. Steacie; 1957, C.S. Beals; 1959, H.G. Thode; 1961, R.M. Petrie; 1963, H.L. Welsh; 1965, H.E. Duckworth; 1967, I. Halpern; 1969, W.G. Schneider; 1971, H.E. Johns; 1973, B.N. Brockhouse★; 1975, W.T. Tutte; 1977, J.C. Polanyi★. (Those shown with an asterisk later won Nobel prizes.)

In 1964-65, I found myself president of the Science Academy and, in 1971-72, president of the Society.

A New Role for the Royal Society of Canada

In general, the science fellows were anxious to achieve greater influence for the society, whilst those in humanities and social sciences were relatively content with its role as rewarder of scholarly achievement. Without much encouragement from academies 1 and 2 (they were called sections 1 and 2 at the time), the Science Academy tried to arouse itself at the 1964 annual meeting in Charlottetown. My chairman's remarks began as follows:

> Some of you will be familiar with the Report *Scholarship in Canada*, prepared in 1945 by the historian J.B. Brebner, an expatriate Canadian then at Columbia University. This Report was 90 pages in length and, of course, appropriate space was devoted to the Royal Society of Canada, in fact, forty-six lines in all. He noted that "its meetings have been rather drowsy gatherings of pleasant urbanity, but little distinction, and the *Transactions* slumber for the most part undisturbed on library shelves" and that "a 'young' FRSC is someone barely under 50 (who) . . . is submerged by easy-going elders." Someone else has stated the Fellows meet once a year to plan how to keep the younger people out.

> With such an honourable tradition, why are we meeting to discuss the support of basic research in Canada? Have we relaxed our vigilance and allowed younger people in? From the appearance of this audience I should say not. I think we've held the line pretty well: Professor Brebner would be proud of us. The explanation of our presence here must be that the subject of the Symposium has actually imposed itself upon us, by its very urgency. Certain specific events have combined to heighten this urgency, and I expect these will be discussed by some of our speakers.

> In addition to these specific events there has been a gradually growing feeling that Canadian Science should emerge from its state of martyrdom

and be permitted to practise its creed without persecution. This persecution of Canadian scientists takes the form of urging them to remain in Canada, of expecting first-class work from them without providing the necessary support, and of deploring their departure if and when they pack up and leave. Of course, many remain – but not enough of the best. The ecstasy of eating pea soup under a maple tree is quite insufficient to atone for the rest.

Following the Charlottetown meeting, it was decided to prepare a brief for presentation to C.M. Drury, then minister of Industry and the minister to whom the NRC reported; that is, he was as close to a minister for science as existed at the time. Some of us met in the office of A.D. Misener, director of the Ontario Research Foundation on Friday, 18 September 1964, to approve the final form of the brief, which we entitled *Towards a Canadian Science Policy.* We then requested an audience with the Honourable Mr. Drury, which we were granted on Thursday, 17 December 1964. By a careless choice of words, we had referred at one point in the brief to native-born Canadians as "native Canadians," and he seized on this trivial aspect of the brief, pretending that he took it to mean Aboriginal peoples. We had only thirty minutes with him, and he managed to kill much of it on the "native Canadian" issue. We did our best with the remaining time but left feeling that we had been the victims of deliberate obfuscation and had sown our seed on barren ground. I later learned that Drury had perfected the technique of seizing upon a triviality to evade serious matters.

Incidentally, another of the symposia at the Charlottetown meeting was devoted to the topic Continental Drift. The idea that North and South America had at one time been part of Europe and Africa (or vice versa) had long been in circulation. In this speculation, the bulge of West Africa had fitted into the Gulf of Mexico, and some of the other parts were conceivable fits before they had drifted apart in prehistoric times. In 1964, University of Toronto geophysicist Tuzo Wilson was championing the cause of this hypothesis, but the Americans were opposed to it, almost to a man. Wilson spoke in the symposium, along with a representative American and William Radforth, chair of biology at McMaster University, who was an expert on muskeg. Radforth was to explain whether pollen evidence shed light on the problem and began his remarks with the perceptive statement, "What we need to find is one half of a log in Nova Scotia and the other half in Scotland." Wilson, who was later principal of Erindale College, University of Toronto, was persistent and persuasive, and even the Americans have since come around to his point of view.

Later, when the Lamontagne Committee began hearings, the RSC presented another brief, but again with little perceptible result.

Royal Society of Canada Symposia

It was against this background of frustration that I suggested at the Winnipeg meeting in 1970 that the society sponsor a symposium entitled "Mercury in Man's Environment." The Society had frequently held symposia as part of annual meetings, but these were offered for the edification of the fellows and had little influence on the outside world. The mercury symposium took place apart from the annual meeting, it involved experts who were non-fellows, and it was aimed directly at the outside world. This type of activity has proven useful and has given the society much-needed visibility at no cost other than the granting of its patronage.

Expert Advice

The National Academy of Science of the United States is frequently called upon to express a view on controversial science questions, for example, the efficacy of a certain drug or the environmental effect of certain industrial activity. If it accepts the challenge, it assembles a panel of experts and delivers an opinion on a cost-recovery basis. During my presidency of the RSC, we paid a visit to Washington to establish fraternal relations with the National Academy of Science and to learn more about its operations. As we approached its splendid building on Constitution Avenue, we felt rather like pussycats visiting the Queen, but they pretended that we were equals, and we returned home with the notion that we might play a similar role in Canada. The first example was a request from the Department of Communications to choose the experiments to be included in a satellite. This has led to several other occasions on which the Society has rendered impartial advice.

A false step, however, was taken a few years ago in an attempt to expand this type of activity by a quantum leap. The Government of Canada was asked to increase its long-standing (but modest) grant to the Society. The government went one better and offered the society large sums of money to undertake specific studies. This deal was struck with the Mulroney government, and the RSC increased its staff dramatically and expanded its premises to undertake these projects. After about three years, the government terminated these contracts, a year earlier than stipulated, and the society incurred termination costs that almost led to its bankruptcy. It was a pact with the devil and left us victim of the vagaries of politicians. I observed these events from a distance and can share neither in the credit nor the blame.

Advising Ottawa

During my period at the University of Winnipeg I was called to Ottawa for a variety of services. I was never as involved in these activities as I had been with the NRC, but the experiences were not without interest.

The Order of Canada

The Order of Canada was established in 1967 as a means of recognizing worthy Canadians who are described by the motto "They desire a better country." At one time, we relied upon the British Crown to perform the task of recognition but, in 1919, the Government of Canada forbade Canadians to accept British honours. The ban was lifted briefly during the administration of Richard Bedford Bennett (1935-1938), but Mackenzie King lost little time in re-instating it when he came to power in 1938. Meanwhile, Bennett had moved to England where, following His Majesty's Birthday Honours List of June 1941, he luxuriated in the title, Viscount Bennett of Mickleham (where he lived in Surrey), of Calgary (which he represented in Parliament), and Hopewell (his birthplace in New Brunswick). Although his title was hereditary, he left no titled heir; indeed, as a bachelor, he didn't even try to do so.

During World War II, a parliamentary committee recommended that British honours be allowed temporarily, in order to recognize civilian contributions to the war effort. Thus, a few now-elderly Canadians were admitted to the Order of the British Empire as "members" (MBE), "officers" (OBE), and "commanders" (CBE). But, thereafter, for more than twenty years, meritorious individuals in Canada lived their lives unrecognized except for honorary degrees and/or citizenships of the year.

At the start, the Order of Canada had two categories: the "companion" and the "officer." The category of "companion" was limited to 150 living members; there was no stated limit on the number of officers. A few years later, the category of "member" was introduced for contributions at a local level.

The Selection Committee for the Order of Canada comprises seven members: the chief justice of Canada (chair), the clerk of the Privy Council, the president of the RSC, the president of AUCC, and three others named by the governor general, who serves as chancellor of the Order but does not attend meetings of the selection committee or lobby for specific nominees. Instead, he receives the recommendations and provides the splendid semi-annual investiture ceremony at his Rideau Hall residence. I served on the selection committee during 1971-72 (as president of the RSC) and during 1976-77 (as president of the AUCC). In 1976, I was invested as officer of the Order.

Hundreds of nominations are received by the chancellery, and most of these are referred to "consultants" before being circulated to the Selection Committee, which meets twice a year, immediately preceding the investiture ceremony. During their meeting, the members of the Committee are entertained for lunch by the governor general and, following their work, they are invited to the investiture, which exudes pomp and circumstance. My wife and I attended five investitures, including my own, and found ourselves in the company of outstanding Canadians of every gender, size, and hue. To my surprise, Kay was particularly pleased to meet two muscular men – Gordie Howe and Jean Beliveau – who entered the Order together.

Before attending my first meeting of the Selection Committee (as president of the RSC), Gerhard Herzberg (who had served on the first selection committee) told me that I would be the only member of the committee looking out for scientists. This was partially true, and I ensured that one scientist was named companion at each meeting. Those four individuals are no longer living, but they enjoyed their deserved celebrity before yielding place to younger candidates.

The Science Council of Canada

In 1966, the Science Council of Canada was established, and it had a rocky start. Criticism of the government's own activities was touchy because almost half of the council members were powerful civil servants. In addition, whatever advice it generated went directly to the prime minister, who was too busy to do anything about it. In 1969, it was re-established as a crown corporation, similar in character to the Economic Council of Canada, with the mandate to give its advice to the public, rather than to the government. If the government chose to pick up on the advice, so much the better.

In 1973, I was appointed to the Science Council for a four-year term. I received the news in a personal telephone call from Madame Sauvé, then minister of state for Science and Technology. Although I have served on numerous federal advisory bodies, this was the only time the call came directly from the minister's mouth. I attended my first meeting with mixed feelings. On the one hand, I had seen the Science Council as no friend of the NRC, with which I had been closely identified for many years. On the other hand, its stated mandate suggested that it could influence significantly the course of events. As time wore on, I realized that the potential for influence had been overblown.

The Science Council operated by initiating studies and publishing reports. At a typical meeting, members would be invited to suggest topics for study, and they would also be asked to consider topics that came from the staff. After a brief discussion amongst the members, a topic would be agreed upon, and four to five members would be named to guide the study, with staff support from one of the permanent employees of the Council. At a brief organizational meeting, some guiding principles would be given to the permanent employee, and the members would forget about the matter until the arrival of the first draft. As any experienced administrator knows, he who writes the first draft determines the nature of the report. The members of the guiding committee might feel uneasy with the entire approach but might find only a few specific points to quarrel with. The end result, in too many cases, was a report carrying the imposing imprimatur of the Science Council of Canada but expressing the view of a member of staff. And since the staff members were infrequently rotated, whatever prejudices they possessed were frequently given the endorsement of some of the best known scientists in the country. It was very difficult for a member spending a few days a year to compete with a full-time employee with an axe to grind.

Each report was released with fanfare at a press conference, and the highlights appeared in the morning paper but, increasingly, the reports had little effect on public policy. In my view, it was the modus operandi that was at fault, but I did little to correct it. I was neither surprised nor disappointed when the Science Council was abolished in the mid-1990s.

The National Library Advisory Board

I served on the National Library Advisory Board from 1974 to 1977. My contribution, if any, was to urge closer connections to public and university libraries. There was already talk that books might be superseded by nonprint media, but the director and her staff seemed aware of the relative developments.

The Canadian Environmental Advisory Council

Arthur Porter, an industrial engineer from the University of Toronto and a man of wide interests and accomplishments, chaired the Canadian Environmental Advisory Council (CEAC), on which I served from 1973 to 1976. Other members came from biology, engineering, political science, medicine, and geology. My son and I co-authored with Porter and J.S.

Rogers a report entitled *Environmental Aspects of Nuclear Power Developments in Canada*, which was of some value. As with the Science Council, the CEAC chose its own topics of study but enjoyed the important difference that we reported to the minister of a mission–oriented department, who could be persuaded to take some action.

The Natural Science and Engineering Research Council

NSERC was one of two new councils created in 1978 to administer the federal support for university research. SSHRC was the other. NSERC took over its function from the NRC, whilst SSHRC's mandate derived from the Canada Council. The creation of NSERC was the culmination of the decade–long campaign to remove the university program from the NRC.

I had been asked for suggestions for the presidency of NSERC and offered some names, all well-known university scientists. To my surprise, and to that of most others, the successful candidate came from the ranks of the civil service, to wit, the deputy minister of Energy, Gordon MacNabb. I was named a founding member of the new council and awaited with interest my first encounter with this bureaucrat, who was clearly an unsuitable choice. MacNabb was low-key but had done his homework and was obviously a fast learner. Soon the members realized that he also knew how the government operated and which channels to follow. Thus, this initial disbeliever was converted to his approach and enjoyed a two-year stint under his systematic and far-seeing leadership.

One important action taken by NSERC resulted from my advocacy. I had expressed concern for the many young Ph.D. graduates who could find no academic posts and yet would be needed by the university system in a few years' time. To use a baseball simile, could they be placed "on deck," awaiting their turn "to go to bat"? This could be accomplished by funding university research fellows, who would be placed in university departments with the understanding that they would be considered for tenure-track positions within five years. MacNabb contained his enthusiasm for the suggestion but gradually warmed to the idea, as did the professors who were on the council. In this way, hundreds of young scientists were attached to universities, at no cost to the universities, and ultimately were appointed to regular university positions. In a sense, they were put in cold storage until the need for them arose. That analogy is misleading, however, because they were anything but "cold"; rather, they brought with them the fire of enthusiasm. In recent years, this program has been phased out, I believe under the pressure of financial exigency.

The Advisory Committee on Nuclear Safety

The Atomic Energy Control Board, a five-member body that regulates all use of atomic energy, had been advised by a group of technical committees. In 1980, these several committees were re-formed into two – the Advisory Committee on Nuclear Safety (ACNS) and the Advisory Committee on Radiation Protection – and some new blood was sought. I was asked to chair the ACNS. A few veteran experts were named to the new committee, and I was allowed to suggest certain other members: Kenneth McCallum (chemist and dean of Graduate Studies at the University of Saskatchewan), Alexander Mackay (lawyer and former president of Dalhousie University), and William Gauvin (metallurgical chemist and director of research at Noranda). Although a novice, I was cordially received by the veterans and continued to chair the Committee until 1988, supported by a knowledgeable vice-chairman, Robert Jervis of the University of Toronto, and two indispensable staff members, Frederick Boyd and Robert Atcheson.

In addition to recommending on specific issues that had been referred to it, the Committee spent much time on two intractable problems: How safe is safe enough? and, Does a threshold exist for radiation damage? Traditionally, the radiation from a nuclear device or installation was governed by the ALARA principle, that is, radiation should be reduced to a level that is *as low as reasonably achievable*. That principle leaves a lot of scope for argument, as any radiation level can usually be reduced further by the expenditure of more money. Thus, underlying the principle (but never expressed publicly) is the assumption that human life has a certain monetary value, and spending more than that value to save an additional life is *not* reasonably achieveable. Application of the ALARA principle led to much negotiation between regulator and regulatee.

The damage to living tissue as a result of exposure to gamma or other radiation increases directly with the length of exposure to and the intensity of the radiation. But does a small enough dose of radiation exist that causes no tissue damage? This possibility is attractive to regulators, inasmuch as doses below that threshold could be disregarded. I see no basis for such an assumption, but it's likely to be argued about for some to come.

It was during my chairmanship of ACNS that two nuclear disasters occurred, Chernobyl (in Russia) and Three Mile Island (near Harrisburg, Pennsylvania). But these disasters differed enormously in nature and scope. Chernobyl was a disaster in every respect: the reactor was destroyed, most of those attempting to deal with the emergency lost their lives, and a wide area was subjected to radiation. That fewer birth defects have been observed than was predicted does not detract from the tragedy of the event. At Three Mile Island, the reactor was destroyed, but no radiation escaped from the encompassing concrete cover. Thus, as far as safety was concerned, it was a technological triumph. At the same time, it was a public relations fiasco, it brought fear to thousands who lived nearby, and it was a financial disaster, throwing doubt (as it did) on the safety of all nuclear reactors in the United States. It did not help that the movie-going public had been sensitized to the danger of nuclear reactors via the Hollywood film *The China Syndrome*. Incidentally, in 1990, the number of nuclear power reactors in operation worldwide was about 450.

The Committee was taken to view many reactor-related activities, including the uranium mines at Eliot Lake (in northern Ontario) and Key Lake (in northern Saskatchewan). At Eliot Lake the mines were underground, and the uranium content of the ore was 0.1 percent. At Key Lake, it was open-pit mining, and some of the ore had uranium content of 8 percent. Yet Eliot Lake mines (which have since been discontinued) were still providing uranium to Ontario Hydro at inflated prices, in accordance with long-term contracts.

The Evaluation Committee for the Communications Technology Satellite

In 1972, Canada and the United States agreed jointly to launch a satellite for the express purpose of testing communications technology and exploring its usefulness. Time on the satellite was to be shared equally between the two nations. In Canada, the project was directed by John Chapman, assistant deputy minister of Communications and anything but a bureaucrat. His department had techniques to be tested but, in addition, he issued an invitation to the country at large for proposed experiments. Then, to ensure that his department was not accused of monopolizing the time available, he asked the RSC to name an evaluation committee to choose which Canadian experiments would be given satellite time. I was asked to chair the committee, the other members being S.D. Clark (sociologist from the University of Toronto) and Leopold Lamontagne (expert in translation).

A meeting was held in Winnipeg, at which interested parties were given further information and I was held up to public view. The deputy minister, Allan Gottlieb, was also present, and I discovered that he had studied for three years at United College and regarded it as his academic home.

During the period between February and July 1973, the Committee reviewed scores of proposed experiments, ranging from the highly technical to ones that even we could understand. The latter included sending video instructions from medical centres to remote locations and providing video connection between widely separated Inuit settlements. When the satellite remained operational for longer than the anticipated two-year period, we re-assembled in the spring of 1974 to recommend time allocations for a third year. This was a good example of disinterested service that the RSC could provide, and it was conceived by Chapman. Since then, the society has been asked on numerous occasions to serve in a similar role. For example, in 1988, I represented the Society as chair of a three-member committee to review Kenneth Hare's report on the safety of Ontario's nuclear power system.

The Killam Committee of the Canada Council

The Killam awards, administered by the Canada Council, have two categories: the Isaak Walton Killam Memorial Prizes and the Killam Research Fellowships. The three prizes, of $50,000 each, honour eminent researchers in science, engineering, and medicine. The research fellowships provide release-from-regular-duties-time to eight to twelve younger, but proven, scholars. During my period on the Committee (1974 and 1975), the research fellows were selected by personal interview. The members of the Selection Committee were also said to be eminent: whether or not they all were, they were a stimulating group to spend three days with, as were the applicants for the research fellowships. The director of the program was Frank Milligan, a former student at United College, and the representative of the Killam Trusts was Albert W. Trueman, who had been president of the University of Manitoba during my brief sojourn in 1945-46. In the meantime, he had presided over the University of New Brunswick, the National Film Board, and the Canada Council, before accepting the chancellorship of the University of Western Ontario. It was good to see both of them again. The whole experience was the most humane of my many in Ottawa.

Isaak Killam began life in 1885 in Yarmouth, Nova Scotia, where he joined the Union Bank of Halifax as the first step in a remarkable career. He became a protegé of Max Aitken (later Lord Beaverbrook) and ultimately controlled Royal Securities. His wife, Dorothy Killam, a native of St. Louis, Missouri, outlived her husband (he died in 1955), and provided for these awards before her death in 1965 and in her will.

The Institute for Research on Public Policy

The Institutue for Research on Public Policy was (I believe) the brainchild of Albert Edgar Ritchie, sometime ambassador to the United States and undersecretary for Foreign Affairs. He persuaded Prime Minister Trudeau of the need for an independent think tank and obtained a promise of $10,000,000 towards an endowment, provided it could be matched from private sources. When I joined the Board of Directors in the late 1970s, the chair was John B. Aird, who served in that capacity from 1974 until his appointment as lieutenant governor of Ontario in 1980. The president was Michael Kirby, successor to the founding president, A. W.R. Carrothers, who had earlier served as president of the University of Calgary. Aird and Kirby – one Establishment to the core and the other ambitious and brash – were in the course of raising the matching ten million dollars. Aird was succeeded by the courtly Robert Stanfield and Kirby by the urbane Gordon Robertson, formerly clerk of the Privy Council. In 1984, Robertson was succeeded by Rod Dobell, director of the School of Public Administration at the University of Victoria. Dobell accepted the position on the condition that he (and certain of the institute's activities) be centred in Victoria. I was associated with the Institute for fifteen years but find great difficulty in assessing it.

My first suggestion to the Board was to plough back some of its income into the endowment fund, as the universities were doing with scholarship and other endowments; otherwise, inflation would soon erode its real value. Any curtailment of the research program was opposed by the staff, and this suggestion fell on deaf ears. By the time Dobell arrived on the scene (or at least came from Victoria for the meetings), the inflation effect was cruelly evident, and it was becoming necessary to seek research contracts. As the RSC later found out, the institute discovered that contract funds do not promote independence. The research program became a patchwork of projects initiated by the institute or financed by special interest sponsors.

Initially, the research program was presented annually to a large group of advisors, or "trustees," representative of governments, universities, and the private sector. The meetings were close to rubber-stamp operations, although the roster of directors and trustees contained many impressive names. For reasons of expense, and/or (possibly) to escape criticism, the Institute has since eliminated the trustees.

In my view, the Institute has not fulfilled its early promise, at least not during my association with it. Clever, well-respected individuals tried to make it work, but the research findings failed to oxygenate the nation. It may be necessary to be part of the political system in order to influence it, as the now-defunct Science Council discovered to its sorrow.

Retirement: 31 August 1981

On 31 August 1981, having reached the statutory retirement age of sixty-five and having served as president of the University of Winnipeg for ten years, I yielded the office to Robin Farquhar, the dean of Education at the University of Saskatchewan. The University gave my wife and me a grand farewell (organized by chancellor R.O.A. Hunter and chair of the Board Robert K. Siddall), appointed me president emeritus, and gave me a lifetime parking permit. My cup was more than filled.

In Retirement: 1981 to 1999

12

On 1 September 1981, I awoke a free man, with nothing to do but drink my coffee and read the *Globe and Mail*. Now I could tour the garden and see if the grass needed cutting, although I had contracted with a strong young man to do it. Later, I could drop into my study to deal with items that I had let slide because of retirement festivities. I was about to enjoy an unlimited period of recreation, cogitation, and vegetation. After a few days, however, this lack of routine began to lose its charm: apparently I needed a transitional stage, a period in a halfway house, before entering upon the idyllic life of leisure that I had so richly earned.

Fortunately, I had carried forward certain obligations and certain per-quisites: I was a director of the Wawanesa Mutual Insurance Company, I still chaired the Advisory Committee on Nuclear Safety of the Atomic Energy Control Board, I was a director of the Institute for Research on Public Policy, I was co-proprietor with Robert Barber of the mass spectrometry laboratory at the University of Manitoba, I was life member of the faculty clubs at both the University of Manitoba and the University of Winnipeg, and *I had free parking privileges on both campuses.* But I needed a core interest, much as a new building needs a principal tenant. It was a psychological need to show the world that I was still a person of conse-quence who had *not yet* been put out to pasture.

I had been sounded out on different possibilities, but my wife and I decided to spend a few weeks in old haunts in London, enjoying each other's company, before making any commitments. We took up residence in Chelsea Cloisters, on Sloane Avenue, just off the King's Road, where we had spent two months in the fall of 1978. There we played house, read the English newspapers, walked daily, attended theatre and opera, visited museums and galleries, bought our food at markets, occasionally patronized Harrods, our neighbourhood department store, and, in general, luxuriated in the London atmosphere. Things slowly came into perspective, and, when we returned to Winnipeg, I reported for work at Canertech on 22 October 1981 as a special consultant.

Canertech: 1981 to 1983

In 1981, the topic of Energy was even more important than that of Inflation. That's saying a lot because, in order to close a house deal, I had taken out a demand loan at 17 percent for five years. But the Arabs had raised the price of oil, and the prediction was that it was heading for $100 per barrel. In these circumstances, the federal government established a crown corporation to promote the development and use of alternative sources of energy. It was to have been called Enertech, but that name had been spoken for by someone else; thus, Canertech was used for this urgent new venture.

The president of Canertech was Lorne Dyke, and its headquarters were located in Winnipeg. Dyke had the instincts of a gentleman and the energy of an entrepreneur, which indeed he was. At one time, he had been deputy minister in the Manitoba Department of Industry and Commerce, but he had also worked in the private sector both for himself and for others. In general, this new crown corporation invested in projects initiated by others but, in one area, Dyke had decided to initiate the project and carry it forward himself. This was to develop a process to extract ethyl alcohol from wood cellulose, the "ethanol-from-cellulose project." Dyke asked me to coordinate this project (as a consultant), aware that I knew nothing of the process but trusting that I could enlist the aid of those who did. Dyke's second-in-command on the technical side was a chemical engineer from Yorkshire, David Free, who would be able to monitor and assist my activities.

I worked for the corporation for about two years. First, we had an assessment of the possibilities by the consulting firm Arthur D. Little of Cambridge, Massachusetts, following which we engaged the services of Wardrop and Associates of Winnipeg in the person of Hadi Hussein, a clever and engaging chemical engineer. With Hussein's help, we selected a process, designed test equipment, and constructed a small-scale experimental unit. During my tenure, the tests were conducted at the University of Manitoba by James Aitken and Steve Ostrovski, and yielded promising results.

I had had previous experience as an employee of the federal government, namely, as employee of the National Research Council during the war years, between 1942 and 1945. At that time, bureaucracy was at a minimum and the emphasis was on speed and results. Canertech had somewhat the same character, largely because of Dyke, but it was evident that the federal Department of Energy, to which Canertech was in certain ways connected, was much more deliberate and conscious of protocol. As I was not jockeying for position and had no eye on the future, I was relatively unaffected by this situation, which is so characteristic of governments. As for Canertech itself, it may have been a bit too freewheeling. Its officers appeared to carry the full authority of the Government of Canada, which led to a touch of arrogance in their dealings with others, and to a degree of recklessness in their investments. For that matter, the investment in the ethanol-from-cellulose project may also have been reckless, although it was justified at the time by the projected cost of oil. Eighteen years later, oil was selling for nineteen dollars per barrel, far short of the projected $100-per-barrel figure, on which the ethanol-from-cellulose program was based. The crown corporation was dismantled a year or two after my departure, and, I believe, there is little to show for the frenzied activity that marked its formation and its first glorious years.

Chancellor of the University of Manitoba: 1986 to 1992

On 16 May 1986, whilst chairing a meeting of the Advisory Committee on Nuclear Safety at York University in Toronto, I was elected tenth chancellor of the University of Manitoba, effective 1 June. Mac Runciman, chair of the Board, called me from the meeting to convey the news. I was stunned: I knew that Ralph Stanton had arranged for my nomination, but I also knew that the election was contested and that few chancellors are elected from the academic ranks. My first duty was to confer degrees eighteen days later at St. Boniface College in Canada's other official language!

I had seen many chancellors in action and was not unfamiliar with their (undefined) responsibilities. Also, I knew that I was entering upon an office that had been imported to Canada from the United Kingdom, where the office was much prized and was held in high esteem. What could I learn from that venerable tradition?

The titular head of a British University is the chancellor, who occupies a symbolic office. Originally the chancellor was the bishop's representative but, with the decline in ecclesiastical influence, he came to be valued for himself. British chancellors are elected for life, and it is they who award the degrees or delegate their vice-chancellors to do so. This convention derives from the time when the chancellor was the keeper of the Great Seal of the university, which had to be affixed to diplomas before they were legal. The disrespectful have described the British chancellor as the *caput non utile sed magnificus.*

The term *chancellor* is used quite differently in the United States, where the holder is a working officer, as opposed to an honorary one. Thus, in the State University of New York, a multi-campus system, the chancellor oversees the entire system, whilst a president oversees each of the constituent parts.

British chancellors have been chosen for their positions in society and/or their personal achievements. For example, members of the Royal Family are well represented: the Prince of Wales is chancellor of the University of Wales; Princess Anne, the University of London; the Duke of Edinburgh, Cambridge, Cranfield, Edinburgh, and Salford. On the other hand, Dorothy Hodgkin, Nobel Laureate in chemistry (1964) was chancellor of Bristol until her death in 1991, dancer Margot Fonteyn was similarly chancellor of Durham until her death in 1991, and in 1992 Margaret (now Baroness) Thatcher was elected chancellor of the University of Buckingham. The latter three are part of a recent trend towards commoners and persons of merit as opposed to persons of inherited position. This trend was accelerated in 1992, when forty-odd polytechnics were elevated to university status and a mad rush ensued to secure the symbolic services of persons whose names could bring distinction to these status-hungry neophytes.

Whatever his or her origin, the chancellor – when garbed in robes of office – is an impressive figure. Following a degree-granting ceremony, but still in full costume, one chancellor is said to have called to a friend, "Neil," – at which several American tourists fell to their knees in adulation.

Elections of British chancellors are normally discreet affairs, but not so at Oxford University. The last two elections have been particularly tempestuous.

The 1960 election featured two candidates – Sir Oliver Franks and Harold Macmillan. Franks had distinguished himself as a student and had later served as provost (head) of Queen's College, ambassador to Washington and chair of Lloyd's Bank; Macmillan was the prime minister. The voters were the 30,000 paid-up masters of the university, graduates who had paid a modest annual fee to be admitted to "master" status. Franks was supported by the dons (professors), whilst Macmillan was supported by the Conservative Party, which felt the honour of the party was at stake. The *Times* supported Franks, arguing (weakly, I believe) that great honours such as the prime ministership and chancellorship of Oxford should be shared. The Conservative Party knew how to get the vote out, transporting old codgers who scarcely knew what they were doing to the polling booth, where they were given the choice: Oliverum Sherwell Franks or Mauricium Haraldum Macmillam. Macmillan won by 1,976 to 1,697 votes. The *Spectator* reported an exchange between two of the elderly imports as they emerged from casting their votes. "Who did you vote for?" asked one, to which the other replied, "Oh, Haraldum What's His Name."

In 1987, following Macmillan's death, four candidates were nominated: Lord Blake, a distinguished historian, a Conservative life lord and provost of Queen's College; Edward Heath, prime minister until dethroned by Margaret Thatcher; Roy Jenkins, former Labour cabinet minister, who was one of the Gang of Four who bolted to form the Social Democratic Party (SDP); and Mark Payne, medical doctor who specialized in alternative medicine. The campaign was bitter and brought a record number of voters to the poll. Jenkins won 40 percent of the vote with Blake and Heath sharing the rest, although Blake was the victor in that internecine struggle. Thus, Jenkins used the SDP tactic of squeezing through an opening created by a split vote, in this case a split within the Conservative party itself. There was general revulsion at the politicization of the university's highest office, which now appears to be completely beyond the university's control.

As Canadians have no members of the Royal Family to call upon, we are left with a mixed bag of individuals. The University of Manitoba chancellors are not untypical: 1877 to 1904, Archbishop Machray (Anglican); 1908 to 1934, Archbishop Matheson (Anglican); 1934 to 1944, John W. Dafoe, editor of the *Winnipeg Free Press;* 1944 to 1952, A.K. Dysart, Court of King's Bench; 1952 to 1962, Victor Sifton, publisher of the *Winnipeg Free Press;* 1962 to 1971, Samuel Freedman, Manitoba Court of Appeal; 1971 to 1974, Peter Curry, businessman; 1974 to 1977, Richard S. Bowles, former lieutenant governor; 1977 to 1986, Isobel Auld, consumer activist and volunteer; 1986 to 1992, Henry Duckworth, emeritus professor of physics; 1992–, Arthur Mauro, lawyer and businessman.

The early reliance on princes of the church was common, with a gradual switch to prominent lay figures. Machray, who became the primate of all Canada, and Dafoe, who was the most respected Canadian editor of his time, were the best known of Manitoba's eleven chancellors.

From fifty-two years of association with universities, as student, instructor, and administrator, I had come to recognize two guiding principles: (1) The chancellor, as titular head of the university, has no authority but a great deal of influence. Most assume that he has authority, which heightens his influence; (2) The chancellor is the chancellor of the entire university and not the chancellor of the administration alone. He must not take sides in disputes between segments of the university unless basic principles are at stake.

My first visit after the election was to Arnold Naimark, president of the University, to assure him that I knew my place and would not second-guess him in the exercise of his duties. I believe that I kept my word: we enjoyed excellent relations to which he contributed at least 50 percent. We occasionally joked that, as vice-chancellor, he was my assistant within the University, but neither of us was in any doubt as to where the authority lay.

On the tangible side, what contribution could I make to the institution apart from a ceremonial one and the occasional *ex cathedra* remark at meetings of the Senate or the Board of Governors? A gift of money was not a major option, because an academic life such as mine does not lead to wealth. Instead, as my contribution I would work to enhance the appearance and the significance of the campus. This would require the cooperation of many individuals, but, in the past, I had shown some ability to interest others in projects of common interest.

Friends, graduates, and members of the University were invited to donate trees to the university as memorials, as celebrations of special events, or simply for their own sake. Two varieties were on offer – twenty-five-year-old Colorado spruce ($400) and six-year-old basswoods ($250) – and choice sites were promised in the centre of the campus. The Colorado spruce are not indigenous to Manitoba but were to be moved from a university arboretum. Winnipeg had no tree spade large enough for the task, but a Jack Holt of Calgary had built one with a diameter of 110 inches, which he brought to Winnipeg, and the transplantees were unaware that anything had happened to them. About sixty were moved, and parts of the campus became instant evergreen groves. The basswoods, members of the linden family, are a native species. They were planted so as to provide a sixty-tree *Unter den Linden* (an equally famous planting in Berlin) in the main quadrangle. These two plantings will adorn the campus for the next century, becoming more imposing each year.

Most of the University buildings are named after individuals who were significant in the institution's history but few of whom are known to the present generation. Handsome plinths of Tyndall stone (from a limestone quarry northeast of Winnipeg) were erected to display bronze plaques with 200-word biographies. Those entering each of the twenty-five named buildings may now pause to read details of the career of the erstwhile luminary whose name the building perpetuates. These handsome units cost $2,500 each, with The Winnipeg Foundation providing $12,500 and the remainder coming from hundreds of individual donors, many of whom had been taught by the people being honoured. For three successive years, as these monuments were being installed, Thomas H.B. Symons, chair of the

Historic Sites and Monuments Board of Canada, participated in the ceremony, which added *gravitas* to the event.

Traditionally the graduating students kneel before the chancellor to receive their degress, and such had been the practice at Manitoba until the chancellorship of Peter Curry. At his first convocation, the kneeling stool was not properly fixed in place, and each kneeler pushed it forward a little until it struck the chancellor's shin. After numerous bumps of this sort, Curry emerged with bloody ankles and declared that either he or the stool would have to go. Thereafter, through the terms of Richard Bowles and Isobel Auld, the chancellor stood throughout the convocation, receiving the graduands, who also remainded standing. I instituted a compromise by sitting in a grand chair whilst receiving the standing students; this indicated a clear difference in status but did not require the students to grovel.

A friend of mine, Gordon M. Shrum, was the first chancellor of Simon Fraser University, an institution that opened for business in 1963 with a combination of radical faculty and radical student body. Shrum, a physicist, had been the first to produce the aurolar green line in the laboratory, which he had done whilst a graduate student with J.C. McLennan at the University of Toronto. He served for years as head of Physics at the University of British Columbia; subsequently, he became chairman of B.C. Hydro and finally was appointed a one-man czar to establish a new university on Burnaby Mountain. At the first convocation, one of the graduating students threw himself to the floor and kissed Shrum's boot. Shrum, whose legs had been crossed, reacted instantly by kicking out with the top leg, barely missing the pseudo-obsequious graduand, an involuntary action that was captured on CTV television. Happily, rebellion had either subsided or taken other forms by the time of my chancellorship.

An occupational peril for chancellors is to award the wrong degree. I'm told that a group of B.A. graduates at Bishop's University once received the Doctor of Divinity. For my part, I surprised one who was expecting to be made *professor* emeritus with the loftier *president* emeritus, but he never tried to exploit my slip of the tongue. I was not expected to announce the class of honours; otherwise, I might have erred (as did another) in awarding not the conventional *summa cum laude,* but the much rarer *semi cum laude.*

As the degree ceremony is a mediaeval pageant, I decided to revive one feature of ancient protocol. The title "doctor" originally signified that the holder was entitled to teach and to examine; only a doctor could promote a candidate to the status of "doctor." Such a promotion was a big event in the mediaeval university; it took place in the cathedral, those involved in the ceremony were in full academic/ecclesiastic dress, and, at the climax,

the fortunate new doctor was kissed by the dean of the faculty to symbol-
ize that they were now academic equals. I stopped short of kissing but I
stood to congratulate each student who had earned a doctorate: Ph.D., M.D.,
or whatever. I also stood for winners of medals.

The respect shown the chancellor is somewhat intoxicating, and the
human tendency is to seek to enjoy it forever, as do the chancellors of
Oxford and Cambridge. But Canadian chancellors are elected for specific
terms, some with the stipulation of one term only. At the University of
Manitoba, the term is three years, with no limit on re-election. In my view,
a three-year period is too brief for most chancellors to make a useful contribution, but two such terms are normally adequate to do so. If the chancellor has not struck oil in six years, it may be time to stop boring.

The Wawanesa Insurance Company

In 1980, through the initiative of my friend W. John A. Bulman, I was
elected a director of the Wawanesa Mutual Insurance Company and of the
smaller Wawanesa Mutual Life Insurance Company. The larger company
had been founded in 1896 in the village of Wawanesa, some 130 miles west
of Winnipeg, and had grown to become the seventh largest casualty company in Canada. The office in Wawanesa is still designated as the head
office, and annual meetings are held there, although the much larger executive offices are located in Winnipeg.

During my fourteen-year period as director, the presidents of the companies were Claude Trites, Ivan Montgomery, and Greg Hansen, whilst the
chairmen were John Laing (a retired stockbroker from Toronto and Victoria) and Victor Binkley (a retired auto dealer from Brandon). Led by these
officers, the Company maintained its remarkable reputation for probity
and integrity. As a *mutual* company, owned by its policyholders, its aim was
to break even, with an adequate provision for reserves; it was not under
pressure to pay dividends to avaricious shareholders.

Advising the Government of Manitoba

I was asked by the Government of Manitoba to assist on two fronts. In each
case I was offered a modest honorarium, but, on the chance that the appointment might be seen as patronage, I declined the offer. I had never
identified with a political party and wanted to maintain whatever reputation I had for objectivity. In that connection, I was once called by telephone on behalf of a Conservative candidate. When I explained, "I am
apolitical," my caller asked, "A political what?"

In 1989, the Minister of Education, Len Derkach, asked me to serve as founding chair of the Manitoba Literacy Council, to advise him on measures to reduce the 15-to-20-percent illiteracy rate in the province. Most other members of the Council had some professional view of the problem and assisted me to gain some comprehension of it. I learned that the country is full of individuals who cannot read, are ashamed of their ignorance, but cannot bring themselves to admit it publicly. Often, it is their children coming home from school and asking for help that drives them to action. Many of the literacy programs are almost cottage industries, with one teacher (often a volunteer) helping a few mature students.

The problem is widespread amongst Aboriginal students, who find traditional schools inhospitable and often drop out of the mainstream. Even if they remain, their level of education may be a mirage. I asked an administrator at Nelson House (in northern Manitoba) how many students were in Grade 12, and was told thirty. When I asked how many would proceed to university, he said, "Possibly, one; the others are 'social passes,'" having been moved forward one year at a time, regardless of performance. I have since learned that social passes are not limited to Native schools.

At a literacy conference, I once chatted with a number of Native women and, to make conversation, said that I had noticed that in Manitoba most Native names were Scottish, such as Ross, Spence, and Sinclair, whilst in Saskatchewan and Alberta they were descriptive, such as White Cloud, Eagle Feather, and Running Water. They pondered this briefly, nodding their heads, and then one said, "Duckworth would be a good Indian name."

I tried to help the cause of literacy by arranging a meeting between professors of education and teachers of literacy. The lieutenant governor (George Johnson) and the minister (Derkach) attended, which gave substance to the event, but most professors of education are more interested in the fast learners than they are in the slow ones, and this filters down to the teachers they are training. For family reasons, I was obliged to resign after two years but was impressed by the variety of efforts that individuals and organizations are making to open the world of books, newspapers, driver's-licence applications, and bank-deposit forms to their less fortunate fellows.

In 1993, the Roblin Commission (chaired by former premier Duff Roblin) reported on the state of post-secondary education in Manitoba and recommended a number of changes. The minister of Education, Linda McIntosh, responded by naming the Post-Secondary Transition Committee to recommend how these proposed changes should be implemented. This committee was chaired by Jeffrey Johnson, a chartered accountant, who presided over seven of us. Most were past or present university students; I was the only professor, and a long-gone one at that. The others were all young enough to be my children or grandchildren. Roblin had noted that, although the participation rate in university studies in Manitoba was comparable to that in other provinces, the rate for community colleges was dramatically lower. One of his recommendations was to repair this discrepancy. There was also much from him, and in the committee, about adaptability, accountability, and transparency, three virtues seen to be lacking in the universities. It was tempting to defend the system, because it was all that I had ever known, but I found myself having to listen to criticisms without taking them as personal. Also, I had to resist describing how things used to be done. My younger colleagues made generous allowance for my antedeluvian digressions, and, collectively, we produced a report that, although somewhat rushed, was a sound document.

One tangible result of these events was the establishment of the Commission on Post-Secondary Education (COPSE), which now oversees both colleges and universities. COPSE replaced the Universities Grants Commission and modified the procedures (within the Department of Education) for regulating and funding the community colleges. The Transition Committee recommended that funding decisions by the new commission be final, as was the case with the UGC, that is, the UGC had been given a total grant that it then allocated amongst the three universities and St. Boniface College. The minister declined to grant similar autonomy to the new commission, requiring it instead to *recommend to the minister.* This, I believe, is a retrograde step, as it may open the door to political interference in what should be objective decisions.

Advising the City of Winnipeg

In 1988, officials in the Canada Department of Health convinced their minister, Jake Epp, that they needed a modern laboratory for disease control. But, before the champagne was uncorked, they were dismayed to learn that the new laboratory, which would rival the world-famous one in Atlanta, Georgia, must be located in Winnipeg, in Epp's home province, Manitoba. To implement this decision, Epp named a committee to recommend a specific site – W.J.A. Bulman (chancellor of the University of Winnipeg), Henry Friesen (professor of physiology and later president of the Medical Research Council), and Henry E. Duckworth (chancellor of the University of Manitoba).

Under Bulman's chairmanship, we received presentations from local advocates and also from the Department of Health itself. We were unanimous in the opinion that, in order to achieve maximum interaction between its staff and other Winnipeg scientists, the laboratory should be located near the University of Manitoba's Faculty of Medicine and the Winnipeg Health Sciences Centre. A possible nearby site was a sprawling area used by the City of Winnipeg for asphalt production and for other noisy and dirty operations. The federal government, however, owned a large tract of land on the outskirts of Winnipeg, where the Royal Canadian Mint and a small federal laboratory were already located. Any other site must be purchased; the site near the Mint would come free.

We conceived the bold idea of asking the City of Winnipeg to donate the dirty, but otherwise desirable, site to the federal government in order to ensure that the City had maximum benefit from the new laboratory. Who ever heard of such an absurd idea, that the cash-strapped City of Winnipeg would *give* a site to the wealthy government of Canada? Sell it at a fancy price, perhaps, but never give it! Notwithstanding the illogicality of the idea, on 2 August 1988, we met with Mayor William Norrie and his four commissioners; I was chosen to drop the bombshell. Norrie, who could visualize grand things, didn't blanch at the suggestion but asked his commissioners for their opinions. Commissioner MacRae, in charge of Works and Operations, endorsed it immediately: it appeared that he had long desired to relocate the asphalt plant and its appurtenances, but had seen no way to do so.

Eventually, with Norrie's prodding, the City of Winnipeg Council reluctantly agreed to subsidize Ottawa, although a federal assistant deputy minister of Health did his best to poison the discussion in the hope that the laboratory would revert to Ottawa by default. On 28 October 1988, the Honourable Mr. Epp announced in Winnipeg that he had selected the City's Works and Operations yards as the site for the Virology Laboratory, as it is now called. Twelve years later, this level-4 complex was opened, within a stone's throw of the other medical-science buildings, in accordance with the site committee's fond hopes.

Susan Thompson, an enthusiastic and public-spirited businesswoman, succeeded Norrie as mayor, with the intention of improving the image of Winnipeg as one of her stated priorities. In 1994, she asked me to chair the Winnipeg Evergreen Committee. Our numbers included Mike Allan (city forester), Penny McMillan (Tourism Winnipeg), Deanna Waters (Take Pride Winnipeg), Lynn Bishop (Winnipeg Airport), John Hreno (Winnipeg Parks), and a clutch of volunteers. Although we had no budget, we had the participation of persons who controlled facilities, and we had the absolute support of the mayor. With the financial help of The Winnipeg Foundation, the Government of Manitoba, the Tree Canada Foundation, Manitoba Hydro,

Versatile Industries, the Winnipeg Fire Department, the Winnipeg Rotary Clubs, Jeffries Nurseries, and many individuals, we were able to festoon several visible areas with foliage that persists through winter's cold. For example, those using the Winnipeg airport can thank the Winnipeg Evergreen Committee for hundreds of the trees that line their arrival and departure routes. When I stepped down as chair in 1996, the project continued under new leadership. Whether it survives in the regime of a new mayor remains to be seen, but, if not, many public areas will remain as monuments to Susan Thompson's vision and the Committee's dedicated work.

Personal Life

On 23 August 1991, my dear wife Katherine Jane died of colon cancer. She had supported me for forty-nine years in everything that I had tried to do. More often than not, she had contributed significantly to those initiatives that were successful. In 1995, I married Shirley Yvonne, widow of Donald Craik, and we are enjoying a happy marriage.

My son, Henry (Harry) William Duckworth, a Ph.D. in biochemistry from Yale University, is currently head of the Department of Chemistry at the University of Manitoba. His wife, Mary Lynn, a Ph.D. in microbiology, is an associate professor of physiology in that same institution.

My daughter, Jane Edmison Maksymiuk, who trained as a teacher and is fluent in French, is married to Andrew William Maksymiuk, a skilled oncologist. They have recently moved from Saskatoon to Winnipeg. My granddaughter, Catherine Jane Maksymiuk, is in Grade 11, my grandson Michael Maksymiuk has spent one year at the University of Saskatchewan, and my grandson Daniel Maksymiuk has earned an M.A. in history from Columbia University, where he is studying for the doctorate with the support of a Richard Hofstadter Fellowship.

Seven Decades of Change

13

The university is conservative by nature – very conservative. It encourages its students to question the status quo and it allows its professors to preach sedition but, as an institution, it is not an agent for change. Not for nothing is it called the Ivory Tower, a place removed from the tumult and the fashionable trends that agitate and seduce the outside world. To a large extent, its inertia is its strength; its reluctance to blow with every wind has enabled it to maintain its unique and precious character. But it has been subject to evolution as surely as have Darwin's birds and beasts, and, like them, it has evolved in response to pressures. Thus, in the main, the credit or blame for these evolutionary changes must be given to social forces or to *agents provocateurs* operating within or without the institution and not to the university bureaucracy.

In these final pages I touch on some of the changes that have taken place in the Ivory Tower since I first entered its sanctuary as a guileless freshman in 1931. I've chosen those in which I've had a special interest and/or personal experience. The views expressed are definitely my own.

From Half-Closed to Open Door

In my undergraduate classes, there were rich kids with British names, there were middle-class kids with British names, and there were the children of the immigrants. In this case, *immigrant* meant "recent immigrant from central and eastern Europe." I belonged to the lower end of the second category.

My graduating class at the University of Manitoba (1935) comprised 440 students in total, of which seventy-two (or 17 percent) fell into the third category, whilst in Wesley College itself the non-British component dropped to 13 percent. These figures were *much* lower than those found in the general population. Pharmacy was the most welcoming to the third category (42 percent), several of these being Jewish students who had hoped to study medicine.

I encountered a much different situation at the University of Chicago in 1939, where I was struck by the panorama of family names from Europe. Blacks were missing, of course, but otherwise the ethnic diversity amongst the students took me by surprise. Until this exposure to the American melting pot, I hadn't realized that in Manitoba my family origin had given me an unequal privilege. But time and circumstance have quite changed the ethnic inequality in our universities. The massive immigration to Canada from Continental Europe, the Caribbean, India, and the Far East, combined with the high priority placed on education by immigrant parents, have transformed our class lists into virtual roll calls at the United Nations. Canadian universities have become the most cosmopolitan in the world and, incidentally, have quite outdone the University of Chicago in that respect.

Women Students

Initially, Canadian colleges and universities did not question the received wisdom that women were intellectually unsuited for higher education. Even if there were some exceptions to that rule, their education would be wasted, as it would never be employed in the world outside the home. As in the United States, it was the Methodists who first broke ranks.

Mount Allison College, in Sackville, New Brunswick, had begun in 1843 as an academy for boys. Five years later, a complementary school for girls was established. When the college evolved from these two schools in 1858, it seemed natural to provide college programs for both sexes. Despite this generous policy, reservations about the awarding of degrees to women persisted, and women at first received the Token of Merit. In 1863, women received the Mistress of Liberal Arts, and then, in 1875, the first B.A. awarded to a woman was to Grace Lockhart, who had received the Mistress of Liberal Arts degree a year earlier. By this enlightened act, Miss Lockhart became the first woman to receive a degree in what was then the vast British Empire. Grace Annie Lockhart was designated a person of national historic significance in 1991, and two years later a plaque in her honour was erected at Mount Allison University by the Historic Sites and Monuments Board of Canada.

The Baptists also early perceived the academic merit of women as McMaster University, founded in Toronto in 1887, was open equally to both genders from its inception.

Elsewhere in the country, women were gradually admitted to the older colleges and universities, whilst the provincial universities in Alberta (1906), Saskatchewan (1907), and British Columbia (1908) were co-educational from the start. Women seeking admission to certain professional schools, however, had a rough time for many years to come.

No attempt was made in Canada to establish a local equivalent of the American women's colleges such as the Seven Sisters. The sole Canadian women-only institution was Mount St. Vincent University, founded in Halifax in 1925 (as Mount St.Vincent College) by the Sisters of Charity. It was intended to provide higher education for women with a Catholic slant, but circumstances have caused that intention to be compromised. It now has a sizeable male component, philosophy and religion are amongst the smallest departments, and lay presidents have recently replaced the Sisters.

There's a vague belief extant that women are poorly represented in the Canadian universities. The fact is that women represented 40 percent of the total enrollment between the wars, they were predominant during World War II, their percentage (but not their number) dropped during the veterans' invasion between 1945 and 1950, and subsequently their share has risen slowly to about 50 percent. Until recently, however, they have been under-represented in studies such as agriculture, dentistry, engineering, law, medicine, and science. Education was a traditional female preserve, as were nursing and social work, when these disciplines were added to the university family. In the past twenty-five years, this situation has altered dramatically; dentistry, law and medicine are now about fifty-fifty, some women have mustered the courage needed to enter the chauvinistic world of engineering, and, encouraged by role models, increasing numbers are seeking careers in science. If nature is now allowed to take its course, I expect that equilibria will be reached that are satisfactory in the light of societal factors that are beyond the control of the university.

Programs for Special-Interest Groups

In Canada, the programs for special-interest groups are mainly Women's Studies and Native Studies. In the United States, the latter is replaced by Black Studies. The pressure for these programs came from lobby groups and provoked an intense discussion – sometimes acrimonious – as to how to bring into the curriculum the aspects of history, literature, and culture that dead white males had failed to recognize. On the women's issue, many thought to modify existing courses to include those aspects relevant to women that had been overlooked or disregarded. The other view, which prevailed, was to institute special courses dedicated to the female side of things. It seemed to me that we had much to gain by studying together as *persons*, and we may yet return to that arrangement. In the meantime, continuation of remedial (or affirmative) action may be necessary to inject the missing curriculum elements into the accepted canon.

In terms of numbers, women's studies is more popular than Native studies. Obviously, there are more women at university than there are Natives, but, even so, it appears that Native students feel more obliged to acquire marketable skills than to learn about their heritage. I once asked a Native teacher if she had taken Native Studies for her degree. She replied, "Let those white guys learn what it's like to be a Native. I already know. I took English."

Professors Lose their Amateur Status

The professors of my undergraduate days (1931–1937) were ones of a kind: they were not replicas of one another, nor were they cast in a mold that would have won them acceptance in the world of business. But they were bound together by a common thread, a desire to learn, and an urge to share their knowledge with others. It might be said that they had been "called" to the professoriate, but, if not, they had at least been "drawn" to it, as if by a magnet. The Germans appear to favour the "call" idea, as the verb *rufen* (to call) is still used when a candidate is invited to occupy a university chair.

These idiosyncratic scholars, who tampered brutally with my naïveté, had gained much of their knowledge by private study without the imprimatur of a Ph.D. Also, many were renowned for the breadth of their knowledge rather than for intensive, specific erudition. At heart, they were amateurs, and the state of knowledge at that time still lent itself to the amateur approach. In physics, for example, important discoveries were still being made with simple equipment and by professors working in isolation, most other advances in the subject were still being described in terms that most physicists could understand, and most professors were prepared to teach any subject that was offered in the undergraduate program. Things soon changed.

The post–World War II university was vastly different from the relaxed institution of the 1930s. Enrollment was climbing rapidly, teaching staff were in short supply, subjects were becoming more complex, demand for graduate study was rising, and government agencies were offering research grants. In the circumstances, especially in the physical sciences, universities sought staff who were qualified to supervise graduate students and who would be eligible to participate in the government grant bonanza. On the other side, ambitious young scientists were viewing university posts as an attractive means of furthering their research careers. True, their research time would be reduced by teaching duties, but graduate students serving as research assistants would quite compensate for that. Further, within some financial constraints, they would be free to choose their own topics of research.

The young professors in the post-war wave saw themselves as entering a profession for which they had been sedulously trained during their doctoral and post-doctoral studies. What had previously been in some ways an avocation quickly became a standard vocation with a well-defined entry requirement (the Ph.D.) and a clear careeer path (assistant professor, tenure, associate, and full professor). This new profession involved the teaching of undergraduates, to be sure, but, in the minds of the new breed, the major emphasis was on research and the training of graduate students. Those of the pre-war professors who had gloried in the transmission of knowledge, rather than in its creation, were seen as fossils from another age. The Ph.D. came to be worshipped, the primary criterion for academic advancement became the number of books and learned papers published, and the value placed on teaching skill declined. In many universities, this is the present situation, and it is not a happy one.

This is not to suggest that research and scholarship are not proper functions of a university, but the current emphasis on research must somehow be squared with the teaching function. It is argued that professors who are not engaged in research are falling behind in their subjects and, ipso facto, are becoming unsatisfactory teachers, as if Newton's Laws of Motion needed to be updated from year to year. The teaching-needs-research argument applies to the teaching of advanced subjects, but much of the undergraduate curriculum changes only slowly and may be best taught by those who have honed their pedagogic skills and have personalities that appeal to undergraduates. On this view, the outstanding scholar and the superb teacher need not be located within the same body. And those who provide this essential undergraduate teaching should not be seen as members of a lower order when tenure, promotion, and salary are being discussed. These dedicated individuals, and, even more so, the undergraduate students themselves, deserve no less.

This apologia for undergraduate teaching in no way diminishes the importance of university-based research. During many centuries, and driven by curiosity, professors of physics and chemistry have pieced together a remarkable model of the physical world. True, scraps of the model have come from elsewhere, but it is universities that have carried the load. Those outside the ivory tower have concentrated more on the application of discoveries made by the professors and their students. No one denies the value of these technological contributions to society: as one perceptive student noted, "Without Edison's electric light, we'd all be watching television in the dark." But the underpinning of virtually all our modern technology has emerged from university laboratories, a fact long known but, until recently, not trumpeted. The advent of the "mission statement" – a pretentious device to mollify critics – has provided a vehicle to emphasize that research forms one of the two pillars of the university and is not simply a useful by-product of the graduate program. The overt acknowledgement that research per se is a required component has taken place during my lifetime and has given rise to some problems.

Research is an intellectual activity that might be seen as a form of creativity. It does not need to be encouraged in a university; it is a natural activity of scholars as they pursue their quest for new insights. Although needing no encouragement, research does need support. Should this support be even-handed, based only on the competence of the researchers, or should account be taken of its possible utility? Slowly, and perhaps inevitably, "usefulness" has become a criterion in the allocation of research support for scientific projects. After all, the university scientists represent a vast body of expertise that could be used to solve society's problems, to improve society's health, and to increase society's wealth. The university could become a vast applied research laboratory operating in the public, or even the private, interest. This, of course, is a huge overstatement, but within it dwells a real and present danger that scarcely existed when I was attempting to determine the masses of atoms. It has not been difficult, for example, using research contracts as the bait, to divert some professors from their chosen researches to investigations that serve vested interests. Much of this new work is appropriate to the university, but some of it is not, and the line between is hard to draw. The universities must find the means to allow their professors and research students to follow their own instincts (which may include applied research) without dictation and without outside pressure.

In general, if university research were to be subjected to a cost-benefit analysis, the report should conclude that the cost is significant and immediate, whilst the benefit is long-term and not necessarily financial. If something of the sort were to be included in universities' mission statements, I could be persuaded to change my mind about the value of the latter.

Decline in Academic Freedom?

Academic freedom is supposed to allow those who know what they're talking about to say what they think. As Milton averred in *Areopagitica*, professors and students have the right "to know, to utter, and to argue freely according to conscience."

I don't think that many Canadian professors have serious problems in this respect with their own administrations unless they are teaching at faith-related institutions. But that is not to say that presidents of universities do not receive complaints about the utterances of their academic staff. These complaints come from political groups (including the government in power), from business and labour groups, from religious groups, from minority and ethnic groups, and from all sorts of individuals. In one form or another, all feel that they have been unfairly commented upon by a professor or by someone speaking at the university and seek an apology and/or a retraction. As president of the University of Winnipeg, I had my share of such complaints and normally took the line that I was powerless to control a professor's opinion. The offending utterance often took the form of a letter to the editor with the writer's name followed by University of Winnipeg, giving the erroneous impression that he or she was acting for the University. I never succeeded in eradicating that misleading practice.

What has become more serious, however, is the action of special-interest groups to prevent those who hold opposing views from expressing them. Take, for example, the physicist who tried to become a social scientist. William Shockley shared the 1956 Nobel Prize for physics with John Bardeen and Walter Brattain for inventing the transistor. In 1963, he joined Stanford University and soon formed the conviction that greater fecundity amongst those of lower intelligence was diminishing the mental capacity of the population as a whole. As much of the concern was directed towards Blacks, he was fiercely criticized for his racism and rudely reminded that his eminence in physics gave him no credentials as a geneticist or demographer. Once his thesis was widely understood, Shockley faced angry crowds wherever he appeared and, more often than not, was prevented from lecturing. The reception accorded Shockley's ill-fated and arguably ill-conceived hypothesis is typical of that faced by many controversial speakers who are foolhardy enough to expose their views on university campuses. Frequently, such speakers are politically incorrect in the sense that they offend groups who have struggled to achieve status or recognition. Ironically, such disadvantaged groups, who have improved their conditions through the exercise of free speech, now often attempt to withhold that privilege from those with whom they disagree. The curtailment of free speech is a high price to pay for political rectitude.

To perform its function, the university must remain a place of diversity, tolerance, and mutual respect. Admittedly, it offers an easy forum to those seeking social or political change, as militant students in the 1960s soon discovered. But, if it were otherwise, it could fall captive to specific orthodoxies that attempt to stifle the spirited discussions that are the essence of the classroom and the seminar. The Nazification of the German universities and the acceptance of Lysenkoism (acquired characteristics are inherited) by the Russian universities are examples that some can still recall. The free discussion of ideas, if left to itself, will soon expose the racist, the charlatan, and the fraud.

University Governance

The pre-war Canadian university was governed by lay board members, most of whom were appointed by provincial governments. Meanwhile, the university senate, which was dominated by deans and senior professors, regulated academic affairs. The senior members of the university had no access to the board, and the junior members had no access to either body, and neither did the students, although they had a worm's eye view of the whole operation.

In the last half of the century, Canadian universities have pretty much succumbed to the demand for participatory democracy, the battle cry that launched many a demonstration in the late 1960s and early 1970s. Students and professors have breached the defences of governing boards and now share the seats of the mighty. Before this assault had succeeded, the governors were seen as dictatorial, conspiratorial, and cavalier, operating in secret and answerable to no one but themselves. That the universities had been able to survive under such benighted rule owed much to Providence. What was discovered by the insurgents, however, when they burst into the boardroom, was not a cabal of villains but a group of dedicated citizens, many of them graduates of the institution and all of them friends of it, who brought a range of expertise and experience to their discussions and decisions. It took many of the insurgents by surprise, and soon the new and the old were working together for the good of the institution.

I saw the "unreformed" board of the University of Manitoba in action during the period between 1966 and 1968 and was a member of democratized boards during more than twenty years at McMaster, Manitoba, and Winnipeg. The addition of professors and students to the supreme body has increased the length of meetings, to be sure, but their presence has also ensured the thorough ventilation of crucial issues. In the new aggregate, professors take a longer view of matters than do the students, whilst lay members intervene less than before, an understandable but unfortunate development.

Special-interest groups should not be represented on the governing board to the point of domination. I've been told that, in the 1970s at the University of Prince Edward Island, it was not unusual for professors to outnumber lay members. On at least one occasion, they voted themselves salary increases that the university could ill afford and that the president opposed. The challenge to professors and students is not to force decisions but to persuade lay members to their points of view. The 1997 decision of the Government of Manitoba to increase significantly the number of students on the boards of provincial universities is, in my view, both inexplicable and undesirable. A microphone is sufficient, a steamroller is unnecessary and could be harmful.

The other innovation in recent times is the opening of board meetings to the public. This action was greeted with relish by the media, who were intent on exposing duplicity and intrigue. When they uncovered instead the prosaic transaction of necessary business, they directed their investigative talents elsewhere, and seats reserved for spectators remained largely unwarmed. Nonetheless, the opening of the door was of huge symbolic significance.

The senate was much less impregnable; indeed, it comprised mostly professors already, albeit senior ones, but it did lack students. Traditionally, it had been the task of the professors to approve programs of study and to determine the standards to be met; the thought of the ill-informed users (students) being involved left the professors uneasy. But, as happened with the governing board, the infusion of a representative group of students did not sabotage the system. In fact, in my experience, student senators intervene less frequently, and more effectively, than student governors, especially when pointing out the difficulties caused by existing or proposed regulations.

Faculty Unionization

Most of the professors in Canadian universities are unionized and use this vehicle to bargain for wages and benefits and, on occasion, to defend union members who are subjects of alleged unfair treatment by their universities.

This move to collective bargaining occurred as professors were taking their places on governing boards and were sitting on search committees for heads, deans, vice-presidents, and presidents. At the very time when they were participating in the management of the university, they formed a separate organization to bargain with the management. The dual system is illogical, complicates the operation of the institution, and sometimes poisons the atmosphere. As the perceptive reader may gather, I regret the incidence of *faculty* unionization.

If we are to have faculty unions – and I fear they are here to stay – I suggest that they bargain with the provincial governments on monetary issues, allowing truly collegial relations to return to the campus. In the United Kingdom, where all universities receive their operating grants from Westminster, the bargaining for academic salaries takes place nationally, and the universities are free to concentrate on academic matters. Similarly, in Australia, the bargaining is with Canberra. The Province of Manitoba was the first in English Canada to certify a faculty union; it could redeem itself by being the first to bargain collectively with the academic staff of its four provincially supported institutions. I suspect it would be unpopular with many professors but would be well received by the general public.

Prospects for Aspiring Academics

Many students in the 1960s observed the burgeoning classes and the many foreign professors who were being brought to Canada to teach them and judged an academic career to be a promising one. But, by the time they had completed their graduate work, the demand for new staff had declined. And, even later (the 1980s), when increased enrollment had created a new need for staff, the universities could ill afford to hire them. Hence, for more than two decades, the prospects for aspiring academics were uncommonly bleak, and the newspapers featured stories of Ph.D. holders driving taxicabs.

Women were an exception, as efforts were made by universities to increase their numbers, but this only worsened the prospects for their male counterparts and discouraged other males from undertaking graduate study.

This unhappy situation is in the process of change, as professors hired in the 1960s approach retirement. I see little evidence that potential academics are being apprised of this impending shortage. Very likely, in the early years of the twenty-first century, Canadian recruiters will be combing the world again, much as they did forty years earlier.

Increasing Dependence on Private Support

Canadian higher education is funded primarily by tuition fees and by grants from provincial governments. The provinces have fallen on hard times and have felt obliged to share their penury with the universities, which, by reversion, have passed on more of their costs to students: much, much more. In these difficult financial circumstances, the role of the private donor has been slowly changing from that of benefactor to that of provider.

In their solicitation of potential donors, development officers often cite the generosity of the American graduate to the alma mater. Although alumni gifts to Harvard, Yale, Princeton, and the other private schools are huge by Canadian standards, the comparison is unfair, as these prestige institutions receive *no* public funds other than for specific research projects; instead, the comparison should be made to American state universities, where the picture is much different. Nonetheless, Canadian graduates and other donors have been steadily increasing their support and so mitigating the relative decline in government support.

One practice that is becoming endemic is to sell the names of university buildings, lecture halls, and entire business schools. Plans for a new building are not complete without a price list for its major components. This seems a bit crass but is forgivable in the present financial climate. Two dangers, however, exist: future government support may presuppose an unrealistic level of private donations, and major donors may exert improper influence on the teaching and research programs. The wise president will hesitate to use private benevolence to balance the core operating budget.

Despite increasing private funding, the financial health of universities is crucially dependent upon public opinion and public funding. It would help if the parents and employers of university graduates were to abandon their *silent* approval and *voice* their endorsement. As it is, governments and the media hear from few supporters of universities who are without self-interest. As the most important institutions in today's society, their successes or failures impinge upon all of us. Long may they prosper!

Conclusion

So ends my account of events and developments in which I have been a participant. I allow for the possibility that *Another Version of the Facts* might see things in a different light. Nevertheless, I have written fearlessly in the knowledge that I enjoy the most secure form of academic freedom: I am on no payroll. Finally, I thank those readers who have stayed with me to this point.

Curriculum Vitae: Henry Edmison Duckworth

Personal

Born: Brandon, Manitoba, 1 November 1915, only child of Henry Bruce Duckworth, D.D., and Ann Edmison Duckworth.

Married: To Katherine Jane McPherson, B.Sc. (home economics), University of Manitoba, 21 November 1942, who died on 23 August 1991; to Shirley Yvonne Craik Hill, 18 August 1995.

Children: Henry William Duckworth, B.Sc., McMaster University, Ph.D., Yale University; Jane Edmison Maksymiuk, B.A., University of Manitoba, post-graduate study at McGill University and Université Laval.

Academic Career

1935: B.A. (University of Manitoba)

1936: B.Sc. (University of Manitoba)

1937: Teaching Certificate (University of Manitoba)

1937-38: instructor in mathematics, Stonewall (Manitoba) Collegiate

1938 to 1940: lecturer in physics, United College, Winnipeg

1942: Ph.D. in physics (University of Chicago)

1942: second lieutenant, Royal Canadian Corps of Signals

1942 to 1945: transferred to defence research work at National Research Council of Canada

1945-46: assistant professor of physics, University of Manitoba

1946 to 1951: associate professor of physics, Wesleyan University, Connecticut

1951 to 1965: professor of physics, McMaster University

1962 to 1965: dean of Graduate Studies, McMaster University

1965 to 1971: professor of physics, University of Manitoba

1965 to 1966: acting head, Department of Physics, University of Manitoba; vice-president (Development), University of Manitoba

1966 to 1970: vice-president (Academic), University of Manitoba

1970–71: professeur visiteur, Université Laval

1971 to 1981: president and vice-chancellor, University of Winnipeg

1971 to 1983: adjunct professor of physics, University of Manitoba

1981: president emeritus, University of Winnipeg

1983: professor of physics emeritus, University of Manitoba

1986 to 1992: chancellor of University of Manitoba

Honours

1940: Sheldon Fellow, University of Chicago

1941: University Fellow, University of Chicago

1954: Fellow, Royal Society of Canada

1954: Fellow, American Physical Society

1955: Nuffield Foundation Travelling Fellowship

1961: University of Manitoba Jubilee Award

1964: Medal of the Canadian Association of Physicists

1965: Tory Medal of the Royal Society of Canada

1966: D.Sc., University of Ottawa

1966: Honorary Fellow, United College

1967: Centennial Medal

1969: D.Sc., McMaster University

1971: D.Sc., Université Laval

1971: D.Sc., Mount Allison University

1972: D.Sc., University of New Brunswick

1976: Officer of the Order of Canada

1976: Fellow, Royal Philatelic Society of London

1978: LL.D., University of Manitoba

1978: D.Sc., Queen's University

1978: Symons Award of the Association of Commonwealth Universities

1979: D.Sc., University of Western Ontario
1982: D.Sc., Brandon University
1989: Duckworth Centre named at University of Winnipeg
1992: Distinguished Service Medal, University of Manitoba
1992: Order of the Buffalo Hunt, Province of Manitoba
1992: Duckworth Quadrangle named at University of Manitoba
1992: ATCO-SUN Medal of the International Union of Pure and Applied Physics
Life/Honorary Member of various societies and organizations

Professional Activities

National Research Council, member, Honorary Advisory Council, 1961 to 1967

Defence Research Board, member, 1965 to 1971

Royal Society of Canada, president, 1971-72

Association of Universities and Colleges of Canada, President, 1976-77

Association of Commonwealth Universities, chairman, 1977-78

International Union of Pure and Applied Physics, chairman of Commission on Atomic Masses and Related Constants, 1966 to 1969

National Library Board, member, 1974 to 1977

Science Council of Canada, member, 1974 to 1977

Canadian Association of Physicists, president, 1960

Canadian Journal of Physics, editor, 1956 to 1962

Canadian Environmental Advisory Council, member, 1974 to 1977

Evaluation Committee for Communications Technology Satellite, chairman, 1973-74

Natural Science and Engineering Research Council, member, 1978 to 1980

Advisory Committee on Nuclear Safety of the Atomic Energy Control Board, chairman, 1980 to 1988

Institute for Research on Public Policy, director, 1979-89

Killam Committee, Canada Council, member, 1974-75

Selection Committee, Order of Canada, member, 1971-72 and 1976-77

Subcommittee on Nuclear Constants of National Academy of Sciences, National Research Council (USA), member, 1958 to 1965

Manitoba Research Council, member, 1966 to 1970

Canertech Ethanol-from-Cellulose Program, co-ordinator, 1981 to 1983

Nuffield Foundation, Canadian Committee, member, 1968 to 1971

Chair, Manitoba Literacy Council, 1989 to 1991

Chair, Winnipeg Evergreen Committee, 1994 to 1996

Director, Wawanesa Insurance Company, 1980 to 1993

Member of numerous other organizations, visiting committees, boards

Publications

Books

Mass Spectroscopy. Cambridge Monographs on Physics Series. Cambridge: Cambridge University Press, 1958.

Electricity and Magnetism. New York: Holt, Rinehart and Winston Inc.; Toronto: The Macmillan Company of Canada, 1960.

Little Men in the Unseen World. London and Toronto: Macmillan and Company Limited, 1963.

The Large Queen Stamps of Canada and Their Use, 1868-1872. Toronto: Vincent Greene Foundation, 1986 (with H.W. Duckworth).

Mass Spectroscopy, second edition. Cambridge: Cambridge University Press, 1986 (with R.C. Barber and V.S. Venkatasubramanian), 1986.

Other

Approximately 100 research papers plus numerous general papers, reviews, and published speeches.

Index